D0849522

New Perspectives in German Studies

General Editors: Michael Butler is Emeritus Professor of Modern German Literature at the University of Birmingham and Professor William E. Paterson OBE is Professor of European and German Politics at the University of Birmingham and Chairman of the German British Forum.

Over the last twenty years the concept of German studies has undergone major transformation. The traditional mixture of language and literary studies, related very closely to the discipline as practised in German universities, has expanded to embrace history, politics, economics and cultural studies. The conventional boundaries between all these disciplines have become increasingly blurred, a process which has been accelerated markedly since German unification in 1989/90.

New Perspectives in German Studies, developed in conjunction with the Institute for German Studies and the Department of German Studies at the University of Birmingham, has been designed to respond precisely to this trend of the interdisciplinary approach to the study of German and to cater for the growing interest in Germany in the context of European integration. The books in this series will focus on the modern period, from 1750 to the present day.

Titles include:

New Perspectives in German Studies
Series Standing Order ISBN 0–333–92430–4 hardcover
Series Standing Order ISBN 0–333–92434–7 paperback
(outside North America only)

You can receive future titles in this series as they are published by placing a standing order.
Please contact your bookseller or, in case of difficulty, write to us at the address below with
your name and address, the title of the series and the ISBN quoted above.

Customer Services Department, Macmillan Distribution Ltd, Houndmills, Basingstoke,
Hampshire RG21 6XS, England

Phantoms of War in Contemporary German Literature, Films and Discourse

The Politics of Memory

Anne Fuchs

Professor of Modern German Literature and Culture
University College Dublin, Ireland

First published 2008 by
PALGRAVE MACMILLAN
Houndmills, Basingstoke, Hampshire RG21 6XS and
175 Fifth Avenue, New York, N.Y. 10010
Companies and representatives throughout the world

PALGRAVE MACMILLAN is the global academic imprint of the Palgrave
Macmillan division of St. Martin's Press, LLC and of Palgrave Macmillan Ltd.
Macmillan® is a registered trademark in the United States, United Kingdom
and other countries. Palgrave is a registered trademark in the European
Union and other countries.

ISBN-13: 978–0–230–55405–4 hardback
ISBN-10: 0–230–55405–9 hardback

This book is printed on paper suitable for recycling and made from fully
managed and sustained forest sources. Logging, pulping and manufacturing
processes are expected to conform to the environmental regulations of the
country of origin.

A catalogue record for this book is available from the British Library.

A catalog record for this book is available from the Library of Congress.

10   9   8   7   6   5   4   3   2   1
17 16 15 14 13 12 11 10 09 08

Printed and bound in Great Britain by
Antony Rowe Ltd, Chippenham and Eastbourne

For Ilse and Klaus

Contents

Acknowledgements

I would like to express my gratitude to the Irish Research Council for the Humanities and the Social Sciences, which awarded a one-year Senior Fellowship to me in 2006/07. Without this support, I would not have been in a position to research the material for this book in such a concentrated way. I also owe thanks to the UCD School of Languages and Literatures, which facilitated the completion of this book by granting me a one-semester period of research leave.

The material presented in this book is original. However, in three chapters I have drawn on previous publications: an earlier version of Chapter 2 appeared under the title "The tinderbox of memory: generation and masculinity in *Väterliteratur*" by Christoph Meckel, Uwe Timm, Ulla Hahn, and Dagmar Leupold, in Anne Fuchs, Mary Cosgrove and Georg Grote (eds), *German Memory Contests. The Quest for Identity in Literature, Film and Discourse Since 1990* (Rochester: Camden House, 2006), pp. 41–65. My analysis of Günter Grass's *Beim Häuten der Zwiebel* in Chapter 6 is an altered version of my article " 'Ehrlich, du lügst wie gedruckt'. Günter Grass's autobiographical confession and the changing territory of Germany's memory culture", *German Life & Letters* 60 (2007), 261–75. The interpretation of Thomas Medicus's book in Chapter 4 is based on "Landscape and the after-images of history in Thomas Medicus's *In den Augen meines Großvaters*", *Gegenwartsliteratur* 5 (2006), 252–71. I would like to thank the editors of the above journals and publications, Jim Walker of Camden House, P. M. Lützeler of *Gegenwartsliteratur* and the editorial board of *German Life & Letters*, for the permission to use this material, which has been in every case revised and adapted for the purpose of this book. The translations in this book are meant to help the reader without sufficient German; they are generally mine unless otherwise indicated.

I am very grateful to the friends and colleagues who have offered astute comments and criticism at various stages of this project, Astrid Schleinitz, Mary Cosgrove, Dirk Göttsche, J. J. Long, Bill Niven and Monika Albrecht. I also wish to acknowledge my MA and Ph.D. students whose vigorous discussions in postgraduate seminars have helped me to sharpen my analytical tools. Linda Shortt deserves special mention here as she has been the most dedicated and eagle-eyed proofreader of the entire manuscript, always returning chapters ahead of schedule with excellent comments. Thanks are also due to Deirdre Creighton, who has proofread the manuscript prior to submission. Last but not least, I would like to express my sincere gratitude to Michael Butler, who, as co-editor of the NPGS series, has offered invaluable editorial suggestions, supporting the completion of this book enthusiastically. Amy Lankester-Owen, editor at Palgrave/Macmillan, has also shown great support for this project, my thanks are extended to her. Finally, I wish to especially acknowledge Helen, who has supported the completion of this book in many different ways.

Anne Fuchs
Dublin

1
Introduction: Family Narratives Between Vernacular and Official Memory

The meaning of being German

Contemporary German discourse has been characterized by a remarkable upsurge in family stories about life in the National Socialist era. Evidence of this can be found in the plethora of fictional and autobiographical narratives as well as an increasing popularity of films that offer experiential representations of the war experience and its long after-life in post-war memory. This book argues that this phenomenon is more than merely a fashion created by the film industry and the publishing houses, which are often portrayed as keen to cash in on the saleability of fascinating fascism. Rather, I view this trend as symptomatic of an "agitated legacy" that continues to ignite public controversies in Germany in spite of more than four decades of analyzing, debating and coming to terms with the Nazi past. Although these debates have established the memory of National Socialism as a cornerstone of German national identity, it appears that they have not yet put to rest the agitated nature of a haunting past. We are now at the historical juncture where the immediacy of first-hand memory of this period is being lost and replaced by new forms of mediated and, at times, imaginary memories by members of the third post-war generation. This shift away from a cultural memory that was anchored in historical experience is a significant factor motivating contemporary Germany's inquiry into family life during and after the Nazi period. As this book shows, 15 years after German unification, a new discourse has emerged about familial origins, legacies and issues of generational identity, which also readdresses important questions of historical agency, choice and responsibility from the perspective of unification.

Before introducing in more detail the notion of family narratives and the attendant issue of the generational experience of history – central ideas that underpin this study – it is useful to illustrate the explosiveness of this discourse with reference to one recent example, the debate that accompanied the publication of Günter Grass's autobiography *Beim Häuten der Zwiebel* (Peeling the Onion, Engl. transl. 2007) and Joachim Fest's *Ich nicht* (Not I) in the summer of 2006. The sheer coincidence of the appearance of the two autobiographies was enough to trigger yet another ferocious controversy about the long-term legacy of National Socialism. Joachim Fest, historian and long-time editor of the influential conservative newspaper *Frankfurter Allgemeine Zeitung*, and Günter Grass, Nobel Laureate and leading representative of political conscience in post-war West Germany, represented two key positions that, from the late 1960s, have polarized public opinion in West Germany. While Grass took the view that the experience of the Third Reich and the Holocaust mark a caesura in German history that needed to be reflected and acknowledged publicly in a discourse of contrition, Fest emphasized the viability of German national identity and the continuity of German cultural traditions after the Holocaust.[1]

The controversy of the summer of 2006 was ignited by Günter Grass himself, who, in a spectacular admission, revealed that at the end of the war he was drafted into the Schutzstaffel (SS). Although Grass had acknowledged on previous occasions that, as a youngster, he was a member of the Hitler Youth who believed in the Third Reich to the end, his revelation about his SS membership discredited for some the integrity of a writer who had enjoyed a high public profile since the publication of *Die Blechtrommel* (The Tin Drum) in 1959. Grass deliberately chose the conservative *Frankfurter Allgemeine Zeitung* for his revelation in order to deflate his critics. However, he could do little to soften the blows of those who believed that the Grass case proved that left-wing commentators had occupied a position of cultural hegemony in post-war Germany for far too long.

In the following weeks, comparisons were drawn between the two texts concerning the question of what it means to be German today. The answers given by both authors in their autobiographies represented divergent evaluations by two members of the Hitler Youth generation who had lived through National Socialism in their youth. Although their stories hardly reflect the experiences of the majority of Germans under the age of 70 today, their narratives were received in terms of German meta-stories about the politics of memory and the quest for tradition. The Grass/Fest controversy resulted in a further German memory contest.[2] As explained elsewhere, in contrast to the old paradigm of "Vergangenheitsbewältigung" (overcoming the past),

> the term memory contests puts emphasis on a pluralistic memory culture which does not enshrine a particular normative understanding of the past but embraces the idea that individuals and groups advance and edit competing stories about themselves that forge their changing sense of identity. The notion of memory contests thus gives expression to the fact that memories always offer heavily edited versions of selves, groups and of their worlds.[3]

The idea of memory contests refers to the special features of German memory debates since unification. Several thematic strands dominate these debates. Firstly, the wider cultural and social divisions between East and West have become the focus of investigation since unification. Secondly, the ever-increasing historical distance from National Socialism has released the hitherto hidden or repressed archives of private family memories. Once these entered the public domain, they challenged the limits of Germany's official remembrance culture, which had been defined by a discourse of contrition. Thirdly, against the backdrop of the ageing of the former students of 1968, the memory debates of the 1990s were characterized by a huge investment in the idea of generation, along with the scrutiny of generational conflict and transgenerational dialogue.

Memory contests are highly dynamic public engagements with the past that are triggered by an event that is perceived as a massive disturbance of a community's self-understanding. In the case of Germany, this disturbance was of course caused by the period of National Socialism, which fundamentally dislodged Germans' shared self-perception as an exemplary *Kulturnation*.[4] According to centre-right promoters of a patriotic German identity, the political normalization that had been achieved by unification should have been followed by what one might call "commemorative normalization": in the eyes of commentators, such as Botho Strauß, Martin Walser, Michael Stürmer or Rainer Zitelmann, the time had come to historicize the significance of Auschwitz in order to allow for a shift away from the idea of an ever-lasting historical burden towards a positive re-imagining of the German nation based on patriotism and cultural heritage.[5] However, the meaning of being German remains a contested issue in contemporary German discourse. This question is at the heart of the Grass/Fest debate, which revolved around the issue of what kind of transgenerational legacy the Third Reich had created and whether the left-liberal or centre-right circles had been the better guardian of German identity since 1945.

Memory – individual, collective and cultural[6] – is always negotiated through symbolic representations that aim to legitimize or challenge a particular set of values.[7] Insofar as it is inevitable that our memories are socially and linguistically constituted, they are never totally authored by the remembering self.[8] As Jeffrey Prager argues, while individual memories are embodied in a particular person, they are always socially embedded.[9] Even where an absolute right to the privacy of remembrance is asserted – as, for example, in the much-debated case of Martin Walser, who, in his autobiographical novel *Ein springender Brunnen* (A Springing Fountain, 1998), attempted to divorce his childhood memories from later knowledge of NS atrocities – this very assertion places individual remembrance in the context of public debate. Accordingly, Alon Confino argues that the link between individual memories and public memories cannot be severed: historical actors simultaneously represent, receive and contest memories.[10] Confino, therefore, advocates the writing of a history of sensibilities that, in the tradition of Lucien Febvre, studies emotions and habits of mind by analyzing "how people make, negotiate, contest and dismantle symbolic representations of legitimacy, authority and values".[11]

History as family narrative

Against the backdrop of current public debates about Germany's memory culture, this study analyzes a wide range of post-1990s' fictional, autobiographical and film narratives that, from a transgenerational perspective, sift through the long after-life of National Socialism within the post-war German family. On the one hand, these texts rediscover the family as a meeting point of competing ideas of what it means to be embedded in tradition. Thus, the family becomes a *lieu de mémoire* (Pierre Nora) that reflects and shapes the cultural topoi of society. On the other hand, the family emerges in these texts as that which Aleida Assmann aptly calls a *lieu de souvenir*, a term that reflects the private and subjective quality of this site of remembrance.[12] While the narratives included in this study make divergent claims about Germany's management of the past, they all explore the family as an intersection of the private and the public, a site where official representations of the past are contested by alternative memories from below. However, the family narratives discussed here capture more than what Jan Assmann designates "communicative memory", that is the living memory that binds together three generations through everyday communication.[13] As self-reflexive artefacts, these narratives also engage with the "figures of memory" that have accompanied post-war German discourse.[14] Exploring the meaning of tradition, they focus on the mutual transfer between individual, communicative and cultural memory. One of the lines of inquiry pursued in this study therefore concerns the question why the remembrance of German wartime experiences has resurfaced with such velocity since German unification. Furthermore, the book illuminates the generational issues that have accompanied Germany's management of the past since the post-war period.

The material discussed in this study includes narratives by first-, second- and third-generation authors. While Günter Grass and Joachim Fest represent the Hitler Youth generation born between 1926 and 1930, second-generation authors include Uwe Timm, Ulla Hahn, Wibke Bruhns and Friedrich Christian Delius. Born around the early 1940s, this generation of authors has few or no personal memories of the Third Reich; their narratives show that 1968 and the subsequent critical engagement with the Nazi period was a defining experience for them. I extend the term "second-generation author" to figures such as Stephan Wackwitz, who, although he was born in 1951, defines himself in relation to the key turning point of 1968. However, in some instances, the question arises whether an author writes from a clearly defined generational position at all, as for example in the case of Sibylle Mulot, who, although she was born in 1950, claims no particular affiliation with 1968. Likewise, authors born in the mid-1950s, such as Thomas Medicus and Dagmar Leupold, could be counted as members of the second or third generation, depending on whether one considers the Hitler Youth generation as the first post-war generation that shaped and influenced the post-war period considerably. We will see later on that the selection of authors implicitly tests the boundaries of the generational paradigm.

Third-generation authors are defined by greater historical and, arguably, greater emotional distance from the events of the Third Reich. Nevertheless, the writings by Marcel Beyer and Tanja Dückers reflect that, despite growing historical distance, National Socialism has remained a symbolically charged topic. Narratives by third-generation authors draw attention to the transition from a memory culture to a post-memorial culture. While the lived experience of historical actors is a vital reference point for the first generation, the latter is characterized by processes of mediation and imagination, a distinction that is developed later on.

A note on terminology: I use the term "family narrative" for all the material included in this study, regardless as to whether the literary and filmic narratives under discussion adopt two or three generational perspectives. While narratives by members of the third generation could, with some justification, be labelled *Enkelliteratur* (literature of the grandchildren) to emphasize the third generation's huge investment in issues of genealogy, family tradition and heritage, I prefer the broader category of "family narrative" for all types of generational narratives that explore issues of lineage and tradition. Arguably, nearly all the examples discussed here are variants of the Freudian family romance, which delineates the child's pathway to independence through a process of re-imagining a noble family background before the child finally accepts the reality principle. Fantasy emerges in my study as a powerful psychological drive behind the reinvention of a better German tradition; it features in texts by second- and third-generation authors alike, and it is also a prime trope of the films included in this study.

Writing on the contemporary family narrative, Harald Welzer suggests that the popularity of such books indicates a move away from the authoritativeness of historical discourse towards what he terms "gefühlte Geschichte" (emotionally experienced history) that blurs the moral boundary between perpetrators and victims.[15] Welzer thus reads these narratives simply as a literary exemplification of wider social and cultural shifts that is the topic of his much-debated book *"Opa war kein Nazi"* (Grandpa Wasn't a Nazi, 2003).[16] In this empirical study, Welzer and his team analyzed the dialogue about the Nazi past in three generations of 40 contemporary German families. Focusing on the transformations of history in the archive of family memories, the sociologists found that even in families in which one or both grandparents were deeply embroiled in National Socialism, the family narratives evinced a high degree of loyalty to the family members. Although the grandchildren showed no signs of sympathizing with National Socialism, and although they regarded the Holocaust as a heinous crime, they tended to represent their grandparents' role during the period in an embellished light. The so-called "family album", that is the family memory, was largely unaffected by the factual knowledge of the Third Reich, for which Welzer and his team coined the term "lexicon".[17] They call such editing of family narratives across generational thresholds a process of "cumulative heroization", which draws attention to the malleability of family memory.[18] According to Bill Niven, "the depressing corollary of such conclusions is that the memory of German perpetration, guilt and suffering of Nazi victims, however intensely cultivated in school education or in acts of commemoration in the 1980s and 1990s, did not percolate down to the level of family memory".[19]

The material discussed in this book suggests, however, that such a pessimistic reading would simplify the interaction between vernacular and official memory, a point made by Niven himself. There is no clear-cut division between the private and the public; both spheres constantly shape and influence each other, often in subliminal ways. It is at best an idealistic reduction to divide post-war German memory culture into three distinct phases: a first phase of repression of the past, followed by an intense period of working through it that establishes the official discourse of contrition from the late 1960s to the early 1990s and, finally, a triumphant recovery of unofficial private memories of the Nazi period since unification. Arguably, from the 1960s onwards, German memory culture has been defined by the intrinsic tension between the emotional need for some kind of positive family and cultural heritage, on the one hand, and the cognitive engagement with the history of the Third Reich, on the other. Otherwise, it would be inexplicable why this topic continues to ignite regular memory contests in the public domain.

There is, however, one striking difference between earlier and present engagements with the past: the growing historical distance and Germany's new national confidence has now made room for a less accusatory transgenerational dialogue, which, by probing the loss of genealogy and tradition, also addresses the persistent "ghosting effect" of the Third Reich. Although Germany has become a much more confident player in the international arena, it appears that this new confidence remains shadowed by a disturbance of tradition. There remains a nearly imperceptible anxiety of influence that manifests itself in the regular assertion that Germany is a normal democracy. Observed from this angle, the emphatic assertion that "grandpa wasn't a Nazi" may mean exactly the opposite, depending on how this assertive speech act is being uttered. Ultimately, Welzer's study does not prove that the third post-war generation is characterized by an erosion of historical consciousness; rather it merely underlines once more that, in the sphere of everyday life, family memories are not normally instruments of critical reflection. Family memories are governed by irreversible kinship relations that exert particular demands on each family member.[20] The power of kinship goes a long way to explain why the family albums of the interviewed German families paint a relatively benign picture of the Nazi period.

Moreover, in contrast to the affective function of communicative memory, the narratives discussed in this book cannot simply be grouped under the heading of "emotionally experienced history". Some examples do, indeed, exhibit the tendency to embellish the memory of National Socialism; however, the majority eschew the cumulative heroization of the past. Instead, they employ generational discourse to explore the function of deferral and transference as important means of indirect communication across generational thresholds. The narratives discussed here explore the meaningful silences and gaps that have shadowed the dialogue about the past in post-war German families. Although they are preoccupied with the shifting gap between vernacular memory, on the one hand, and official memory, on the other, they do not resolve this tension in a one-sided fashion. On the contrary, the best examples of this new genre adopt a meta-critical perspective that resists the temptation to remythologize history.

This book also challenges the view that the new family narrative prioritizes familial continuity above and beyond the ruptures that characterized the 1968 generation's antagonistic engagement with their parents.[21] The direct comparison of examples of the so-called *Väterliteratur* of the 1970s and early 1980s with contemporary family narratives illustrates that, insofar as the contemporary family narrative adopts a self-reflexive perspective on inner-familial communication, it upholds the dialectic between rupture and continuity that already marked the earlier version of the generational narrative at least on a subliminal level. The new family narrative does not simply abandon this dialectic in favour of a new transgenerational solidarity between actors of the third generation and their grandparents. Rather, they subscribe to an enhanced meta-discursive approach to issues of genealogical inheritance and tradition. It is this meta-discursivity, combined with an analytical perspective on the narrator's own emotional investment in the past, that gives the new generational narrative its contemporary tonality. On the other hand, this study supports Friederike Eigler's observation that the new family narrative lacks the ideological and utopian urgency of earlier novels by Günter Grass, Christa Wolf, Uwe Johnson or Peter Weiss, all of whom were iconic figures in the 1970s and early 1980s.[22] In contrast to the older literature, the new family narrative tends to be sceptical towards all ideological offerings, underlining the historical pessimism that characterizes our globalized age.

This study deals with a range of films in order to illuminate how the quest for affiliation, lineage and belonging has surfaced in popular cinema and television productions. Both media tend to be labelled as trivial and commercial in current German memory debates and thus not worthy of academic consideration. Matthias Fiedler has argued that intellectual reservations about popular cinema in Germany today is a reflection of Siegfried Kracauer's and Walter Benjamin's early assessment of film as well as of the Frankfurt School's lasting influence on theories of popular culture.[23] It is in line with this viewpoint that Peter Reichel, writing on popular films about the Third Reich and the Holocaust, concedes the trivialization of history in popular cinema before defending its potential to make this period accessible to later generations by turning an abstract macro-history into stories about individuals.[24] Arguably, Reichel's well-meant defence underestimates the media literacy of contemporary viewers who are well versed in reading diverse film genres and their cinematic languages. Although cinema and television have a huge appeal, the media's visual immediacy does not necessarily result in a less critical engagement with issues of historical representation than in examples of "high culture". In any case, as popular cinema and television are two of the most powerful carriers of cultural identity today, we must take them seriously.

However, before these issues can be explored in greater depth, it is necessary to introduce the key ideas that have underpinned German memory debates in recent years, namely the ideas of generation and genealogy, on the one hand, and the "Germans as victims" discourse, on the other.

Generation and genealogy

In the majority of these narratives, the unifying experience of a generation is used as an explicit reference point that either validates or questions a particular set of historical explanations. However, the relationship between a generation and its historical experience is far from clear; it requires critical attention. The common understanding of the concept of a "generation" is based on membership of an age group, which exposes individuals to similar historical experiences and cultural influences. Birth date alone is an insufficient criterion for establishing a generational identity; it must be complemented by a shared historical perspective and a sense of generational cohesion. The idea of generation operates at the intersection of natural and cultural processes. Because it straddles the biological factor of birth and the cultural influences that shape a generation, the term carries the risk of explaining historical phenomena with reference to natural processes. In order to avoid this pitfall, the term requires careful handling and historical analysis. Cultural critics have come up with a range of explanations. In the 19th century, Wilhelm Dilthey defined the concept in terms of a harmonious relationship between the individual's biography and his times.[25]

Dilthey's explanation implicitly presupposed that it is great men who make great history. His concept of a generation did not really encompass the lives of ordinary people; rather it referred to the biographies of great men whose lives provide an age with a mirror of its historical and cultural achievements. In an article entitled "The problem of generations", the sociologist Karl Mannheim tried to move away from Dilthey's understanding of a "geistige" (intellectual) bond between a generation by analyzing the concept in analogy to class: like class membership, membership of a generation was not a question of choice but one of birth; however, a generation needs its members' conscious awareness to form a generational bond.[26] Mannheim advanced the level of analysis considerably by putting forward a social understanding of the idea of a generation. And yet, in spite of his achievement in this regard, he too ultimately subscribed to the notion that the *Zeitgeist* of a particular age is the product of the intellectual élite that puts its stamp on its times. Writing on the same subject, the art historian Wilhelm Pinder introduced the idea that an historical epoch is not defined by homogenous time; rather it is made up of a polyphony of generational voices that exist simultaneously with one another.[27] Having established the idea of historical simultaneity, that is the co-existence of different generational positions at any given point in time, Pinder went on to argue, however, that epochs are characterized by the emergence of an inborn and predetermined generational voice (the "entelechia") that gives its age a unique identity.[28] We can see how the debate of the concept of generation runs up against the problem of naturalizing cultural and historical processes.

Mannheim and Pinder presented their interpretations of the idea of generation in the inter-war era when the so-called "lost generation" had returned beaten and demoralized from the war.[29] Some of the former soldiers retreated into a group identity that was largely modelled on their camaraderie during the war. Resentful of the Weimar Republic, this generation channelled its disappointments into a feverish form of nationalism that wanted to tear down class barriers in favour of a community like theirs that had been forged in the trenches of the First World War. In the discourse of the generation of young men that had participated in the war, the concept was largely used to refer to particularly male forms of bonding in response to national humiliation and defeat. It is hardly surprising that the concept became increasingly contaminated by proto-fascist notions of the German nation as a "Schicksalsgemeinschaft", a community shaped by fate. From here it was only a step to the idea of a racially defined community that was predestined to change history.

The fascist contamination of the concept of generations explains why the term played little role in the humanities after the Second World War. Although the generation of defeated soldiers expressed its shared set of experiences within a generational framework, the concept of generations had become too enmeshed in National Socialism to help with the critical analysis of cultural and historical change. While it continued to play a role in everyday life, especially in youth culture, it was written out of academic discourse by the 1960s. Instead, the 1960s saw the upsurge of paradigms that emphasized the structural or functional perspective on historical change. Marxism, structuralism, functionalism, feminism, psychoanalysis and, finally, deconstructivism swept away the biographical method that had underpinned much of generational discourse; these intellectual movements also challenged the idea that great men change and write history.

Against this background, the question arises why the concept of the generation has become such a fashionable idea in contemporary memory debates. Why has it been embraced by popular culture and academics alike? Finding plausible answers to these questions is a main concern of this study, which, on the one hand, examines recent cultural expressions of generational discourse in literature, film and political culture, and on the other, offers a range of critical perspectives on the usage of the term itself.

Germans as victims of war

The trend towards the stylization of German identity as victims of Hitler's Third Reich and of the war can be seen in countless television documentaries as well as populist historical and autobiographical books that appeared from around the turn of the millennium. Sebald led the way with his public lecture series in Zurich on *Luftkrieg und Literatur* (1999; Engl. transl. *On the Natural History of Destruction*, 2003).[30] Sebald's thesis that Germans had repressed their own wartime suffering unleashed a public debate about the traumatizing effects of the war on the Germans' individual and collective psyche. Subsequently, a plethora of books and television programmes promoted Germans as victims of the war, amongst them Jörg Friedrich's controversial *Der Brand* (The Fire, 2002), and his illustrated volume *Die Brandstätten* (Sites of Burning, 2003), Christoph Kucklick's volume *Feuersturm: Der Bombenkrieg gegen Deutschland* (Firestorm: The Bombing-Raids on Germany, 2003), K. E. Franzen and Hans Lemberg's *Die Vertriebenen: Hitlers letzte Opfer* (The Expellees: Hitler's Last Victims, 2001), as well as Guido

Knopp's television documentary *Die große Flucht* (The Great Flight, 2002).[31] An early literary example of the representation of perpetrators in terms of victims of historical circumstance was Bernhard Schlink's controversial bestseller *Der Vorleser* (The Reader, 1995).[32]

The question arises whether this rediscovery of German suffering 60 years after the war is evidence of a new revisionist victim discourse that is specifically German.[33] Alternatively, there is evidence that this recoding of the war experience is a reflection of wider international trends. In a similar context, Eigler points to the cosmopolitan interpretation of the Holocaust through its endless representation in our media-dominated world. While for some the simulation of history as a form of reality television show ultimately dehistoricizes history, for others this has created a transnational memory culture characterized by solidarity.[34] Regardless of how one evaluates such trends, it is apparent that the broad relativization of the Holocaust and of the Second World War have also begun to de-demonize perpetrator nations. One interesting example in this respect is Clint Eastwood's recent anti-war film *Letters from Iwo Jima* (2006), which adopts a Japanese perspective throughout on the eponymous battle fought in February and March 1945 towards the end of the Pacific Campaign. It was released shortly after Eastwood's *Flags of our Fathers* (2006), which filmed the same battle from the American perspective. The popularity of Christian Carion's *Joyeux Noël* (2005) is another pointer in this regard: set in the trenches of the First World War on Christmas Eve 1914, the film revolves around the unofficial cease-fire between French, British and German soldiers who emerge from the trenches to play football together and exchange gifts. While Eastwood's double perspective on the same event breaks down old dichotomies, Carion's movie celebrates a moment of transnational solidarity. Two recent German television dramatizations about the end of the Second World War ought to be placed in this context: *Dresden* (ZDF, 2006; directed by Ronald Suso Richter) and *Die Flucht* (The Flight, ARD, 2007; directed by Kai Wessel). Co-financed and broadcast by Germany's main public broadcasters, they offered highly sentimental interpretations of the Third Reich, without, however, subscribing to an historical revisionism that denies or downplays German responsibility for the war. Rather both films offer a message of transnational reconciliation from the point of view of a post-Wall united Europe.

Hailed by ZDF as the first German film about the bombing of Dresden on 13 February 1945, the two-part *Dresden* is a melodrama in Hollywood style. The horror of the bombing raids is refracted through the implausible love story between the young German nurse Anna Mauth (Felicitas

Woll) and the British bomber pilot Robert Newman (John Light), who is shot down near Magdeburg and, injured, manages to make his way on foot to Dresden, where he is saved by Anna.[35] While the romance between the British pilot and the German nurse sidelines historical conflict through images of a transcending love, the dramatization of the bombing creates an apocalyptic scenario that engulfs perpetrators and victims alike: the burning Dresden is a hell on earth that consumes everybody. However, in spite of drastic images of the burning city, where a firestorm rages through the streets sucking people to its centre, of air-raid shelters full of suffocated people, of mummified corpses in the streets, of traumatized children and adults after the fire, the film's overriding message concerns the idea of inter-cultural loyalty and love. Accordingly, the sub-plot revolves around the story of a German–Jewish "inter-married" couple, who, like Robert and Anna, are also allowed to survive the bombings. In this way, the film solicits consensus about the achievements of today's multi-cultural post-Wall Europe. With its present-day message, the film thus underlines the transformation of memory according to changing views on gender, ethnicity and politics. On the other hand, it also gives expression to a residue of German resentment about the wanton destruction of one of Germany's cultural gems. The film represents this through two complementary scenes: prior to the bombing, we see how Anna and Robert climb the cupola of the famous *Frauenkirche* (Church of Our Lady), where they cast an admiring eye over Dresden's architectural grandeur; after the bombing, Robert climbs the cupola once more before it collapses to look at a devastated cityscape where endless ruins extend to the horizon. Wherever his gaze falls, there is nothing but total destruction. His speechless gaze over this ruined cityscape could be viewed as a moment of perpetrator guilt: by making a British pilot look at such a scene, the German script enacts a fantasy of punishing the victor for his deeds, thus reversing the real power relations that existed between the victorious Allies and the defeated Germans in the post-war era. In the end, however, the consensual message prevails: the film closes with documentary footage from the actual celebrations on the occasion of the opening of the re-built *Frauenkirche* in 2005, a project that had been accomplished through German–British collaboration.[36]

Dresden was followed only one year later by a complementary victim narrative, the ARD-financed two-part drama *Die Flucht*. Like *Dresden*, this melodrama employed a love story between an attractive German woman, this time the aristocratic Prussian Lena von Mahlenberg (played by Maria Furtwängler), and the enemy, a communist French PoW

(Jean-Yves Berteloot), to dramatize the expulsions from the eastern territories at the end of the war. Like *Dresden, Die Flucht* sets aside national and class differences in the face of historical calamity: crossing the frozen "Haff" (lagoon), the fugitives are attacked by bombers; the ice breaks and when the Frenchman sinks into the frozen water, Lena drags him out single-handedly. Clearly, both films centre on stories of human solidarity that subsume the historical antagonisms of the war period under the notion of an all-encompassing trauma of warfare. Although both films are politically correct in that they explicitly refer to Germany's responsibility for the war, they nevertheless exploit the popularity of trauma discourse to represent Germans as victims of war alongside other established victims. Watched by millions of Germans – each film attracted more than 10 million viewers –, the reception of these dramas was, however, extremely varied.[37] For example, writing for *Die Zeit*, Evelyn Finger criticized the television dramatizations for satisfying the desire for collective reconciliation with Germany's past by replacing historical reflection with visual icons that undermine all differentiated understanding of history.[38] The lively debate in the press and the wider public underlines once more the pluralization of Germany's memory culture. I thus agree with Bill Niven's comment that "for all the tendency towards uncritical empathy with German victimhood, then, the theme is nevertheless subject to a genuine discourse in Germany in which different views compete for public attention".[39]

A few words on Sebald's *Luftkrieg und Literatur* are necessary to outline the trajectory of this ongoing debate about the memory of history. In his contentious *Luftkrieg* essay and its by now well-rehearsed argument on the repression of German wartime suffering in the post-war period, W. G. Sebald ultimately represented older arguments that had already been made by the psychoanalysts Alexander and Margarete Mitscherlich in their widely cited work *Die Unfähigkeit zu trauern. Grundlagen kollektiven Verhaltens* (The Inability to Mourn, 1967).[40] According to the Mitscherlichs, Germans responded in the post-war period to the sudden loss of self-esteem, caused by the loss of Hitler as an object of narcissistic love, by way of "de-realizing" the past. In other words, instead of working through the Nazi past, post-war Germans chanelled their energies into the material reconstruction of West Germany. Few participants in the Sebald debate noticed that he had simply transferred the Mitscherlichs' psychoanalytic argument on the effects of repression from the Germans-as-perpetrators perspective to Germans-as-victims.[41] Furthermore, the public debate on collective repression ignored earlier criticism directed at this type of argument: in 1983 Hermann Lübbe challenged the common interpretation that repression was negative by arguing that after the war Germans needed to remain silent about National Socialism in order to build up functioning democratic institutions.[42] Lübbe interpreted this silence in terms of an "asymmetrical discretion" between the minority of Nazi opponents and the majority of Nazi supporters. For Lübbe, this discretion was essential for enabling former Nazis to become citizens of the emerging democratic order. Even from a psychoanalytical point of view, the moral interpretation of repression is problematic: as a psychological mechanism, repression is not a moral stigma but a basic psychological function that is indispensable for the operation of the human psyche.[43] While long-term repression can inhibit the individual's development, in the first instance, it is a coping mechanism when the individual can no longer process events adequately. Similarly, Alon Confino points out that, as a morally charged argument, the repression thesis resulted in a sweeping condemnation of post-war society. The myth of repression replaced the analysis of how people actually remembered the war with the notion of atonement. Confino writes, "in this dichotomous relationship, Germans could either fully atone for their crimes or else they were repressing them". And he concludes, "Rather than asking why Germans did not remember their criminal past, a better question would be what in fact they did remember of the Nazi period."[44]

The popularization of the debate on German wartime suffering in the media is governed by the idea that after unification the time had come at last to discover Germans as victims of war. However, this discussion ignored the fact that this topic had already preoccupied the public domain in the 1950s. As Robert G. Moeller has shown, the loss of the *Heimat* in eastern regions and the fate of the German Prisoners of War (PoWs) in Russia featured prominently in the political campaigns and parliamentary speeches of most post-war parties; furthermore, it was a regular concern in popular cinema where *Heimat* films were the staple diet.[45] These films managed to fuel sentiments of victimhood while simultaneously advocating West Germany as the new *Heimat*.[46] Moeller further shows that the discourse of German victimhood never left the stage: although it was sidelined in the wake of the ruptures of 1968 and the emerging critical engagement with the Nazi past, it continued to claim public attention at regular intervals.[47]

Returning to the recent debates of German wartime suffering, one ought to emphasize, however, that this topic is by no means confined to popular discourse; it also surfaced in the domain of "high literature". In contrast to the populist representations of Germans as victims, literary representations of German suffering are in most (successful) cases underpinned by an ethics of remembering that never loses sight of the basic issue of historical responsibility. Self-reflexivity is thus a hallmark of a range of books in which the end of the war and the treks from the East feature prominently. After Günter Grass had broken the ice with his novella *Im Krebsgang* (2002, Engl. transl. *Crabwalk*, 2003), other publications followed, including Reinhard Jirgl's *Die Unvollendeten* (The Incomplete, 2003). Jirgl's novel relates the story of three generations of women who, after being driven from their home in Czechoslovakia, make their way to the eastern sector, where they settle without giving up their emotional attachment to the lost *Heimat*. Similarly, Christoph Hein's *Landnahme* (Taking Possession of the Land, 2004) tells the story of a male expellee who, through a deliberate strategy of social conformism, overcomes his status as a social pariah in a small village in the East. Both narratives deal with the lives of the expellees in the GDR where, by contrast to the FRG, expellees were not awarded special status. The fate of the expellees also features in Ulrich Treichel's novella *Der Verlorene* (1998, Engl. transl. *Lost*, 1999) and in Angelika Overath's *Nahe Tage. Roman in einer Nacht* (Near Days. A Novel in One Night, 2005). Treichel focuses on an expellee family that lost one of their children on the trek, a loss that can never be compensated for by the younger son who was born after the war. By concentrating on a nuclear expellee family in the post-war period, Treichel carefully draws out the characteristic shadow of a haunting past. Similarly, Overath relates how the loss of *Heimat* was a trauma that produces a pathological mother – daughter relationship. While these literary representations examine the long-term effects of memories of the war and of the expulsions within post-war families, they reject any revisionist historical agenda. Their interest lies squarely in an exploration of the mechanisms and long-term effects of transgenerational communication and silence.[48]

A reader's guide to this book

Each chapter offers a self-contained reading of a range of family narratives. However, the chapters are arranged in such a way that they develop and fine-tune my argument about family narrative as a site where alternative visions of the past are shaped. Chapter 2 introduces the notions of generation and genealogy from an historical perspective; I then compare and contrast an example of the so-called *Väterliteratur* (fathers' literature), Christoph Meckel's *Suchbild. Über meinen Vater* (In Search of a Portrait. About my Father, 1980), with a range of contemporary family narratives, Ulla Hahn's *Unscharfe Bilder* (Blurred Images, 2003), Uwe Timm's *Am Beispiel meines Bruders* (The Example of my Brother, 2003; Engl. transl. *In My Brother's Shadow*, 2005) and Dagmar Leupold's *Nach den Kriegen* (After the Wars, 2004). Here the analysis focuses on how these narratives treat issues of affiliation, lineage and generational rupture. While the privatization of history emerges as an important feature of this literature, it is also characterized by a degree of self-reflexivity that prevents a naïve investment in a new transgenerational solidarity. Indeed, the examples of Timm and Leupold underline an analytical perspective that helps the narrators of these family stories to identify a specifically masculine code of honour as one of the reasons for the breakdown of communication in post-war families. In this way, Chapter 2 also illuminates that generational discourse is always accompanied by a discourse on gender.

Chapter 3 explores the shift from a dyadic to a triadic perspective on family history. A theoretical discussion of the idea of postmemory in the context of current trauma theory prepares the ground for a critical reading of three postmemorial narratives. I compare Günter Grass's *Im Krebsgang* with Tanja Dückers's *Himmelkörper* (Heavenly Bodies, 2003) as both stories take the same historical event, the sinking of the *Gustloff* in 1945, as a point of departure for a transgenerational exploration of hidden family legacies. The reading of Dückers's narrative highlights the danger of fetishizing the past by means of a postmemorial discourse that turns the past primarily into a site for a titillating trail hunt. In contrast, the analysis of Marcel Beyer's *Spione* (2000, Engl. transl. *Spies*, 2005) illuminates how postmemory in this novel defies our conventional understanding of historical time. We will see that Beyer's narrative challenges modernity's historical disenchantment, while also exposing the ploys of the postmemorial imagination.

Chapter 4 pursues the postmemorial investment of the past through an analysis of the significance of place in two family narratives, Thomas Medicus's *In den Augen meines Großvaters* (In my Grandfather's Eyes, 2004) and Stephan Wackwitz's *Ein unsichtbares Land* (2003; Engl. transl. *An Invisible Country*, 2005). Although both narratives are clearly derivative of Sebald's intermedial games, they deserve particular attention for their exploration of place as a prime carrier of family memory. Both narratives explore the multi-layered connections between family history, cultural memory and geopolitics through a rediscovery of former German territories in the East. Unearthing a history of violence that is embedded in these territories, they mobilize intertextuality to draw out the haunting quality of a hitherto hidden past that has shadowed family history. However, we will also see that in spite of this demonstratively self-reflexive effort, both narratives entail strong moments of identification with the very traditions they so painstakingly deconstruct.

Chapter 5 deals with a topic that has received scant critical attention beyond historical circles: resistance narratives in East and West Germany during the Cold War period and in contemporary discourse. The chapter adopts an interdisciplinary approach to analyze the symbolic value of resistance from the post-war period to the present day. I deal first with the changing historical paradigm and its interaction with wider public debates; I then discuss the representation of resistance in the *Gedenk-stätte deutscher Widerstand* (GDW) in Berlin, before turning to a range of literary examples, including Wibke Bruhns's *Meines Vaters Land* (My Father's Country, 2004), Friedrich Christian Delius's *Mein Jahr als Mörder* (My Year as an Assassin, 2004), Sibylle Mulot's *Nachbarn* (Neighbours, 1995) and Michael Wallner's *April in Paris* (2006). The chapter concludes with an in-depth discussion of three recent films about resistance: Jo Baier's *Stauffenberg. Der 20. Juli* (Stauffenberg. The 20th July, 2004), Marc Rothemund's *Sophie Scholl. Die letzten Tage* (Sophie Scholl. The Last Days, 2005) and Margarethe von Trotta's *Rosenstraße* (2003). My analysis places these films in current debates on the so-called "heritage genre" to investigate the representational choices made in each of these films. I ask to what extent these films aid a symbolic reconciliation with Germany's past either through a re-heroization of resistance or by means of a nostalgic cinematic code. All the examples discussed in this chapter underline the enormous adaptability of resistance as narrative: resistance narratives change over time because they promote our self-image.

Chapter 6 returns to the Grass/Fest controversy mentioned earlier. Against the backdrop of current debates on autobiography and life writing, I compare and contrast Grass's and Fest's respective narratives as two examples of Hitler Youth autobiographies that negotiate the need for biographical continuity in the context of massive historical upheaval. We will see that both books also gave rise to a public re-evaluation of the Hitler Youth generation's prominent role in post-war West Germany. However, a brief comparison of other autobiographical narrat-ives by Ludwig Harig, Martin Walser and Christa Wolf underscores once more that one ought not to apply the generational paradigm rigidly as an interpretive straightjacket because it can limit the under-standing of generational diversity in terms of political and other differ-ences. My in-depth discussion of Grass and Fest explores how the two authors employ the autobiographical paradigm to give expression to diametrically opposed versions of the meaning of personal memory in the context of history. Grass engages in a highly self-conscious narrative that, on the one hand, exposes the gulf between his former and his present selves and, on the other, scrutinizes the constant interplay between his own biography and his fictional work. In sharp contrast, Fest displays strong authorial confidence vis-à-vis his own life, his understanding of the NS past and of the post-war period. The self in this narrative is represented as heir of a better Germany that was embodied by the educated bourgeoisie. The enthusiastic reception of Fest's autobiography in the press suggests that the conservative project of re-instating German patriotism has gained support beyond right-wing circles.

And yet, on the other hand, the books, films and public debates included in my study demonstrate that this quest for a viable tradition in unified Germany remains ambivalent and, ultimately, strongly contested. While all of the narratives discussed here rediscover generational identity and family as a way of recouping notions of heritage and belonging, the majority of examples shows up tradition as a trope of fantasy, a phantom that continues to haunt those who want to anchor the self in a stable past. Freud's family romance ends with the acceptance of the reality principle. Similarly, in the family romances discussed here, the dream of a better German past remains bounded by the ethical obligation to acknowledge history as it actually happened. The contemporary German family narrative also engages in a dialogue with the historical narrative proper: by ignoring the institutionalized boundaries between the past and the present, it confronts the reader with the persistence of non-historicizing visions of the past. Faced with the uncomfortable uncertainties of our own globalized age, it enacts a necromantic drama that involves the dead and the living. By making the memory of loss one of its prime concerns, the contemporary family narrative challenges the expulsion of ghosts from our technology-driven, supermodern world. The past in this narrative may be a site of violence, but it is also a site of missed historical agency that can be retroactively imagined as an alternative history that, unfortunately, never happened.

2
Generational Conflict and Masculinity in *Väterliteratur* by Christoph Meckel, Uwe Timm, Dagmar Leupold and Ulla Hahn

Väterliteratur and the language of silence

Väterliteratur (fathers' literature) could be considered a late by-product of the student movement of 1968 in that some of its former members embarked on a literary exploration of post-war German family life in the late 1970s.[1] Concerned with the authoritarian father figures that, according to these authors, dominated the family dynamics of the post-war period, *Väterliteratur* attempts to show how the National Socialist past of the war generation infiltrated post-war family life. Wavering between a whimsical style, on the one hand, and outright aggression towards the domineering father figure, on the other, these narratives have been dismissed by some critics for their apparent lack of critical distance and the shrillness of their tone.

A case in point is Ernestine Schlant, who discusses the genre in her 1999 study, *The Language of Silence*, and notes that the majority of these narratives share so many substantive, linguistic and structural similarities that they are "virtually formula novels".[2] For Schlant, the genre largely fails to make the important connection between family life and political practice. This narrative insufficiency is further compounded by the genre's failure to come to terms with the Holocaust. Although she concedes that many of the narratives "approach the Holocaust subjectively, through the narrator's attempt at conversations with their elders", she deplores the peripheral role of Jews in this literature: "In narratives that are full of one specific sort of affect – anger against the parent and rage at the mistreatment of the child – there is a curious lack of affect when it comes to the Holocaust."[3]

Schlant's dismissal of the genre reflects the normative approach underpinning her entire book, which posits that all German narratives about National Socialism must also foreground the Holocaust and its victims. In clear contrast to Schlant's view, this chapter argues that *Väterliteratur* made a valid contribution to German memory contests by exposing the intergenerational dynamic that shaped post-war family life. Notwithstanding the emotional style of many of these narratives, the best examples of the genre helped to deconstruct a particular notion of masculinity, which has its bedrock in the *völkisch* ideology of the early 20th century.

Using Christoph Meckel's *Suchbild. Über meinen Vater* (In Search of a Portrait. About my Father, 1980) as a point of departure and as an example of many of the original characteristics of the genre, I will move on to a discussion of three recent versions of the genre: Uwe Timm's *Am Beispiel meines Bruders* (The Example of my Brother, 2003), Ulla Hahn's *Unscharfe Bilder* (Blurred Images, 2003) and Dagmar Leupold's *Nach den Kriegen* (After the Wars, 2004). Three of these narratives aim to create a high degree of authenticity: they are not works of fiction but autobiographical narratives written in an analytical-discursive style that embeds family history in the history of the German nation. Timm, Meckel and Leupold build their own biographies into their narratives to ensure that their analysis of post-war family life is read in terms of a psychological diagnosis of a collective condition. The continuities and discontinuities between Meckel's father book and the contemporary revival of the genre will be examined with reference to their respective treatment of the intergenerational dynamic and, in particular, the theme of masculinity in the four narratives. Before discussing these narratives in some detail, it is, however, necessary to elaborate the concept of "generation".

Between rupture and continuity: Generational discourse

"It is difficult to think of a notion that has become more commonplace yet at the same time more opaque than that of 'generation'."[4] The opening sentence of Pierre Nora's analysis of the establishment of the concept of generations through the French Revolution summarizes well the semantic ubiquity and elasticity of the term. From a contemporary German point of view, the business of talking about generational experience appears to have become particularly fashionable in the last decade, that is, precisely at the historical juncture when the aging members of the generation of 1968 began to examine critically their youthful protest in the 1960s and the long-term effect this had on society.[5] While this already points to a crucial link between the modern usage of the term "generation" and youthful revolutionary zest, in the post-war landscape the term had, of course, wide currency among other social cohorts, above all the war generation, whose first-hand involvement with and experience of National Socialism and of the Second World War was a constant reference point for its self-understanding. Born around 1905, this generation had actively supported National Socialism and, after the war, adopted a position that the historian Norbert Frei describes as characterized by the "reflexive denial of guilt" and the "refusal to communicate".[6] It was precisely this generation's self-understanding that triggered the intergenerational contest between fathers and sons and fathers and daughters in the wake of 1968. Sandwiched between the war generation and the generation of 1968 are members of the so-called "sceptical generation". Born between 1925 and 1930, its members, including Günter Grass, Martin Walser and Hans Magnus Enzensberger, were socialized during National Socialism but emphatically embraced the project of a critical engagement with Germany's past in the post-war period.[7]

As Sigrid Weigel observes, such counting of generations can be observed in disciplines where history is interpreted with reference to a massive historical caesura, above all in German historiography since 1945, in Holocaust studies, and also in postcolonial studies. A generational genealogy appears to have the dual advantage of providing us with a clear model of periodization and of anchoring these periods in collective memory. However, Weigel rightly points out that our modern, largely synchronic usage of the term "generation" as membership in a given age group with a shared experiential horizon has taken the place of a much older semantics that encompasses the idea of genesis and genealogy. Etymologically, the term goes back to Greek *genos* and Latin *generatio*, which connote genealogy, reproduction, lineage and thus the historical continuity of a people, race or species. Clearly, genealogy and lineage are diachronic ideas, spanning several generations and thereby establishing the continuity of history by means of the genealogical ordering of origin and sequence. The notion of generation is rooted in biological meaning, but at the same time it regulates legal, social and cultural issues of affiliation through inheritance laws.[8]

As Pierre Nora shows, a shift away from genealogy occurred during the French Revolution. With the revolution of 1789, youth burst onto the political scene, eradicating the *ancien régime's* hereditary rule in favour of democratic principles of free individuals, unburdened by lineage and heritage. It is therefore not coincidental that the Declaration of the Rights of Man of 1793 proclaims, "a generation has no right to subject any future generation to its laws".[9] This implies that generations as a social and political force are bound up with the idea of constant regeneration and thus the notion of youth. What Nora terms the "eschatology of rupture" makes the revolution an intrinsically generational phenomenon that gives birth to an egalitarian world in which historical change accelerates.[10] However, in clear contrast to the real caesura of 1789, the rupture of 1968 is for Nora merely symbolic: he reads 1968 in terms of "a revolutionary mime" in which nothing really happened other than "a violent affirmation of horizontal identity that suddenly dominates and transcends all forms of vertical solidarity".[11] Blasting away older forms of solidarity, such as family or class, the idea of generation took the place of other social allegiances. "In a world of constant change", writes Nora, "in which every individual has occasion to become his or her own historian, the generation is the most instinctive way of converting memory into history. Ultimately that is what a generation is: the spontaneous horizon of individual historical objectification."[12]

With its emphasis on regeneration through rupture, Nora's analysis highlights the revolutionary evolvement of the modern meaning of the term "generation"; however, he also draws attention to the concept's underside, namely a sense of lack and mourning about those moments of historical grandeur that later generations have not experienced. His reading is firmly embedded in French historiography in that it posits a melancholy relationship of the Romantics to the French Revolution who, in their historical writings, reflect on their own sense of belatedness. The lack of participation in the formative moment of the nation's history becomes a source of melancholy reflection. The same sense of being born in history's aftermath informs the post-war generation's perspective on the Second World War as a further momentous historical event. Nora's reflection on melancholy as the underside of generational renewal shows that, in spite of the French Revolution, the concept remains ultimately entangled in a discourse about origins and heritage.

It is precisely this ambiguity that characterizes German *Väterliteratur* of the late 1970s and early 1980s. On the one hand, *Väterliteratur* refutes the importance of tradition and lineage in quite an aggressive fashion and, on the other, many of these narratives also express a melancholy longing for the very ideas that they attack so vehemently. However, since the rejection of tradition is the main ideological force behind

Väterliteratur, this longing for lineage is never properly addressed in these texts; it only finds indirect expression on the level of subtext. The need for tradition and heritage thus remains an unresolved issue in the first wave of *Väterliteratur*. This helps to explain why a new version of the genre has become popular in German literature since the late 1990s: the repressed longing for tradition now resurfaces in terms of a transgenerational legacy that requires further working through. In today's Germany, what Pierre Nora calls "the tinderbox of memory" has ignited a new interest in generational identity and genealogical traditions.[13] Analyzing the genre's characteristic oscillation between rupture and continuity, this chapter demonstrates that many of these narratives locate the need for a break with the past in a particular form of masculinity.

Of damaged fathers and ruined families: Christoph Meckel and Uwe Timm

Väterliteratur is, of course, not an invention of the generation of 1968. Its paradigmatic precursor is Franz Kafka's *Brief an den Vater* (Letter to My Father, 1919), which, with its accusatory style, sets the tone for the genre. Referring to his deep-seated fear of his father Hermann, Kafka in the opening sentences paints a picture of a physically and mentally domineering father, whose greatest failing, however, is assimilation. Focusing on the lack of Jewish rites and traditions in the family's life, Kafka's text makes the disturbance of genealogy and tradition one of its main concerns.

While the patriarch in Kafka's narrative is a powerful ogre of sorts, in Christoph Meckel's *Suchbild*, the father is portrayed simultaneously as a despot and as a helpless figure.[14] Opening with the happy memory of a ride in the father's car, a significant moment that the narrator associates with a feeling of safety and blind trust, a sense of reassurance in the father's proximity (*S*, 9), the narrative then sets out to dismantle this image. Christoph's father, Eberhard Meckel (born in 1907), was a traditionalist poet and literary critic, who, throughout the 1930s, continued to write poetry and stories untouched by the times. For Meckel, his father's lyrical escapism is a signature of an entire generation of intellectuals, who, unlike the émigrés Brecht, Döblin and Mann, relied on a depoliticized belief in universal values:

> Allerlei Literaten seiner Generation (eine ganze Phalanx der jüng-
> sten Intelligenz) lebten erstaunlich zeitfremd weiter. Man kapselte

sich in Naturgedichten ab, verkroch sich in die Jahreszeiten, im Ewigen, Immergültigen, Überzeitlichen, in das Naturschöne und Kunstschöne, in Vorstellung von Trost und in den Glauben an die Hinfälligkeit zeitbedingter Miseren. (*S*, 22)

[All sorts of writers of his generation (a whole phalanx of the youngest intelligentsia) continued to live a life untouched by the politics of the day. They shut themselves away into their nature poetry, seeking refuge in the seasons, the everlasting and eternal and transcendental spheres, in nature and art's beauty, in notions of comfort and the belief that the wretched state of things was a temporary affair.][15]

This generation's subscription to a catalogue of humanistic values goes hand in hand with a strong belief in the Prussian military tradition that is seen in opposition to the vulgarity of National Socialism. For Meckel, it is highly significant that the father abhors National Socialism not so much for its ideology but for its lack of style (*S*, 34). He shows that the father's snobbish disinterest in politics only disguises his support for brutalized forms of violence that National Socialism legitimized. Interspersing the biographical narrative about the father with quotations from the father's war diaries, the narrator draws out the father's growing collusion with National Socialism. For example, an entry of 24 January 1944 mentions Auschwitz in the following way:

Im Abteil eine Frau, in Lemberg zivilangestellt; sie erzählt von einem Frühstück in einem Warschauer Lokal, das 4000 Zloty gekostet hat, von den Schiebereien und Geschäftsmethoden der Deutschen allenthalben in der Verwaltung. Bestechungen Überpreise und dergleichen mehr, vom KZ in Auschwitz usw. – Als Soldat ist man doch so fern all dieser Dinge, die einen im Grunde auch gar nicht interessieren; man steht für ein ganz anderes Deutschland draußen und will später im Kriege sich nicht bereichert haben, sondern ein sauberes Empfinden besitzen. Ich habe nur Verachtung für diesen zivilen Unrat. (*S*, 43)

[In my train compartment was a woman who was employed as a civilian in Lemberg; she talks about a breakfast in a café in Warsaw that cost her 4000 Zloty, the racketeering of the Germans everywhere in the administration. Bribes, higher charges, and things like that, she also mentioned the KZ in Auschwitz etc. – As a soldier one is quite removed from all this stuff, things that don't really interest one; one stands for quite a different Germany in the field and after the war one does not wish to have profited from the war but one wants to come back with a clean conscience. I can only despise such civilian vermin.]

The laconic reference to Auschwitz and the ensuing reflection on the soldier's emotional distance from the reality of war and persecution brings into relief the image of the cold persona, detached from all empathy and emotional involvement. The entry of 27 January 1944 reinforces this image drastically: the diarist describes how, on his way to lunch, he witnessed the public execution of 28 Poles. Noting the "wüster Leichenhaufen" (horrible pile of corpses) after the atrocity, he emphasizes that, in spite of the ghastliness of this scene, it left him completely untouched as the execution was simply the "Muster eines Volksschauspiels der neuen Zeit" (*S*, 43–44; an example of the popular drama of our new times). It is precisely the shocking coldness of these diary entries that motivates this investigation of the father's life: having read the war diary, the son can no longer treat his relationship with his father merely as a personal affair. The diary turns the seemingly private into a case study of an entire generation. What follows is an anatomy of this generation's value system, which, with its deep-seated authoritarianism, relied on the military code of honour, conformity and duty to the fatherland to sidestep the notion of individual responsibility and conscience. Taking over the "Toilettenjargon der Herrenmenschen" (*S*, 50; the lavatory slang of the superior race), the father is shown to also adopt the eliminatory racism and anti-Semitism of Nazism.

Meckel's anatomy of a generation thus goes far beyond a mere accounting of personal childhood injuries. His portrait of a father makes an important connection between National Socialism and a code of honour that goes back to Wilhelmine society and fully flourished during the First World War. As Helmut Lethen has shown in his brilliant study of the German anthropology of the interwar period, the loss of the First World War mobilized a culture of heroic shame.[16] In contrast to a culture of guilt, which operates on the basis of introspection, a culture of shame employs social fears and conventions to produce a functionalized notion of selfhood that is built on appearance and image rather than on subjectivity and self-expression.[17] Against the backdrop of defeat in the First World War and in the face of the massive social transformations of the Weimar Republic, the figure of the cold persona emerged in the 1920s, advocating the masking of pain and emotion behind a protective shield. The experience of the First World War had already produced what Lethen calls the "cold armour of honour, courage, fame and hardness", the paradigmatic expression of which is the figure of Ernst Jünger's "steel warrior", a point to which I return later. As Lethen shows, the cult of coldness emphasizes techniques of mimicry and masking in order to disguise the subject's vulnerability; with its code of honour, it reflects specifically male fears of exposure and maps out a masculine notion of selfhood.

The total exclusion of woman from this arena of self-construction is exemplified by Helmuth Plessner's anthropology of the interwar period: according to Plessner, the self must only enter the public arena equipped with a knight's armour. He writes, "everything psychological that shows itself in its nakedness runs the risk of being ridiculous".[18] Without his protective shield, the self is reduced to the powerlessness of the creature. Bereft of social status, membership of a class and the protective shield of social conventions, the creature leads a pariah existence at the bottom of the social pile.[19] The creature is the unmasked self, the self without protection, human existence as "terrified organism in fear of death"[20] or, in the words of Georgio Agamben, it is bare life.[21] The anthropology of the 1920s thus reacted to the perceived risk of social degradation by formulating a theory of social self-constitution based on the idea of the social mask and a hard masculinity. Only in the safety of the private home can the cold persona drop his mask. Plessner's male subject is thus an extremely guarded self that can only find temporary relief from the demands of constant self-control through a woman's gift of love. As Lethen comments, woman is thus excluded from this "fencing arena of the subject's constitution".[22]

In Meckel's *Suchbild*, the extracts from the narrator's father's war diaries display how, in the course of the war, he adopted the cold persona, turning himself into a steel warrior who remained untouched by the suffering of the Polish and Jewish civilian population around him. Far more than a settling of old scores, the book aims to deconstruct precisely this notion of masculinity that spans the two world wars and reaches into the post-war period. After his imprisonment as a prisoner of war, the father returned as a dethroned, helpless despot, wavering between sudden outbursts of rage and moments of tearful sentimentality. Although the father is shown to accept the idea of German collective guilt, according to his son, he ultimately failed to deal with the far more pressing question of his personal responsibility. His anecdotal stories about the cruelty of war glossed over his own involvement and engaged in a settlement of guilt, based on a "Punktsiegstrategie" (*S*, 86), a scoring of moral brownie points that utilizes precisely the same code of honour that had fuelled NS ideology. A good example of this is the father's insistence that his behaviour during the war was always "TADELLOS"[23] (*S*, 86; irreproachable); it betrays a breathtaking clouding of conscience that, according to Frei, is the signature of the war generation's attitude to the past. The total ruination of Germany's infrastructure is reflected in the ruination of the German family:

> Der Krieg hatte die Familien zugrunde gerichtet. Die Väter taumelten nach Hause, lernten ihre Kinder kennen und wurden als Eindringlinge abgewehrt. Sie waren fürs erste verbraucht und hatten nichts Gutes zu sagen. Der für den Vater freigehaltene Platz wurde von einem Menschen besetzt, der fremd und feindlich oder zerrüttet war und Position als Erzieher bezog – das war nicht glaubhaft. Beschädigte Ehen und verstörte Gefühle, Ruinen, Hunger und schlechte Aussichten auf Zukunft, zehnmal geflickte Strümpfe und kalte Öfen – wie sollte da Freude in den Familien sein. (*S*, 95)

[The war had ruined the families. The fathers staggered back home, meeting their children who rejected them as intruders. They were exhausted and had nothing positive to communicate. The place that had been reserved for the father was now taken by a person who was alien and hostile or shattered and who assumed the position of educator – that was hardly credible. Damaged marriages and disturbed feelings, ruins, hunger and bad prospects, socks ten times darned and cold stoves – how could there have been any sense of joy in the families?]

Meckel's narrative is scathing, but offers a highly analytical reading of the problem of masculinity in the post-war period. Entitling his narrative "Suchbild" (in search of/an attempt at a portrait), Meckel draws attention to the fact that, as a narrative combining the selection and evaluation of the biographical data of his father's life, his portrait necessarily entails a degree of fictionalization: "Die Erfindung offenbart und verbirgt den Menschen" (*S*, 55; invention always reveals and disguises a human being).

The title of Uwe Timm's *Am Beispiel meines Bruders* seems to suggest a significant shift of emphasis: instead of homing in on the father, the narrative is triggered by the figure of Timm's older brother Karl-Heinz, who joined the Waffen-SS at the age of 18 and was killed on the eastern front on 16 October 1943.[24] Timm's narrative analyzes how, after his death, the older brother assumed an iconic status in the family's collective memory of itself; representing the notion of "der tapfere

Junge" (*AB*, 16), the brave boy who never lied and was always obedient (*AB*, 21). The family legend turned the figure of the brother into an exemplary icon, embodying precisely those problematic male virtues that ignited the conflict between fathers and sons and fathers and daughters in the post-war period. Unlike Meckel, who erases his mother and siblings from his account[25] in order to accentuate the father–son conflict, Timm includes all family members: the story about his brother is primarily a story about the brother's phantom-like existence in the post-war family. Notwithstanding this important widening of scope, the book can be read as a variant of *Väterliteratur* because it too unmasks the patriarchal underpinnings of post-war German society.

However, Timm's narrative investigation of post-war German family dynamics can only take place on the basis of historical distance: only after his mother and older sister have died, is he at liberty to scrutinize the family legend (*AB*, 12). As in Meckel's *Suchbild*, it is a diary, in this case the brother's shocking war diary, that necessitates the narrator's inquiry. Beginning on 14 February 1943, the diary records every day at the front until it suddenly terminates on 7 August of the same year. Devoid of any emotional involvement or subjective reflections, the diary makes highly disturbing reading: "75m raucht Iwan Zigaretten, ein Fressen für mein MG" (*AB*, 19; 75m away Ivan smoking cigarettes, fodder for my MG).[26] As in Meckel's case, the narrative opens with a happy and emotionally charged childhood memory:

> Erhoben werden – Lachen, Jubel, eine unbändige Freude – diese Empfindung begleitet die Erinnerung an ein Erlebnis, ein Bild, das erste, das sich mir eingeprägt hat, mit ihm beginnt für mich das Wissen von mir selbst, das Gedächtnis [...]. (*AB*, 9)
>
> [Lifted up into the air – laughter, jubilation, boisterous delight – that sensation accompanies my recollection of an experience, an image, the first to make a lasting impression on me, and with it begins my self-awareness, my memory [...]. (*MB*, 1)]

Describing a hide-and-seek game between the toddler and his older brother, the narrative begins with a Proustian scene, a unique moment of exuberant reunification. However, for all of its uplifting symbolism, this iconic moment of togetherness will remain isolated. Instead of insisting on the depoliticized innocence of one's childhood memories as Martin Walser has done in *Ein springender Brunnen* (A Springing Fountain, 1998), Timm shows how deeply the personal is affected by the political. The complete absence of any dreams, desires and hopes from the brother's war diary exemplifies this; with its exclusive focus on the war, the technical preparation of the attacks, target practice and war technology, it bars access to the brother's inner self: "Um die eigene Geschichte und um die Erfahrbarkeit eigener Gefühle betrogen, bleibt nur die Reduktion auf Haltung und Tapferkeit" (*AB*, 31; cheated of his own story, of a chance to experience his own feelings, he was reduced to putting a brave face on things; *MB*, 22). What comes into relief here is how the military code of courage that masks the brutality of the war also erases the self's sense of subjectivity and self-expression to a point where it makes little sense to speak of selfhood.

The post-war family legend does not reflect on the brother's reduction to a functionalized soldier during the war; his name continues to be shorthand for the still unquestioned masculine code of honour that was carried into the post-war period by the war generation born around the turn of the 20th century. Like Meckel, Timm analyzes how this generation of fathers responded to its degradation at the end of the war by exercising its deeply ingrained authoritarianism within the four walls of the family unit: "Die Kommandogewalt hatten sie im öffentlichen Leben verloren, und so konnten sie nur noch zu Hause, in den vier Wänden, herumkommandieren" (*AB*, 69; our fathers had lost the power of command in public life and could exercise it only at home, within their own four walls; *MB*, 59). Politically, militarily and mentally dethroned, this generation is also shown to be morally and emotionally obtuse: its inability to mourn is paradigmatically reflected in conversations of the "Kameraden" (fellow soldiers), which routinely revolve around missed opportunities to win the war:

Sie kamen abends, saßen zusammen, tranken Cognac und Kaffee und redeten über den Kriegsverlauf. Suchten Erklärungen, warum der Krieg verloren gegangen war. Es wurden noch einmal Schlachten geschlagen, Befehle korrigiert, unfähige Generäle abgesetzt, Hitler die militärische Befehlsgewalt entzogen. Kaum vorstellbar, daß das abendfüllende Themen für diese Generation waren. (*AB*, 78)

[They came round in the evening, sat together, drank coffee and cognac and talked about the war. They tried to find explanations for why it had been lost. Battles were fought all over again, wrong orders put right, incompetent generals dismissed, Hitler deprived of his command of the army. It is hardly imaginable now to think of that generation discussing such subjects all evening. (*MB*, 67)]

This moral obtuseness, which turns the war into an adventure park of sorts, goes hand in hand with massive linguistic deformations that affect the discourse of the post-war period. Dodging the question of individual moral responsibility, the parental generation hides behind linguistic stereotypes that allow the construction of a victim identity: "Hitler der Verbrecher. Die Sprache wurde nicht nur von den Tätern öffentlich mißbraucht, sondern auch von denen, die von sich selbst sagten, *wir sind noch einmal davon gekommen.* Sie erschlichen sich eine Opferrolle" (*AB*, 106–7; Hitler the criminal. Language was publicly misused not only by the killers but also by those who said of themselves, *well we got off again.* They slipped into the victim's role under false pretences; *MB*, 95). Peppered with the Nazi jargon of the *Endlösung* and the *Untermensch* or the countless abbreviations of the Nazi apparatus, the war stories of these war comrades display a far-reaching mutilation of the German language and mentality (*AB*, 101). The physical expression of this generation's moral deformation is the ubiquitous image of the damaged male body:

> Die Kommißsprache, die Sprachverstümmelungen, die ihre Entspre-chungen in körperlicher Versehrtheit fanden; die Hinkenden, an Krücken Gehenden, die mit einer Sicherheitsnadel hochgesteckten leeren Jackenärmel, die umgeschlagenen Hosenbeine, die quiet-schenden Prothesen. (*AB*, 101)

> [Army terminology, linguistic mutilations that found their counter-part in physical injury: men limping on crutches, an empty jacket sleeve fastened with a safety pin, trouser legs turned up, squeaking artificial limbs. (*MB*, 90)]

Here, Timm draws attention to the fact that the German war narrative always included stories of the bombing raids. Referring to the bombing of his family's home on 25 July 1943, Timm traces the slow conversion of the traumatic experience into an entertaining anecdote in the family legend: the repetitive re-telling of the family's flight through the burning streets of Hamburg produced eventually a formulaic narrative that disguised the original trauma: "Das Eigentümliche war, wie der Schock, der Schreck, das Entsetzen durch das wiederholte Erzählen langsam faßlich wurde, wie das Erlebte langsam in seinen Sprachformeln verblaßte" (*AB*, 41–2; it was strange the way in which shock, alarm, horror gradually became comprehensible through repeated telling, the way experiences slowly faded when put into words; *MB*, 31).

Like Meckel's father, Timm's father subscribes to a code of behaviour that aims to mask the self's vulnerability. A polished host and gifted after-dinner speaker, the father lives in permanent status anxiety. With a constant eye on what people might think of him, he embodies the culture of shame that Lethen's book analyzes. Fearing ridicule and public exposure, the father evaluates himself only in terms of his public appearance: "Was die Leute denken, das war die immerwährende Sorge um die eigene Geltung. Nicht in der oberflächlichen Bedeutung, was die anderen von einem halten, sondern als Spiegel dessen, was man selbst von sich halten kann, was ist man, als was erscheint man" (*AB*, 82; what would people think? He was constantly anxious about his status. Not in the superficial sense of what others thought of him, but as reflecting his own idea of himself, of what he was and what kind of figure he cut; *MB*, 72). This fear of embarrassment, which again has its historical roots in the Wilhelmine code of honour and the experience of defeat in the First World War, internalizes the gaze of the onlooker, the social other. Lethen suggests that the cold persona's refusal to mourn after the Second World War points to the repetition of an attitude that, after the end of the First World War, had great resonance in the public.[27] An important example in this respect is Carl Schmitt, who in 1947 described his imprisonment as an American PoW in terms of a degrading nakedness.[28]

Entangled in their code of honour, this generation of fathers also re-enacts the erasure of women, which had already characterized the anthropology of the interwar period. For the father, girls simply do not count: the father's chauvinistic desire to be a father of sons leads to the complete marginalization of Timm's older sister, who, as the first-born child with the wrong gender, is shunned by the father – none of the family photographs show the father in physical contact with his daughter; as the narrator emphasizes, she is never in his arms or holding hands or on his lap (*AB*, 51 and *MB*, 41). Dismantling the enshrined status of the absent dead brother, Timm also questions the gender politics of the post-war period. His reading of the family dynamic is a counter-reading that investigates the place of the female actors in the post-war family. The book therefore gives detailed portraits of the mother and the older sister: carefully restoring the place of the sister in the family romance, Timm shows how she lived under the shadow of the idealized dead brother.

Timm portrays his mother as a realist, a breadwinner and a loving caregiver who adjusts to the harsh conditions of 1945 and who continues to run the family business into old age. Unlike Meckel, who in his *Suchbild*.

Meine Mutter launches a shrill attack on his mother, Timm is careful to respect the integrity of his mother's life. Although she is a member of the war generation and ultimately shares its value system, her realism is shown to be an important counterpoint to the ideological rigidity of the *pater familias*. Timm empathizes with this generation of mothers and daughters who, subordinating their own needs, saw their families through the post-war period.

Timm's dialogic investigation of the past marks a significant shift away from the antagonistic examination of the parental generation in the father books of the late 1970s and 1980s. However, it would be a mistake to suggest that this indicates the neat transition from the earlier paradigm of rupture towards a new paradigm of transgenerational continuity and understanding. Although Timm demonstrates a heightened self-awareness and the ability to empathize with his family members, like Meckel he too distances himself from the male protagonists with their cold persona and false code of honour. And although Meckel's first impulse is the desire for rupture, the force of his antagonism points to a latent desire for a family life that would be unaffected by the war and National Socialism. Motivated by the anxiety of influence, he engages in a narrative exorcism that aims to destroy all traditional forms of transgenerational solidarity. And yet, the flipside of such monologic gestures of self-proclamation and conflict is an underlying sense of loss of meaningful traditions and models of lineage. The violent affirmation of renewal through a generational break remains willy-nilly wedded to the concept's genealogical dimension.

Between sentimental empathy and historical analysis: Fathers as soldiers in Ulla Hahn and Dagmar Leupold

In contrast to Timm's inclusion of the females in the narrative, Ulla Hahn and Dagmar Leupold return to a more narrow focus on the father – daughter relationship, a precursor of which is Elisabeth Plessen's *Mitteilung an den Adel* (Message for the Nobility, 1976). Hahn's *Unscharfe Bilder*, the only text discussed here that is not autobiographical but a novel, exploits one of the most significant memory contests of the 1990s, namely the debate around the controversial exhibition *Vernichtungskrieg. Verbrechen der Wehrmacht 1941–1945*, which documented the large-scale involvement of the so-called "ordinary" soldiers in war crimes. When some of the captions of the photos were proven to be historically inaccurate, the exhibition was withdrawn and re-launched after the necessary corrections were made. Some 850,000 visitors saw the exhibition in Germany and Austria, with many visitors looking at the photos with magnifying glasses to identify family members.[29]

In Hahn's novel, the exhibition is used as a ploy that ignites a conflict between father and daughter.[30] The protagonists are Hans Musbach, a retired school teacher, and his daughter Katja, who has followed in her father's footsteps and embarked on a teaching career. Musbach is introduced as a refined and enlightened person who embraces the same belief in education and humanism that features in Meckel's *Suchbild*. But unlike Meckel, Hahn's Katja maintains a cordial and warm relationship with her father until she visits the Wehrmacht exhibition, where she believes she recognizes her father in one of the photographs. However, this revelation comes only at the end of the novel: at the beginning, Katja gives a copy of the exhibition catalogue to her father to jog his memory, an unwanted gift because, in his view, he has done his bit as a teacher by analyzing and discussing the past with his students for decades (*UB*, 18). The structure of the detective novel allows Hahn to record the daughter's intermittent interrogation of her father.

Forcing the father to confront the past, Katja seeks an admission of personal guilt. The narrative uses a quotation from Wittgenstein's *Philosophische Untersuchungen* (Philosophical Investigations, posthumously published in 1953) as a recurring leitmotiv: "Ist eine unscharfe Fotografie überhaupt ein Bild eines Menschen? Ja, kann man ein unscharfes Bild immer mit Vorteil durch ein scharfes ersetzen? Ist das unscharfe nicht oft gerade das, was wir brauchen?" (is a blurred photograph really an image of a person? Indeed, is it always in our interest to replace a blurred image with a sharp one? Is not the blurred image often exactly what we need?). In the dialogue between father and daughter, the notion of the blurred image is a contested issue: while Katja insists on "sharp images", that is the need for historical objectivity and documentation, her father emphasizes the truth of his subjective memories. Nevertheless, he accepts his daughter's challenge to immerse himself once more in the past and narrates a series of war stories that include all the formulaic elements of war narratives, such as the soldiers' plight at the Russian front, the experience of hunger, coldness, camaraderie, cruelty and the loss of a best friend. As Helmut Schmitz has shown, Musbach's experiences can be traced back to Hans Joachim Schröder's *Die gestohlenen Jahre* (The Stolen Years, 1992) and the collection *Kriegsbriefe gefallener Soldaten 1939–1945* (1952, Letters from the Front by Soldiers Killed in Action), which Hahn consulted for her book.[31] Another important ingredient in this cocktail of youthful innocence and suffering is his love story about his time with Wera, a Russian partisan whose life he claims to have saved. Seeing through this story as a screen memory,[32] the daughter eventually musters up her courage and asks him directly whether he was the soldier in the Wehrmacht exhibition photo who is shown to execute someone. The father now tells a new story about how an SS soldier who knew him from school had forced him to kill a Russian civilian (*UB*, 268–9). The execution scene converts the perpetrator into a victim of sorts and reintroduces the dubious notion of "Befehlsnotstand" (following orders) into the debate: the father portrays himself here as an ordinary soldier who was forced to carry out a war crime against his will. Although Hahn appears to subject this scene to historical scrutiny by having Katja discover that, in the photograph, nobody was standing behind the soldier (*UB*, 274), the narrative ends on a highly ambivalent and ultimately unsatisfactory note: when in a final twist the broken father admits that nobody had forced him to shoot, the daughter absolves him from her charge because the date of the photo does not coincide with the father's purported biography (*UB*, 275). The novel ends with the tearful reunion of father and daughter and the daughter's sense of guilt for having subjected the father to the terror of historical investigation. Harald Welzer rightly observes that, with this novel, Hahn legitimizes precisely the blurred images that make up much of the reservoir of German transgenerational family memories.[33] Shifting focus from the question of the parents' guilt to their children's lack of empathy for their plight, the novel, according to Welzer, constructs the convenient notion of a guiltless guilt.[34]

Hahn's novel presses nearly all the buttons of contemporary memory contests: in addition to the context of the Wehrmacht exhibition, there is an implied allusion to the Walser debate when Musbach, like Walser in *Ein springender Brunnen*, reminds Katja that the era of National Socialism was not just characterized by Hitler's speeches, Nazi parades, terror and military drill, but also by his youthful preoccupations outside the political frame (*UB*, 58). A little earlier, the novel directly refers to the victim–perpetrator debate as triggered by Günter Grass's *Im Krebsgang* (Crabwalk, 2002) (*UB*, 27); this is followed by Musbach's reflection on generational dialogue (*UB*, 52, 54), two episodes that recall the generation of 1968 and its members' antagonism towards their parents (*UB*, 64, 255), a brief discussion of Peter Weiss's seminal *Die Ästhetik des Widerstands* (Aesthetic of Resistance, 1975–1981) (*UB*, 70) and two references to Ernst Jünger's contested notions of the steel soldier and of sacrifice (*UB*, 119, 172). With its superficial inventory of current memory contests, the novel resolves the dialectic of the desire for a complete break with the family heritage, on the one hand, and the longing for genealogy and tradition, on the other, a hallmark of *Väterliteratur*, in favour of a one-sided and forced harmonization. At the conclusion of the novel, transgenerational empathy overrides crucial historical distinctions: in the end, the father appears as just another victim of history's cruelty.

In contrast to Hahn's narrative, Dagmar Leupold's *Nach den Kriegen* offers a more self-reflexive perspective on the issue of family heritage.[35] As in Meckel, it is the death of the father that triggers the daughter's investigation of his life story. Framed by the daughter's journey from the United States back to Germany to attend her father's funeral – which she misses due to her flight being delayed – the daughter remembers her final visit to her father when he was gravely ill in hospital. The memory of seeing his naked body in its raw physicality before death is an uncanny reminder of a shared lineage and genealogy:

> Daß ich von ihm abstammte – eine Abzweigung, ein Ausschnitt war –, schien mir im Zustand der Nacktheit auf die wörtlichste Bedeutung reduziert, alles Potentielle war gelöscht zugunsten einer fest berechneten Summe. In den Anzügen, die er trug, war er im Auftrag unterwegs: Zum Bridgeturnier, auf Klassenfahrt, zu Symposien, Kleidung war etwas Öffentliches, war Lebensstoff, Kleidung erzählte vom Vater und wies nicht auf die Tochter zurück. Im nackten Körper dagegen war der Vater – auf dem Kind unheimliche Weise – ohne Vorwände zu Hause und ähnelte darin allen anderen Menschen. Also auch der Tochter. (*NK*, 19)

> [That I descended from him – that I was a branch of his, an extract of sorts – seemed to me to gain a literal meaning when I saw his nakedness, everything that had been a potential dimension was now erased in favour of a sum total that was calculated in an exact manner. Wearing his suits he was always on his way to some official assignment: the bridge competition, a school trip, symposia; clothes were of a public nature, the material of life, his clothes represented the father without pointing back to his daughter. However, in his naked body the father suddenly seemed to be at home without reservations, which the child found uncanny. He resembled all other human beings. And this also included his daughter.]

Without the protective shield of his well-groomed public persona, the father in his illness appears as precisely the unmasked self, the helpless creature that the cold persona had tried to fend off. This exposed nakedness is uncanny because it brings to the fore an existential semblance and relatedness that makes it impossible for the daughter to draw a line between herself and her father. In many ways, this hospital scene with its imagery of the dying father and the daughter's recognition of the inevitability of familial affiliation signifies the return of the repressed by pointing to her own mortality. It also highlights the interdependence of genealogy and generational renewal: while the daughter's move to the United States and the start of her own family exemplifies her desire for a new beginning, the death of her father forces her to see herself as a daughter and thus as part of an unwanted genealogy, the symbolic expression of which is a wax stamp that the father had made in order to vouch for the life story that he always wanted to write but never managed to put on paper (*NK*, 7). Inheriting this wax stamp, the daughter sees it as a posthumous assignment to give shape to his damaged life and to their damaged relationship. According to the narrator, the disturbed relationship between father and daughter was a legacy of the Second World War because the unmastered war experience had created deep trenches within post-war German families (*NK*, 7). The task of giving shape to the father's life through narration entails the unmasking of the family legends that, according to the daughter, are the product of the type of familial co-fabulation that inevitably constructs a sense of familial togetherness (*NK*, 33–4). And yet, although the daughter's narrative is a counter-reading to the father's self-image, she views her enterprise in terms of a self-imagining that assigns to the fragmentary selves of father and daughter the dignity of a wholeness that only the written word can provide (*NK*, 34). It is precisely this dialectic between a need for *Gestalt* (form) and the realization that the gaps and ruptures of life cannot be healed that make this a particularly compelling example of *Väterliteratur*.

Like Timm's book, Leupold's *Nach den Kriegen* offers an analysis of post-war family life, which appears, with its emphasis on economic reconstruction and the accumulation of status symbols, in a phrase coined by F. C. Delius, as the "Steinzeit der Demokratie" (the stone age of democracy).[36] The narrator juxtaposes memories of her childhood, such as the image of herself roller-skating in the streets, with the critical analysis of the ideology of the economic boom of the 1950s (*NK*, 76). But in spite of the parental focus on the future and the "Verwaltung der Wohlstandsträume" (*NK*, 77; the administration of their dreams of prosperity), the war still haunts the present.

The father, who in the course of the war lost three fingers, continues to fight various imaginary wars at the dinner table so that eating and conducting warfare become intertwined in the child's imagination. In order to understand the deep-seated failure of communication between father and daughter, the daughter reconstructs his biography. Family photographs, the father's war diary, his post-war literary writings and other historical documents are used to reconstruct the formative stages in the father's biography: we learn that he was born as a member of the German minority in Polish Bielsko in 1913, and that after finishing secondary school and his father's suicide he studied mathematics and physics in Lemberg supported by his sister. His Germanness, or rather his status as a member of the German minority, becomes the touchstone of his identity as well as a career choice (*NK*, 116). Refusing to accept a Polish teaching post, the father moves to Vienna until he becomes a school inspector, in the German-occupied territory known as the *Generalgouvernement*. He joins the Nationalsozialistische Deutsche Arbeiterpartei (NSDAP) in 1941 and is drafted into the Wehrmacht in 1942, which he spends in Russia until he is wounded; recovering in Stettin, he begins to keep a diary, which is composed, according to his daughter, with an eye on the posthumous reader. Interspersing quotations from the war diary with her personal reflections and historical documents such as quotations from the notorious *Generalgouverneur* of the occupied Polish territory, Hans Frank, or from the party programme of the German *Jungdeutsche Partei* in Poland, the narrative adopts a variety of angles to give form to the father's life.

The resulting hybridity of this narrative must, however, not be read in terms of a polyphony that gives voice to the relativity of all historical interpretations but rather as a documentary technique that ensures a high degree of historical objectification. By placing the father's diary in a wider historical context, the narrative shows that the emotional and psychological make-up of his generation was steeped in *völkisch* ideology and its core idea that the alleged superiority of the German people necessitated the colonial subjugation of eastern Europe. Citing various passages from her father's diary that record conversations between Hans Frank and the founder of the *Jungdeutsche Partei*, Rudolf Ernst Wiesner, about the imminent extermination of the Jews, the daughter highlights the father's complete emotional detachment from the subject of these conversations (*NK*, 127). As in Meckel and Timm, the father's stylization in terms of the cold persona is the focal point of the daughter's analysis. In her eyes, the complete absence of empathy with the suffering of the Jews and Poles draws attention to the double vision of the diary writer: on the one hand, he adopts the mask of the cold strategist who only registers the civilian population's suffering in terms of collateral damage; on the other, he is shown to be fired up by his ideological mission (*NK*, 129). After the war, the father views neither his own life nor history in terms of the sum of individual and collective deeds, but rather "als eine nach eigenen Gesetzen sich vollziehende, periodisch wiederholende Dynamik, die sich die Geschichte unterwirft" (*NK*, 167; in terms of a periodically repetitive dynamic that subjects history to its own laws).

The great role model for this generation's characteristic attitude to the war was Ernst Jünger. His name crops up in Meckel, Timm and Hahn: while Meckel mentions his father's admiration of Jünger (*S*, 28), Hahn has Hans Musbach distance himself from the Jünger cult of his generation and from the notion of sacrifice (*UB*, 172). Timm also comments on Jünger's pervasive influence: he highlights the paternal generation's failure to make the connection between the absolute values of courage in the face of death, duty and sacrifice, as paradigmatically expressed in Jünger's *In Stahlgewittern* (The Storm of Steel, 1920), and the later application of these values to even more deadly purposes in the Nazi era (*AB*, 153). But it is Leupold's narrative that offers an in-depth analysis of Jünger's formative influence on this generation of males. Drawing out stylistic similarities between her father's post-war diaries and Jünger's *Strahlungen* (Radiation, 1949), she shows to what extent the father adopts the Jüngerian pose of the cool observer who scans the world unemotionally with a scientific eye. Jünger's modernist interest in the surface of appearances, in a world free of cause and effect, has been analyzed as an example of a modernist aesthetic that realizes the dream of man's synchronization with modern technology.[37] In Jünger's work, the anthropology of the cold persona is fetishized in the figure of the steel warrior who in the death zones of war immunizes himself against the experience of pain. Encountering the first soldier with a steel helmet, Jünger describes this significant moment in terms of the erasure of subjectivity as symbolized in the levelling of a man's personal voice:

Er war der erste deutsche Soldat, den ich im Stahlhelm sah, und erschien mir sogleich als Bewohner einer fremden und härteren Welt. [....] Das vom stählernen Helmrand umrahmte unbewegliche Gesicht und die eintönige, vom Lärm der Front begleitete Stimme machten einen gespenstischen Eindruck auf uns. [....] Nichts war in dieser Stimme zurückgeblieben als ein großer Gleichmut. Mit solchen Männern kann man kämpfen.[38]

[He was the first German soldier who I saw wearing a steel helmet; and he immediately appeared to me like the inhabitant of an alien and tougher world. [...] Framed by the steel-rim of the helmet, his immobile face and his monotonous voice, which was accompanied by the noise of the front had an uncanny effect on us. [...] This voice retained nothing but a great indifference. One can fight with such men.]

As Lethen comments, readers of the right-wing camp tend to feel attracted to this iconic steel warrior but repelled by the modernity of Jünger's analysis of the modern type; in contrast, readers of a left-liberal persuasion tend to focus on Jünger's quasi-Marxist concept of the modern worker, but they reject his iconography of the warrior.[39] Leupold's interest lies squarely with the ethical consequences of this modernist separation of the aesthetic from the moral domain. Applied to the political sphere, this sidelining of the moral contributes to the fascist ideology with which so many intellectuals, including her father, identified. As Jünger's disciple and epigone, the father in his diary mimics Jünger's language down to the level of style. Dagmar Leupold describes Jünger in terms of the first observer who surveys the surface of objects without any interest in cause and effect (*NK*, 169). For Leupold, an episode in *Strahlungen I*, Jünger's war diary, a copy of which she inherited from her father, illustrates paradigmatically the moral consequences of such a studied and sterile objectivity. Jünger's diary entry of 29 May 1941 relates how he had been asked to witness the execution of a deserter. Leupold cites the opening passage, in which Jünger refers to this as one of a "Flut von widrigen Dingen" (a flood of inopportune things) that he has to attend to, but in the end he accepts the assignment because he is driven by a "higher curiosity":

Im Grunde war es höhere Neugier, die den Ausschlag gab. Ich sah schon viele sterben, doch keinen im bestimmten Augenblick. Wie stellt sich die Lage dar, die heute jeden von uns bedroht und seine Existenz schattiert? Und wie verhält man sich in ihr?[40]

[It was really a higher curiosity that made me decide. I have seen many people die but nobody at a predetermined moment. What is this situation that threatens all of us, shadowing our existence? And how does one behave in it?]

Jünger's amoral observation of the world goes hand in hand with a metaphysical leap that turns man into a being that is driven by higher forces. In the post-war era, this notion of a higher determinism allowed the convenient move from the troubling question "who am I?" to "who are we?"; a shift from the individual to the collective, from introspection to external factors (*NK*, 173). While Jünger's detached observation of the world might be an aesthetically interesting experiment, for Leupold it produces a highly reductive notion of the intellectual who merely takes note of the phenomena of the world without judgement:

> Wir werden bewegt, von außen, eben von den Stürmen, und ihre Kraft, ihre Richtung verändert uns – auch innerlich. Aber wir bleiben Zuschauer, Getriebene. Die Aufgabe des aufmerksamen (Selbst-) Beobachters – also nach Jüngers Auffassung des Intellektuellen – ist folglich die eines Protokollführers. Er muß genau verzeichnen, was vorfällt; er macht die Bestandsaufnahme, er inventarisiert die Welt. Den Käfern, der Liebe, dem Massenmord und der Hauptmahlzeit wird dasselbe, genau abgewogene Interesse gewidmet. Das Sichtbare und das Ereignishafte haben immer Vorrang vor dem Inneren. (*NK*, 174)

> [An external force is moving us, the storms, and their force and direction changes us – even on the inside. But we remain spectators who are tossed around. The task of the alert observer (of his own self) – that is according to Jünger the intellectual – is that of a minute taker. He must note down precisely what happens; taking stock he produces an inventory of the world. He dedicates exactly the same calculated attention to beetles, to love, to mass murders or the main meal of the day. That which is visible and eventful always has priority over introspection.]

Leupold's analysis of the iconic status that Jünger occupied in this generation of men thus helps to explain the causes of their disastrous moral blindness. Jünger appealed to a man like Leupold's father because Jünger's aesthetic perspective on all the phenomena of this world justified the generation's profound lack of moral judgement, and, furthermore, he provided them with a metaphysical determinism that allowed them to avoid the painful business of introspection.

However, in spite of her astute critique of the generation's ideological make-up, Leupold's book does not close on an acrimonious note. Having worked through her father's diaries and other writings by him, she visits his grave and remembers another family legend. But this time, it is one that concerns her own birth: according to her father, he nurtured her after she and her twin sister were prematurely born:

Frühgeburt im Niederlahnsteiner Krankenhaus ohne Brutkasten, da sei er es gewesen, der mich gefüttert habe, ebenso habe er, zwei Monate später, nach unserem Einzug zu Hause, in der Nachtschicht mich übernommen, in seinen Schoß gebettet, den großen Glatzkopf in der Armbeuge – das machte er pantomimisch vor –, habe gestaunt über das häßliche Kind, dem Wimpern, Haare und Nägel fehlten. Grottenmolch, sagte er, du sahst aus wie ein Grottenmolch. Bei einem Ausflug von Kärnten nach Slowenien besuchten wir eine Tropfsteinhöhle; in den Tümpeln darin zeigte er mir die transparenten, nachtschattigen Molche und wiederholte: So hast du ausgesehen. Ich habe dich trotzdem gefüttert.

Im Grunde spielt es keine Rolle, ob es so war oder nicht. Es ist der Anfang einer Geschichte. (*NK*, 221)

[Premature birth in the hospital of Niederlahnstein, without an incubator. So it was he who fed me, and two months later after we had moved into our house – it was he who took me over during the night shifts, placing me in his lap, my big bald head in the crook of his arm – he mimicked this for me – astonished about this ugly child who had no eye lashes, hair or nails. A water newt, you looked just like a water newt, he said. On a trip from Carinthia to Slovenia we visited a cave full of stalagmites; in the puddles he showed me a water newt, transparent and with a night-shady appearance. And he repeated: that's what you looked like. But I fed you anyway.

It doesn't basically matter, whether it's true or not. It is the beginning of a story.]

By reinstating a family legend at the centre of which is an image of unconditional love and care, Leupold also reinstates the notion of genealogy and affiliation and of a lineage that engenders stories. The final conciliatory gesture of putting a bunch of flowers (the highly delicate mimosa) on his grave does not, however, in any way negate her previous critique of a particular version of Germanness and German maleness. But now that she has given the missing shape to her father's life, distance and affection, generational renewal and the recognition of her own familial lineage are poised in a delicate balance.

Conclusion

All four narratives discussed in this chapter adopt a bottom-up, specifically inner-familial perspective on major historical events. The privatization of history is thus one of the main signatures of this literature in that it views the political, social and economic factors that motivated National Socialism through the lens of family history. This conflation of history with personal memory can be used to very different effects: Hahn's novel resolves the complex dialectic between rupture and continuity, a defining characteristic of *Väterliteratur*, in favour of a rather forced harmonization that is at the expense of historical analysis and objectification. In contrast to the sentimental denouement of *Unscharfe Bilder*, Meckel, Timm and Leupold provide an anatomy of the paternal generation in order to lay bare the ideological underpinnings that continued to influence the post-war period well into the 1950s. All three narratives identify a specifically masculine code of honour as one of the main reasons for the breakdown of communication in German post-war families. While all three narratives aim to dismantle those family legends that have produced negative legacies which haunt the sons and daughters, Uwe Timm adopts a highly self-reflexive and dialogic stance that takes account of the narrator's own affective position and leaves the integrity of his siblings and parents intact. By contrast, Meckel's book offers a far more scathing and unrelenting account of the long-term damage caused by a generation of helpless despots in the post-war family. However, Leupold's analytical investigation of the paternal generation's Jünger cult shows that contemporary *Väterliteratur* cannot be simply read in terms of a new investment in transgenerational understanding and solidarity. To varying degrees, the narratives by Meckel, Timm and Leupold maintain the dialectic between continuity and rupture, between the desire for a generational break and affiliation and between historical analysis and subjective memory. If this dialectic is abandoned, as in Hahn's case, the genre runs into the danger of a sentimentalized harmonization of memory, which ultimately diminishes the factuality of history. Only when and if this transgenerational literature manages to negotiate the potential gaps between history and memory does it avoid the pitfall of a historical revisionism that abandons the notion of personal responsibility.

This privatization of history thus also results in a significant rediscovery of autobiographical modes of writing about the past and a new investment in authorship: abandoning the 1960s' declaration of the death of the author and the analysis of the social and linguistic structures that precede individual agency, these intergenerational authors emphatically embrace autobiographical forms of writing in order to restore the notion of individual historical agency and responsibility. Furthermore, these family narratives shift focus from the question of what happened in the past to how these repressed events have disturbed post-war familial relations. They often investigate personal diaries, letters and photographs in order to exorcise the family's negative legacy. As meta-narratives, they examine the belatedness of their own engagement with this topic and explore the function of deferral and transference as a latent but nevertheless crucial means of communication across generational thresholds.

3
Family Narratives and Postmemory: Günter Grass's *Im Krebsgang*, Tanja Dückers's *Himmelskörper* and Marcel Beyer's *Spione*

The new German family narrative

The analysis of some of the more recent examples of *Väterliteratur* in Chapter 2 has shown that, in contemporary German literature, National Socialism is increasingly viewed through the lens of family history. While this new focus on the internal family dynamic has a precursor in the father novels prevalent in the late 1970s and early 1980s, my analysis suggests that the new family narrative is, on the whole, more dialogic and self-reflexive than the earlier *Väterliteratur*. In the same breath, however, I have argued that this must not be misread in terms of a one-sided investment in transgenerational understanding and solidarity at the expense of a critical perspective on post-war family life. The examples of Timm's and Leupold's narratives demonstrate that the dialectic between continuity and rupture, between discontinuity and affiliation and between historical analysis and subjective memory is a hallmark of the contemporary discourse too. Chapter 2 has also argued that these new examples of *Väterliteratur* share some important traits with their precursors: both Timm and Leupold continue the tradition of *Väterliteratur* as exemplified by Meckel by dissecting the anatomy of *völkisch* masculinity in order to lay bare the ideological underpinnings that continued to influence the post-war period well into the 1950s.

This chapter addresses the shift from a dyadic towards a triadic exploration of family history and the prevalence of a postmemorial engagement with the past in many of these narratives. Unlike the earlier father texts with their focus on father–son or father–daughter relationships, the contemporary German family narrative often deals with the experiences of three or more generations, as for example in Günter Grass's *Im Krebsgang*, Reinhard Jirgl's *Die Unvollendeten* (The Incomplete, 2003), Eva Menasse's

Vienna (2005), Thomas Medicus's *In den Augen meines Großvaters* (In my Grandfather's Eyes, 2004), Tanja Dückers's *Himmelskörper* (Heavenly Bodies, 2003), Sibylle Mulot's *Die Fabrikanten* (The Factory Owners, 2005) or Arno Geiger's *Es geht uns gut* (We Are Fine, 2005).[1] With the exception of Grass's narrative where the story is narrated from a second-generation male perspective, these texts predominantly deal with approaches to the family's past from the postmemorial position of the third generation. However, this shift from second to third generation should not be equated with a smooth transition from personal memory to postmemory. In most cases, second-generation narrators also have few or no personal memories of this period: for example, in Grass's *Im Krebsgang*, the narrator, Paul Pokriefke, has no conscious memories of the family trauma – that is, the sinking of the Strength-through-Joy cruise liner, the *Wilhelm Gustloff* – because he was born exactly at the moment when the traumatic event occurred. The uncanny coincidence of trauma and birth is one of the main themes of the novella. Similarly, in Treichel's *Der Verlorene* (1998, English transl. *Lost*, 1999), the narrator has no personal recollections of the trauma that haunts his family, the loss of his brother during the flight from the advancing Russian troops at the end of the war. The narrative explores to what extent the second son is a phantom of this unmastered trauma: conceived as a compensation for a loss, he can never fill the void left by the first son who functions as an emotionally charged symbol of historical loss in the parents' lives. While in Timm's *Am Beispiel meines Bruders* the autobiographical narrator does possess a few Proustian memories of his older brother, these have a fleeting and phantomatic quality. The transgenerational communication of trauma is a signature of all these texts.

Irrespective of its dyadic or triadic generational spectrum, the contemporary family narrative is characterized by some salient features: it relates past events as well as how these events have been concealed and yet subliminally transmitted within the family unit. In this way, this literature adopts a meta-critical narrative perspective towards the belatedness of this engagement with family history, exploring the function of deferral and transference as important means of communication across generational thresholds. Preoccupied with the malleability of historical memories more than 60 years after the end of the Second World War, the narrators of these family stories are equally concerned with the silences and gaps in the family narrative and the overt family legends that have been passed down through the generations. Tuning into the unsaid that punctures the archive of family legends, they play the part of "phantomologists" who probe an unmastered inheritance within the domain of the family.

The departure point of the family narrative is the insight that, in the first instance, history is always experienced and managed by people who entertain willy-nilly a genealogically defined relationship to their parents and – where relevant – their own offspring. As an intergenerational node that binds together members of two, three or even four generations, the family is represented by these narratives as the ideal site of a new experiential historiography that charts history's disruptiveness in terms of multiple familial dysfunctionalities. The implication here is that history, like Freud's concept of the family, is inherently dysfunctional and that its prime trope is repression: that which is repressed will inevitably resurface and haunt later generations unless it is submitted to a thorough working-through that aims to produce affective recognition of the past rather than mere cognition. Accordingly, Sigrid Weigel argues in her study of the complex career of the ideas of generation and genealogy that the new family narrative makes a particularly relevant intervention in German identity debates precisely because it shows up tradition as a trope of fantasy, a Freudian family romance that concerns unfulfilled libidinal desires, rivalries and archaic fears.[2] Weigel goes so far as to propose that this literature has managed to free itself from the "Authentizitätssucht", the quest for authenticity, of historical discourse in favour of a return to a genealogical exploration of family history.[3]

The following chapter takes a more critical line, discussing some of the epistemological consequences of the implied equation of history with family history. Focusing on the idea of postmemory as developed by Marianne Hirsch in her influential study *Family Frames*, I analyze two narratives in which the third generation's narrative viewpoint goes hand in hand with a postmemorial reflection of the past. In dialectical fashion, I shall first suggest that Tanja Dückers's *Himmelskörper* (Heavenly Bodies, 2003) exemplifies the limits of postmemory. In a second step I proceed to turn this on its head by showing that Marcel Beyer's *Spione* (2000, English transl. *Spies*, 2005) realizes the concept's opportunities. However, before embarking on these readings, the notion of postmemory must be properly introduced.

Postmemory and trauma theory

Family Frames defines postmemory as follows:

> postmemory is distinguished from memory by generational distance and from history by a deep personal connection. Postmemory is a powerful and very particular form of memory precisely because

its connection to its object or source is mediated not through recollection but through an imaginative investment and creation.[4]

In the first instance, postmemory captures the transgenerational transmission of the Holocaust as a defining trauma of 20th century history; it conceptualizes the second and third generations' growing distance to this historical event. The concept reflects how descendants of survivors invest history with varying degrees of imaginative fantasy in order to produce a family narrative that bridges the generational gap. Although designed with reference to the dynamic of Holocaust remembrance, the application of the concept exceeds the framework of Holocaust discourse by far. Potentially, it can be applied to any historical event and any historical subject that relates to a transgenerational traumatic legacy. Postmemory is an extension of the idea that traumatic memory is always belated and symptomatic and that the process of working-through is necessarily delayed. However, it is important to note that this process of working-through no longer requires historically verifiable remembrance of what happened but that it embraces an imaginary mediation and recreation of the past. In a persuasive critique of the epistemological implications of postmemory, J. J. Long has therefore argued that this "shifts epistemological authority from the first to the second generation, which implicitly devalues the first generation's experience, while also hollowing out [...] the subjectivity of the second generation and replacing it with the effects of the previous generation's trauma".[5] One could perhaps contend that the second and subsequent generations only manage to work through such transgenerationally active trauma by adopting a self-reflexive position towards the past that maps the self's experience of trauma onto the trauma narrative of previous generations. Good examples in this respect are Art Spiegelman's famous cartoons *Maus I* and *Maus II*: Hirsch reads the multiple mediations that characterize the cartoons in terms of an "aesthetic strategy" that provides "affirmation of identity as construction".[6] The second generation is not just a passive vessel for the transmission of the first generation's experience but co-author of a collaborative narrative which, in this instance, is told by father and son. However, Long's suspicion that postmemorial narratives tend to privilege the second generation epistemologically is borne out by Hirsch's own analysis of *Maus*: although she describes the relationship between Art Spiegelman and his father in terms of a collaboration, her actual reading of Spiegelman's aesthetic choices gives far greater weight to the son's creative authorship above and beyond the father's testimony. Furthermore, Long rightly criticizes the fact that

Hirsch's claim that the practice of inscribing the traumatic experience of others into one's own life story produces an "ethical relation to the oppressed or persecuted" sits uneasily with the notion of imaginative investment and creation, which is a defining feature of postmemory. Long comments, "Imagination and creation, after all, contain the possibility of unregulated fantasy that need pay no attention at all either to historical accuracy or to the otherness of the other. The question is: how can this imaginative investment and creation be policed in order to prevent appropriation or even usurpation of the other's experiences?"[7] According to Long, the documentary dimension of postmemory, that is its reliance on photographs, documents, diaries and so on, does not help to resolve this ethical dilemma either. For Long, this "guarantees little when one takes into account the ineluctably selective and partial nature of memory, the imbrication of archival processes in structures of power, the necessarily incomplete state of the documentary record, and the capacity of photographs not only to be manipulated, but to generate widely divergent and conflicting interpretations".[8]

Long's critical appraisal thus draws attention to some of the risks that accompany postmemorial discourse. Designed to conceptualize the inevitable transformation of memory work that arises when the eyewitnesses are replaced by later generations, postmemory is a symptom of this shift itself. Postmemory prioritizes what one might call feeling-structures over the traditional business of history, which is the representation of the past on the basis of documentary evidence and argument. It runs the risk of obscuring important epistemological distinctions, such as that between experience and fantasy, past and present, evidence and fabrication or fact and fiction.

In the following, I want to demonstrate that postmemory derives from the type of trauma theory, which is currently fashionable in the United States. As a clinical category, trauma refers first and foremost to a painful psychological condition produced by an event in the past, which the subject could not process adequately on a cognitive or emotional level when it occurred. By contrast, current trauma theory has widened the concept's meaning significantly, turning it into a prime agent of history itself. Proponents of this type of theory suggest that the idea of historical trauma does not just designate a specific type of historical event, such as mass murder or genocide, that is deemed to have a traumatizing effect on its victims and survivors; rather historical change as such is recoded in terms of trauma. In her book *Unclaimed Experience*, Cathy Caruth puts forward the argument that we are always separated from historical experience by the repression inherent in trauma.[9] We can therefore only ever approximate historical experience belatedly through traumatic re-enactment. Caruth goes so far as to align the displacement and latency of trauma with the literality of the historical event itself. She writes, "For history to be a history of trauma means that it is referential precisely to the extent that it is not fully perceived as it occurs; or to put it somewhat differently, that a history can be grasped only in the very inaccessibility of its occurrence."[10] In this view, the truth of history is always latent, submerged and belated; history is repetitive and pathological; it is acted out compulsively. As Ruth Leys has shown in her compelling critique of Caruth, the theoretical linchpin for this type of trauma theory is a performative theory of language derived from Paul de Man.[11] For, according to Caruth, language succeeds in testifying to the traumatic horror of history only when its referential function begins to break down. A mode of expression must be found that gives expression to the gaps in meaning as a direct emanation of the trauma. Leys rightly cautions that the deconstructive version of trauma theory ends up resembling "an extremely literalist version of history as chronicle, conceived as a nonsubjective, nonnarrative, and nonrepresentational method of memorializing the past".[12] She concludes that it is as if "representation is imagined as itself a kind of subject who risks murdering or distorting the moral truth of facts concerning the traumatic pasts, facts that should and do 'speak for themselves' ".[13]

It should come as no surprise, therefore, that Caruth's work takes the Holocaust specifically as the defining benchmark of historical experience, a problematic argument that has been analyzed and criticized by a growing number of scholars.[14] Historians are unlikely to subscribe to Caruth's sweeping reading of history as trauma because, ultimately, this position results in an ontologization of trauma, eradicating the very notion of historical experience itself.[15] Caruth's version of history as trauma proposes not so much a mode of historical inquiry but rather the performance of trauma through postmemorial modes of writing that favour mediation and indirection over discursive expression. Her categoric assertion that history can be grasped "only in the very inaccessibility of its occurrence"[16] turns historical inquiry into a performance that attempts to maintain a mimetic relationship to trauma by way of the gaps and breaks in discourse. Ironically, this deconstructivist vision of history as trauma is a remake of the Naturalist's dream of a language that aimed to register reality as it occurred. While the experiments of the Naturalists in the late 19th century encountered the problem that the gap between the world and the word cannot be closed even by the most radicalized form of mimesis, Caruth suggests that the gaps and fissures in discourse do actually indicate the literal presence of trauma. This conveniently ignores the fact that silences, gaps and all other possible disruptions in the flow of language are part of the language system itself. Indeed, in literature, they belong to a sophisticated and highly troped rhetoric of indirection that aims to evoke the unmastered traumas of the past. The stylized and, at times, studied register of W. G. Sebald's postmemorial narratives is a case in point. As I have shown elsewhere, Sebald's poetics of memory relies on a range of sophisticated intermedial and intertextual games in order to turn history into a kind of phantomology that favours absence over presence, evocation over representation and historical loss over progress.[17] Of course, Sebald is not the only German-language author who embraced an aesthetic of the oblique as a response to the unrepresentability of historical suffering. Other prominent writers in this respect would be the poets Paul Celan, Ingeborg Bachmann or, more recently, Anne Duden. They all situate their writing in the context of a fundamental critique of the issue of representation in discursive language; they employ metonymy, montage, synecdoche and musical allusion as counterpoints to discursive language. In this way, they animate the utopian potential of language in the attempt to overcome what Bachmann calls, the "schlechte Sprache", the bad language of the post-war era that has been fundamentally damaged by National Socialist violence.[18] Insofar as the writings of these and many other authors respond to the caesura of Auschwitz by way of a poetics of the oblique that, in the words of Sebald, evokes the "Schmerzensspuren der Geschichte", the painful traces of history, they do indeed all subscribe, in varying degrees, to the interpretation of history as trauma.[19] However, it is one thing to evoke trauma poetically but quite another to insist, "history can be grasped only in the very inaccessibility of its occurrence".[20] Ironically, the upshot of Caruth's conversion of history into trauma is not an enhanced recognition of the otherness of the past but rather the erasure of the category of the past altogether. For in her reading the past resembles a gothic house peopled by phantoms and ghosts that haunt its inhabitants eternally.

My analysis thus far has highlighted the neat convergence between trauma theory and postmemory. While trauma theory proposes that history can never be witnessed due to its intrinsically traumatic nature, postmemory suggests that the eyewitnesses' testimonies, as well as our cognitive approaches to the past, are always subject to repression, displacement and distortion. In this way, both trauma theory and postmemorial discourse reinforce each other, depreciating the role of cognition in our understanding of history. This is not to suggest that postmemory is a useless concept that should be abandoned altogether on epistemological grounds but rather that its dissemination must be premised on a meta-critical debate that explains both the attractiveness and limitations of postmemorial engagements with the past. The following readings attempt to show that postmemory can be used to very different effects. While, for example, in Tanja Dückers's *Himmelskörper* it is presented as an alternative to historical discourse, in Marcel Beyer's *Spione* the category of postmemory is itself deconstructed in the process of narration.

Günter Grass's *Im Krebsgang* and Tanja Dückers's *Himmelskörper*: From historical self-reflexivity to postmemorial confidence

Tanja Dückers's *Himmelskörper* appeared in 2003, that is one year after Günter Grass had explored the long-term psychological legacy of the Second World War in his acclaimed novella *Im Krebsgang*. As both narratives thematize the same historical event, the sinking of the *Gustloff*, which was carrying German refugees at the end of the war, it may be useful to briefly summarize the salient features of *Im Krebsgang*. In Grass's novella, the metaphor of the crabwalk gives expression to the manifold difficulties that the narrator, Paul Pokriefke, encounters in his attempt to finally reconstruct the traumatic circumstances of his birth, which coincides with the sinking of the *Gustloff* in January 1945.[21] Originally built as a holiday cruiser for the NS "Strength-through-Joy" propaganda campaign, the ship was used at the end of the war to transport several thousand German refugees from Gotenhafen in former Prussia, now in Poland, to Kiel in Northern Germany. However, the boat was torpedoed and sunk by the Russians after it left the harbour. Since the overcrowded *Gustloff* carried an insufficient number of lifeboats, only a very small number of passengers survived the sinking. According to Grass's plot, Tulla Pokriefke is one of these survivors: surrounded by drowning fellow passengers and children, she gives birth to her son Paul on board the *Löwe*, a torpedo boat that came to the *Gustloff*'s rescue. The co-occurrence of mass death and his birth produces a haunting legacy that Paul only manages to address when he finds out that his own son has adopted a Neo-Nazi outlook on the NS past. Crabwalking through his story, the narrator, Paul, finally revisits his strained relationship with his mother, Tulla, in order to understand the estrangement from his own son. While Tulla is caught up in an endless cycle of repetitive retelling of the original trauma, Paul slowly works through the trauma, situating the family story in the context of both NS and post-war German history. Since its publication in 2002, Grass's novella has attracted a wide range of critical responses.[22] For example, Kirsten Prinz argues that *Im Krebsgang* exceeds the limiting horizon of current German victim discourse by debating the complex relationship between memory and the media. In her view, Grass's narrator, Paul, responds to the deficits of Internet communication by way of a narrative counter-strategy that undermines both the alluring presentness of the chat-room and the confident representational claims of traditional historical narrative.[23] By contrast, Ulrike Vedder criticizes Grass for equipping Paul with enormous narrative superiority towards his topic.[24] She argues that the novella makes Paul the spokesperson not only for his mother and for his son but also for the entire post-war generation of intellectuals with left-wing credentials who have failed to address this theme. Indeed, the novella does represent an older first generation of post-war intellectuals through the figure of the old man, a Grassian alter ego, who explains to Paul that his generation never managed to deal with German suffering because of the moral obligation to remember Auschwitz. According to Vedder, this narrative constellation gives Paul far too much narrative authority over both family history and national tradition. In fact, she sees in him "an uncurtailed transmitter", a type of omniscient narrator who services the resurrection of national tradition by way of a soft reconciliation with the NS past.[25] In order to arrive at this conclusion, Vedder needs to downplay the significance of Paul's own failures and disappointments that are thematized throughout the novella and that concern both his private and professional life. His failed marriage, dented professional ambition, vaguely liberal attitudes as well as his inability to communicate with his mother, his wife and his son combine to make Paul a disoriented, somewhat melancholy and self-pitying character who has little confidence in his professional and private authority. Not so much a transmitter, as a researcher, Paul carefully reconstructs the historical role that the *Gustloff* played as a major propaganda tool of NS social policy. In this way, he filters the trauma through a historical-analytical lens, which objectifies the circumstances of the sinking. Grass's novella manages to thematize German war trauma without any hint of revisionism. In the end, Paul's story exceeds the framework of trauma narrative precisely because it sets the personal and the historical in dialogue with one another.

While the figure of the old man in the novella points to the anchoring of the story in Grass's personal memories of the NS past, Tanja

Dückers,who was born in 1968, relates to this issue from a postmemorial position characterized by growing emotional distance and an increased sense of historical relativism. Dückers made her debut with *Spielzone* (Zone of Games, 1999), a novel that portrays life in the post-unified Berlin of the late 1990s in the idiom of youth cult. Dückers's humorous depiction of an array of identity games, which revolve around membership of the latest scene, the right fashion accessories and the staging of gender roles, established her as an author of the contemporary Berlin novel. Although the legacy of National Socialism only plays a peripheral role in this novel, it features in an amusing scene that captures the difficulties of a normative memory culture. Laura, a 14-year-old girl who desperately wants to be part of her older cousin's cool scene, is invited by her mother to stay at home and watch a television documentary about Plötzensee, the Nazi prison in Berlin where many German resisters had been executed. Turning down this pedagogic invitation, Laura comments,

> "Nein danke!", sage ich laut.
> Ich bin schon zweimal höchstpersönlich in Plötzensee gewesen, einmal mit der Schule und einmal, falls sie sich erinnern können, mit meinen Eltern. Ich habe jedesmal Alpträume nachher gehabt, mich hat das überhaupt nicht kaltgelassen, wie mir Wolf vorwarf, bloß weil ich da drin 'ne Tüte Chips gegessen habe, was er aus irgendeinem Grund "sehr unpassend" fand.[26]
>
> [I say loudly, "No thanks!"
> I've been to Plötzensee myself twice, once with the school and once, supposing they could remember it, with my parents. I suffered from nightmares afterwards each time, it didn't leave me untouched at all, which is what Wolf accused me of simply because I ate a bag of crisps there, which he, for some reason, found inappropriate.]

In many ways, this scene captures the different generational attitudes to the legacy of National Socialism: while Laura's parents embody the archetypical enlightened liberal type with a belief in the benefits of a pedagogy of remembrance, Laura does not share their pedagogic piety any longer: eating a bag of crisps, she is nevertheless affected by the visit to Plötzensee. While this remains a passing episode in *Spielzone*, Dückers's *Himmelskörper* homes in on the issue of the transgenerational communication of the past within German post-war families. The publication of the novel was marked by an interview with Dückers in

Die Zeit, which focused on her own generational attitudes to the legacy of National Socialism. Unlike Grass and his narrator, Paul, Dückers made extremely confident claims about her ability to represent the past from a postmemorial position. Shifting epistemological authority from the first to the third generation, she asserted that her own generation's enhanced historical distance to National Socialism has now made room for a more objectified perspective devoid of the emotional entanglements of previous generations:

> The generation of 1968 had an emotionally strained relationship to their parents, to the generation of perpetrators; this was a confrontation between two generations who had both experienced the war. My generation is the first one that is in a position to cast a sober glance on this theme. I would consider it ominous if an arrogant authenticity of the older generation were to grow out of the fact that my generation did not experience the war.[27]

The epistemological naiveté of this postmemorial position is striking. By making historical distance from the event the yardstick for enhanced objectivity, Dückers simply bypasses the problematic nature of historical representation which concerns difficult issues of linguistic representation through narrative, the imbrication of archival processes in structures of power, the fragmentary status of documentary records and so on.[28]

Dückers addressed postmemory at greater length in a foreword to a collection of short stories entitled *stadt land krieg* (city countryside war), which she co-edited together with Verena Carl in 2004.[29] The collection contains prose writings about the long afterlife of National Socialism in post-war Germany by contemporary authors who were mostly born in the 1960s or 1970s and who have no personal memories of this watershed period. Discussing the merits of postmemory, the foreword refers to Harald Welzer's aforementioned study *Opa war kein Nazi*, which analyzed the dialogue about the Nazi past in three generations of 40 contemporary German families. Drawing on Welzer, Dückers and Carl point out that the abstract and numerical communication of the facts of National Socialism in post-war discourse disconnected family memory from official memory. The deficits of public discourse necessitate a different approach to the unofficial reservoir of family memories. Accordingly, they argue that the latter can be best tapped from a postmemorial position that combines historical distance with experimental narrative forms. For Dückers and Carl, a new generation of postmemorial writers had to emerge before the inconsistencies, the memory gaps and the secrets in the family could be brought into proper relief.[30] Returning to the issue of a generational difference between second- and third-generation writers, the foreword concludes on the same confident note as Dückers's aforementioned interview in *Die Zeit*. Dückers and Carl claim that, in contrast to the writings by older writers, their collection showed no revisionist tendencies because the younger writers approached their topic without pathos and belittlement, but also without coldness and distance.[31]

This self-proclamation by a new generation of writers once more underlines that generational topoi always makes strong claims about regeneration and renewal. As Pierre Nora argues, generational discourse tends to embrace an "eschatology of rupture" that privileges the youth as a site of revolution, renewal and regeneration.[32] For Nora, the idea of generation exudes such tremendous appeal in the modern era of accelerated change precisely because it is "the most instinctive way of converting memory into history. Ultimately, that is what a generation is: the spontaneous horizon of individual historical objectification."[33] However, as a spontaneous horizon of historical objectification, generational discourse always runs the risk of naturalizing history. In many ways, Tanja Dückers's *Himmelskörper* shows that such investment in the concepts of generation and postmemory does not in itself resolve the epistemological difficulties that are always associated with historical writing; rather it simply masks them behind gestures of generational self-proclamation.

Unlike Grass, Dückers furnishes her first-person narrator, Freia, in *Himmelskörper* with a great deal of unbroken narrative authority.[34] Similar to her author, Freia is a member of the third generation who is confident that she can look through the screen memories that have surrounded her family history since the end of the Second World War. Freia's sudden interest in her family's history during the Second World War is triggered by the death of her grandparents and by her own pregnancy. The ensuing reconstruction of the real circumstances of the family's flight from Prussia is accompanied by a number of other narrative strands, which thematize Freia's own childhood and youth in a wealthy suburb of post-war West Berlin. Dominant themes here are her changing relationship to her twin brother Paul, her first love with Wieland, her brother's coming out and her father's many affairs with other women. While the pregnancy makes Freia aware of issues of lineage and genealogy,[35] her meteorological research project – Freia is a Ph.D. student in meteorology cataloguing cloud formations – is supposed to equip her with a quasi-scientific credibility, which is elaborated through her conversations with Paul, who is an artist. Throughout the narrative, Freia's search for the elusive cloud "Cirrus Perludicus" is used as a rather laboured metaphor for this new postmemorial engagement with an equally elusive past.

At the heart of the story are the real circumstances of the family's flight from Gotenhafen on board the *Theodor* in 1945. According to family legend, the family managed to board the *Theodor* rather than the ill-fated *Gustloff* because of sheer luck and the grandfather's intuitive foresight that the *Theodor* would be the safer option. However, step by step, Freia peels back a different narrative layer that concerns the privileged treatment of members of the NS party even during the last months of the war: although a neighbour and her son would have been next in line to board the *Theodor*, Freia's grandmother Jo and her five-year-old daughter Renate were allowed to jump the queue because Renate informs on the neighbour for no longer practising the "Heil Hitler" salute. The effect of this childish telling on others is that the two families swap places and that the grandmother and her daughter end up on the right boat while the neighbour and her son are left behind. Step by step, Freia reveals that the grandparents' story of their dramatic escape from the Russians glossed over the real circumstances of their rescue in order to cover up their continued belief in NS ideology.

The unearthing of this family secret is accompanied by Freia's meta-critical engagement with three distinct types of memory discourse[36]: historiography as exemplified in post-war West German school curricula, the reservoir of family memories, and the cultural memory of the Third Reich. Freia criticizes all three discourses as inadequate in terms of their ability to communicate historical experience to later generations. It should comes as no surprise that Freia's dismissal of the history lessons in secondary school is delivered in sweeping and polemical fashion. So what objections does she level against taught history? First, she claims that history in school presented students with nothing but a hotchpotch of disconnected facts and figures, the main purpose of which was the reproduction of correct dates in examinations (*HK*, 92). Secondly, to make matters worse, the history lessons made the rise and fall of National Socialism appear like an abstract event, in fact a quasi-natural law beyond the sphere of human intervention (*HK*, 93). Thirdly, according to Freia, the majority of history teachers let their students down by failing to connect their history lessons with their own historical experiences of the Third Reich (*HK*, 94). The one and only exception is a particular Herr Dolle, who, for all his enthusiasm and pedagogic mission, appears to be an "Alleinunterhalter" (*HK*, 94; a solo entertainer), who at the end of the year unfortunately allocated grades to his students. In many ways, Freia's (and her author's) polemical rendition is symptomatic of a postmemorial discourse which, instead of engaging with historical discourse, simply trivializes it. My point is not that the novel is deficient because it fails to deliver a detailed appraisal of history lessons in post-1960s West Germany where the historiographical shift towards social history in the 1960s had led to a radical overhaul of the post-war curricula. Rather, I argue that this kind of polemical rendition does little to enhance our understanding of the complexities that surround the historical representation of perpetration and the attendant problematic nature of an ethics of remembering.

It could be argued that Freia's third polemic suggests that the reservoir of family memories could act as a productive way of filling the historical void created by historical discourse precisely because family memories have the capacity to communicate historical experience from below. However, according to Freia, this too ultimately fails to open up a viable perspective on history. For the grandmother's story of their flight from Prussia shows that family memories tend to solidify into formulaic parts that bury all experiential traces in a sea of stereotypes. Freia tells us that she knew the story of their flight by heart with every pause and linguistic embellishment (*HK*, 98). Like Timm in *Am Beispiel meines Bruders*, Dückers puts her finger on the conversion of a traumatic experience into a key anecdote of the reservoir of family memory. Jo's repetitive telling of the family's flight from Gotenhafen has produced a formulaic narrative that disguises the original experience. Freia's focus on repression and displacement as key drivers of family memory thus makes the psychological mechanism underpinning this type of memory visible. However, her eagerness to unveil the real Nazi story behind the grandparents' screen memories ultimately prevents her from giving voice to the traces of trauma that are nevertheless often inherent in such stereotypical renditions. In fact, the clichéd language in some of the dialogue is not so much the product of a metalinguistic critique, rather an emanation of Dückers's own indulgence in it. This is particularly evident when the grandfather relates the sinking of the *Gustloff* and the drowning of small children as follows: "Dann ging der Kopf zuerst unter Wasser und der Unterleib durch Auftrieb nach oben. Besonders bei den kleinen Kindern. *Schöner Mist*" (*HK*, 141, my emphasis; the head went underwater first and the bottom was driven upwards. Particularly in the case of small children. A nice piece of crap). As Adolf Höfer rightly comments, "schöner Mist", a nice piece of crap, indicates a change of register that seems to originate more in the author's idiom than in the grandfather's inability to communicate.[37] A direct comparison with Grass's very different handling of stereotype shows that a clichéd and repetitive language can be used as a particularly effective way of evoking trauma. For, although in Grass's novella Tulla Pokriefke keeps recycling the same image throughout the narrative, her dialect makes the reverberations of the trauma audible: "Die sind alle falsch runterjekommen vom Schiff, mittem Kopf zuerst. Nu hingen se in die dicken Schwimmwülste mitte Beinchen nach oben raus...."[38] The tonal quality of Tulla's rendition does indeed communicate something about the haunting quality of war trauma.

The deficits of the third type of memory discourse, official cultural memory, are thematized during Freia's trip to Warsaw, which she undertakes to investigate the suicide of uncle Kazimierz, a maternal cousin. In the course of their stay, Freia and her boyfriend Wieland also pay a visit to the memorial of the Warsaw Ghetto. Surrounded by flocks of tourists, ice-cream vendors, Polish taxis that play loud music and other signs of a flourishing tourist industry, Freia fails to make a meaningful connection with this site of Jewish suffering. Instead of preserving the historical site, the memorial has taken its place, thus displacing historical memory in the very act of officially remembering the Holocaust (*HK*, 170). Freia's failure to respond to the memorial in a meaningful way draws attention to the pitfalls of a didacticized memory culture that has long translated the Holocaust into a merely pious message.[39]

This three-pronged critique of memory discourse begs the question what kind of alternative postmemory offers to the impasse of distorting family remembrance, on the one hand, and the dead end of didacticized historical discourse and official cultural memory, on the other. What key has Freia found that enables her to reveal a hidden truth? In order to answer this question, one must look at the narrative model that underpins Freia's hunt for the truth. In Grass's story, Paul Pokriefke is a journalist who uses the research methods typical of critical journalism to make sense of family history. However, while Paul keeps crabwalking sideways, questioning his ability to come to terms with his material, Freia plays the part of a detective who chases a number of hot trails, dead ends and so on until the right clues are found. The classic detective novel is normally set in motion by a crime, which, once it has been committed, opens up an epistemological gap between seeming and being, between a false appearance and a hidden truth. It is the detective's job to close this gap by unearthing the truth behind a false reality. In this way, the classic detective story restores order and reassures our belief in a world anchored in truth. The application of this narrative model is most obvious in Freia's visit to Warsaw which she undertakes to find out the real reasons for uncle Kazimierz's suicide. Like a proper detective, Freia interviews his close friends, his employer, and she visits the pubs and cafés where Kazimierz was a regular, in the hope of revealing the clues that would possibly explain his suicide. Although the chase for evidence is in vain, and although the trip to Warsaw proves to be a dead end, this dead end is not without purpose: it fuels the suspense of Freia's Nazi trail hunt, which finally leads her to a secret jewellery box that contains important evidence of the grandparents' deep immersion in NS ideology. The narrative represents the grandmother's jewellery box as a miniature horror chamber, hiding a whole range of titillating Nazi memorabilia: there are seven postcards showing the "Führer", three pictures of the Nazi pilot Hanna Reitsch, a draft of her grandmother's letter congratulating Göring on the birth of his only child, even a bike reflector with an engraved swastika and – last but not least – a map delineating the eastern front that is used as a book cover for a copy of Hitler's *Mein Kampf* (*HK*, 262). Obviously, the grandmother's jewellery box is a sort of Nazi shrine, preserving cherished fetishes of the Nazi era. An object becomes a fetish when we invest it with a particular animistic, magical, demonic or spiritual power to influence the world. As Hartmut Böhme argues, fetishes are characterized by their performative structure and agency. This means that they can themselves reveal the powers that are attached to them.[40] Fetishes thus function in a magic milieu that invites affective participation rather than cognitive reflection. As a performative symbol, the fetish destroys the distance between subject and object.[41] Because it always activates its inherent meaning through participation, the fetish is particularly attractive to – what Max Weber calls – "charismatic leadership", which is built on the notion of a community, based on blind belief.[42] One might therefore draw the conclusion that the main function of the discovery of the jewellery box in *Himmelskörper* is the exposure of the grandparents' continued fetishization of Nazism in the post-war period. However, I argue that instead of de-fetishizing the past, the subconscious of the narrative achieves the opposite effect: it ends up re-mythologizing National Socialism by way of the very trails and secret objects that Freia chases to unmask the grandparents' Nazi fetish.

In everyday language, a secret is an object or fact that has been buried or hidden away somewhere so that it cannot be found out; or rather, so that it cannot be found out by the wrong party. The implication here is that a secret carries a special meaning that needs to be concealed from general circulation. It speaks to a denominated group of insiders or code-crackers; it is thus a highly loaded signifier that is encoded with reference to the idea of revelation. Secrets are thus not simply the forgotten of history but encoded facts that are suppressed in order to enhance their significance. Secrets are libidinally invested signifiers; like absent lovers, they must be chased and sought after, courted and cherished. The power of secrets and the attractions of code-cracking are perhaps best exemplified by the global success of Dan Brown's *Da Vinci Code*, which recasts the hunt for the grail in the register of a fast-paced contemporary thriller, entangling the readership in a labyrinthine world at the centre of which is the Vatican and the idea that there is a secret genealogy going back to Christ.[43] Trashy as it may be, Brown's *Da Vinci Code* is an exaggerated version of the family novel: by claiming that direct descendents of Christ people the earth today, it invests the idea of genealogy with an aura that is further heightened by the fact that this is a secretive lineage. Similarly, the trails and clues that circulate in Dückers's *Himmelskörper* imbue history with the type of meaning that can be typically found in gothic novels. Dark attics, secret drawers, strange paintings, hidden-away photographs and diaries are common props that achieve a gothicization of the past. And this is precisely the effect of the trail hunt in *Himmelskörper*: by reducing historical knowledge to the unearthing of fetishized secrets, the narrative subliminally remythologizes National Socialism. Ultimately, the secret at the heart of Dückers's story could not be any less surprising: like many Germans, the grandparents were active supporters of National Socialism and, presumably, like many Germans they tried to save their own skin at the end of the war at the expense of others. Yet the circulation of this secret through a range of narrative guises, including the language of Paul's paintings or Freia's plaits, which are a fetishized object of adoration for both grandmother and mother, produces a network of overdetermined symbols that ironically re-fetishizes the past in the very act of de-fetishizing it. The discursive-analytical approach to history that is evident in Grass's novella is replaced here by an historical exorcism that purports to undo the hidden power of National Socialism. The problem with this is that, as a ritualized performance, exorcism belongs to the magic milieu in which the fetish flourishes. By exorcizing the past, Dückers's narrator Freia participates in the affective investment of the fetish. In this way, the narrative transmutes the grandparents' NS devotion underhandedly into the grandchild's shocked excitement, titillation and the thrills that accompany her search. Ironically, although this postmemorial engagement with the past invokes the idea of not knowing all the time, it ultimately eradicates the otherness of the past by turning it into the alluring fantasy that history consists of tantalizing secrets. It is a further irony that the revelation of a dark family secret elides from the narrative lens the real phantoms of the family past, that is the woman and child who were left behind in Gotenhafen.

Undoing disenchantment: Necromancy in Marcel Beyer's *Spione*

Dückers's answers to the diagnosed deficits of historical discourse only effect new authorial gestures, which, in the attempt to legitimize the third generations' postmemorial position, ends up remythologizing the NS past. And yet the issue of historical disenchantment cannot be put to rest that easily. It figures as a major trope in much of contemporary German literature, which embarks on an investigation of our canonical understanding of historical time. In order to understand the significance of this engagement, the issue of historical time needs to be addressed.

As is widely documented, the secularization of time with its division into distinct categories of past, present and future was fully accomplished in the theatre of Enlightenment Europe, where notions of human progress and the perfectibility of man fed into a rationalization of thought that fundamentally affected modern man's conception of temporality. In this process, alternative notions of time, such as the medieval wheel of fortune, pagan versions of the co-existence of the dead amongst the living or even the Christian idea of an eschatological time, were designated as anti-rational and pushed beyond the concerns of philosophical or academic investigation. In the words of Walter Benjamin, the result was the "homogeneous, empty time" of capitalist modernity in which the individual is alienated from self, history and the material environment.[44] Benjamin's critique of homogeneous time had been preceded by Nietzsche's scathing attack on the tenets of 19th-century historiography in his essay *On the Uses and Abuses of History for Life*: singling out positivism as the dominant paradigm of his times, Nietzsche waged war against it for its inherent tendency to give equal weight to everything without evaluating anything.[45] For Nietzsche, the result of the positivists' historical indifference was an antiquarian mindset that was cut off from the living horizon of culture. Since Nietzsche's and Benjamin's seminal writings, these self-destructive aspects of the modernizing project have been the subject of continued academic debate. Deconstructivist and postcolonial criticism has helped to oust Hegel's belief that the modern state is the vehicle of human progress and the *sine qua non* of history. Indeed, the very positing of a radical break between an earlier cyclical temporality and the modern linearity of progress has come under scrutiny alongside the phallocentric imaginary of European thought. In the words of Stuart McLean,

> it is from such a retroactively imagined split that both the modern subject and the modern conceptualizations of history can be seen to have sprung. History, as the ideological self-knowledge of history-making human subjects, has sought to subsume other configurations of temporality and subjectivity by recasting them as its own retrojected antecedents, bygone moments in a teleology of human advancement that would, so it was claimed, subsume pockets of seeming backwardness both on the margins of European societies and in their burgeoning overseas empires.[46]

Although the move towards a history from below in the second half of the 20th century has done much to rectify the ideological biases and omissions of the modern mind, McLean notes that alternative accounts of time continue to pose a challenge for the historian.

However, what for McLean constitutes the "greatest scandal for academic historiography", that is "the contemporary persistence of nonhistoricizing visions of the past with their disregard of instituted boundaries between past and present",[47] has been the age-old prerogative of the poetic imagination. From antiquity to Shakespeare, the Romantics to the Victorian Gothic Novel, the desire to speak with the dead has been the motor of a poetic imagination that punctuates the linearity of time with spectral visions. The recent re-animation of this supernatural lineage in contemporary German literature is further evidence that the spectres of the non-modern have never ceased to confront modernity with its founding exclusions. In the light of this, one must therefore ask what kind of exclusion the postmemorial imaginary attempts to rectify. Or to put it differently: what alternative mode of knowing emerges from the spectral orchestration of history?

In order to explore the potential of the postmemorial imagination, the chapter discusses necromancy in Marcel Beyer's *Spione*. Beyer made his name with his second novel *Flughunde* (1995)[48], which explores NS crimes from the point of view of the shifts in media technology that helped to optimize Nazi propaganda.[49] While *Flughunde* conveys the penetration of NS ideology through the recorded human voice – Karnau, the main protagonist, is a recording technician who gets involved in Nazi medical experiments – *Spione* exploits a visual metaphor to both stage and scrutinize the postmemorial imagination. The novel enacts a necromantic drama of disavowal and a return that challenges the modern rationalization of historical time. On one level, the novel invokes a non-disenchanted version of history that seems to undo the strict demarcation between the dead and the living, between subject and object. However, on a second meta-critical level, the novel exposes the tricks and ploys that the postmemorial imagination mobilizes to reverse modernity's historical disenchantment. In order to achieve this double effect of invocation and effacement, *Spione* employs the idea of a dark family secret, which is at the centre of the contemporary German family novel.

The economy of secret is already set in train in the first scene where we encounter a nameless first-person narrator who is spying through the spy-hole in the door of his apartment. He developed this penchant for spying in his childhood when he stood on a stool or a box, peeping through the spy-hole whenever possible. However, the activity of spying is accompanied by the prohibition of touching the lens:

> Ich darf die Linse nicht berühren. Das Treppenhaus liegt keinen Schritt entfernt, nur diese Tür trennt mich von ihm. Das Bild aber erreicht mich von weither. Hält mein Auge dem Ausblick stand, rücken die Gegenstände langsam näher, dann auch die Schatten an den Rändern. Die unscheinbarsten Einzelheiten draußen treffen das geschliffene Glas, als wollten sie die Netzhaut gleich durchdringen.[50]

> [I'm not allowed to touch the glass. The stairwell is just a step away, blocked only by the door. But the image comes from a great distance. If I watch steadily, the objects slowly draw nearer, as do the shadows on the perimeter. The most inconspicuous details outside strike the polished glass as if attempting to directly penetrate my retina.[51]]

Although the iconography of this scene immediately conjures up images of the proverbial dirty old man that gets his voyeuristic kicks from the simultaneity of proximity to, and distance from, the object of desire, here the male gaze is strangely desexualized. In fact, the opening scene detaches the peeping completely from the economy of desire with its sexual motivation and reframes it instead in terms of a child-like engagement with the world that manages to convert the drabness of the immediate surroundings into an exciting playing field for the child's imagination. And yet, in spite of this alternative semantics, the prot-agonist's peeping has no air of innocence at all; on the contrary, it is introduced here as an obsessive activity that registers the smallest phenomena in terms of threatening appearances that might pierce the observer's retina. Instead of controlling the observed reality, the constant spying has completely engulfed the peeping self.

In many ways, this opening encapsulates the logic of the narrative as a whole, which concerns a family secret that is produced in the very act of unmasking it. The plot of the narrative revolves around four cousins who, during their summer holidays, roam their surroundings in search of juvenile adventures. According to the narrator, they all share the same physical trait: a pair of mysteriously dark Italian eyes, "Italieneraugen", which set them apart from the other family members. When they are confronted by the leader of another youth gang, who demands to know why they have such dark eyes, they make up a story about their dead grandmother, who, they claim, lives a grand life as an opera singer in Rome. The ringleader's request for proof of this exotic family background sets a trail hunt in motion that centres on the figure of the grandmother. According to the cousins' co-fabulated story, the grandmother was ousted from family memory by the grandfather's second wife, who, after marrying the grandfather, attempted to eradicate the grandmother from living memory, a point to which I return later. The family album, which the cousins happen upon in their search for the grandmother's operatic past, provides physical evidence of the second wife's destruction of family memory. Leafing through the old-fashioned album with its black-and-white photographs, they discover a whole range of portraits of their grandfather as a young man, a strange snapshot of the grandparents' damaged apartment after an air-raid during the Second World War, and several group photos. However, there is not a single portrait of the grandmother (*S*, 38). The cousins interpret the grandmother's omission from the album as a significant absence that points to a dark family secret. With this scene, Beyer enacts the translation of a gap into a secret, thus sparking off the necromantic imagination, blurring the boundaries between the dead and the living, present and past, or the visible and the invisible. In the ensuing narrative, the cousins' refracted stories about the grandmother's operatic career aim to create a magic milieu in which the evacuation of the supernatural from the modern world is reversed. The family album, with its striking epistemic instability between the seen and the unseen, is one of the main conduits that invests the past with the power to interrupt the present. Iconographically, the family photograph evokes a redemptive vision of a family's togetherness in the here and now; however, as an object of a later familial gaze, it is always a spectral reminder of time passing and of death.[52] Beyer cleverly exploits photography's epistemic instability to ignite the necromantic imagination that reinstates a way of thinking about the past that unsettles the rationalistic division of time. From now on, a whole range of visible and invisible photographs are circulated that sharply disturb the linearity of time.[53]

However, the above-cited episode is more than a mere trigger for necromancy: for the cousins' ensuing speculation about the possible fate of the grandmaternal portraits both reflects and addresses the politics of looking that defines the familial gaze. According to a recent theory of photography, the looking relations of the familial gaze "situate human subjects in the ideology, the mythology, of the family as institution and project a screen of familial myths between camera and subject".[54] With regard to the family album, this would mean that it constructs norm-ative roles of domination, of subjection and of interconnectedness on the basis of finite representational choices. The two main sub-genres of the family album, the group photo and the portrait, are perhaps the most important representational means through which the familial gaze is organized: while the group photo demands to be seen with reference to the family's togetherness, the portrait gives expression to the indi-vidual's identity based on his or her role in the family. It is precisely this normative power of the family album, which the cousins have in mind in their reaction to the absence of their grandmother's portrait from the album. Imagining a whole range of photos showing the grand-mother's face and above all her Italian eyes, they speculate that some unknown viewer must have removed "sämtliche Bilder, auf denen man die Italieneraugen sehen kann. Vielleicht hat der direkte Blick unserer Großmutter einen Betrachter dieser Bilder so beunruhigt, wie unser Blick die Menschen zu beunruhigen scheint" (*S*, 40; all the pictures in which one could see her Italian eyes. Perhaps the direct gaze of our grand-mother disturbed someone viewing the pictures as much as our gaze seems to disturb people; *Sp*, 31). With this interpretation, Beyer makes the four cousins a mouthpiece of current theories of photography that pose an opposition between the normative familial gaze on the one hand and an alternative subversive way of looking on the other; while the first is an instrument of social domination, the latter is constructed as a subversive alternative that – in the words of Kaja Silverman – is "on the side of flux, memory, and subjectivity".[55] Metaphorized here in the "Italieneraugen", which the cousins claim to share with their grand-mother, this look has an unsettling effect on the onlooker, destabilizing the usual relations of power and domination that are upheld by the economy of the familial gaze. It is in line with this that the cousins proceed to imagine a scene in which an unknown observer cuts out all photographic representations of the grandmother with the help of a pair of nail scissors or nail-clippers to remove, once and for all, the disturbing spell of the grandmother's Italian gaze from the family album (*S*, 40). While Beyer has so far exploited the polarity of looking and gazing to spur the cousins' spectral visions, the humorous depiction of an assault on the grandmother by such powerful weapons as nail-clippers gives this gothic fantasy a self-knowing twist.[56] As the scene progresses, the notion of spectral evidence becomes so over-determined that it appears to be an effect of narratological orchestration, which has its origins in Beyer's skilful handling of the postmemorial paradigm.

Piecing together the grandmother's biography as an opera singer, the cousins also sketch a highly romanticized picture of the grandfather's courting of the grandmother. They offer alternative accounts of this first encounter, discussing the drawbacks of each version until they decide to entrust the first-person narrator with the task of extracting further information on the grandmother's life from their parents (*S*, 78). Although his mission fails, the power of this co-fabulated story is such that it casts a spell over the first-person narrator, whose life is increasingly absorbed by the workings of the postmemorial imagination. With the help of a few recurring spectral props such as the kitsch souvenir of a Spanish dancer[57], which pops up throughout the narrative as a fetish of desire, he (re)constructs an alternative necromantic world in which love-making and spying become interchangeable. The conversion of romance into a spy narrative is already set in motion in the opening scenes of the postmemorial narrative, which zooms in on the figure of the grandfather in the opera. A pair of binoculars in his lap, the grandfather scans his surroundings while thinking about his future career as a pilot in the *Luftwaffe*, which, as we are told, was in the process of being secretly built up by the NS State in defiance of the Treaty of Versailles (*S*, 11). The grandfather is introduced here as a bearer of a political state secret who spies on the mystery of the opera singer's desirable Italian eyes:

> Schon während der Ouvertüre will er nach den Italieneraugen Ausschau halten, er kann es nicht erwarten. Die Leute in der Reihe vor ihm räuspern sich. Er dreht am Schärfenregler, wischt die Linsen noch einmal. Die Nachbarn werfen ihm auffällige Blicke zu. Sie wissen ja nicht, wer er ist. Er wird sich schon zurechtfinden, er wird schon lernen, nicht mehr aufzufallen, still zu sein. Der Vorhang wird gelüftet. Eine Frau erscheint. Das muß sie sein. (*S*, 13)

[During the overture he waits to search for her Italian eyes, although he doesn't expect to find them.[58] The people in front of him clear their throats. He adjusts the focus, wipes the lenses again. The people next to him are glancing at him openly. They don't know who he is. He'll soon settle in, learn to be inconspicuous, quiet. The curtain rises. A woman appears. It must be her. (*Sp*, 7)]

The economy of this scene is such that it makes spying a form of desiring and desire a form of spying. In this way, the narrative provides an original scenario, in fact, a romanticized lineage for the visual obsessions of the narrator who has already been introduced as the peeping Tom behind his spy hole. A little later, the narrator provides authentification for this postmemorial scenario by means of a photograph in the family album, which, so he claims, shows the grandfather in the opera balancing the programme on his knees. The drama of desirable spying is enlivened once more but brought to an intermittent halt when the singer finally appears to turn her attention to the young man (*S*, 17). Later on in the narrative, the opera scene is being rewritten when the opera singer shows him the set. Deprived of the alluring splendour of performance, the world of opera shows itself here in its off-stage drabness, pointing to the vast gap between a prosaic reality made up of papier-mâché props and the performance that needs constant re-enactment to create a powerful illusion of an alternative world ruled by desire. Off-stage, the world of the opera thus makes visible the illusionary quality of desire, which hinges precisely on the kind of idealization that the opera performs on stage. When the young man, who is clearly unsettled by the illusionary dynamic of desire, asks his lover whether she can make out any faces in the audience, she replies that nothing exists at the edge of the stage. If it appears to a member of the audience that she would look into his eyes, this is simply a coincidence, an illusion (*S*, 64). But the dynamic of desire is not put to rest with this scene: a few paragraphs later, the opera singer is shown peeping from behind the curtain, checking whether her lover is watching her performance (*S*, 65).

The recycling of the opera scene with its complex matrix of looking and being looked at keeps reinvesting the story with libidinal energy, inviting the portrayal of further details in the romance. The motif of the grandfather's career as an officer in the newly built-up *Luftwaffe* in 1930s Germany, however, allows for the introduction of a gothic dimension into the story that reverberates through the narrative as a whole. Gradually, the narrator reveals that the grandfather was a member of the Condor Legion that supported Franco in the Spanish Civil War and bombed Guernica. Because he has to keep this mission secret even from his fiancée, a gothicized climate envelops her, feeding on rumours about Guernica, and her own growing suspicions that her fiancé has dished up a "Tarngeschichte", a lie. This climate of suspicion is further fuelled by the appearance of a strange officer who pretends to pass on her fiancé's regards while in reality spying on her. When, after their wedding, the newly wed husband eventually reveals the truth to his wife, they make a pact that they will keep his mission in the Spanish Civil War a secret (*S*, 180). Evidently, for the narrator this secret assignment, together with the seeming erasure of the grandmother from the family album, is the driving motor behind his own investigations.

However, the exaggerated emplotment of this story ultimately draws attention to the mechanics of the two genres employed here, namely romance and the gothic spy narrative. It is increasingly evident that the superimposition of these genres produces the very family secret that the narrator actively chases throughout the story. Narrative over-determination of genre thus opens up a meta-textual distance to the first-person narrator, who, after the summer holiday with his three cousins, continues his necromantic hunt for the grandmother. In the course of his obsessive investigations, the narrator employs a whole range of narrative strategies to authenticate his necromantic story: in addition to the employment of a range of props that are cited as evidence of a hidden past, he breaks up the monologic perspective of the first-person narrative, giving his cousins and each grandparent their own narrative voice. However, while the polyphony of voices plays on the idea of multi-perspectivist testimony, thus lending credence to the story, the narrative over-determination of genre constantly calls into question the truth of this construct. This is particularly evident in the story of the grandfather's second wife, who is represented as a figure plucked straight from the Brothers Grimm fairy-tales: she makes her entry as the proverbial evil witch who drove her step-children out of the house with an axe raised high above her head. According to the narrator, the figure of "die Alte", the old hag, is the source of a foundational memory ban that prohibited their grandfather from maintaining any contact with his children. Worse than the Butzemann, or even Vitzliputzli, the old hag represents for the narrator a supernatural power that enthrals all family members (*S*, 79). Employing a range of hyperbolic expressions, he claims that she rules not only the front garden, the path to the house and the entire edge of the town, but also the grandfather and through him she commands his offspring. In his view, she has dominated the family since time immemorial, as her reign began before any of them were born (*S*, 79).

The over-determined iconography of the old hag, in particular, seems to invite a Freudian interpretation. From a psychoanalytical angle, it makes sense to read the grandfather's second marriage and his estrangement from his first family as the root of a transgenerational disturbance in communication that the cousins attempt to repair by co-fabulating a hidden lineage. In line with this, the story they tell about their grandmother's grand operatic past bears all the hallmarks of a classic family romance. According to Freud, the family romance marks a stage in the child's development when the child attempts to overcome the first experience of disillusionment with his parents by way of fantasizing an alternative ennobled birth.[59] Freud views the family romance as an essential but transitory coping strategy through which the child rejects the harsh demands of reality. In the end, the child must abandon this fantasy and acknowledge the reign of the reality principle. From a Freudian perspective, the story which the four cousins invent during their summer holiday and which is later elaborated by the narrator would thus compensate for disillusioning experiences with their own parents: it invests the dead figure of the grandmother with a surplus of (nec)romantic significance. Further evidence for such a reading is provided later on when we learn that Nora's, Paulina's and Carl's parents divorced shortly after that fateful summer and that an extended period of estrangement ensued between the three siblings. All this clearly points to a psychoanalytical meta-level from which the whole narrative seems to be orchestrated. In this way, Beyer seems to invite his reader to unravel the grandparents' past with its secret signals, passwords and clues as nothing but a classic screen memory produced by the mechanism of condensation and displacement.

This interpretation with its typically rationalized approach to the necromantic imagination is actually put forward by one of the cousins themselves who is visited by the narrator 20 years later in his continued search for the grandmother. Carl is now a successful diplomat with wife and children who has lost his "Italieneraugen" (*S*, 237). Accordingly, he attempts to dissuade the narrating self from his obsessive preoccupation with the ghosts of the past by means of several tropes of disenchantment. First, he claims that the photograph of the grandfather in the opera could never have been taken for technical reasons, such as poor lighting conditions and an impossible depth of field (*S*, 249). He argues that as a result of too much emotional investment in the story the narrating self has lost all ability to distinguish clearly between fact and fiction, between an irretrievable past on the one hand and the demands of the present on the other. Diagnosing what amounts to a paranoid condition in the narrating self, Carl reminds his obsessive cousin that the story of the Italian opera singer was originally nothing but a childish invention meant to fob off the other children in the neighbourhood (*S*, 251). Furthermore, he explains that a notice that the four cousins had put in the paper announcing the death of the grandfather's second wife was a macabre and bad joke that luckily failed to have the desired effect on the woman who survived the shock of reading her own death notice (*S*, 252). However, although the cousins had made everything up, in the end their hateful fixation on the figure of their stepmother did cast a spell on their own lives. For, despite the evidence to the contrary, Paulina continued to believe that they had killed the old woman: as a result of this, he argues, her life was being destroyed by the inventions of their youth (*S*, 252). Carl concludes by expressing his hope that at some stage the four cousins might be able to sit down together again without the weight of the past and the weight of their family history bearing down on them (*S*, 253).

Foregrounding the psychological mechanisms at work behind the original co-fabulated story, Carl posits a radical break between their former youthful enchantment with family history on the one hand and a disenchanted grown-up version of this history on the other. From the perspective of the adult, all the strange secrets of the past must be either read in terms of rationally analyzable psychological conflicts or simply erased from memory to make space for future orientations. Carl, the diplomat, embodies here the outlook of the modern history-making subject that seeks to control alternative notions of subjectivity and temporality by designating them obsolete antecedents on the road of human development and progress. His rationalized interpretation of the past dispels its ghostly revenants and presences by locating them inside the self. As an effect of the human psyche, the uncanny loses all enchantment: it becomes open to the type of rationalist unmasking that Carl performs with his interpretation of the family past. A disenchanted self, he thus paradigmatically repeats here the modern evacuation of all presences and forces beyond human control from the environment. His reading of his cousin's continued pre-occupation with the grand-mother's past bears all the hallmarks of modern historical consciousness with its founding exclusions.

And yet in spite of this rationalizing rhetoric, Carl seems to be haunted by his discarded anti-self. For when he admonishes his cousin that the spell of the past must be broken, he ultimately attests to the power of that spell: "Wir haben die Macht der Worte unterschätzt, vielleicht waren wir noch nicht alt genug, um zu begreifen, wie vorsichtig man mit Worten umgehen muß" (*S*, 251; we underestimated the power of words. Perhaps we weren't old enough to realise how carefully they have to be handled; *Sp*, 220). Ironically, what is meant here as a trope of disenchantment turns out to be a figure of re-enchantment: instead of effacing necromancy, the notion of an unbroken power of words invokes a magic milieu in which the spectres of the non-modern flourish. Likewise, Carl's confident assertion that the spell of the past will be broken in the near future (*S*, 253) only testifies once more to the persistence of an alternative vision of the past that continues to punctuate the linearity of historical time. Carl's great effort to oust his cousin's spectral visions from family memory can be read as a contrapuntal invocation of a disenchanted world. Ironically, this makes the ghostly residues of a non-historicizing temporality visible.

At first sight, it appears that Carl's admonitions have a sobering effect on the narrating self who, step by step, begins to unravel his own story about his stepmother, the old hag. Relating once more the over-determined scene of the second wife's violent destruction of all family memorabilia that are associated with the grandmother's spectral presence, he concludes this scenario by deflating his own necromantic vision: "So kann es nicht gewesen sein" (*S*, 270; it can't have been like that; *Sp*, 237). But this apparent rationalization of the postmemorial imagination is turned on its head when the narrator realizes that the power of words that Carl talked about subliminally rehabilitates an ostensibly pre-rational worldview. He therefore decides that he no longer needs to search for evidence of his grandmother's operatic past because his postmemorial imagination will suffice to keep her alive without further proof (*S*, 272). What follows is the account of an imaginary meeting between him and the elderly grandmother in which she relates her life story to the grandson. In a kind of postmemorial séance, the grandmother constructs a gothic story at the heart of which is life after her own staged death. She relates that, when she had unexpectedly survived a period of serious illness, the grandparents took a joint decision to keep her recovery a secret from their children by seeking a divorce. According to the grandmother's account, the grandfather's second marriage was part and parcel of their cunning plot that allowed the grandmother to reinvent herself as an opera singer in Italy after the divorce. While, on the one hand, the grandmother's story appears to rationalize her gothic disappearance from family memory, on the other hand, the emplotment of her story allegorizes once more the drama of disavowal and return that characterizes the necromantic imagination. In this way, the imaginary meeting between grandmother and grandson reinstates a way of thinking about the past that runs counter to the rationalistic demarcation between the past and the present. But this scene is crucial in another respect: it makes necromancy a form of transgenerational communication with the dead. For the grandmother's account culminates in a vision of an afterlife through a gifted grandchild who would follow in her operatic footsteps. This vision hinges on the idea that as an opera singer she has always inhabited an in-between space where fantasy and reality become inseparable. In its unsettling ambiguity, this in-between space is the ideal meeting place for the dead and the living:

Mit seinem ersten Ton wird der Sänger zu einer erfundenen Figur. Für die Dauer seines Gesangs befindet er sich in einem Zwischenraum, ihm ist bewußt, er ist nicht derjenige, als dessen Verkörperung die Zuschauer ihn erkennen mögen, und zugleich weiß er auch, er ist nicht mehr derselbe wie noch eben in der Garderobe. In diesem Zwischenraum, wo eine Sängerin sich selbst als Erfindung begreifen muß, könnten Großmutter und Enkelin zusammentreffen. Das würde sie sich wünschen. (*S*, 289–90)

[With the first note, the singer assumes a character. For the length of her song she exists between two states: she knows she's not the person the audience sees, but she also knows she's no longer the same person she was in the dressing room. Between these two states, when a singer recognizes herself as an invention, a grandmother might meet her grandchild. That's what she'd like. (*Sp*, 253)]

The grandmother's vision of a necromantic communication with the dead has been put into practice throughout the narrative by means of various postmemorial techniques, ranging from the circulation of ghostly props to the employment of *mise-en-abîme*. In this way, the narrative keeps refracting the pressing question whether the evacuation of ghosts from modernity's landscape is really such a desirable effect of the establishment of modern historical consciousness. By setting a busy traffic between the dead and the living in motion, Beyer turns the postmemorial imagination into the playing field for a non-historicizing relation to the past. This postmemorial rehabilitation of an ostensibly lost world is simultaneously nostalgic and self-knowing: nostalgic because it transmutes vestiges of the past into a redemptive vision of renewal, as is evidenced in the above scene; self-knowing because the narrative constantly points back to its postmodern orchestration, ultimately undermining any authorial authentification of the necromantic play. Nevertheless, in spite of these ironic gestures, this postmemorial staging of necromancy highlights the impoverishment of the modern historical consciousness that has lost all ability to speak with the dead. In this way, *Spione* shows that the postmemorial imagination can be much more than an unregulated fantasy in the service of historical forgetfulness. Although the novel employs fantastical props and supernatural conduits, its self-knowing discourse rehabilitates alternative modes of knowing the past.

Conclusion

This chapter illuminates how in recent years humanities discourse has embraced the idea of postmemory as a key concept, guiding the investigation of the transgenerational transmission of the memory of the Holocaust and of the NS period. Designed to take account of the growing historical distance to this defining event of the 20th century, the concept prioritizes an imaginative appropriation of the past above and beyond documentary or historical representations. Postmemory conceptualizes the mediated nature of transgenerational memories from the point of view of those generations that no longer share a personal connection with the past. This chapter suggests, however, that the idea of postmemory feeds into currently fashionable, but highly questionable, trends to emphasize the intrinsically traumatic experience of all history. My reading of Cathy Caruth alongside Marianne Hirsch therefore challenges the equation of history with trauma. Where it is applied uncritically, it runs the risk of obscuring important historical distinctions. It replaces historical analysis with the idea that history's intrinsically traumatic nature requires a performance that mimics the ungraspable nature of history's vagaries. From an historical point of view, this reconfiguration of history in terms of trauma theory would constitute a serious depreciation of historical analysis, which, in the last analysis, would eradicate the very notion of the past.

Notwithstanding the critical appraisal of the academic reception of this discourse, postmemory remains a powerful poetic device that can be exploited to very different effects. A first comparison of Günter Grass's *Im Krebsgang* and Tanja Dückers's *Himmelskörper* underscores once more the generational topoi that tend to accompany German identity debates today. However, by contrast to Grass's careful handling of the transgenerational memory of the war period, Dückers exploits her postmemorial position primarily to make sweeping claims about the deficits of Germany's official cultural memory of the NS period. The postmemorial subject position in *Himmelskörper* represents the grandparents' embroilment with National Socialism in terms of a range of titillating memorabilia which have a fetishized hold over the present. Ironically, instead of de-fetishizing National Socialism, Dückers's postmemorial narrative ends up re-mythologizing the period through a network of textually over-determined symbols. By contrast to the discursive-historical approach to history that guides Grass's inquiry into the transgenerational legacy of National Socialism, Dückers advocates a kind of historical exorcism that merely reduces historical knowledge to the unearthing of family secrets. In this way, the privatization of history obfuscates in this text a meaningful perspective on the important question whether the notion of historical responsibility is transgenerationally active.

On the other hand, Marcel Beyer's sophisticated postmemorial novel *Spione* highlights the real deficits of our canonical understanding of historical time as it emerged in the modern period. As the ideological horizon of the history-making subject, modern history underlines modernity's unbroken faith in a rational temporality that can be controlled, archived and preserved. Modernization set in trains a number of interrelated processes that presupposed a teleological understanding of history. The standardization of industrial production processes, the exploitation of natural resources alongside colonialism and the development of modern technologies all depended on the propagation that time is homogeneous and linear. Faced with unprecedented historical acceleration from the late 18th century onwards, modern society discovered memory as a way of overcoming the dislodged and uncomfortable reality of modernity's alienating reality. The obsessive concern with memory is thus not just a signature of our own age in which massive technological transformations on a global scale have eroded traditional notions of place and time in favour of a threatening synchronicity.[60] As Peter Fritzsche argued in his study *Stranded in the Present*, this trend can already be located in the melancholia that characterizes post-revolutionary France, where the emergence of a new historical consciousness was accompanied by frenzied memory work.[61] According to Fritzsche, the French aristocrats' experience of exile and loss led to the attempt to preserve melancholy remnants of a lost past.

Analyzed from this angle, one could argue that postmemory is a similarly melancholy category that makes the memory of loss an imperative, thereby connecting the modern subject with an alternative vision of the past that defies the linearity of historical time. This is precisely the horizon of Marcel Beyer's *Spione*, which confronts modernity with its founding exclusions. By enacting a necromantic drama that involves the dead and the living, Beyer invokes a non-disenchanted version of history that subtly calls into question the evacuation of ghosts from modernity's landscape.

4

Heimat and Territory in Thomas Medicus's *In den Augen meines Großvaters* and Stephan Wackwitz's *Ein unsichtbares Land*

The geography of memory

Stephan Wackwitz's *Ein unsichtbares Land. Familienroman* (2003, Engl. transl. *An Invisible Country*, 2005) and Thomas Medicus's *In den Augen meines Großvaters* (In My Grandfather's Eyes, 2004) are exemplary of the contemporary German family narrative that, as the previous two chapters demonstrate, examines history through the lens of family history, exposing the floating gap between the official historical discourse of the post-war period, on the one hand, and the unofficial archive of private memories, on the other.[1] By piecing together the jigsaw of family history with the help of family photographs, albums, diaries and other stranded objects from the past, these narratives produce a patchwork of sorts, an historical *bricolage* that draws attention to the constructed nature of historical truth. They reproduce, re-arrange and scrutinize these biographical and historical materials in order to set the personal and the historical, the private and the public, imagination and fact in dialogue with one another.

However, while these traits are shared by many family narratives, Wackwitz's and Medicus's narratives reintroduce an important dimension into the debate: the idea that the environment, built or natural, is a prime vessel for the transmission of both family memory and cultural memory. Exploring the multi-layered and deep-seated connections between a particular location and family life, Wackwitz and Medicus produce thick descriptions of those localities that have played a formative role in their family histories. The narrators of both stories embark on multiple journeys to former German territories in Poland, where their families had lived prior to the war. In both narratives, these trips are sparked by the narrator's subconscious remembrance of eastern European landscapes that have been communicated subliminally within the family across generational thresholds. In order to understand the significance of this transgenerational legacy, it is necessary to briefly mention the role of the German expulsions in post-war German discourse.

At the end of the Second World War, between 12 and 14 million Germans fled or were expelled from their homes in the eastern provinces of Prussia, Silesia, Pomerania, regions that are now Polish, and the western parts of the Czech Republic, the so-called "Sudetenland".[2] In the eastern sector, the later GDR, expellees never managed to gain special recognition as the GDR needed to be on good terms with Poland, a socialist brother state; they were therefore quickly distributed across East Germany in an attempt to assimilate them into the local population. Whereas expellees were not recognized as victims of war in East Germany, the situation was very different in West Germany, where expellee organizations were quickly founded in the immediate post-war era. Here the so-called *Landsmannschaften* (compatriot associations), later amalgamated by the *Bund der Vertriebenen* (Association of Expellees), became a powerful platform for representing the financial, political and cultural interests of refugee Germans.[3] As expellees comprised a significant segment of the West German vote, their demands were formally acknowledged by the Ministry for Expellees, Refugees and the War-Damaged which was set up especially to deal with this situation and which existed from the 1950s until the 1960s. In addition to seeking financial compensation for lost property in the East, granted by law in 1952, the expellee organizations also made political demands: for a long time, they refused to recognize the western boundary of Poland, the so-called "Oder-Neiße Line". Culturally, their outlook was conservative, if not reactionary, as the organization fostered a revisionist *Heimat* discourse, which ignored the changes of the geo-political landscape of the post-war era. However, as the historical distance from the expellations of 1945 grew, the political demands of the expellees became increasingly obsolete and divorced from the realities of the post-war era. Willy Brandt's *Ostpolitik*, built on the principle of "Entspannung" (Change through Rapprochement), initiated a new dialogue with Germany's eastern European neighbours, effectively recognizing the western border of Poland.[4] Although the *Bund der Vertriebenen* kept appealing publicly to the lost *Heimat* in the East,[5] the memory of the former German territories in Poland was marginalized in German memory discourse, until the events of 1989 revised the geopolitical map dramatically. The lifting of the Iron Curtain suddenly made these forgotten territories visible, and they were quickly rediscovered by the media and the tourist industry. Both Wackwitz's and Medicus's treatments of these historically contested territories draw attention to the interrelationship of collective and cultural memory and geo-politics: without any hint of revisionism, they explore the complex emotional and historical connections between their families and the areas that were erased from Germany's official memory map. However, in order to avoid the pitfall of revisionist *Heimat* discourse, both narratives reflect continuously on the meaning of place as landscape and territory.

In both narratives, the first impulse for these trips to Poland stemmed from the desire for a Proustian recognition of areas that neither narrator ever visited as a child. However, a memory imprint of these areas was kept alive within both the families. In this way, the "madeleine" experience of these stories is not the effect of an authentic childhood scene but rather the product of the indirect transmission of *Heimat* images within these families. In both narratives, *Heimat* discourse and, as we will see, landscape images are represented as subconscious deposits that are opened up and explored once the grandsons visit these localities in the 1990s. Although both narratives thus re-enact a Proustian recognition, they both subject this moment to erasure by simultaneously exposing the historical and the political violence embedded in the landscape. Adopting an archaeological perspective that unearths traces of a history of violence and destruction, both narratives switch between landscape discourse as an aestheticized variant of *Heimat* discourse, on the one hand and territorial discourse, on the other. Landscape discourse is underpinned by the idea of a harmonious relationship between a contemplative self and a framed nature, which is both domesticated and yet an image of "Herrschaftsfreiheit" (indominability).[6] With its transcendental appeal, landscape promises freedom from the alienating effects of social organization.[7] Likewise, German *Heimat* discourse establishes an organic link between the German people and the environment. By contrast, territory suggests a patch of land in its geopolitical and historical sense. Territories are fought over, revised, destroyed, built up, and their boundaries are contested or agreed.[8] While landscapes are the product of the painterly and poetic imagination, territories are represented by maps. In the following, the notion shall be explored that Wackwitz and Medicus project their landscape and *Heimat* images onto the territorial map of the National Socialist colonization of the East, thereby exposing the ideological connections between landscape, *Heimat* and territory. Examined from a different angle, their trips to the East could be interpreted as exercises in "dark tourism" that also bring the titillating attraction of death and disaster to the fore.[9] Their highly self-conscious engagement with sites of destruction, death and warfare also exposes a postmemorial longing for participation in history's vagaries.

Landscape as screen memory: Medicus's *In den Augen meines Großvaters*

Medicus's investigation of the hidden family history revolves around the question whether his grandfather Wilhelm Crisolli, a German *Wehrmacht* general with an Italian name, was responsible for war crimes committed against the Italian civilian population in the Apennine mountains in 1944. However, while this inquiry is thus overtly motivated by the desire to establish historically verifiable facts, the author's autobiographical alter ego is equally driven by the fear of an uncanny repetition effect: his grandfather was shot by partisans at the young age of 49, and it is suggested that his father committed suicide at the same age. Approaching this dangerous threshold in his own life, Medicus embarks on the self-conscious reconstruction of his grandfather's biography and of the circumstances that led to his death.

Interweaving memory discourse and landscape discourse, Medicus employs different media to explore the potential and the limits of landscape discourse: a landscape painting by the German painter Walter Leistikow, known for his paintings of Grünewald near Berlin; a photograph of an Italian garden, showing his grandfather in a bucolic setting; and the sonnets by the English poet Rupert Brooke. While Medicus's engagement with Leistikow's painting and Brooke's poetry draws attention to the idealized quality of landscape discourse, which is always at a remove from reality, the photograph of the Rococo garden appears to anchor landscape in the real world. The switch from painting and poetry to photography as a mimetic medium is an intermedial game that allows the self in Medicus's narrative to reimagine the grandfather's past along the following lines: if the grandfather inhabited an Arcadian garden in Italy, then he could not possibly have carried out violent deeds against the Italian population or died a violent death himself. Step by step the narrative exposes and dismantles the garden image as a Freudian screen memory that disguises a troubling historical reality. Drawing on landscape discourse, Medicus's narrative also offers a critique of the limits of postmemorial discourse.

From its opening, the narrative introduces a series of landscape memories that move from the remembrance of the narrator's *Heimat* in Franconia to Berlin and finally to the pine forests of eastern Europe that, as we are told, are already imprinted on the narrator's subjective memory map. This imaginary map is made up of layers of the East-Elbian landscape that, as we are told, have sedimented inside the self from early childhood. The narrator mentions a range of East-Elbian place names such as Kolberg, Stolpmünde or Belgard. In his memoryscape these do not signify a real topography but evoke the iconography of an imagined landscape, which is composed of a few simple elements, including sand, pine trees and lakes. The highly stylized and iconographic composition of this inner landscape is underlined by the insertion of a small-scale black-and-white reproduction of Walter Leistikow's painting *Abendstimmung am Schlachtensee* (Evening Atmosphere on Schlachtensee). The narrator reads this painting as the "Ausdruck eines ebenso unsagbaren wie unwiederbringlichen Verlustes" (*AG*, 14; expression of an unspeakable and irretrievable loss). He notes that the depth of the painting is an effect of the interplay between the dark pine trees in the foreground and the glowing sunset in the background. The intensity of the light is further emphasized by the reflection on the surface of the lake. This lends the picture a quasi-religious iconic appeal, carrying precisely the transcendental promise traditionally associated with landscape painting. Accordingly, Georg Simmel argues that nature, presented as a landscape, demands a sense of isolation, a singular and yet characteristic detachment from the inseparable unity of nature.[10] For Simmel, the aesthetically idealized quality of the landscape that is evident in landscape painting is a defining feature of all experiences of landscapes. The perception of nature as landscape depends on the right mood, which evokes a correspondence between man and nature:

> The most important carrier of this unity seems to be what we commonly call the mood of a landscape. For if a person's mood designates this sense of unity which colours the entirety of the particularities of his soul for a short or enduring time; and if this cannot be reduced to a single aspect but if it must be understood with reference to something general in which all singular aspects of the landscape come together, then this means that the mood of a landscape impregnates all its individual components; so that we cannot pin it down to something particular.[11]

It is precisely this "mood", in Simmel's sense, that unleashes Medicus's longing for a place that is not so much the site of his family's real history as the highly aestheticized carrier of a transcendental promise. Not surprisingly, Medicus introduces the topos of the paradisiacal garden at this point. We are told that his childhood bedroom overlooked the park of a small castle, which was covered by pine trees and which the child imagined in terms of an exotic island full of evocative secrets (*AG*, 17). By planting the pine tree in this childhood scene, the narrator aligns the idea of the paradisiacal garden with the earlier landscape image. The imaginary quality of the eastern European landscape, already thematized through the Leistikow painting, is thus considerably heightened. The childhood memory draws attention to the paradisiacal expectations associated with the inner landscape. This can have no match in reality because it evokes man's non-alienated existence in harmony with nature prior to the Fall and prior to man's entry into history.

When the investigating self begins to travel to eastern Europe, he appears to abandon landscape discourse in favour of the historical exploration of the remnants of the former German culture. A first indication of this change of perspective is the self's developing interest in pine forests. Although he concedes that, unlike other mythically laden trees, the pine tree hardly ever spurred the poetic imagination, the travelling self associates a certain degee of uncanniness with this mundane tree (*AG*, 25). An image of the black-dotted map of the *Atlas Florae Europaeae*, which is inserted at this point, underlines this dark omnipresence of pine forests; it shows that pine forests cover most of the northern hemisphere and reach as far as Siberia. Medicus's usage of images is clearly modelled on W. G. Sebald's: both writers employ photographs as objects of desire as well as uncanny icons of a past that haunts the present.[12] Through the insertion of this map, Medicus signals the switch from landscape discourse to territorial discourse, in Sebaldian fashion. Evidently, the forests and planes of the East are not a pastoral landscape but the former territory of Hitler's expansionist war. As a haunted landscape, it necessitates a different approach from the aetheticized optics that the self had previously modelled on the Leistikow painting. But at this point in the narrative, the travelling self merely poses as an "Archäologe einer verschütteten Kultur" (*AG*, 20; archaeologist of a submerged culture). Instead of digging into the complex cultural and political history of the former German territory, he indulges in alluring and self-consciously kitschy fantasies of fascinating fascism. The chapter ends with a passage in which Medicus's alter ego imagines himself as a member of camouflaged *Wehrmacht* troups (*AG*, 27).

That such romanticization of the war leads the self up the proverbial garden path is made demonstrably clear in the next chapter. Medicus relates how, during a trip to Britain, he came across a portrait of the English poet Rupert Brooke in a tea garden near Cambridge, frequented by a number of famous Cambridge intellectuals, including Brooke himself. In the setting of this English garden, he reads Brooke's famous war sonnet "The Soldier" of 1915, which, as Medicus points out, invokes the war as a "schwärmerisch-patriotischer Hymnus" (*AG*, 32; enthusiastically patriotic hymn): "If I should die, think only this of me: / That there's some corner of a foreign field / That is forever England".[13] Beguiled by this pastoral representation of the war, the traveller begins to immerse himself into Brooke's life and works. The English poet becomes his spiritual *doppelganger* precisely because he imagined the war in terms of exotic landscapes. Returning from a trip to Tahiti at the outbreak of the war, Brooke, like many young men of his generation, welcomed the war: "Die feurigen Landschaften, von denen er immer häufiger geträumt hatte, waren Wirklichkeit geworden. Das Verheißungsvolle war da, das Wunderbare: der Krieg" (*AG*, 34; the firey landscapes which he had been dreaming of more often became reality. The alluring promise, the marvel: the war). Such aestheticization of the war was only possible because Brooke never saw a real battlefield; he died as a result of a fever while travelling from Egypt to Greece on board a ship. Brooke appealed to the British public of the time because of the apparent unity between the poet's life and work. His early demise seemed to verify the idealized picture of a beautiful death, which his sonnet had evoked in such lyrical style. Obviously, this had nothing to do with the bloody massacre that took place in the trenches of the First World War. As the narrator comments, Brooke offered him Arcadian warscapes in which, although one was surrounded by blood and horror, pain and screaming, one did not die a wretched death (*AG*, 37). But this is an insight that his travelling alter ego has not yet realized; he remains Brooke's *doppelganger* in search of an Arcadian war.

The deconstruction of the Brookean pastoral fantasy only occurs in the course of two trips to Italy, which the self undertakes to reconstruct the final months of his grandfather's life. The main source for this reconstruction are 51 photographs that were taken by the grandfather and his staff during the Italian occupation in 1944. Medicus uses these photographs to explore the limits of landscape discourse. By looking at landscape through a photographic lens, he exposes the gap between aesthetic representations of the environment and a concealed historical reality that is blatantly absent from these pictures. Landscape discourse and the self's postmemorial engagement with the grandfather's photographs thus mutually reinforce each other: they both derealize history and provide appealing smokescreens for a highly disturbing family history. It is in line with this phenomenon that – driven by a Brookean desire for a complete erasure of the manifold rifts between self and other, self and nature, present and past – the investigating self studies these photographs, arranges them into thematic groups, scans them into his computer to magnify each and every detail, until he seems to have merged with the world depicted in these images: "Ich hatte den Wunsch, die Vergangenheit, die diese Bilder fixierten, läge hinter Türen, die ich nur zu öffnen bräuchte, um hinüberzutreten" (*AG*, 56; I wanted the past that was fixed in these photographs to lie behind doors which I only needed to open in order to cross over). Referring to the depth of field in a series of photographs that depict a brief stay of Wilhelm Crisolli's division in Denmark in 1943, the investigating self is struck by the exaggerated presence of the past in these photographs: "Der Tiefenschärfe gelingt es, der abgebildeten Vergangenheit eine gewisse Überpräsenz zu verleihen. Als ob sie eingefrorene Gegenwart wäre, ist die Vergangenheit auf diesen Fotografien einfach da" (*AG*, 61; the depth of field succeeds in lending the photographed past a certain supra-presence. As if it were a frozen present, the past in these pictures is simply there). Here, Medicus exploits the apparant mimetic appeal of the photographs to highlight the epistemological difficulties that accompany all reconstructions of the past, whether fictional or historical. The photograph's mimetic quality makes the self forget that, in the words of L. P. Hartley's novel *The Go-Between* (1953), "the past is another country. They do things differently there." The confusion of his own imaginative investment in these photographs with the past itself is helped, of course, by photography's unique relationship to its referent. As Roland Barthes argues in his classic essay *La chambre claire*, the "has-been-ness" of the photograph distinguishes it from other iconic images. "Contrary to these imitations, in Photography I can never deny that *the thing has been there*."[14] As an emanation of reality rather than its copy, photographs have a highly evidential appeal. According to Marianne Hirsch, this makes them an ideal medium for postmemorial work. Commenting on our special relationship to family photographs of victims of the Holocaust, Hirsch argues that it is "precisely the utter conventionality of the domestic family picture that makes it impossible for us to comprehend how the person in the picture was, or could have been, annihilated. In both cases, the viewer fills in what the picture leaves out: the horror of looking is not necessarily *in* the image but in the story the viewer provides to fill in what has been omitted."[15] For Hirsch, family photographs are an ideal medium for the postmemorial work of later generations because their fragmentary status invites an imaginative response to the past. She writes, "They are leftovers, the fragmentary sources and building blocks, shot through with holes, of the work of postmemory. They affirm the past's existence and, in their flat two-dimensionality, they signal its unbridgeable distance."[16] But, as the previous chapter argues, this postmemorial engagement with the past must maintain a self-critical impetus. Otherwise it runs into the danger of producing nostalgic versions of history that make the past the site of alternative identities.

This is precisely the focal point of Medicus's metacritical engagement with photography as an appealing but highly problematic medium for memory work. His intense study of the photographs does, of course, not open the door to the past, rather it results in a titillating fetishization of images that give expression to the self's semi-conscious longing for a "Männerbund" (men's club) and the Prussian military tradition. Accordingly, the self admires the flawlessness of the appearance and the physical discipline of these officers, which he reads as an expression of their inner countenance, their virtuousness and honesty (*AG*, 63). He further describes how he surrenders to what he perceives as a rather dandyesque performance, which, in his eyes, has the air of quiet aesthetic opposition (AG, 63). Although such passages show that the self studies these pictures from a meta-critical perspective that exposes the construction of ideology in the composition of these photographs, there is an underlying sense of identification with the idea of tradition and social exclusivity. Throughout the narrative, the self displays a fascination with such aestheticitized representations of Prussian manliness. While the polished perfection of the officers' appearance displays a moment of slippage, the pictures nevertheless exude for the self the aura of old Prussian military tradition (*AG*, 62–3). Accordingly, Medicus relates how his alter ego places the photographs on black cartons that produce a fitting aesthetic frame and a meaningful sequence for the story of Wilhelm Crisolli's death (*AG*, 56). The meaningfulness of these photographs is thus the result of a range of carefully orchestrated intermedial games through which the grandson fetishizes the past. The postmemorial story the grandson provides at this point does not just fill in the gaps of meaning that are inherent in portrait or group photographs, but it generates an overdetermined iconography that heightens his own role in the text. In this way, the narrative underlines the proximity between a postmemorial representation of the past and its fetishization.

Singling out one photograph from a batch of Italian pictures that show gardens with Wilhelm Crisolli always in the middle (*AG*, 64), the narrative explores how such fetishization of the past drives the investigating self into a complete impasse. It is a photograph depicting his grandfather and Adjutant Maak in an Italian garden. Labelling this seemingly bucolic garden scene, the "Rokoko-Foto", the narrator mentions a range of inter-textual associations that transport the imaginary quality of the scene. He likens this photograph to paintings by Watteau or Fragonard in order to connect the picture with the idea of mythological Arcadia: "Wer hätte der Aura solch eines Bildes widerstehen können? Das Rokoko-Foto war das perfekte Erinnerungsbild" (*AG*, 68–9; who could have withstood the aura of such a photograph? The Rococo-Photo was the perfect memory icon). The grandson's overdetermined gaze turns the grandfather from a *Wehr-macht* general who is enmeshed in a bloody war against Italian partisans into an innocent inhabitant of Arcadia. The Rococo picture is the perfect memory icon precisely because it derealizes the war.

The self's first trip to Italy is a disappointment. Embarking on his journey without the photographs, the traveller is caught up in a series of self-delusions (*AG*, 82), resulting from his continuous projection of remembered images and expectations onto the environment. While the failure of the first trip has to do with a disregard for the epistemological gulf between a remembered landscape and its real equivalent, the second trip appears at first sight to be more successful. Equipped with the right maps and the photographs, he now manages to locate the original scene of the Rococo photo; a Renaissance villa that has been in the hands of the same family since the 16th century. Its young owner identifies the garden in the photograph, and the search seems to culminate in a recovery of the bucolic scene. According to the narrator, they jumped a few steps down into the garden and walked directly into the photograph (*AG*, 84).

Clearly, Medicus's discourse on landscape draws here on the concep-tual framework of Italian Renaissance gardens.[17] Characterized by a geometrical arrangement and a careful orchestration of house and garden, the Italian Renaissance garden embodies the idea of the *natura educata*, of a nature that requires man's hand to achieve perfection. It is for this reason that the terrace gains central importance in Italian Renais-sance gardens; linking house and garden it serves both as a viewing platform from which man can view nature in terms of a landscape and as a stage for man's own mastery of nature. Furthermore, the formal and geometrical qualities of the Italian garden are enhanced by the applica-tion of strict geometrical forms, such as squares, circles and semi-circles. These create the impression of interlocking garden rooms that display a perfect harmony between man and nature. In the Rococo picture, the grandfather and his Adjutant are thus surrounded by a *natura educata* that exudes order, tranquility and harmony. The stylized quality of the garden is heightened considerably here by the stylized sharpness of the black-and-white photograph. Both the architecture of the Italian garden and the iconography of the photograph thus indicate that this garden scene is removed twice from the reality of the war.

The traveller, however, is as yet unaware of the imaginary quality of the garden scene. In his eyes, the discovery of the garden of the Rococo picture shows that history can be interpreted in terms of landscape discourse. However, his suspicions are eventually aroused when the Italian owner of the villa and garden tells him that, although partisans shot a German officer at the end of the war, no reprisals were taken against the Italian population. He reflects that this story must be an embellished version that suits the Arcadian illusion (*AG*, 86).

Yet in spite of such methodological doubts concerning his Brookean immersion in the past, the travelling self continues to pursue a mimetic reconstruction of the events of 1944. Beguiled by the strong impact of the images, he attempts to re-enact the events by, for instance, adopting an imaginary partisan optic during a walk over the mountains (*AG*, 91). However, further research, including various conversations with eye-witnesses of the events of 1944, reveals a series of contradictions that expose the fantastic moment of landscape discourse; step by step the Arcadian landscape is exposed as a "Landschaft des Verrats" (*AG*, 105; landscape of betrayal). The traveller now realizes that he has been entrapped by a web of rumours, legends and half truths, all of which feed the screen memory that a German officer with an Italian name could not possibly have pursued and killed Italian partisans. According to local legend, the dying officer even forgave his assassins and forbade reprisals for his killing (*AG*, 104). Having discovered both the site of the garden scene and the site of the assassination, the traveller has to relinquish the appealing aura of the Rococo garden. Admitting that his method of uncovering the past through the immediacy of visual experience had served its purpose, he finally abandons the Robert Brookean desire for fusion (*AG*, 111).

The two trips to the historical site of the events of 1944 thus show that history cannot be deciphered in terms of landscape or garden discourse. Effectively, the various landscape images and garden scenes that accompany the self's search for the past are screen memories barring access to a deeply troubling historical reality. In order to unearth the events of the past, the self must change his methodology and adopt a critical–archaeological perspective that places the grandfather's and his family's life squarely on a historical–geographical map. The time-lessness of the landscape images begins to be superseded by a more historical perspective that makes the traces of the Second World War visible. Surrounded by relics of German culture, he now perceives the environment in terms of a former landscape of war.

This emerging historical perspective also helps him recognize the gendered nature of his inner landscape. On his memory map, Pomerania is a space primarily occupied by the females in the family. We learn that his mother and grandmother had escaped in one of the last refugee treks in 1945. After the war, they did not participate in the activities of the expellee organizations; nevertheless, they projected a longing for the lost *Heimat* onto their grandson, who became a subconscious medium for these memories (*AG*, 50). Adopting his mother's viewpoint, Medicus shows how the end of the war continued to shape her outlook on life. Although his mother adapts quickly to the requirements of the emerging post-war order, she hangs on to her Pomeranian values of old. The status anxiety of the eastern refugee is now channelled through the accummulation of property and the middle-class lifestyle of the 1950s, which attempts to mimic the Pomeranian childhood (*AG*, 170). However, unlike the grandmother, who persists in such role play until she dies, the mother eventually manages to break with the past. After her husband's death, she sells up the Franconian property and moves to Munich, where she embarks on a new career. By contrast, the grandmother continues to view Pomerania in terms of an idealized space where she could lead a quasi-aristocratic existence that, until 1945, was completely untouched by the turbulent political events of the inter-war period, the rise of Hitler and the war. When Wilhelm Crisolli and Annemarie Rosetzki, Medicus's grandparents, met in the 1920s, they felt that the remoteness and rural structures of Pomerania could really erase the defeat of 1918. Their marriage in 1927 stood for a continued "Junker" existence based on Wilhelmine patriotism. For all the family members it was a piece of the lost empire. We are told that whenever the highly decorated World War participant and future husband materialized, the watershed of 1918 appeared to be eradicated (*AG*, 126). Similarly, Countess Johanna – a maternal cousin whom Medicus visits towards the end of the book – talks about the war in terms of a novel that is peopled by attractive Prussian officers who upheld the Wilhelminine ideal of a masculinity steeped in chivalry, Lutherism, Prussian patriotism and military courage. It is in line with this Prussian narrative that Johanna relates how Crisolli was sidelined in the *Wehrmacht* after he refused to carry out an order against the civilian population in one of the eastern European campaigns where the *Wehrmacht* ravaged entire villages. Medicus realizes that the motif of disobeying orders is a fixed element of the "preußische Erzähltradition"

(*AG*, 222; Prussian narrative tradition), fuelling the family myth about Crisolli's integrity and honour. For Johanna and his grandmother, the war remains a love story, ending with the tragic defeat of the German man (*AG*, 216).

The analysis of the genderized experience of the end of the war shifts emphasis away from the Arcadian imagery towards an historical–psychological perspective on the long-term effects of the war. After the second trip to Italy, the investigating self switches from landscape discourse to territorial discourse. Poised between empathy and critical analysis, he now focuses on the ideology and belief system that guided his grandparents lives, exemplary for a generation that continued to believe in Germany's cultural mission and in *völkisch* nationalism even after the defeat of 1918. He represents his own garden fantasies as an effect of the grandparents' Pomeranian garden existence, in which the German ideals of Lutherism, Prussianism and militarism had survived until the end of the Second World War. The marriage with Annemarie gave Wilhelm access to a quasi-aristocratic lifestyle that was sealed off from the events of the Weimar Republic. While the First World War polished his character with the necessary "Schliff" (toughened manliness), the marriage embedded him in the social environment of the *Kaisertum* (*AG*, 152–53). However, as the couple's engagement photograph revealed, their lives were based on an anachronistic role play that barely disguised their underlying feelings of shame, degradation and disorientation that war, defeat and the post-war situation had brought them (*AG*, 137). The fall from the Pomeranian paradise comes at the end of the Second World War, when Wilhelm is assassinated in Italy and the family flees from the approaching Russian army.

Medicus's empathic and yet critical analysis of the wider family history prepares a better ground for his final investigation of the events surrounding his grandfather's assassination. Instead of indulging in Arcadian fantasies, the self now embeds his grandfather's military moves in 1944 in the history of the end of the war. In this process, the Apennine region is transformed from a camouflaged garden into a bloody war theatre where the retreating German army committed war crimes against the civilian population. After the landing of the Allied forces in Normandy on 6 June 1944 and the Russian advancement towards Berlin from the East, partisan activities increased in Italy. Commanding the *20. Luftwaffen-Felddivison* (20th Airforce Field Division), the grandfather was in charge of defending the coastlines and securing the so-called "Green Line" against partisan attacks. On 24 July, the SS arrested a local priest and two women who were then charged with partisan activities and who, under the command of Crisolli's division, were shot dead three days later (*AG*, 193). After the war, some of Crisolli's superiors were charged and sentenced for their Italian war crimes. Haunted by the unspoken fear that the grandfather might have been implicated in such war crimes and that his assassination could have been a direct reprisal, the remaining members of the Crisolli family passed on the hidden fear about the grandfather's complicity in war crimes as a family secret that the grandson attempts to unravel. However, when – after extensive historical research, interviews with eye-witnesses, consultation with military historians – he finally receives a copy of the relevant records of the War Crimes Office in the United States, he only manages to establish for certain that the grandfather was indeed responsible for the execution of the Padre and the two women. Although these executions played no role in the war crime trials against Crisolli's superiors, the calculated killing of the three Italians betrays a specific will to annihilate (*AG*, 240), which, in principle, makes the grandfather's participation in other war crimes possible. Further research shows that the worst war crimes took place after the grandfather had been shot dead. In the end, however, the grandson cannot delete the grandfather's name from the list and the suspicion continues to live on (*AG*, 240). Unable to establish with absolute certainty whether or not his grandfather was involved in any other war crimes, he returns to his metacritical analysis of (post)memory, subjecting the various research methods to a final evaluation. It now becomes clear that all the evidential materials used during his investigations have intrinsic limitations: the eye-witnesses misremember events, and the photographs – with their beguiling depth of field – are equally fictional. Medicus comments that the linguistically remembered reality and the reality that had been photographed 60 years previously opened a room of many voices filled with facts, fictions, legends and rumours, in which weighing the probable against the improbable was one of his main concerns (*AG*, 245). The photographs of the Italian gardens which triggered the original investigation are screen memories that drape a troubling reality in the acceptable and aestheticized language of the pastoral. Like Brooke's poem "The Soldier", which imagined death through warfare as a beautiful transformation of the poetic soul, Medicus's alter ego needed to imagine a beautiful war where masculine soldiers carried out gentlemanly deeds. The switch from landscape discourse to territorial discourse enables the self to view landscape eventually as one aspect of an historically grown and contested environment. In the end, Pomerania and Italy are seen neither simply in terms of a landscape nor merely in terms of a territory; as sites of conflicting memories, they are sedimented environments, shaped by verifiable historical events, legends, rumours and myths that are attached to a region. If history can only be heard in a polyphonous space where facts, fiction, myths and legends are voiced, then the metacritical reflection on one's reasons for prioritizing certain interpetations over others must be built into the historical account.

This does not mean that the interpretation of history is arbitrary; on the contrary, it requires a careful evaluation of all sources, including the investigating self's personal motivations for embarking on this research. The self's conclusion, therefore, concerns not so much the grandfather's alleged violent deeds or his death but rather his own attitude towards the past. Citing the example of an Italian academic who, after beginning to research his own grandfather's story, became so absorbed by it that he lost sight of all concerns in the present, Medicus concludes laconically: "Man mußte sich erinnern, aber auch vergessen" (*AG*, 248; one had to remember, but also to forget).

Heimat discourse and colonialism in Stephan Wackwitz's *Ein unsichtbares Land*

The idea of an organic link between the German people and its environment was one of the most powerful ways of grounding modern German national identity. Elizabeth Boa's and Rachel Palfreyman's rich study of German *Heimat* discourse from the late 19th century highlights the semantic elasticity of a concept that, on the one hand, invites identification with family, locality, language and the nation and, on the other, already carries within it a sense of dislocation and alienation.[18] This view is further supported by Thomas M. Lekan's incisive study of German environmental and landscape discourse between 1885–1945. In his book, Lekan shows how the German landscape preservation movements, which emerged in the Wilhelmine period, were a form of cultural politics that articulated middle-class anxieties about national identity, the pace and scope of industrialization and urbanization.[19] With their emphasis on *Heimat* as a site of emotional identification, the Wilhelmine preservationists drew on a rich tradition of literary and artistic representations of *Heimat* from the early 19th century onwards. Furthermore, the emerging discipline of political geography had provided a "scientific" underpinning for this cultural interpretation of the land. A good example of this is Wilhelm Heinrich Riehl's *Die Naturgeschichte des Volkes als Grundlage einer deutschen Social-Politik* (1855; Engl. transl.

The Natural History of the German People, 1990), which proposed that the national character emerged organically from the interplay between the topography of a particular region and its culture. For Riehl, landscape is thus a cultural repository that anchors a community in space and time. Accordingly, Wilhelmine preservationist movements, such as the *Naturdenkmalpflege* (Care of Natural Monuments) and the *Deutscher Bund Heimatschutz* (German League of Heimat Protection), believed that "environmental and moral improvement went hand in hand, with Heimat sentiments providing a levelling bulwark against levelling tendencies of modernity".[20] They favoured the cultivation and preservation of the local region as a way of achieving the desired harmony between the people and the environment. However, by the late 1930s the moral geography of the Wilhelmine movements with their focus on a regional meaning of landscape had been replaced by the colonial vision of the "Lebensraum" (living space). This redefinition involved a move away from the provincialism of the *Naturschutz* (Protection of Nature) movement towards a Darwinist vision that recast the idea of "Kulturlandschaft" (cultural landscape) along racial lines, positing a natural symbiosis between blood and soil. The ensuing militarization of the landscape thus introduced ethnic determinism into *Heimat* discourse.[21]

The nationalization and colonization of landscape discourse provides the backdrop for Stephan Wackwitz's *Ein unsichtbares Land*. Like Medicus, Wackwitz reconstructs a hidden family history that concerns the family's life in a former German colony in Poland. Wackwitz's engagement with this topic is particularly poignant because the family lived in a German village in close proximity to Auschwitz. We are told that the grandfather had worked in Anhalt as a pastor from 1921 until the family emigrated to South-West Africa in 1933. Although the family had left the area long before the Holocaust occurred, their family history in Anhalt is under erasure as a result of a geographical proximity that is never openly articulated in the family.[22] Unable to deal with the meaning of this proximity, the family members withdraw into a communicative silence that produces a haunting legacy, which is transmitted across generational thresholds. What at first sight appears like an historical coincidence, the family's geographical proximity to the site of Auschwitz, is thus reconfigured in terms of Freud's uncanny.[23] In a recent analysis of *Ein unsichtbares Land*, Friederike Eigler rightly argues that this discourse on the uncanny goes beyond the legacy of National Socialism; it also concerns its subliminal repetitions and reverberations in the generation of 1968 to which Wackwitz claims to belong.[24] For the narrator, repression of the family's history has produced a series of repetition effects that makes him an uncanny *doppelganger* of his grandfather. Like his grandfather, who spent many years of his working life as a German expatriate in Poland and South-West Africa, the grandson has chosen a career abroad. Similar to his grandfather, who was a religious and patriotic missionary, the grandson, who works for the Goethe-Institut, sees himself as a cultural missionary in the service of a new Germany. These rather contrived resemblances – contrived because the work of a protestant pastor in the 1920s and 1930s can hardly be compared to the cultural–political work of a Goethe Institute employee – produce the very repetition effect, which Wackwitz proceeds to analyze with reference to German national identity and the quest for tradition after the Holocaust. Right from the start, the narrative makes the invention of tradition one of its overriding concerns.

Although the project of making the invisible country visible is thus motivated by a therapeutic impulse, the narrative attempts to go far beyond such a psycho-hygienic framework. By mapping out the family history in Anhalt and South-West Africa, Wackwitz constructs a German tradition which in his view lays bare the ideological underpinnings of the German colonial fantasy.[25] In this way, the narrative aims to contribute to what Dirk Göttsche describes as the ongoing rediscovery of the cultural history of colonialism in that it traces the inherent connection between the *völkisch* dream of Germany's eastern European expansion and the colonial fantasy.[26] As Göttsche points out, a cultural history of German colonialism should not just bring into relief the overseas colonial narrative, but it must also reflect on the preconditions and effects of colonialism in European societies.[27] This double perspective is precisely the achievement of Wackwitz's book: first, the narrative sets Holocaust discourse and postcolonial discourse in dialogue with one another, thus providing an in-depth analysis of two versions of the *völkisch* colonial dream. Secondly, by reading Germany's colonial and NS history through the lens of family history, he shows how deeply enmeshed the personal is in the political. Instead of simply pitting the personal against the political, Wackwitz's narrative traces the deep structures of ideology in everyday life.

In Wackwitz's narrative, Freud's uncanny is the prime trope guiding the self's transgenerational investigation of the idea of tradition. However, as the opening chapter unfolds, it becomes clear that the uncanny is the effect of a particular way of reading family history. For Wackwitz mobilizes a range of intertexts that produce a sense of uncanniness which the narrator always connects back to his family history. In this way, the narrator's intertextual games convert his family history into a site of the overdetermined 20th-century German history. This technique of superimposing layers of intertexual meaning onto family history occurs already in the opening chapter. Wackwitz relates a number of local Polish and German ghost stories that are attached to Anhalt. There is, for example, the story of a procession of candle lights that upon entering a house then suddenly blow out, thus announcing a death of a family member; or the legend of the dead pastor who sat every night outside his house, reading a book while an invisible hand was turning the mangle (*UL*, 8). Such sagas and legends give poetic expression to an archaic belief in the influence of the dead over the living; they are the product of a collective imagination that imbues the region with a mythology, thus establishing a strong sense of community and identity. It is therefore important to know that his grandfather contributed some of these stories and sagas to a collection published in 1930 under the title *Sagen der Beskidendeutschen* (The Legends of the Beskidy Germans).[28] The grandfather's involvement with this publication reflects his belief in precisely the type of mythological landscape that came under erasure after Auschwitz. The uncanny effect of the local ghost stories articulates and masters archaic fears by way of a collectively anchored poetic imagination. By contrast, the historical uncanny, which affects the family after Auschwitz, cannot be worked through on the basis of such a mythologizing tradition.

After the war the grandfather was unable to accept that the type of poetic imagination that was at work in the *Sagen der Beskidendeutschen* cannot cope with the shadow of Auschwitz. He became an obsessive diarist locked in the minute reconstruction of his life and his beliefs for more than 25 years. Each year, on the occasion of a family reunion, he gave bound copies of this "fortlaufende Ich-Erzählung" (*UL*, 25; serialized autobiography) to each of his five children.[29] Later in the narrative, we learn that the grandfather had planned his diary project as a counter-narrative to the emerging Auschwitz discourse in the early 1960s. When the Auschwitz trials took place in Frankfurt, he continued to write about the German settlement of Anhalt in the elegiac manner of a Stifter, Storm and Keller (*UL*, 144). However, such poetic descriptions do not manage to elide the Holocaust completely as his landscapes are written over by the uncanny. Drawing our attention to the echoes of 19th-century writers in the grandfather's writing, Wackwitz unwittingly also brings to the fore the double-edged nature of the transgenerational legacy that preoccupies his alter ego throughout the narrative. On the one hand, this haunting legacy originates in the historical coincidence that the family lived in close proximity to Auschwitz, a coincidence that gains further sinister meaning because it is erased from the grandfather's memoirs. However, on the other hand, the intertextual ploys used here and elsewhere create an overdetermined iconography that charges family history with additional symbolical meaning. For example, highlighting the resonance of a Hebel or Stifter in the grandfather's writings, the narrator employs a sentence structure and tonality that mimics W. G. Sebald's writings. Clearly, the superimposition of Hebel, Stifter, and the deliberate affinity with a Sebaldian style is not coincidental: it achieves what one might call a melancholy effect that heightens the gothic representation of family history.

Die Echos aus Johann Peter Hebels Geschichte vom "Unverhofften Wiedersehen" sind in dieser Passage unseres Familienromans manchmal fast wörtlich zu hören [...]. Und als Bewohner der stillen kleinbürgerlichen Welt des Dorfes fallen meinem Großvater als Erstes die Toten ein, die im Schatten der Kirche ihre Ruhe haben, was mich wie einer der unheimlichen Züge berührt, die Stifter noch seinen traulichsten Schilderungen oder eben Hebel seiner Geschichtsidylle über den wiederaufgetauchten Bergmann von Falun beigegeben hat. Die sinistren Bewandtnisse der Gegend um Anhalt, die in der Beschreibung meines Großvaters als jener Stifter- oder Hebelton anklingen, haben sich in den seither vergangenen Jahrzehnten bis ins fast Unerträgliche verstärkt, und ich bin bei eigentlich jedem Besuch dort froh gewesen, am Abend schnell wieder nach Krakau zurückkehren zu können. (*UL*, 146–47)

[Occasional echoes of Johann Peter Hebel's story "Unexpected Reunion" are unmistakable in this passage of our *family romance*. [...] And, as my grandfather writes, it is first of all the dead who rest in the shade of the church that come to his mind – an association that moves me as do the uncanny features added by Stifter to his cozy descriptions, or by Hebel to his idyllic story about the resurrected miner of Falun. The sinister quality of the area around Anhalt has become almost unbearably intense in the decades since my grandfather wrote these paragraphs, and whenever I'm there, I find that I'm relieved to be returning to Kraków as soon as possible. (*IC*, 122)]

The overdetermination of this passage and others shows that the grandson has not just inherited a troublesome legacy passively, but that he constructs a particular version of tradition actively by superimposing a range of intertexts onto his family history. Although Auschwitz undoubtedly features as the source of the disturbance of tradition, Wackwitz's construction of this tradition relies heavily on a range of intertexual games that reinforce the sense of uncanniness throughout the narrative.

A good example of this occurs in an earlier chapter entitled after the famous Hebel story "Unverhofftes Wiedersehen" (Unexpected Reunion). The chapter relates how in 1993 an old Kodak film camera was returned to his father after more than 50 years. The camera had been confiscated by the Royal Navy in 1939 when the Wackwitz family left South-West Africa to return to Germany on board the *Adolph Woermann*. After leaving the harbour, the passengers and the crew were arrested and the ship was sunk. While in Hebel's well-known story, the discovery of the dead miner's body leads to an unexpected reunion of the now old bride with her young groom, here the discovery of the camera awakens the hope in both Wackwitz and his father that the family past may have been preserved on film. However, the film has been destroyed by time and there is no such dramatic moment of recognition. Reflecting on the questionable nature of the turning point of a classic anecdote, Wackwitz proclaims that the meaning of his own narrative will emerge as the invisible centre of the confused, hidden and interlocked twists of a family romance (*UL*, 18). Evidently, Wackwitz refers here to the psychoanalytical meaning of the term "family romance", which Freud had conceived in terms of a generational conflict, at the heart of which is the child's realization that his parents are not as singular and exceptional as he imagined them in early childhood.[30] A family romance in Freud's sense thus concerns the inevitable disappointment that a child has to experience with his parents in the process of growing up. By denominating his narrative a family romance, Wackwitz draws attention to a hidden psychological dynamic that is enacted across generational thresholds. Clearly, this cannot be represented in terms of Hebel's anecdotal construction of historical truth; it requires the analysis of the agents of repression in the family.

A prime source for this analysis is the grandfather's memoirs. Because the grandfather's response to the erasure of Anhalt in Germany's cultural memory is the erasure of the significance of Auschwitz in his own narrative, his memoirs do not overcome the communicative silence in the family; rather they effect a double erasure that short-circuits the transgenerational postal system. For, in the eyes of the grandson, the grandfather's silence about the impact of Auschwitz transforms this cultural history of a forgotten region into a dehistoricized idyll. It is for this reason that the grandson rejects the grandfather's message.

In a chapter entitled "Im Palast des Kaisers" (In the Emperor's Palace), Wackwitz employs Kafka's "Eine kaiserliche Botschaft" (The Emperor's Message) to enact the failure of the transgenerational postal system. The opening sentence of Kafka's story runs thus: "Der Kaiser – so heißt es – hat Dir dem Einzelnen, dem jämmerlichen Untertan, dem winzig vor der kaiserlichen Sonne in die Ferne geflüchteten Schatten, gerade Dir hat der Kaiser von seinem Sterbebett aus eine Botschaft gesendet" (The Emperor – so they say – has sent you the individual, the miserable subject, who, as a tiny shadow, has fled from the Emperor's sunshine into the far distance – of all people the Emperor has sent you a message from his death bed).[31] The caveat "so heißt es" (so they say) already points to the logic of the remaining story; the emperor's message can never reach its destination because it has always been the product of a mythologizing tradition. In the course of Kafka's story, there is a switch from perfect tense to present tense, which indicates how the belief in an imperial message is reinvested each time this story is told. As Elizabeth Boa argues, "such a dream of non-alienated communication evokes what in deconstruction is termed a metaphysics of presence, the belief that the spoken word and the presence of the speaker provide the guarantee of stable meaning".[32] In the course of Kafka's story, this metaphysics of presence is literally lost. On his way through the vast palace with its endless corridors, doorways and courtyards, the messenger and reader get entangled in a labyrinthine structure that, with its twists and turns, contradicts the notion of an imperial message based on the unquestioned authority of one speaker. Kafka's story hinges on the idea that the Emperor's message is an act of grace which the addressee, the "jämmerliche Untertan" (miserable/pitiable subject), is longing for. By contrast, in Wackwitz's narrative the relationship between Emperor and subject is reversed; here it is the grandfather who is longing for his message to reach his grandson, while the grandson protests that he no longer desires this message.

Significantly, this rejection of the grandfather's message is made most explicit when Wackwitz's alter ego visits the site of the grandfather's childhood memories in Laskowitz near Breslau. We are told that this section of the memoirs was the most elaborate, the saddest, the most beautiful and the most humane part of the description of his life (*UL*, 112). Equipped with the grandfather's account of his childhood, he searches and finds the village and park that his grandfather evoked in such lyrical terms. Interspersing his own impressions with quotations from the grandfather's memoirs, the self compares the "geschriebene Erinnerungslandschaft" (written memory landscape) with the park environment today. To his surprise, the park presents itself as a more or less unchanged arrangement in the manner of Caspar David Friedrich (*UL*, 115). And when the traveller finally comes across the forester's lodge in which his great-grandfather had lived, he is shocked by the high degree of resemblance between the scenery today and an old photograph of the forester's lodge that survived the war (*UL*, 115). But unlike Medicus, who mistook the Italian garden scene for reality itself, Wackwitz maintains intellectual distance to this mimetic appeal of the park setting. Citing seven pages of the grandfather's highly evocative description of life in the forester's lodge, the grandson realizes that it represents an effigy of order (*UL*, 116), which the grandfather re-erected in his diary against the post-war order. With its beguiling love of detail, the iconography of the forester's lodge evokes a homeliness and familiarity, erasing the grandfathers' experience of dislocation that affected him from the end of the First World War. According to the grandson, with its park setting as an idyllic backdrop, the cosy interior of the lodge disguises the underlying connections of this vision of *Heimat* with the colonial fantasy. Referring once more to Freud, he reads the grandfather's childhood memories as an inversion of the Freudian family romance. In his view, the grandfather indulged in fantasies of an ideal empire, to which he desperately wanted to belong, precisely because this fantasy reproduced the circumstances and events of his father's life (*UL*, 123–24). Wackwitz's commentary satirizes the grandfather's imperial aspirations by exposing their anchorage in a petty-bourgeois lifestyle:

> Die Revolution, der Weltkrieg, die narzisstisch-wuterfüllte Zerstörung der im Krieg geprüften und zu leicht befundenen Nation und ihr unbestimmt-grandioser Wiederaufbau in Jahrhunderten, von denen er in seinem Tagebuch von 1918 phantasiert, schließlich der neue Lebenskaiser und das Reich von 1933 – all das, scheint es, sollte irgendwie dem Teckel, dem Sofa, dem Oberförster und dem Mittagsschlaf gleichen. Auf die unbestimmte, wenig durchdachte und merkwürdig verantwortungslose (sozusagen fahrlässige) Weise, in der sich Andreas Wackwitz über politische Zusammenhänge zeitlebens Meinungen bildete, scheint er sich das gute Leben und das richtig regierte Land nie anders gedacht zu haben als ein Forsthaus, in dem es nach Hunden, Leder und Zigarren roch. (*UL*, 123–24)

[The revolution, the world war, the enraged and narcissistic destruction of a nation that had been tested in war and found wanting, and its vague and grandiose restoration in future centuries fantasized by my grandfather in his diary of 1918, and finally the new Reich of 1933 – all this, apparently, should somehow resemble the dachshund, the sofa, the Chief Forester, and the nap. For his entire life, Andreas Wackwitz, in the vague, poorly thought-out, and peculiarly irresponsible way in which he formed his political opinions, seems never to have imagined a properly governed country any differently than the forester's house that smelled of dogs, leather, and cigars. (*IC*, 100–101)]

In the course of the narrative, we learn that the grandfather's belief system was deeply steeped in the colonial fantasy of *völkisch* nationalism. Unable to accept defeat in the First World War and the Treaty of Versailles, especially the allocation of German Anhalt to Poland, the grandfather participated in the rightwing Kapp-Putsch. Writing in 1956, the grandfather still couched his participation in this rightwing revolt in terms of "die Erhaltung der Volksubstanz" (*UL*, 104; The salvation of our German essence; *IC*, 86). For the grandson, this continued subscription to "die merkwürdig wirren und national-autistischen 'Ideen von 1914'" (the strangely confused and nationally autistic "ideas of 1914") is symptomatic of a generation of veterans who channelled "eine gefährliche, eigenartig verschleierte Schwermut" (*UL*, 106; a dangerous, strangely veiled melancholia) into the NS version of the German colonial fantasy. The clearest expression of this is a diary entry entitled "Ein Traum vom Osten" (a dream of the East), in which the grandfather imagines the subjugation of eastern Europe alongside the colonization of Africa (*UL*, 98). Against such colonial fantasies, the grandson pits his own alternative "Traum von Amerika" (dream of America), which is shorthand here for the emergence of Western democracy in the post-war era. In contrast to his grandfather's vision of a country governed in the paternalistic manner of the forester's lodge, the grandson sees the rubble years of the immediate post-war era as the promise of a new beginning, a view that is not too far removed from the common myth that 1945 was a "Stunde Null" (zero hour), divorcing post-war Germans from their NS past. Evoking the phantasmagorical beauty of summer periods in the first post-war years, Wackwitz explains that, although he was only born seven years after the war, these summer images provided him with a small utopian background picture, connoting "ein Aufatmen, ein Gefühl des Neuanfangs, eine plötzliche Ahnung von

Luxus und Weite, ein Traum von Amerika" (*UL*, 98; a sigh of relief, a feeling of a new beginning, a sudden awareness of luxury and vastness, a dream of America). In the end, the grandson explicitly denounces what he calls the grandfather's "memory palace" as impenetrable, impermeable and depressingly indistinct junk (*UL*, 124). In a rather emphatic gesture, he asserts once more that the Emperor's message will never reach him (*UL*, 124).

Wackwitz dramatizes the conflict between grandfather and grandson as a territorial dispute that concerns the emotional and the geopolitical attributions of place: "Solang er redete, war sein Land stärker als meines und die Vergangenheit wirklicher als Gegenwart oder Zukunft. Aber er würde nicht mehr lange reden" (*UL*, 157; as long as my grandfather kept talking, his country was stronger than mine, and the past was more real than the present or the future. But he would not be talking for much longer; *IC*, 131). And a little later, the narrator adds that even his aunts, for years the most loyal audience of his lectures, began to shake their heads and orientate themselves towards their children: "Mein Land hatte gewonnen" (*UL*, 163; my country had won; *IC*, 131). In order to underline the ideological connotations of place, Wackwitz then reconfigures the conflict between grandfather and grandson in terms of the 19th-century dispute between the philosophers Johann Gottlieb Fichte and Friedrich Schleiermacher, which concerned two opposing versions of German national identity and tradition. In 1808, Fichte reacted to the Napoleonic occupation of Prussia in his *Reden an die deutsche Nation* (Addresses to the German Nation), in which he advocated a German nationalism based on the purity of the German race. Anchoring German freedom in the idea of an "Urvolk", a primal people, uncontaminated by Roman influences, Fichte adopted a phobic rhetoric that saw foreignness as a source of alienation from the predestined aims of the German nation.[33] Wackwitz emphasizes that the Fichtean notion of nationalism re-emerged after the German defeat in the First World War when his grandfather's generation embraced "ein leerer Stolz auf eine ungreifbare deutsche Tiefe" (*UL*, 173; an empty pride in an unreachable German depth; *IC*, 145).[34] Against this generation's construction of the Germans as a chosen original nation (*UL*, 172) in the Fichtean tradition, the grandson pitches the Habermasian idea of a pluralist constitutional democracy, which he sees as a modern variant of the philosophical tradition represented by Schleiermacher. For Wackwitz Schleiermacher and Habermas stand for a viable conception of national identity based on the insight that our engagements with the past are always acts of self-interpretation in the service of the invention of an usable tradition (*UL*, 179–80).[35] He cites Schleiermacher's ironic review of Fichte's "Vorlesungen über die Grundzüge des jetzigen Zeitalters" (Lectures on the Characteristics of the Present Age) as an example of a more playful and ironic engagement with questions of national identity. This conversion of the conflict between grandfather and grandson into a philosophical dispute calls attention to the way in which Wackwitz superimposes a range of intertexts onto the family history in order to probe the conflicting meanings of place. For the grandson, this dispute gains such importance not least because Schleiermacher's father had been the pastor of the very German parish which Andreas Wackwitz took over in 1921. Early on in the narrative, Wackwitz recounts the history of the Protestant German settlers who, after the Polish counter-reformation, had resettled from Seibersdorf/Kozy to Anhalt under the protection of Frederick II. In this context, he cites a passage from his grandfather's memoirs which mentions that the philosopher's father, Johann Gottlieb Adolph Schleyermacher, had designed the garden of the vicarage (*UL*, 76). In Wackwitz's narrative, Schleiermacher thus signals an alternative tradition which is embedded in the very locality that for the grandfather embodies the German colonial dream.

And yet, on the other hand, to a certain degree the grandson himself is shown to be under the spell of the colonial fantasy. Although the narrative exposes the racist and *völkisch* underpinnings of the grandfather's belief system, there are moments of identification with the colonial fantasy. One such example occurs early on when the grandfather relates how the passengers of the *Adolph Woermann* had to board the life-boats before the ship was sunk by the British Navy:

> *Der Wind drückte die Boote an die Schiffswand, und die Wellen ließen sie steigen und fallen. Was würde nun mit uns geschehen? Da öffnete Dr. Lehfeld, ein aus Sumatra heimkehrender Studienrat, bedächtig seine Zigarrentasche und bot mir eine seiner Zigarren an. Ich sagte: "Donnerwetter, Lehfeld, das werde ich Ihnen nie vergessen!" und wir setzen in aller Ruhe die Glimmstengel in Brand und rauchten mit Gelassenheit.* (*UL*, 32)

> [*The wind pushed the boats against the side of the ship where they were lifted and lowered by the waves. What would happen to us now? Then Dr. Lehfeld, a high-school teacher returning home from Sumatra, carefully opened his cigar case and offered me one of his cigars. I said: "Egad, Lehfeld, I will never forget you for this!" Calmly we lit our stogies and smoked at leisure.* (*IC*, 25)]

According to this fantasy with its obligatory Freudian equipment, the phallus remains the master of history even in the face of calamity. In his commentary on this highly staged scene, Wackwitz shows how his alter ego is attracted by this fantastic moment of self-aggrandisement in the grandfather's narrative. We are told that he would like to own a photograph of the cigar scene in order to place it right next to that of his son (*UL*, 33). This desire to exhibit the grandfather's phallic fantasy alongside the image of his own son pinpoints in paradigmatic fashion the grandson's latent identification with the idea of a patriarchal gene-alogy. This scene thus undercuts the grandson's earlier deconstruction of his grandfather's imperial message. In spite of his claim that it was dispatched in vain, the grandson is shown to share a phallic inter-pretation of history with his grandfather; both associate the power to procreate with historical mastery.

This latent identification flourishes fully when the narrator cites a hunting story which takes place in the Namib Desert. Published in *Welt und Haus* (World and House) in 1935, the grandfather's story is a classic colonial narrative that revolves around the white man's burden. This story has to be seen against the backdrop of Germany's colo-nial vision. Although Germany was a latecomer on the colonial stage, from the mid-19th century, Africa played an increasingly important role in the German colonial imagination. An early indication of this is Wilhem Raabe's novel *Abu Telfan oder die Heimkehr vom Mondgebirge* (Abu Telfan or the Return from the Mountains of the Moon) published in 1867, which offers an astute critique of the discursive construction of exoticism.[36] While Raabe cast a critical eye on the colonial imagina-tion, other authors, such as Frieda von Bülow, Gustav Frenssen and Carl Falkenhorst, helped to popularize the colonial narrative. The ideolo-gical underpinning for the colonial project found expression in pamph-lets, such as Friedrich Fabri's "Bedarf Deutschland der Colonien?" (Does Germany need Colonies?) of 1879, in which the author argued for Germany's overseas expansion on the basis of her "Cultur-Mission". Andreas Wackwitz's own colonial narrative should be placed precisely in this context; although it was written long after the end of the German colonial enterprise, it reflects the tradition of colonial literature. Gustav Frenssen's novel *Peter Moors Fahrt nach Südwest* (Peter Moor's Trip to the South-West, 1906), which thematizes the defeat of the Herero Uprising in 1904 from the point of view of *völkisch* nationalism, inspired the grandfather's African memoirs (*UL*, 189).[37]

Central to the Namibian hunting episode mentioned above is a ride through the Namib Desert with insufficient quantities of water. This story is a classic colonial narrative that draws on stereotypical elements, such as a journey through the desert, the imperial view over a moon-lit nature, the endurance of the male riders and – last but not least – the notion of male camaraderie. Once adversary had been overcome, reward was at hand. The episode culminates in a scene in which the male hunters feast in the wilderness, while trading stories about their own prowess without the fear of social correction (*UL*, 54). The grandson's engagement with the colonial fantasy is characterized by a degree of ambivalence. On the one hand, he criticizes the archive of colonial narratives that informs his grandfather's colonial dream, on the other, he identifies with the iconography of the above episode which includes standard narrative elements such as the hunters' exchange of stories from the battlefield when they are gathered around a crackling fire. Instead of simply exposing the latent connection between the grandfather's idealized representation of the German colony in Poland and the colonial fantasy, the narrative also traces how this connection resurges in the grandson's own dreams.

Wackwitz stages these moments of identification in a highly self-conscious fashion, thus opening them to precisely the kind of critical scrutiny that is applied to the grandfather's colonial fantasy. Towards the end of the book, he recounts one further episode which exposes the phallic anxiety that is at work behind the grandpaternal fantasy of the white man's camaraderie. The grandfather's memoirs contain a symbolically laden story of a misfired prank that he and his friend Gerhard played on a black Herero servant. The memoirs recount how, on a trip to the north of South-West Africa, the grandfather and his friend stopped one day at a military graveyard where German soldiers, who had fought in the colonial campaign against the Herero people, were buried. When the two white men come across a black cobra on one of the graves, they flog it to death in a violent rage, piercing its head with a stick. They then decide to place the dead snake on the backseat of their car to frighten the black man. But when the snake disappears under a rug, the prank backfires and the two white men are startled by the snake's survival. Grabbing it by its tail, Gerhard flings it far away. However, the snake glides under the car and the two men spend a few hours searching in vain for the snake. Eventually, they drive on and spend the night with friends when the snake reappears once more, frightening the lady of the house before it is killed by one of her sons. The story ends with the grandfather relating this turn of events to the Herero servant who was the original target of the dangerous prank. He is far less surprised by this uncanny reappearance of the supposedly dead snake than his "master" (*UL*, 217).

The symbolism of this "unerhörte Begebenheit" (unprecedented event) is quite stark. Although the story speaks to the reader on its own grounds, the grandson offers lengthy interpretations of it to ensure that the reader draws the right conclusions about the disturbance of tradition in the wake of National Socialism and the German colonial fantasy. This hermeneutic over-engagement on part of the narrator underscores once more the urgency of his inquiry of what it means to be German after 1945. In the first instance, the narrator reads the story as an expression of the colonizer's latent anxiety that the colonized might take revenge. As one of the few survivors of a people that were nearly exterminated by the German colonial campaign, the Herero descendant would have had good reasons for taking his own revenge by placing the snake back in the car. From the defeated Herero's point of view, the snake could also stand for the ghost of a dead Herero chieftain who returns to haunt the colonizers. Wackwitz also comments on the psychoanalytical symbolism of the snake story; noting the excessive anger with which the two men kill the snake and then pierce its head, he reads the episode in terms of a phallic competition between the colonizer and the colonized. With its slapstick-like phallic iconography, the snake story is a parody of the colonial enterprise in which the white men mimic a colonial power they no longer really possess (*UL*, 221). But the snake is, of course, also one of the most powerful symbols of evil in the biblical narrative. For Wackwitz, it is, therefore, one of the grandfather's biggest failings that he managed to misread the symbolism of the story. While the grandfather believes that the Herero people embody evil and that the death of the snake repeats once more the colonial victory, the grandson knows that the real source of evil was awaiting the grandfather at home (*UL*, 222).[38] Through his overly explicit interpretation of the snake story, Wackwitz reverses the gaze and returns to the German stage of the 1930s and early 1940s, where the *völkisch* imagination sought to transform eastern Europe into a "Lebensraum" (living space/habitat) fit for Aryan settlement. It is in line with this that Wackwitz explores the intrinsic connection between the colonial narrative proper, the Wilhelmine *völkisch* imagination and its resurgence and resonance in National Socialism and the Final Solution. This is not to say that *Ein unsichtbares Land* reduces the complexity of the relationship between the colonial fantasy and the Holocaust to a simple cause-and-effect chain, but rather that it draws out the intellectual and emotional factors that fed into a racialized view of the German nation and a territorial interpretation of the land.

While taking the conflict-laden family dynamic as its cue, Wackwitz's narrative exceeds the framework of the psychological analysis of trans-generational communication. The conflict between grandfather and grandson concerns two incompatible views of German national identity. Even in the post-war period, the grandfather was hampered by his "deutschnationale Behinderung" (*UL*, 175; German nationalist impairment), which made him view the lost *Heimat* in terms of the very ethnic and *völkisch* categories that had fuelled its destruction and loss through war in the first place. Against this racialized understanding of place the grandson pitches his highly self-reflexive narrative that explores, tests and imagines alternative readings of the environment.

Although the grandson deconstructs the ideological foundation of the grandfather's colonial narrative, he shares the vision of happiness that finds expression in the grandfather's stories about his adventures in South-West Africa. Reflecting on the recurrence of park settings in his own dreams, the grandson observes that such dreams are the effect of a cross-generational transfer: "Wie die Rohre eines ausziehbaren Fernrohrs, sagen die Generationssoziologen, seien die Erinnerungen und Träume der Väter und Söhne und Enkel ineinandergeschoben, und wahrscheinlich lebt wirklich keiner sein innerstes Leben für sich" (*UL*, 188–89; Sociologists tell us that the memories and dreams of fathers, sons and grandsons fold into one another like the tubes of an extendable telescope, and that probably that no one really lives his innermost life on his own; *IC*, 158). Through this passage, Wackwitz reinstates the genealogy of tradition which, according to the logic of Kafka's "Kaiserliche Botschaft", is the driving force of human desire.

However, it remains a textual irony unnoticed by the author that, in spite of the accumulation of cultural – historical reflection, the grandson gives expression to precisely those male fantasies that underpinned the grandfather's colonial dream in the first place. On a subconscious level, the grandson remains deeply immersed in the grandfather's dream of tradition. This secret alliance between grandfather and grandson also explains the marginalization of the father who, as a representative of the liberal post-war generation, is hardly present in the narrative.[39] The absence of female protagonists from the grandson's family romance is even more striking. The narrative thematizes only one episode where the mother features as a central player; her memories of the air-raids on Stuttgart in 1944, in which she was badly injured, act as a counterpoint to the "Fremdsprache" (foreign language) of the grandfather's war memories (*UL*, 92). And yet, although the mother's memories make the reality of death and war visible, her story does not become the point of departure for a gender-critical analysis of the ideas of generation and tradition. It is one of the blind spots of this narrative that it continues to generate male versions of tradition.

Conclusion

In this chapter, we could see how Medicus and Wackwitz make use of a range of intertexual devices and narrative techniques which help to explore the multi-layered connections between family history, collective memory and geopolitics. Both narrators engage with the *Heimat* discourse of their grandparents' generation in order to probe their own emotional attachment to landscapes and areas that turn out to be repositories of family memories. However, we could see throughout the chapter that this exploration goes beyond a merely psychological reading of family history; it also lays bare the grandparents' ideological beliefs that fuelled the conversion of *Heimat* discourse into territorial aggression. Although German colonialism and Hitler's aggressive war in eastern Europe are geographically and historically separate events, according to Wackwitz, they share nevertheless a common ideological foundation in *völkisch* nationalism and its dream of a German Empire. Medicus and Wackwitz adopt a distinctly archaeological perspective that aims to unearth those traces of a history of violence and destruction that have been embedded in their own family history.

Furthermore, the thematic focus on former German territories in both narratives underlines the current trend to revise the normative boundaries of Germany's cultural memory. However, this chapter argues that the two narratives discussed here do not fuel the Germans as Victims discourse, which has been popularized in the German media in recent years. For the complexity of both narratives resists such political instrumentalization, highlighting instead the deficit of a revisionist engagement with the past that fails to reflect on the derealization of history in a highly nostalgic *Heimat* discourse. *Heimat* in both narratives is an imaginary *lieu de mémoire* at a remove from the troubling experience of the violence of lived history.

By deconstructing the notion of an original and non-alienated *Heimat* in the East, Wackwitz and Medicus implicitly challenge all forms of political revisionism, such as the recent political campaign by the *Bund der Vertriebenen* for a Centre Against Expellations in Berlin. This project ignited a ferocious controversy in the public domain, which revolved around the question whether such a centre would equate German wartime suffering with Jewish suffering during the Holocaust.

Opponents of the centre pointed to the absence of any credible international involvement with the centre as evidence of its revisionist orientation. Similarly, its proposed location in the city centre of Berlin was seen as highly symbolic in that it seemed to challenge the established hierarchy of suffering, the formal expression of which is the Holocaust Memorial in Berlin. So far the present coalition government has respected the established boundaries of German cultural memory.

Against this backdrop, it is not difficult to see the political energy of the two narratives discussed here. For, by exploring the imaginary nature of the lost eastern *Heimat* in their works, both Medicus and Wackwitz also expose the ideological core of a transgenerational memory that reproduces the gendered and *völkisch* implications of a colonial dream. Both narratives effect this deconstruction of an established discourse through the way in which they play with various forms of intertextuality and intermediality: Medicus employs different genres of landscape discourse (painting, poetry and photography) to expose *Heimat* as an imaginary space that covers over an unpalatable historical reality. In its play with intertexuality, the narrative probes the make-up of a transgenerational legacy that has been communicated to the grandson by the surviving members of previous generations. In the end, the narrator has unravelled the myths and legends that surround the family memories of the grandfather and of life in Poland. Instead of Arcadia, he unearthed a contested war territory, which is composed of conflicting memories, legends, feelings, rumours as well as verifiable historical facts. Similarly, Wackwitz in his narrative also exposes his grandfather's sentimental attachment to the lost *Heimat* as a version of the colonial fantasy. Here the intertextual engagement with a range of literary and philosophical traditions, including Hebel, Kafka, Schleiermacher, Fichte or the German colonial writers, draws out the uncanniness of such transgenerational memories as well as the racial dimension of the *völkisch* dream. It is important to note that both narratives employ very literary techniques to unmask the imaginary attributions of space and place that make up the discourse about the lost *Heimat* in the East. In this way, they also give prominence to the enhanced ability of literary discourse above and beyond historical analysis to represent and deconstruct the allure of the imaginary. Historical discourse has no register for the desires and fantasies that humans attach to place. But as these non-rational factors combine to form a powerful drive that influences our perception of history, they must be recognized as an important historical force. However, while both narratives thus bring to the fore the contested nature of space and place, they also show traces of a repetition effect.

For in both narratives there are significant moments of identification with the traditions they so painstakingly deconstruct. My analysis has shown that on a subliminal level Medicus and Wackwitz are fascinated by and attracted to their grandfathers' display of masculinity. We could see that Medicus's narrator experiences moments of strong identification with the Prussian military tradition and an old canon of an elitist masculinity. Similarly, Wackwitz fetishizes the grandfather's fantasy of historical mastery and of a patriarchial genealogy. This partial authorial blindness underlines once more the gendered nature of tradition.

5
Narrating Resistance to the Third Reich: Museum Discourse, Autobiography, Fiction and Film

The symbolism of resistance

From a strictly historical point of view, the story of German resistance to the Third Reich could be summed up quickly: organized opposition to Hitler was on the whole ineffective and had no discernible impact on the demise of the Third Reich. Neither left-wing nor right-wing resistance managed to change the course of history before the Allied forces finally defeated Germany in May 1945.

By contrast to an historical evaluation of the failure of resistance, this chapter looks at resistance through a cultural lens, highlighting, above all, the symbolic value of resistance in German post-war discourse and the rediscovery of resistance narratives in unified Germany. The chapter focuses first on the emergence of competing resistance narratives in East and West Germany that, as we will see, helped to underpin the ideological antagonisms of the Cold War period. The circulation of two opposing resistance narratives draws attention to a striking feature of cultural memory: in both East and West Germany, official commemorations of resistance articulated two specific versions of a viable tradition. Resistance became a retrospective narrative that legitimated the identity of each state with reference to what was interpreted as an heroic struggle in the past. The implication here is that official resistance narratives are inherently conservative: they put forward the idea that tradition concerns the uninterrupted transmission of a heritage that is supposed to provide models for the future. However, secondly, the chapter examines how this conservative notion of resistance has been challenged by recent counter-narratives that expose the gulf between enshrined cultural memory on the one hand and the sphere of personal memories on the other. The mutation of the post-war resistance narrative, above all the undermining of the heroic dimension in recent museum discourse, films and literary texts, is the main subject of this chapter. The story of resistance emerges as a fundamentally ambivalent and contradictory narrative that questions all those notions of heritage and lineage that aim to place the individual in a secure tradition.

Resistance narratives and the construction of a moral legacy in East and West Germany

For more than 50 years, German resistance to the Third Reich has been the object of historical research. As a result of continued critical debate, the historical understanding of German resistance has become ever more differentiated and fragmented.[1] In contemporary discussions, the idea of resistance includes not only widely divergent movements and people, covering the entire ideological spectrum from the elitist military plotters of the 20 July 1944 to the communist resisters, but it also reflects a whole range of activities, including organized resistance, individual acts of resistance or even spontaneous acts of non-conformity and civil disobedience in everyday life. However, the definition of the term "resistance" remains a contested issue: some historians argue in favour of a flexible terminology that is capable of grasping different degrees of non-cooperation; others, however, warn against the erosion of the core idea of resistance. Influential historians in the first camp are Peter Steinbach and Hans Mommsen, who make a case for the analysis of the variety of "resistance practice".[2] Others, such as the British historian Ian Kershaw, favour a more normative understanding of the term, restricting its application to "the description of active participation in organized attempts to work against the regime with the conscious aim of undermining it or planning for the moment of its demise".[3] Notwithstanding such differences, there is consensus that the changes brought about by the methodological shift towards "social history from below" has led to the demythologization of the resistance movement. In the words of Ian Kershaw, the turn towards social history and the history of everyday life approach have thus helped to take the resistance narrative out of "the realms of unreachable heroics down to the level of ordinary people".[4] Furthermore, this removal of the heroic dimension of resistance and the widening of the term have also drawn attention to the social context in which resistance did or did not develop. The story of resistance is thus often a story of partial collaboration and conformity with the National Socialist system.

In contrast to the nuanced understanding of resistance in historical circles today, the reception of resistance in the post-war era was at first reticent. In the immediate aftermath of the war, the Allied occupiers in the western zones had little sympathy for any public remembrance of German resistance. Such reservations were founded in legitimate fears that public recognition of German resistance would have fuelled popular notions that the German nation had been Hitler's first victim. On the other hand, the Allied Control Council swiftly rehabilitated the resisters by overturning all court sentences by Nazi courts that had been based on political, religious or racial grounds. In the early 1950s, the rehabilitation of the resisters in West Germany was further helped by the so-called *Bundesentschädigungsgesetz* (Federal Compensation Law), which regulated financial compensation of those persecuted under Nazi rule.[5] While such legislation was a first and indispensable step towards legal recognition of resistance, further critical legal debate was needed to overthrow the established idea of positive law. In this respect, Gustav Radbruch, a former minister of the Weimar Republic and a renowned Professor of Law, wrote a ground-breaking article "Gesetzliches Unrecht und übergesetzliches Recht" (Legal Injustice and Translegal Justice, 1946), which tackled the prevalent idea that the written law must always be upheld. By prioritizing the principle of justice above and beyond the letter of the law, Radbruch helped to legitimize the attempts of the resisters to overthrow Nazi rule.[6]

Because of the aforementioned reservations of the Allied powers about the effect of a resistance narrative on the German population, the first accounts of the 20 July 1944 were published abroad, mainly in Switzerland. Written by surviving participants of the plot or their family members, these accounts had a dual purpose.[7] On the one hand, they addressed the Allied occupiers by refuting the idea of German collective guilt. Although it is a contested issue amongst historians whether the notion of collective guilt was indeed official Allied policy[8], certain re-education measures, such as poster campaigns and films about the concentration camps, were understood in terms of the charge of collective guilt.[9] By highlighting the role of resistance, these narratives thus constructed the idea of a positive German tradition as the basis for the emerging democratic order. On the other hand, these resistance narratives attempted to refute a notion that was widespread amongst the German population: that the resisters had been traitors who had stabbed Germany in the back for a second time. This view was publicly voiced by the former Wehrmacht commander Otto Ernst Remer, who had played a decisive role in defeating the 20 July plot in Berlin.

After the war, he became a leading representative of the West German *Sozialistische Reichspartei*, which was later banned for its Nazi outlook. During the election campaign of 1951, Remer infamously declared that the men of July 1944 had been traitors in the service of foreign powers. The Minister for Domestic Affairs, Robert Lehr, took Remer to court for defamation and slander. The charges were brought by Fritz Bauer, who later became the State Prosecutor in the Frankfurt Auschwitz trials of the early 1960s. Bauer saw the case against Remer as an opportunity to rehabiliate the resistance movement once and for all. In his famous closing speech, he drew upon a long and rich body of law, including the oldest Germanic legal codex, the so-called "Sachsenspiegel", to show that the right to resistance had a basis in the old notion "rex eris, si recti egeris" (you shall be king as long as you govern righteously). The denial of human rights and the abolition of all control mechanisms and means of parliamentary democracy legitimized for Bauer the right to resistance. He concluded by citing the famous lines of Schiller's *Wilhelm Tell*: "Nein, eine Grenze hat die Tyrannenmacht" (no, there is a limit to the tyrant's power). Bauer's learned citation of a long tradition of law as well as of the German cultural heritage shows how little acceptance the idea of resistance had in the 1950s. In its judgement, the Braunschweig court followed Bauer's argument to a large extent and sentenced Remer to a term in prison, explicitly acknowledging that the systematic abuse of law by the NS Regime had necessitated its violent removal. With this landmark case, the plotters of 20 July had finally reached a central place in West Germany's resistance narrative.

The conservative and bourgeois opposition to Hitler thus began to play a pivotal role in West Germany's memory culture. Other publicly celebrated resistance movements included resistance by church circles (Martin Niemöller and Dietrich Bonhoeffer are the most prominent figures), and resistance by the members of *Die Weiße Rose* (the White Rose), which features later in this chapter. All these resistance movements represented conservative, Christian or middle-class opposition. Communist and left-wing resistance movements continued to be sidelined or even denounced in West German public discourse. A prominent example in this respect is the Harnack/Schulze-Boysen group, which is more generally known as the *Rote Kapelle* (Red Chapel). In post-war West Germany, the organization was considered to be a group of communist agents who had been in the service of Stalin's Soviet Union, a view which was first circulated by prominent members of the conservative resistance and then regurgitated in later publications.[10] Although some leading figures in this group did indeed attempt to pass on information to Moscow about Germany's imminent war against the Soviet Union, the Red Chapel had no Soviet-style vision for Germany. Made up of socially diverse members, its activities concerned the distribution of leaflets, helping Jews and PoWs wherever possible. According to recent research, its social and political vision was not at all in line with the position of the exiled communist party in Moscow. A revaluation of the diversity of this group has only become possible after the opening of eastern archives in the early 1990s.[11]

But the ideological myopia in the FRG was matched by a parallel defect in the GDR. For, in both parts of Germany, the critical understanding of the complexity of resistance was fundamentally hampered by the ideological faultlines of the Cold War period. While West Germany's memory culture centred on bourgeois conservative and Christian resistance movements, East Germany prioritized communist resistance, denouncing as imperialist the conservative bourgeois resistance and Social Democratic resistance. From the 1950s right into the 1960s, resistance discourse in East and West Germany thus reflected and reproduced Cold War antagonisms. After the division of Germany in 1949, both German states began to circulate their own resistance narratives that in their one-sidedness consolidated two opposing but nevertheless complementary memory cultures.

This phenomenon stands in marked contrast to the initial post-war period when, for a very short period prior to the Cold War antagonism, the reception of resistance by Germans had been at first inclusive. One example of a much more open approach is the big anti-fascist demonstration held in remembrance of the victims of fascism in Berlin's Tiergarten on 22 September 1946. The speakers included members of the conservative resistance (Countess Marion Yorck von Wartenburg), communist resistance (Anne Saefkow), Christian resistance (Werner Haberthür) and other left-wing and mixed groups.[12] However, this anti-fascist platform was soon smashed. In East German discourse, the official Soviet doctrine began to rule, according to which the bourgeois-conservative resisters were ultimately not much more than a disgruntled extension of Hitler's "imperialist" rule. A distinction was made between the real anti-fascist resistance and bourgeois resistance. For example, an article published in 1947 by a leading member of the Communist Party argued that the men of 20 July had acted primarily as representatives of the ruling class which wanted to protect its own imperialist interests by toppling Hitler.[13] After the enforced amalgamation of the Kommunistiche Partei Deutschlands (KPD) and Sozialdemokratische Partei Deutschlands (SPD) into the Sozialistische

Einheitspartei Deutschlands (SED), it did not take long for Social Democratic resistance fighters to be submitted to this type of ideological denunciation too: in the wake of the SED's increasingly aggressive anti-Social Democratic campaign, leading figures of the Social Democratic resistance movement, such as Julius Leber, were demonized as agents of US imperialism.[14] This division between real anti-fascist communist resistance and resistance movements based on "false consciousness", reflecting a lack of Marxist beliefs, dominated East German historical discourse well into the 1970s.

In the West, the hidden alliance between official cultural memory and historical research began to break up in the 1960s, when social history and the aforementioned history of everyday life instigated a move away from the elitist conception of resistance. Research on regional resistance showed the divergence of resistance movements, widening the scope of the concept "resistance" significantly. Alongside such new studies, the 20 July was also being reassessed. By the 1960s, the 20th July 1944 plot had been firmly embedded in West Germany's public memory culture with annual speeches and acts of remembrance. Against the backdrop of an increasingly enshrined memory discourse, historians began to analyze critically the social and political vision of the conservative resisters.[15] To a certain degree, this move towards enhanced differentiation was even replicated in the GDR. Although communist resistance continued to be the yardstick for all resistance movements, the discussion of conservative resistance in the GDR began to loosen the straight-jacket of Marxist–Leninist historiography. For example, when in 1967 the first GDR-biography on Stauffenberg appeared, it drew a comprehensive and more nuanced picture of Stauffenberg and his fellow plotters.[16]

This brief survey of the history of the reception of resistance in East and West shows that, in the post-war period, the cultural memory of resistance in both German states was characterized by the mutual exclusion of alternative resistance stories. From today's perspective, such monolithic and monopolizing discourse on resistance appears like another chapter in the dark Cold War narrative. However, while it is easy to dimiss the antagonistic dynamic of the discourse on resistance in this period, one should remember that a defining function of official cultural memory is to articulate and negotiate versions of a viable tradition. The circulation of two opposing cultural memories of resistance allowed both German states to see themselves in terms of the legitimate offspring of "das andere Deutschland" (the other Germany). Although diametrically opposed in terms of ideology, both cultural memories share some salient features:[17]

1. While resistance as political intervention aims to undermine, damage or overthrow the ruling regime with a view to creating a better future, resistance as a narrative only comes into public circulation after the defeat of the regime. It is obviously a retrospective narrative that attempts to express a heroic struggle for national liberation.

2. Resistance narratives legitimize certain forms of violence against the state in circumstances that can be defined as "the state of exception" (Carl Schmitt). But once tyranny has been defeated, legitimization of violence is strictly confined to the past. It is in line with this relegation of resistance to the past that both the FRG and the GDR saw themselves as the only legitimate German state. Both claimed to be democratic states. Remembrance of resistance in both the FRG and the GDR thus precluded any idea that violent resistance to their own respective constitutional frameworks could ever be lawful. This is so despite the fact that the Federal Republic had actually enshrined the right to resistance in Article 20 of the Basic Law.[18] The right to resistance exists only if and when the constitutional principles of parliamentary democracy have been suspended.

3. Resistance is a prime *lieu de mémoire*; its appeal is founded in the remembrance of a tragically heroic past. Once circulated as a mode of cultural remembrance, resistance narratives are not instruments of critical analysis, but rather stories that service the "invention of tradition". They offer powerful symbols of non-conformity which bolster a flattering self-image.

4. Resistance narratives construct a moral legacy for later generations; they give expression to a strong transgenerational appeal that makes later generations the heirs of resistance movements. Despite their retrospective cast as stories, they gesture to the future in order to make a particular narrative the "traditional" cornerstorne of a future cultural identity. Despite the historical ineffectuality of German resistance in the Third Reich, resistance narratives convert this tragic failure into a transgenerational duty that concerns the adherence to and defence of the principles of democracy. Insofar as the death of the tragic hero asserts notions of individual freedom, agency and civic responsibility, resistance narratives have a strong pedagogic purpose.

Resistance narratives thus highlight paradigmatically the instrumentalized nature of cultural memory, which always reflects present cultural,
social and ideological needs. This does not mean that resistance narratives cannot be constructed against the grain but that their message
reflects the cultural–political framework of the present. Against this
background, the following sections engage with a range of resistance
discourses of the past decade, including museum discourse, films and
recent literary representations of resistance. I will first discuss the representational choices made by the GDW before analyzing a range of literary
texts and films that have made powerful interventions in the debate
on resistance. My overriding concern is to ask to what extent resistance
narratives of the past decade service the reinvention of a viable moral
and political tradition in unified Germany.

The memorial site for German resistance: *Gedenkstätte Deutscher Widerstand*

Located in the so-called "Bendlerblock" in Stauffenbergstraße in Berlin's
Tiergarten, the organizational centre of the 20 July plot, the GDW is both
a product of and a response to the ferocious memory contests that have
increasingly characterized the public and historical debate of German
resistance. From a conceptual point of view, the GDW reflects the
steady shift towards a pluralist conception of resistance: while the first
memorial site of 1968 focused on the military opposition against Hitler,
the present exhibition and memorial site adopt an "integrative" concept,
representing the diversity of resistance movements and activities.

In 1983, the then Mayor of West Berlin, Richard von Weizäcker,
commissioned the historian Peter Steinbach to create a permanent
exhibition, covering the breadth and diversity of the German resistance.
Opened in 1989 in the very rooms in which the July plot had been
attempted and eventually defeated, the exhibition displays more than
5000 documents and pictures in 26 rooms. It covers the end of the
Weimar Republic, the rise of National Socialism, resistance by workers'
movements, Christian resistance, resistance by the arts and sciences,
youth resistance, Social Democratic resistance, liberal and conservative
resistance, the 20th July 1944 plot, the Kreisauer Kreis around Count
von Moltke, the White Rose, the Red Chapel, resistance in exile, resistance by the Nationalkomitee Freies Deutschland, resistance by Jews,
Sinti and Roma, smaller groupings and resistance by soldiers during
the war. In order to destabilize the entrenched dichotomies of the
post-war resistance discourse, the exhibition does not simply group all

left-wing and right-wing movements together. Instead it traces the difficult development of various resistance groups over the course of NS rule.

While the exhibition thus carefully avoided the Cold War categorizations of "left" versus "right" wing resistance, these distinctions resurfaced in 1994 on the occasion of the 50th anniversary of the 20 July, igniting yet another German memory contest. In essence, various members of the conservative Christian Democratic Union (CDU) objected to the inclusion of communist resistance, especially the display of photos depicting the later GDR leader Walter Ulbricht and GDR minister Wilhelm Pieck in exile.[19] Although considerable political pressure was exercised on Peter Steinbach to alter the exhibition, the GDW resisted such political interference successfully. However, as Bill Niven argues, despite a lot of party-political wrangling over the right kind of remembrance, in the end, entrenched positions were worn away. According to Niven, "gradually, a tentative sense of consensus evolved that it was what the 20 July conspirators and the communists had in common that really mattered, namely their opposition to Hitler, not what separated them".[20] Ten years later, this pluralist conception of resistance has been largely accepted. For example, Chancellor Schröder's speech on 20 July 2004, when 500 Bundeswehr recruits swore their constitutional oath in the courtyard of the Bendlerblock, emphasized the diversity of resistance. Underlining a European perspective, he highlighted the significance of the Polish uprising against German oppression in 1944 alongside the 20 July plot.[21]

In many ways the 1994 controversy over the inclusion of communist resisters missed the point of the exhibition entirely. Rather than discussing the overall conceptual and artistic design of the exhibition and of the entire site, the debate isolated a few photographs of communists. Furthermore, by focusing on the right kind of moral legacy for unified Germany, it illustrated once more the instrumentalized nature of cultural memory. The public reception by some conservative circles thus ran counter to the overall aim of the exhibition which is to undermine all such one-sided claims of ownership. Located on an historically evocative site, the curators of the GDW insist on the need for a differentiated historical understanding of the diverse resistance movements. According to Peter Steinbach, it is not the GDW's first mission to honour resistance fighters but to display the historical contexts in which resistance did or did not develop. Underlining the pluralist concept of the GDW, Steinbach stated emphatically that the main purpose of historical exhibitions is to exemplify and analyze the particularities of historical contexts. These contexts, he explained, are significant because of their sheer historical factuality and not because of the changing symbolic meaning attributed to them by later generations.[22] Steinbach thus drew a very strict line here between historical analysis on the one hand and commemoration on the other, arguing that the latter always fuels secondary contemporary interests that have little to do with the complexity of resistance under NS rule.

However, although Steinbach rightly rejected various attempts to instrumentalize the exhibition for political purposes, it is questionable whether the demarcation between historical analysis and commemoration can or should be as clear-cut as Steinbach suggests. What makes the GDW such a compelling resistance narrative is the productive tension and dialogue between commemoration and historical analysis. For the GDW is both a site of the historical analysis of the complexity of resistance during the Third Reich as well as a site of commemoration. As visitors enter the courtyard of the Bendlerblock, they first come across the following inscription: "Hier im ehemaligen Oberkommando des Heeres organisierten Deutsche den Versuch, am 20. Juli 1944 die nationalsozialistische Unrechtsherrschaft zu stürzen. Dafür opferten sie ihr Leben" (here, in the former Army Headquarters, Germans organized the attempt on the 20 July 1944 to topple the NS dictatorship. To this end they sacrificed their lives). In line with traditional commemorative practice, the emphasis is put on personal sacrifice in the service of the German people. Strikingly, there is no reference to the military nature of the conspiracy but only to the fact that Germans attempted to topple the system. The centre piece of the courtyard is Richard Scheibe's bronze figure of a man with bound hands. Originally erected in 1953, it was maintained after the conceptual overhaul of the Bendlerblock in the 1980s. The sculpture is accompanied by Edwin Redlob's inscription "Ihr trugt die Schande nicht – Ihr wehrtet Euch – Ihr gabt das große ewig wache Zeichen der Umkehr – Opfernd Euer heißes Leben – Für Freiheit, Recht und Ehre" (you could not bear the shame, you rose up, signalling a true and everlasting sign of change. You sacrificed your young lives for freedom, justice and honour). The sombre nature of the courtyard is completed by a plaque on the wall which marks the location of the executions on the night of the 20 July. The courtyard is thus entirely dedicated to commemoration; it is the site of annual commemorative events, and in 1999, as we have seen, for the first time a group of Bundeswehr recruits swore the constitutional oath in the courtyard.

The historical exhibition is housed on the second floor of the Bendlerblock in 26 interconnecting rooms and hallways which comprise the actual nerve centre of the 1944 plot. As previously mentioned, the exhibition avoids a harmonizing representation of resistance by exploring the difficult evolution of resistance over time, and especially the grey zones between conformity and resistance. The critical impetus of the curatorship is perhaps most evident in the section dedicated to church resistance, where the photowall juxtaposes a variety of church reactions, both Catholic and Protestant, to National Socialism. The photos document outright support, accommodation of National Socialism as well as principled opposition in both the churches. Underlining the diversity of responses within church circles, the accompanying materials show that resistance was not always based on principled opposition straightaway but was often "the culmination of a long process of deliberation".[23] The gradual move towards opposition is made particularly evident with reference to the position of the Catholic Church which, after the 1933 concordat with the Nazi state, saw a quick erosion of this unholy alliance. For example, a folder with letters and other documents by and on Cardinal Faulhaber invites the visitor to trace how he shifted from welcoming the Nazi rise to power to opposing National Socialism.

The ambiguity of resistance is further explored with reference to some of the right-wing or conservative resisters, many of whom had at first welcomed the demise of the Weimar Republic and actively supported the aims of National Socialism. Some had worked as high-ranking officials during the Weimar Republic but managed nevertheless to rise to significant positions within the Nazi State after 1933. A case in point is Johannis Popitz, who features in the room dedicated to conservative resistance. Popitz was Prussian Finance Minister between 1933 and 1944. However, although a high-ranking official in the Nazi State, he was connected to the conservative Goerdeler resistance circle and the so-called "Wednesday society".[24] He even drafted a "Vorläufiges Staatsgrundgesetz" (provisional constitution) for the time after Hitler's removal from power. According to the plotters' plans, Popitz would have become Finance Minister after a successful coup d'état. After his arrest on 21 July 1944, he was sentenced to death by the infamous *Volksgericht* (People's Court) on 3 October 1944 and executed on 2 February 1945 at Plötzensee Prison. Individuals such as Popitz exemplify the contradictory and highly ambivalent attitudes of many members of the right-wing and ultra-conservative resistance. By documenting the complex pathway from active support of National Socialism, the idea of containment to ambivalent opposition or outright resistance, the exhibition, however, does not adopt a teleological perspective; it attempts to highlight the irresolvable contradictoriness of the core beliefs of many conservative resisters who, as Hans Mommsen has shown, shared a deep-seated distrust of mass democracy based on anti-rational and anti-individualistic attitudes.[25]

However, the GDW's critical perspective must not be misunderstood as a dismissal of the conservative resistance from the point of view of the pluralistic values of our contemporary society. It is one of the great achievements of this exhibition to point to the historical distance that separates the visitor from all resistance movements, be they left-wing, liberal, Christian or ultra-conservative. As Hans Mommsen argues in his study, *Alternatives to Hitler*, the evaluation of German resistance by today's standards erases "the historical dimension in which the political thought of the resistance must be situated, and which reveals an unmistakable conflict with present-day theories of democracy."[26]

The analysis so far seems to suggest that the GDW has resolved the intrinsic tension between historical analysis and commemoration by way of a clean division of labour: while the courtyard is dedicated to pure remembrance, the exhibition itself subscribes to the idea of critical enlightenment. But this separation is not clear-cut, as a closer look at the museum design reveals. When Hans Peter Hoch, a renowned designer of museums and exhibition spaces, was entrusted with the artistic design, he was faced with the problem that he needed to underpin the exhibits with a sensual dimension without, however, using fake stage props. Rejecting the idea of a naturalistic representation of resistance, Hoch employed a quiet language of symbols. The visual display of photographs and documents is thus supported by evocative lighting and frames that display the content in a restrained manner.

The commemorative dimension of the exhibition is perhaps most evident in the rooms dedicated to the 20th July 1944 plot. The exhibition carefully avoids a theatrical imitation of the events that actually took place in these very rooms. Instead of recreating the original furnishings of the rooms, for example, the three rooms are divided into three interconnecting sections that document the plot, its execution and failure. While the exhibits in Stauffenberg's office focus on his biography and on his attempt to kill Hitler in the Wolfsschanze, the room connecting his office with that of Generaloberst Friedrich Fromm displays the photographs of 181 plotters and on the opposite wall the plotters' constitutional plans. These materials are supported by folders which can be studied in detail on tables with benches. The third room where the plotters were finally overcome and arrested by Fromm and his supporters displays the defeat and aftermath of the plot. Although this arrangement emphasizes the historical analysis of the events, there are subtle symbolic reverberations, drawing the visitor's attention to the location itself. For example, the centre piece in Stauffenberg's former room is a black table, echoing his original desk, which can be seen on the only black-and-white photograph of the original room of 1944 displayed on the wall. The interplay between the blurry photograph and the black table creates a shadowy impression that makes the exhibits phantoms of a bygone and ultimately irretrievable past. Although conceptualized from an historical perspective, the exhibition thus produces an uncanny effect, drawing attention to the dialectic between absence and presence. Similarly, the interconnecting room plays on its original usage: while during the war it housed the military maps, it now forms an archive on the 20 July and its plotters. In this way the room points to the original purpose. The third room deepens these reverberations further by displaying the defeat of the coup d'état in the very room in which it took place. No props are used at all to achieve a mimetic effect. The curators rely entirely on the interplay between the location of the defeat and the exhibition; a simple plaque on the wall marks the place where General Beck had been forced to commit suicide. The visitor is also reminded that this was not only the room in which Fromm sentenced Stauffenberg and his co-conspirators to death[27], but that it was here in this room that Hitler had explained his vision of an eastern expansion to the Wehr-macht officers as early as 1933. The curators thus appeal to the visitor's historical knowledge without visual melodrama to produce an uncanny effect that pervades the atmosphere of the room. It is an uncanniness, however, that does not obscure historical analysis and distinctions but that points subtly to the long afterlife of National Socialism.

The highly evocative artistic realization of the conceptual design of the exhibition thus overcomes the dichotomy between remembrance and historical analysis. Although the GDW offers a differentiated historical understanding of resistance movements in all their fragmentation and diversity, it also makes room for a new type of commemoration that undermines the ossification of the resistance into a symbol of modern mass democracy. Advocating critical commemoration of resistance, the GDW thus demonstrates that the historical analysis of the complex and sometimes contradictory motives and pathways of different resistance movements can go hand in hand with the respectful recognition of the resisters' courage in the service of a different Germany.

Sixty years after the end of the war, the historical distance from National Socialism has grown to such an extent that resistance and the search for a viable moral tradition have made their way back into literature. The following two section discuss four recent resistance narratives that engage with resistance as a prime *lieu de mémoire* that intersects with the private *lieu de souvenir*: Wibke Bruhns's *Meines Vaters Land* (My Father's Country) published in 2004, Friedrich Christian Delius's *Mein Jahr als Mörder* (2004, My Year as an Assassin), Sibylle Mulot's *Nachbarn* (1995, Neighbours) and Michael Wallner's *April in Paris* (2006). The narratives of Bruhns, Delius and Mulot are based on historical figures and events associated with resistance in Germany and in France; Wallner's narrative, however, is a piece of fiction, in fact a postmemorial fantasy inviting the reader to suspend disbelief. While Bruhns and Delius deconstruct aspects of the German resistance narrative, Mulot and Wallner home in on resistance in France.

The impairment of tradition in Wibke Bruhns's *Meines Vaters Land* and Christian Friedrich Delius's *Mein Jahr als Mörder*

When Wibke Bruhns, a well-known journalist and television news presenter, published *Meines Vaters Land* in 2004, the book became an immediate bestseller.[28] Hailed by the reviewers as an exemplary narrative that traces the pathway of a bourgeois merchant family from conservativism to National Socialism, the book reconstructs the story of the author's father, Hans Georg Klamroth, a lesser-known figure of the 20 July plot, who was tried for treason in August 1944 and hanged in the same month.[29] As the title indicates, the book goes far beyond a simple reconstruction of her father's life: it offers a comprehensive analysis of the mindset of the German bourgeoisie by tracing the family's rise to economic and social power from the late 18th century through the 19th century to the NS period. The Klamroths appear in this narrative as kith and kin of Thomas Mann's Buddenbrooks, combining a middle-class belief in entrepreneurship with a strong investment in the ideas of family and tradition. As Volker Ulrich of *Die Zeit* observes, the book drops the accusatory tone of the generation of 1968 in favour of a dialogic exploration of the past.[30]

In many ways the book thus exemplifies the current trend to localize German history in family history. Like many narratives in this genre, Bruhns's story incorporates a range of materials such as photographs, diaries, personal letters, oral stories and historical sources. By interweaving the private and the political through such narrative hybridity, Bruhns – like so many contemporary German authors, ranging from Uwe Timm, Monika Maron, Stephan Wackwitz to Thomas

Medicus – explores the enormous gap between reified cultural memory on the one hand and intensely personal memories on the other. It shares with other family narratives a keen psychological interest in the dynamic of cross-generational communication and in the mechanism of transference as an important means of establishing tradition.

However, while these traits characterize the new German family narrative, Bruhns's book is particularly interesting in the present context because of the way in which it punctures the reified discourse on the events of 20 July. Reconstructing her family history, the author ultimately investigates notions of tradition and heritage by raising the question of what kind of inheritance her father's generation has left behind for her own and future generations. We are told that as a younger woman she rejected this inheritance, embracing the notion of a radical new beginning: "Mein Glück war die Zäsur. Ich habe angefangen, als alles aufgehört hatte" (*MV*, 21; the caesura was lucky for me. My life began as all this had finished). But this notion of a historical caesura that would disconnect the post-war generation from the NS past is a type of subconscious forgery: for Bruhns was born in 1938 and thus six years old when her father was killed. Over time, the denial of her father's inheritance has a shadowing effect, preventing the analysis of why her own generation feels so damaged by the war. In order to escape this negative burden, the narrator needs to unravel the family history, in particular the entanglement of her own generation in the legacy of the war (*MV*, 21).

Johannes Georg Klamroth, Bruhns's father, was born in 1898 as the first son of Kurt and Gertrud Klamroth. His family were successful Prussian merchants who had steadily expanded their business throughout the 19th century. As a member of the wealthy upper middle class, his father, Kurt Klamroth, had joined the *Königlich Preußische Kürassierregment* to gain the title "Hochwohlgeboren", which was an entry ticket to a Prussian society that was still largely dominated by the nobility. According to his granddaughter, the Klamroths' belief in the service to the nation, Protestantism, manliness and self-control provided the guiding educational principles for their children's education (*MV*, 44). After the First World War, in which both father and son served as officers, Johannes Georg (who is called Hans Georg by all the family) was sent as a trainee to a company in Hamburg, where he met his future wife Else Podeus. However, the couple was only allowed to marry on completion of his traineeship with several overseas internships in South and North America. After the move to Halberstadt, Hans Georg joined the family business, managing it with his father. Father and son managed to steer the company through the tumultous times of the Weimar Republic with hyper-inflation, revolutionary upheavals and, finally, Hitler's rise to power. Although initially distrustful of Hitler's mass appeal, Hans Georg joined the NSDAP and the SS in 1933. After the beginning of the Second World War, he was drafted into the Wehrmacht and stationed in Denmark as a counter-intelligence officer. Transferred to the Lithuanian border in 1942 as commander of the *Abwehrkommando 111* (counter intelligence unit), he was responsible for fighting Russian partisans. He was recalled to the *Abwehr III* unit of the *Oberkommando der Wehrmacht* (OKW) in Berlin in March 1943, where he was responsible for espionage and counter-espionage. We learn that over the course of the war Klamroth had become increasingly disillusioned with National Socialism. In February 1944, he travelled to Mauerwald in eastern Prussia, which was the seat of the OKW whenever Hitler resided in the nearby *Wolfsschanze*. During this visit he met his son-in-law Bernhard (who had married the oldest daughter Ursula), Generalmajor Helmuth Stieff, Major Joachim von Kuhn and Albrecht von Hagen, all of whom were involved in organizing the explosives for the plot against Hitler. In the course of this visit, he probably learned about the planned coup which attracted his passive support. After the defeat of the plot, Hans Georg Klamroth was arrested, stripped of his military honours, tried for treason by the People's Court and hanged on 26 August 1944 together with other resisters such as Adam Trott von Solz (*MV*, 379).[31]

It is evident from this sketch that the facts of Hans Georg's biography make him in many ways a paradigmatic case study of the mindset of many conservative resisters whose negative attitude to the Treaty of Versailles, to mass democracy as well as their strong belief in Germany's cultural mission led them at first to support National Socialism until the events on the eastern front turned their growing sense of unease into outright opposition. However, in Bruhns's narrative, the exemplariness of her father's biography is never allowed to detract from the experiential dimension of history. Reading diaries and personal family letters, the narrator attempts to portray the experience of living in and through history by highlighting the manifold incongruities between domestic concerns and the unfolding world history. For example, when Hans Georg and his wife Else go through a serious and final period of estrangement in the early 1940s over Hans Georg's many affairs with other women, Bruhns draws up a long list of the ongoing liquidations of Jews and other mass executions in the East (*MV*, 337). The direct juxtaposition of the domestic concerns within the Klamroth family with these crimes against humanity does not, however, belittle the seriousness of the quarrel between Else and Hans Georg; rather it draws attention to the limited horizon of family identity.

Bruhns's narrative thus aims to privatize history, exposing the gulf between personal experience of history and later historical analysis. This privatization of the historical does not obscure important historical distinctions or subscribe to historical exculpation. On the contrary, the book succeeds in dismantling the heroic dimension of typical resistance narratives by locating one of its stories within the social context of family history. A range of minor but highly symbolic attitudinal and emotional shifts comes into focus which normally escapes the historian's analytical framework. Moreover, by tracing Klamroth's slow mutation from a convinced Nazi into a Nazi with growing doubts, Bruhns undermines the idea that resistance was always based on conviction. Her narrative probes the moral legacy of the resisters which, according to West Germany's official memory culture, was supposed to provide role models for future generations. In this way, she reinvests the generic features of official cultural memory, replacing the idea of resistance as a prime *lieu de mémoire* with an alternative notion of resistance as a mode of critical and empathetic enquiry. Rather than reifying the 20 July plot as a symbol of heroic resistance, the narrative rejects the idea of heritage in favour of the narrator's personal investigation of family history.

The narrative begins with the confession of the narrator's intellectual and emotional distance to her father: we learn that her memory of her early childhood was obliterated by the trauma of the war, especially the bombing of their home town Halberstadt on 8 April 1945 (*MV*, 23). After the war, any personal memory of the father was equally erased by the official remembrance culture that arose around the events of 20 July (*MV*, 14). The official plaques and rites of commemoration have turned the father into an abstract symbol devoid of any traces of the messiness of lived history. According to the narrator, the mother avoided dealing with her estrangement from her husband by delegating her memories to the public discourse on 20 July:

> Else (Wibke's mother, A. F.) habe ich gefragt, andere, die ihn noch gekannt haben. Doch da war es schon viel zu spät, die Sprachregelung längst gefunden. Die hatte etwas zu tun mit den in staatlichen Gedenkreden apostrophierten Helden des Widerstands; dazuzugehören, und sei es auch nur als Kind, war Ehre. Privat teilte Else ihr Leben in ein vorher und nachher: Vorher war Glanz, nachher war Fron. Der Verlust des einen und die Mühsal des anderen wurden

mit Haltung ertragen, die Trauer über beides dem Kind gegenüber als Tabu manifestiert. (*MV*, 15)

[I asked Else and others who had known him. But by that time it was far too late, the correct language had already been established. It reflected the invocation of the heroes of resistance in the official commemorative speeches. Being part of that community, even as a child, was deemed to be an honour. Privately Else divided her life into a before and after: the time before was glorious, the time after drudgery. The loss and the hardship were endured with composure. The grief about both communicated itself to the child as a taboo.]

With this passage, Bruhns criticizes the generic features of the official post-war remembrance culture which, as I have demonstrated before, converted the tragic failure of German resistance into a duty transferred to later generations. Debunking the official commemorations as a screen memory, the narrator shows that, as an officially enshrined memory icon, symbolizing the idea of an heroic death in the service of the nation, the father was dislodged from the sphere of conflicting and highly ambivalent private memories. What comes into perspective here is the public management of the past by way of a language of symbols that have been hollowed out: the idea of heroic death, for example, is devoid of the contradictory impulses, ideas, feelings and motives that characterized the father's life. The circulation of iconic symbols in the public domain thus disembodies personal memory to the extent that Hans Georg's life is reduced to a "noble" death stripped of its inhumanity, degradation and utter painfulness. And this is so because of the ritualized invocations of the inhumanity of the Third Reich: the regular speeches and commemorative rites obscure all traces of that which they evoke. Instead of coming to terms with the past, these symbols are thus little more than symptoms of an unmastered condition which Bruhns aptly calls the "umschiffte Schmerzzone" (*MV*, 14; bypassed zone of pain) in her mother's and, ultimately, in her own life. However, it is important to note that erasure never achieves final deletion. On the contrary, the fact that interconnecting traces of personal and "objective" history are struck off the official record only serves to make more visible that which has been obscured. Or, to put it differently, as a denial of a speech act that has already been uttered, erasure is a mnemonic technique whose prime tool is repression. Assigning certain unmasterable memories to the realm of the subconscious, erasure thus produces phantoms of the past that continue to haunt the present.[32] The role of these phantoms in her own life is precisely the focal point of Bruhns's investigation.

From a psychoanalytic point of view, phantoms are more than simply the dark bits in the great narrative that we call tradition. As Nicolas Abraham explains in his commentary on Freud's metapsychology, phantoms are the representations of the gaps left behind by the absence of a loved one. They are hallucinatory inventions through which a hidden legacy makes itself felt.[33] However, if phantoms communicate the gaps that have been created by secrets within families or communities, then this also implies that phantoms are powerful transmitters of an unmastered past. Sigrid Weigel comments that phantoms are produced by the imagination which puts something in place of these gaps.[34] One could add that they are stakeholders in a secret account of an otherwise publicized past. As ghostly evocations of that which has been repressed, phantoms thus signal a fundamental impairment of tradition. Shadowing our discourse on the past, phantoms communicate across generational thresholds that an unspeakable event has been buried by tradition.[35]

In Bruhns's story, the father is just such a phantom, whose dreadful death is buried inside the mother. Because the mother has become her husband's grave, the daughter needs to unearth the untold story of her father's life. Significantly, her investigation is triggered by a television documentary that shows film scenes of her father in the People's Court. The shocking recognition that her father was not after all an abstract icon in the service of the nation but "ein Mensch aus Fleisch und Blut" (*MV*, 14; a man of flesh and blood) points to the physical and emotional reality of the pain he suffered at the end of his life. In the official memory culture, this pain has been erased through constant evocation. Self-consciously adopting the phantom of her father, Bruhns goes far beyond a dialogic investigation of the past; her autobiographical alter ego transforms herself into a new type of historian who recognizes the double-edged nature of facts. While facts are indispensable for the analysis of history, they need to be shadowed by that which they conceal. Drawing out a fundamental blindness of facts towards the reality of historical suffering, the narrator therefore turns herself into a sort of phantomologist, who approaches the buried past with imagination and acumen.

At the beginning of the narrative there was the shocking image of her father in front of the People's Court and the realization that he suffered an intolerable death. At the end, there is a brief but poignant account of this death based on historical sources (*MV*, 380).[36] Significantly, the narrative does not finish with this grim picture but instead with the narrator's imagined address to her father in which she finally accepts his complex and highly ambivalent inheritance. This acceptance finds grammatical expression in the change of address: throughout the narrative, Bruhns referred to her father as "HG", an abbreviation that has a distancing and ironizing effect. Here, however, she uses the personal pronoun to mark her emerging emotional identification with her father (*MV*, 380). While these closing reflections give expression to a yearning for proximity, Bruhns never allows the critique of her father's conformism to be eclipsed by her emotions. Constantly switching from the private to the political sphere and back, her address highlights once more the father's disturbing lack of empathy for the victims of the Third Reich before, in a final gesture, the narrator accepts this difficult paternal legacy:

> Ich bin verstört über das, was ich als deine Gleichgültigkeit verstehen muß gegenüber dem Schicksal der Juden, der Zwangsarbeiter, der Geisteskranken, der Häftlinge in den KZs, Himmlers "Untermenschen" in den besetzten Gebieten. Habe ich dich mißverstanden, weil du nie etwas gesagt hast? Jetzt stirbst du als "Untermensch". Sie haben dir den geistlichen Beistand versagt, um den du gebeten hast. Doch du hast deinen Ölberg hinter dir und du bist ein Held in deinem Tod. Dein Leben lang in einer fürchterlichen Zeit, und wenn es denn für die Kinder besser werden sollte, das ist gelungen. Du hast den Blutzoll gezahlt, den ich nicht mehr entrichten muß. Ich habe von dir gelernt, wovor ich mich zu hüten habe. Dafür ist ein Vater da, nicht wahr? Ich danke dir. (*MV*, 380–81)

> [I am disturbed by what I must understand as your indifference towards the fate of the Jews, the slave workers, the mentally ill, the prisoners in the camps, Himmler's *Untermenschen* in the occupied areas. Have I misunderstood you because you never spoke up? Now you are about to die as an *Untermensch*. They did not give you access to a pastor, your last request. But your Mount of Olives is behind you, and you are a hero in your death. You lived your life in a terrible time, and if your children were to have a better life, then it was a success. You paid the high price of your own life, a price I will not have to pay. Your example has taught me what I have to be on guard against. That's what a father is for, isn't he? Let me thank you.]

The narrator's final words are full of pathos and inscribed with Christian images that transform the father into a martyr. However, in spite of this traditional rhetoric of remembering the dead, this speech of reconciliation does not simply resurrect the ossified notion of tradition as secure anchorage in an otherwise unstable world. For if the father's legacy concerns the avoidance of his historical mistakes, then this implies that tradition as an unquestioned heritage has been replaced by the idea of an exemplariness that remains ambivalent to the end. By addressing the wound of her fatherless youth, the narrator's final gesture of reconciliation thus makes visible the irreparable impairment of tradition after the Second World War. In many ways, the narrator's own changing attitudes to this heritage underline the multiple mutations of resistance in post-war discourse. What emerges in Bruhns's story is a form of empathetic dialogue that challenges the ossification of conservative resistance in Germany's cultural memory.

While Bruhns's autobiographical narrative deals with conservative resistance and its after-life, Christian Friedrich Delius tackles the repression of left-wing resistance in West Germany's post-war culture. Here the diagnosis of the impairment of tradition goes hand in hand with an analysis of the mutilation of the German language by National Socialism. Tracing residues of Nazi jargon and thinking in the post-war period, Delius also shows that the antagonistic language of the generation of 1968 showed similar signs of frenzied fanaticism. In this way, the novel highlights the German language as a damaged heritage that, for many decades after the war, communicated unmastered phantoms of the past.

The narrator and protagonist of Delius's novel *Mein Jahr als Mörder* (2004) is a student during the upheavals of 1968, who, through his narrative, makes a belated confession that at one point in his life he was planning to assassinate a former Nazi judge.[37] Combining fictional elements with documentary materials, the narrative uses the device of the self-proclaimed confession to relate the story of Hans-Georg Groscurth, a lesser-known figure of the German resistance who had been sentenced to death in 1944. Groscurth, a medical doctor at the famous Moabit hospital in Berlin, was a member of a small socialist resistance group, the so-called "European Union", which comprised a few doctors and scientists, including Robert Havemann, the later GDR dissident. The group helped Jews, politically persecuted people and soldiers who wanted to avoid being drafted into a lost war. The group also distributed leaflets, advocating the end of National Socialism and the formation of a united free socialist Europe. In 1943, the group's cover was blown when some members attempted to make contact with the Soviet Union through the communist Paul Hatschek, who was already under observation by the Gestapo. When Hatschek was arrested, he revealed the names of the group members who were swiftly arrested, tried and sentenced. With the exception of Robert Havemann, who survived because his research was deemed "kriegswichtig" (important for the war), all the other group members were executed in 1944. Delius's narrative thus makes an important contribution to the cultural memory of German resistance by reconstucting in detail one of its many forgotten stories.

However, in addition to adding another building block to the cultural memory of resistance, the novel also investigates the ruthless instrumentalization of the resistance narrative during the Cold War period. The post-war story of Groscurth's widow Anneliese exemplifies the crude logic of Cold War politics: working in West Berlin as a doctor in the public health system, in 1951, Anneliese became a member of a public committee that demanded a popular referendum in East and West on German unity and the threat of remilitarization. The West German authorities in Bonn and Berlin banned the referendum, arguing that the committee had been orchestrated by East Berlin. Subsequently the West Berliner *Tagesspiegel* published an article, revealing the names of those who had supported the referendum.[38] Anneliese Groscurth was especially singled out by the paper's anti-communist witchhunt because the committee met in her home. Publicly typecast as a communist, she was sacked by the West Berlin authorities and stripped of her special pension for the victims of National Socialism. Caught up between the fronts of the Cold War, she lost all financial entitlements, her status as victim of National Socialism and even her right to a passport in several lengthy court cases, spanning two decades and involving the highest West German courts before a settlement was finally reached in 1972. The detailed case study of Anneliese Groscurth's prolonged struggle for justice thus highlights the lengthy persistence of NS attitudes in the post-war period. Her story offers an anatomy of the "restaurative" climate of the Adenauer era, which chanelled the Nazis' deeply ingrained anti-Bolshevism into the staunch anti-communism of the Cold War.

The plot is set in train on 6 December 1968, when the newsreader of radio RIAS in Berlin announces the non-guilty verdict in the case against the former Nazi judge Hans-Joachim Rehse, who had served in Freisler's People's Court and had sentenced more than 230 people to death, including Hans Georg Groscurth. However, the novel's protagonist hears more than the announcement of the acquittal: in his imagination the "feste männliche Stimme" (*MJ*, 7; the firm male voice) of the

RIAS newsreader commissions him to take revenge on Rehse for his abuse of law during the Third Reich. His initial determination to accept this imaginary assignment is bolstered by his childhood friendship with Axel Groscurth, one of the Groscurth sons whom he had befriended in the 1940s when Anneliese and the children sought refuge in his hometown of Wehrda. As the narrating self explains, this sense of indignant outrage at the lack of justice was further fuelled by the political upheavals of the late 1960s in which a range of iconic events, such as the assassinations of Martin Luther King, Robert Kennedy or the massacres in Vietnam, highlighted the repressiveness of the post-war order in the West (*MJ*, 13).

In this way, the narrative assumes a dual perspective, analyzing both the stifling climate of the post-war era as well as the formulaic reaction of the generation of 1968 against the West German process of "restauration". The narrator's attitude to the representatives of 1968 is highly ambivalent: on the one hand, his astute analysis of the 1950s illuminates the far-reaching legacy of National Socialism, thus contextualizing the ferocity of the revolt by the members of 1968 against authoritarian parents and those post-war institutions which, like the judiciary, had absorbed National Socialists without much ado. According to the narrator, 1968 can only be understood with reference to the immediate post-war era, the "stone age of democracy" which had buried all the conflicts that eventually erupted in the late 1960s (*MJ*, 126). On the other hand, he shows that the generation of 1968 shared with their opponents a blind ideological dogmatism which silenced the voices of the victims of National Socialism. An excellent example of this is a demonstration against the Rehse judgement in which the protagonist participates, albeit reluctantly, because he wants to convey the image of anti-Nazi Germany to the wider world. Surrounded by various Marxist splinter groups, he is repelled by the omnipresence of Maoist slogans and posters which have nothing to do with the reason for the demonstration: "Die uniformen Bilder des Vorsitzenden aus Peking schlugen, so empfand ich das, die Widerstandskämpfer noch einmal tot" (*MJ*, 49; in my view, the uniform images of the Party Leader from Beijing killed the resistance fighters all over again).

Although his age makes him a contemporary of the 1968 movement, the protagonist is a Hamlet figure who tries in vain to bridge the gap between word and action, intention and deed. His original plan is to write a book about his motives before carrying out the murder. However, he ends up deferring action in favour of detailed research until the judge's sudden death releases him from the assignment. In the end, the narrative is the displaced deed: interweaving the story of the Groscurth-Havemann resistance group with the story of Anneliese Groscurth's persecution by the West German authorities in the post-war era and the story of the 1968 generation's emotional entrapment in the past, the narrator finally manages to produce precisely the "kleiner Beitrag zur Aufklärung, zur Demokratie, zur Gerechtigkeit" (*MJ*, 13; the small contribution to enlightenment, to democracy and justice) that he abandoned 30 years earlier. This project also entails the analysis of the damaged German language in the post-war era, a theme that is introduced in connection with the narrator's childhood memories.

In a significant childhood scene, the narrator recalls how he first learned of the grusesome death of Axel's father. A conversation between the young protagonist, who is depicted as a naive village boy with little knowledge of the wider world, and his friend Axel, the more grown-up city boy, revolves around the absence of fathers in the post-war era. The village boy has many friends whose fathers are "Foto-Väter" (photo-fathers) who have disappeared from life behind words such as "gefallen" (killed in action) or "vermisst" (missing), which have become omnipresent in post-war discourse (*MJ*, 22). While these photo-fathers adorn the sideboards of many homes, the village boy has never heard of a father who was killed by his own people. His shock is further aggravated when Axel reveals that his father was beheaded:

Kopf abgehackt, das macht man bei den Hühnern, die werden mit der Hand an den Flügeln gepackt, auf den Hackklotz gelegt, wo sie zappeln, und dann hebt die Bäuerin die Axt, das ist Frauenarbeit, und hackt den Kopf ab, das Blut spritzt, der Kopf fällt zu Boden, das Huhn zuckt und zappelt weiter. [...] Schon bei Kaninchen wird nicht mehr der Kopf abgehackt, Schweine kriegen den Bolzenschuss in die Stirn, Rinder karrt der Viehhändler ins Schlachthaus, keinem Tier wird sonst der Kopf abgehackt, warum hackt man den Menschen den Kopf ab? Das Dorfkind ist allein mit den Wörtern Kopf abgehackt, darüber kann es nicht mit dem Freund reden, der hat schon zuviel gesagt, es bleibt allein mit den Wörtern: Kopf abgehackt. (*MJ*, 23)

[Head chopped off, that's what you do with chickens: you grab their wings with one hand, put them on the butcher's block where they continue to struggle, and then the farmer's wife lifts up the axe – because this is a woman's job – and chops off the head. With the blood spurting out, the head falls onto the ground, while the chicken keeps twitching. Even with rabbits you don't chop off the head any more, pigs are killed with a bolt in their forehead, cattle are sent to the abattoir; there is no other animal whose head is chopped off – so why do they chop off a person's head? The village boy is left all alone with the words "head chopped off"; he can't talk with his friend about it since he has said too much already. He's left alone with the words: head chopped off.]

The shocked child attempts to make sense of the incomprehensible words "head chopped off" by incorporating them in the domestic world of the countryside. These comparisons with the world of animals, however, only accentuate the absolute incongruity and incomprehensibility of this death. Delius constructs here an original scene of a trauma which is at the heart of the protagonist's later revenge fantasies. When the stuttering child asks his own father for an explanation for the death of Axel's father, the child's deep shock and sense of fear are brushed aside by means of the language of the Cold War:

Ja, es war schlimm damals, ist die Antwort des Vaters, ich glaube, er wurde erschossen, aber er war ja ein Kommunist. Das Aber, denkt das Kind, was ist das für ein Aber? Kommunist ein Wort zum Gruseln, trotzdem wagt das Kind noch eine Frage: Was ist das eigentlich? Nun kommt die Antwort schon fester, weniger irritiert: So einer wie die in der Ostzone, wo es keine Freiheit gibt und wo sie den Glauben verbieten wollten. (*MJ*, 24)

[Yes, that was terrible, the father answered, I think he was shot, but he was a communist after all. But – what type of "but" is this, the child thought. The word "communist" was terrifying, and yet the child dared to ask another question: what is that precisely? Now the answer is more confident, less irritated: Someone like those in the eastern Sector, where they have no freedom and where they wanted to suppress religion.]

While the child's stutter gives expression to an unmastered trauma, the father's sterile and clichéd response serves to repress memory. In this way, the scene cleverly deconstructs the notion of symptom: here it is not the boy's stutter which indicates an unmastered disturbance, but the fluency of the father's formulaic explanations which swiftly bridge the abyss of National Socialism. "Die in der Ostzone" (those people in the eastern zone) provide the convenient alibi in the West for the collective repression of the past.

For Delius the impairment of tradition is thus most evident in the impairment of the German language at the end of the Third Reich. While the father's words make manifest the collective resistance to introspection and analysis, his grown-up son is by no means immune to such linguistic acting-out of an unmastered past. Although he realizes the debasement of the German language by Nazi jargon, his own language shows up traces of an aggressiveness that turns language into a weapon of assault. And this is so in spite of the protagonist's linguistic sensibility: when he reads the judgement against Groscurth, he stumbles across the shocking proclamation: "Für immer ehrlos, werden sie mit dem Tode bestraft" (*MJ*, 86; stripped of their honour for eternity, they shall be sentenced to death). While the eternal timeframe of this speech act demonstrates the psychotic megalomania of the Nazi ideology, the terminology of the judge's "reasoning" shows that this ideology has damaged the German language itself: "Das Maschinengewehrfeuer der Wiederholungen: *defaitistisch, kommunistisch, schamlos, intellektualistisch.* Allein die Sprache zeigte, wie das Recht gebeugt wurde" (*MJ*, 91; the machine gun of repetitions: defeatist, communist, without shame, intellectualist. The language itself showed the abuse of law). Studying the judgement, the protagonist experiences this German as a foreign language, in fact, as a dangerous minefield that is, however, strangely familiar (*MJ*, 87). Delius brings into perspective here a subliminal ghosting effect which marked the language of the post-war era. After the war the specific jargon of the Third Reich had been collectively dropped in East and West; however, the mode of expression and the tonal quality still carried traits of a deeply ingrained aggressiveness and authoritarianism which produced its own legacy. For in spite of his own linguistic sensibility, the son is shown to employ linguistic patterns which display precisely the defensive aggressiveness that he had sensed in his father's anti-communist justifications. This is exemplified in an episode with his mother at Christmas 1968, where he submits her to a self-righteous interrogation. He overtly attacks her religious world view, but in reality his aim is to deflect her justified concerns about his prolonged studies which she is still financing. Remembering his former self, the narrator takes issue with his own selfishness that draped itself in terms of ideological superiority: "Ohne Skrupel setzte ich sie matt und verschaffte mir so die Freiheit, von ihr nicht weiter gestört zu werden" (*MJ*, 117; I had no qualms about shutting her up and was thus freed from being disturbed by her any more). Whereas in Bruhns's narrative the public celebration of the father as an iconic symbol of heroic resistance produced a ghosting effect in the family, in Delius's novel the German language as such becomes the haunting ground for the ghosts of the past. Not what was said but how it was said, not a shared belief system but unmastered emotional attachments thus yoke the generations together.

It is important to note that Delius does not stop at deconstructing the West German resistance narrative. He equally highlights the instrument-alization of the resistance narrative in East Germany. Robert Havemann, the only survivor of the EU resistance group and, after the war, Professor of Physics at the Humboldt University, played a prominent role in building a socialist Germany before becoming a dissident, and from the point of view of the SED, an enemy of the state. However, in Delius's narrative he appears as a highly ambivalent figure who manip-ulates Anneliese Groscurth into accepting a series of political assign-ments in which the emerging GDR had a vested interest. One of them is her involvement with a committee that was set up under Havemann's auspices to investigate the events surrounding the *Weltfestspiele* (Youth World Games) of 1951, held in Berlin. These games became the arena for competing western and eastern propaganda: when East German youths marched into the western sector, singing songs and carrying socialist flags, the West saw this as a deliberate provocation. The West Berlin police subsequently beat up and arrested a large number of socialist youths. While for the eastern press the events were indicative of western repressiveness and anti-democratic police brutality, the western media depicted the demonstration of the socialist youth as a provocation orchestrated by the GDR. Against the backdrop of rapidly deteriorating relations between East and West, the narrator imagines a conversa-tion between Havemann and Anneliese Groscurth in which Havemann recruits her for his public inquiry into the events surrounding the *Welt-festspiele*. Seeking Anneliese's agreement to name the committee after her dead husband, Havemann is also shown as coaching her into signing a public petition which was published in the *Berliner Zeitung*. The narrator shows how Havemann used a form of emotional coercion that instru-mentalized his dead friend for post-war political aims (*MJ*, 164, 167). Trapped in the binary mindset of Cold War politics, Havemann repro-duces the sterile language of anti-fascism which rendered abstract the memory of Hans Georg Groscurth in the same way as the western remembrance culture rendered abstract the memory of the participants in the events of 20 July. What all these speech acts have in common is a monologic orientation that seeks to remove legitimacy from other polit-ical beliefs. By incorporating these warring voices into his novel, Delius makes the language of the post-war period a prime site of investigation.

As a damaged code, this language is full of "agitated words" that point to the presence of unmastered phantoms of the past.[39] In the register of the Cold War period, "resistance", "communism" and "anti-fascism" are not abstract nouns denoting political movements, but emotionally charged and highly contested terms that, from a psychoanalytical perspective, indicate that denial and transference operate across generational boundaries. The novel analyzes how through such agitated words phantoms entered tradition within families and even national cultures.[40]

Resistance in France in German narratives: Sibylle Mulot's *Nachbarn* and Michael Wallner's *April in Paris*

While Delius and Bruhns's resistance narratives highlight the impairment of the very notion of tradition in post-war German discourse, Sibylle Mulot's *Nachbarn* steps outside the German frame of reference, tackling long-cherished myths of the French *Résistance*. Mulot, who was born in 1950 in the southern German town of Reutlingen, lives in the Départment Haute-Saône in France, where her novel is set. The plot of *Nachbarn* is loosely based on real local events that, for the author, exemplify in many ways the ambivalent inheritance of French resistance and the dynamic of local communities. Here, as in her other works, Mulot writes in the register of what one might call "ethnographic realism", which aims to probe the interconnections of national history with local history.[41] *Nachbarn* is of particular interest in our context because it deconstructs the myth of the French *Résistance* from the point of view of the outsider who does not belong to the community that is the subject of the narrative. Unlike Bruhns's and Delius's narrators, who are emotionally embroiled in the world they describe, Mulot writes from the perspective of a detached ethnographer who studies the local community with a mixture of empathy and objectivity. The fact that a German author could choose this particular role and subject illuminates once more the growing historical distance from the Second World War. Although the novel's theme tackles resistance as a prime *lieu de mémoire* of French post-war cultural memory, the narrative's ethnographic perspective also contributes to the mutation of Germany's cultural memory of resistance. Its deconstruction of the invention of tradition in a small French community highlights the instrumentalized nature of cultural memory.

The novel is set in the fictional town of Parisey in Franche-Comté. Employing the structure of the detective novel, the plot revolves around the circumstances of the death of René Pasteur, who was accused of being a *collaborateur* and killed by local resisters in August 1944. The narrative pursues the question of Pasteur's alleged collaboration, tracing the ostracization of the Pasteur family in the post-war period. Like Anneliese Groscurth, who was denied a widow's pension because of her alleged communist beliefs, Judith Pasteur was denied a widow's pension because of her husband's alleged collaboration. In the 1970s, she fought and lost a court case in which she tried to prove that her husband had not been a traitor. In both Delius's and Mulot's narratives, the children are shown to be affected by overt or subliminal stigmatization.

Adopting the perspective of an ethnographer who is studying the codes and symbols of a tight-knit community, Mulot's narrator begins with an extensive description of the town itself, its history and customs. Against the backdrop of this ethnographic map, the events are triggered by the death of old Delmont, a local printer who was a hero of the *Résistance* and survivor of Dachau. Since Delmont was a neighbour of the Pasteur family, his widow Judith and her daughter Renée discuss the question of whether or not they should attend the funeral. Right from the start the narrative interweaves the community's notions of neighbourliness with the post-war discourse on *Résistance*: while good manners would normally demand the widow's presence at the funeral, the officially enshrined gulf between resisters and "collabos" make this impossible for Judith Pasteur. When the daughter announces that she will attend the funeral, the mother replies wryly, "Geh nur. Dir haben sie ja nur den Vater umgebracht. Aber mir meinen Mann" (Alright, you go. For you it was only your father they killed, but for me it was my husband).[42] The narrator shows how "collabo", "Résistance", "maquis" function as agitated words in the community, indicating the presence of unresolved conflicts in the French narrative about resistance. A prime *lieu de mémoire*, the reification of *Résistance* in French post-war discourse bolstered the idea of France as *la grande nation* steeped in the tradition of the French Revolution.[43] In de Gaulle's post-war France, the resistance narrative emphatically underlined the Frenchness of the democratic principles of *liberté, fraternité* and *egalité*; it universalized the activities of the *Résistance* to such an extent that the entire nation could see itself as legitimate heir of the resistance. Hand in hand with the universalization of resistance went the demonization of collaboration. The discursive construction of a strict dichotomy between resisters and "collabos" thus underpinned the national fantasy of a nation of resisters with only a small minority of black sheep.

As the events in Mulot's narrative unfold, the idea of neighbourliness comes under scrutiny too: a binding force of the community, the norms of neighbourliness are shown to function as a smokescreen, barring access to a critical examination of the past. Reified by official rites of commemoration, the moral gulf between resisters and "collabos" turns out to be the product of deliberate adaptations of the resistance narrative in the post-war period. An instrumental figure in this respect is Marcel Gibet, the successful mayor of the neigbouring community St. Sauveur, who has modelled his biography on the idea of resistance in the service of the nation. Posing as a resister of the first hour, it is, however, widely known that he only joined the *Résistance* after the Normandy landing. Prior to that he had worked as a Gendarme, supplying the German occupiers with information. Hunting down the printer of various resistance leaflets, it was he who probably denounced Delmont, who was subsequently arrested and deported to Dachau. However, because Gibet played a leading role in the local resistance towards the very end of the war, carrying out brutal executions of alleged collabos, he became an officially acknowledged and decorated resistance fighter after the war, whose social standing in the small community remained unchallenged despite various rumours of his true role during the occupation. Things begin to change with Delmont's death when papers about the activities of the *Résistance* are passed on to Charles Lorain, a leading figure of the resistance, who now begins to investigate some of the murkier deeds of the local resistance towards the end of the war, including the brutal killing of René Pasteur. In a letter to the daughter, who is named "Renée" after her father, old Lorain announces his intention of documenting all executions that were carried out under his leadership of the local resistance group, including the information he has on her father's death which was carried out by Gibet's maquis. The old resister and the daughter of the alleged collabo join forces in the attempt to reconstruct the events that led to the denunciation and execution of René Pasteur. While Lorain wants to replace the sanitized version of the *Résistance* that dominates French discourse with a "möglichst vollständiges Bild der Zeit und ihrer Akteure" (*N*, 138; most comprehensive picture possible of the times and its agents), Pasteur's daughter is motivated by the need to deal with the figure of her absent father. In the lives of the Pasteur children the father was nothing but a "Fotografie, nicht einmal eine vage Erinnerung" (*N*, 34; a photograph, not even a vague memory). In the first instance, old Delmont's death does not trigger in Renée thoughts about her father but rather memories about André Delmont, old Delmont's son, with whom she once had a relationship. However, in a crucial mirror-scene, Renée realizes that she can only deal with her own psychological baggage, that is her inability to maintain a relationship with André Delmont, if she deals with the figure of her father. Studying her own mirror image, she compares herself with the only photograph of her father. On an impulse, she holds up the photograph to the mirror and begins to detect a hidden resemblance:

Man hatte ihr immer gesagt, sie wäre nach der Großmutter geraten, einer mageren Frau mit braunen Locken [...]. Aber Renée sah, daß ihre eigenen Augen wie die ihres Vaters geschnitten waren. Das Haar war ganz anders, auch das Kinn. Sie hatte eine spitzes, ihr Vater ein weiches, rundes Kinn mit Grübchen. Zum wiederholten Male kam ihr der Gedanke, daß etwas von dem großen Unbekannten, der angeblich ihr Vater war, auch in ihr stecken könnte. Diese Idee verwirrte sie und machte sie nachdenklich. (*N*, 72–3)

[People had always said that she looked like her grandmother, a skinny woman with brown curls. [...] But Renée saw that her eyes had the same shape as her father's. Her hair was completely different, the chin too. Hers was pointed whereas her father's chin was soft and round with dimples on his cheeks. She found herself thinking again that something of her unknown father might be part of her, a confusing thought that put her in a pensive mood.]

This reinscription of the Lacanian mirror-scene transforms the jubilatory moment of self-recognition into the recognition of a selfhood based on lineage and inheritance. Interestingly, the daughter can only recognize this resemblance once the image of the father is reflected back to her by the mirror: identification thus occurs here on the basis of a doubled-up distance. The mirror image of her father's photograph and the mirror image of herself create the right conditions for this recognition of resemblance. The reflections of father and daughter in the mirror thus transport the fundamental paradox of all identification: in Lacan's mirror stage the child's jubilatory recognition of its own image goes hand in hand with the fragmentation of selfhood. Likewise the recognition of a transgenerational resemblance is here accompanied by a significant moment of self-alienation. As in Bruhns's narrative where it was a television documentary that caused the daughter to embark on her transgenerational investigation of the past, here it is the sudden realization of a hitherto unacknowledged lineage that triggers in Renée the desire to unearth the fateful events of the summer in 1944. In the course of the narrative, Renée and old Lorain form a transgenerational pact to illuminate the shadowing effect of a hidden past. In the end, they establish that her father was wrongly denounced by a real collaborator who saved his own neck by projecting his many denunciations onto a range of innocent people, including René Pasteur. Although the precise manner and probable location of his murder are revealed, the names of the killers remain hidden. The novel thus debunks the myth of the clean *Résistance*; however, it carefully avoids the naive illusion that myth and truth can be neatly separated. Just as the resistance figure, Gibet is shadowed by a murky past, the truth remains accompanied by gaps, rumours and myths.

As a German narrative about French resistance, the book also underlines the growing historical distance from the Second World War. The narrator's ethnographic perspective objectifies the events without, however, passing judgement. Mulot's analysis of the rifts and rumours that make up public life in this small French town also touches on the very notion of community. This story about conflicting memories of the French *Résistance* thus pinpoints paradigmatically the manner in which communities construct their sense of local identity. Although loyalty and security are core ideas of the community, these key terms turn out to be agitated words, indicating a fundamental disturbance of communal identity. The constant invocation of the need to be neighbourly in this small town thus highlights a basic feature of the very notion of community itself: once it is the subject of self-conscious discourse, it loses its binding force.[44]

While Mulot's ethnography of French *Résistance* thus makes an important contribution to the ongoing debate on the legacy of resistance, the same cannot be said of Michael Wallner's *April in Paris* (2006).[45] Wallner is an Austrian writer (born in 1958) who had published two previous novels before *April in Paris* became an international bestseller at the Frankfurt Book Fair in Autumn 2005, when the translation rights for 13 countries were snapped up by the publishers' agents.[46] This enthusiastic reception of what is effectively a melodrama highlights the current fashion in a postmemorial discourse that has freed itself completely from the constraints of historical veracity and plausibility. A brief summary of the main plot may be useful: set in Paris in 1943, the story revolves around the 22-year-old Wehrmacht soldier Roth, who one day is seconded to the SS Headquarters in the Rue de Saussaies, where he has to translate the interrogations. Taking up his post, Roth begins to lead a double life. After his daily duties which require him to translate the confessions that are beaten out of the prisoners by the SS, he swaps his uniform for a checkered suit and walks the streets of Paris, playing perfectly the part of a Frenchman called Antoine. He falls in love with Chantal, a young woman who turns out to work for the *Résistance* alongside her father and a local barber. Back in his hotel, he is confronted by Anna Rieleck-Sostmann, a German dominatrix, who has seen him in his civilian outfit and now demands regular sexual favours in return for her silence about his excursions into French civilian life. Roth manages to maintain his double life until his superior, SS Hauptsturmführer Leibold, informs him of the imminent arrest of a resistance group. Returning to the bookshop where he met Chantal for the first time, he reveals his real identity as a German Wehrmacht soldier, warning her and her father, the old bookseller, of the threat of arrest. Chased by the SS, the three make a dramatic escape through the cellars of the apartment block. After a passionate night with Chantal, Roth resumes his duties at the Rue de Saussaies and is present when the SS beat up and torture the barber who was caught. In a final meeting with Chantal, she warns him not to attend a nightbar which is frequented by the SS. However, when Leibold asks him to accompany him and a group of SS officers to this bar, he cannot turn the invitation down: after their arrival a bomb goes off, several SS men are killed or injured, and Roth, who had already attracted Leibold's suspicion, is duly arrested, imprisoned and tortured in the Rue de Saussaies until he receives a coded message that he will be freed with the help of the *Résistance*. After another spectacular escape, he hides once more in a friend's apartment and tries to find out Chantal's whereabouts. When the SS appears suddenly with Leibold, it turns out that Roth has been under surveillance all the time; against all odds, he manages to make yet another spectacular get-away, this time over the roof of the house. He falls off the roof, loses a finger when trying to catch the gutter, breaks his arms and legs and other bits of his body (his jaw has already been broken and fixed with a piece of wire). Waking up badly injured, he finds himself in the apartment of the concierge who has rescued him and who nurses him until he is fit enough to walk on crutches. Disfigured and disabled, he manages somehow to limp from Paris to Normandy in search of Chantal. On his way, he comes across members of the *Résistance* who nearly kill him together with alleged collaborators. Arriving at the farm where Chantal's family is hiding, he learns that she was shot dead by the Germans for stabbing a soldier who was raping her sister. Before her demise, however, she gave birth to their daughter who is called Antoinette.

This plot with its exaggerated twists and turns, which moves back and forth from romantic love to gratuitous violence, is typical of melodramatic fiction. Eschewing subject-centered models of identity, the emotional economy of melodrama revolves around excess and restraint.[47] Or as the first-person narrator, Roth puts it: "Alles begann sofort und ohne Übergang" (*AP*, 18; everything began immediately and without transition). Melodramatic types are therefore characterized by the "singleness of feeling that gives one the sense of wholeness".[48] In such a world, characters "behave in the same way, think in the same way and act in the same way throughout".[49] Thus the protagonist of Wallner's novel is an immediately transparent type who, once he has spotted Chantal outside the bookshop, is solely driven by his desire for her. His regular metamorphosis into Monsieur Antoine is a theatrical performance that glamorizes the "entrepreneurial kind of individualism" which is the driving force of melodrama.[50] As Peter Brooks argues, melodrama makes the world morally legible; its structural backbone is the ethical fantasy that good triumphs eventually over evil.[51] Chantal's death merely underlines this fantasy: for the birth of their child and Roth's own survival ensure that the emotional economy of melodrama is maintained to the kitschy end.

The problem with Wallner's novel is not so much the utterly implausible plot but rather its resurrection of the popular cliché of the innocent Wehrmacht soldier. Feeding the fantasy that love can overcome all ideological and political barriers, the novel also nurtures the notion that self-interest is a form of resistance to the system. Although Wallner makes no effort to equip his hero with any political beliefs, Roth's switching of sides at the right moment only magnifies his innate virtue. The economy of this novel thus transforms the apolitical soldier from a passive or active agent of National Socialism into the figure of the subversive resister. Encoding romantic love as an act of resistance, the novel illustrates the consequences of a postmemorial discourse that embraces fantasy and abandons the ethical distinction between perpetrator and victim. The novel thus depoliticizes the concept of resistance. While in Bruhns, Delius and Mulot the telescoping of history through family history magnifies the agitated nature of resistance discourse, here the privatization of history results in its trivialization. *April in Paris* thus highlights the seductiveness of a postmemorial engagement with the past that gives absolute priority to fantasy over factuality. In spite of the overwhelming historical evidence to the contrary, the reader of this text is invited to indulge in the absurd idea that the war was one great romance. My argument does not resurrect the epistemologically untenable opposition between fact and fiction; rather it insists that imaginary representations of the real must probe reality and open new avenues of understanding. Although novels must not be subjected to the same criteria of verification as historical writing, they too operate within a framework of historical reflection. The problem with *April in Paris* is not simply that it is a bad piece of fiction but rather that it supports a tendentious appropriation of the past. Wallner's clichéd adventure story is symptomatic of the post-1990s culture of fabulation in which titillation and consolation are endlessly recycled.

Resistance as family romance: Jo Baier's *Stauffenberg. Der 20. Juli 1944*

The 60th anniversary of the 20 July plot was not only marked in public ceremonies and commemorations but also by a new television drama entitled *Stauffenberg. Der 20. Juli 1944*. Commissioned and financed by a range of public broadcasters, including ARD, WDR and ORF, the drama was directed by Jo Baier. The cast included well-known German actors, such as Sebastian Koch in the lead role of Claus Schenk von Stauffenberg, Ulrich Tukur as Henning von Tresckow and Nina Kunzenberg as Nina von Stauffenberg, amongst many others. In many ways this film – which was screened by ARD on 25 February 2004 and reviewed by the leading broadsheets[52] – exemplifies the return to classical narrative in German cinema since unification. According to Sabine Hake, post-1990 German film-making tends to "enlist the harmonising effects of genre in the rewriting of the German past and the remapping of the German present within the cultural and geopolitical topography of post-Wall Europe".[53] Hake argues that, with their heavy reliance on production design, these films turn German history into a visual spectacle that underscores the normalization of German history.[54] Similarly, in his discussion of the new German heritage film, Lutz Koepnick emphasizes the genre's overt nostalgia which attempts to solicit a new consensus for the Berlin Republic.[55] Popular films, such as the *Comedian Harmonists* (Joseph Vilsmaier, 1997) or *Aimee & Jaguar* (Max Färberböck, 1999), employ melodrama to collapse the difference between past and present. For Koepnick, the problem with recent heritage films is that they attempt to master any residual anxiety about Germany's past by converting "bad history into a good story".[56]

Jo Baier's *Stauffenberg. Der 20. Juli 1944* is such a heritage film in that it gives expression to a symbolic reconciliation with German history. By reclaiming the 20 July 1944 as a symbolic moment of failed resistance, the film arguably also recoups the very notion of a "better German tradition" and reinstates a conservative version of German national identity. The Stauffenberg drama interweaves a re-enactment of the events of the 20th July plot with a family narrative that articulates questions of allegiance to family and the nation. By depicting Stauffenberg as an heroic individual who is torn between his duty to the nation and his love for his family, the film exemplifies the allegorization of history through family history which attempts to make German history morally legible.

Before analyzing this privatization of history more closely, it may be useful to refer briefly to two earlier films on the topic: the 1955 production *Der 20. Juli*, which was directed by Falk Harnack and based on a script by Günther Weisenborn and Werner Jörg Lüddecke[57], coincided with Georg Wilhelm Pabst's *Es geschah am 20. Juli* (It happened on 20 July) with popular actor Bernhard Wicki starring as Stauffenberg. As Peter Reichel points out, the reception of both films was heavily influenced by the controversies over Germany's rearmament in the 1950s.[58] Against the backdrop of the heated moral and political debate over the foundation of the *Bundeswehr*, the two films helped to make a case for re-armament and, above all, to popularize military resistance in the public's imagination. It is important to remember that only four years earlier, former Major Remer, a decisive figure in the defeat of the plot, had publicly denounced the men of July 1944 as traitors. While both films thus marked a watershed in the post-war reception of resistance, the press especially praised Harnack's film for its comprehensive depiction of the groups and individuals who had prepared the events of the 20th July plot. At a time when the critical engagement with the Nazi past was still confined to rarefied academic and intellectual circles or to the literary fringe, the film tried to communicate a positive image of the conspirators by focusing on their humanitarian motivations and beliefs. For example, a few scenes are set in the so-called *Mittwochsgesellschaft* (Wednesday Society) in Berlin, where the national-conservative resisters around the former mayor of Leipzig, Carl Goerdeler, debated Germany's social and political future after Hitler's removal from power. The film's dramatization of the social, political and philosophical discussions that had preceded the plot against Hitler shows how the nationalist-conservative resisters proceeded tentatively from criticizing the system to the idea that a coup d'état was inevitable to safeguard Germany's future. But the film does not stop at highlighting the immense psychological barrier to breaking away from the national war effort, it also addressed the diversity of resistance movements: while some scenes deal with church resistance – for example, Bonhoeffer is shown preaching – others depict Social Democratic resistance cells. Furthermore, the representation of resistance is accompanied by scenes showing Germany's ruination, the loss of life at the front or the deportation of Jews. In this way the resisters' motivations are objectified and historically validated from an authorial point of view. The latter part of Harnack's 1955 production offers a detailed reconstruction of the 20th July plot, including the important events in Paris where General Stülpnagel attempted to support the coup by arresting members of the SS. Harnack's film communicates a comprehensive picture of the 20 July 1944, highlighting both the historical context in which resistance emerged as well as the technical obstacles that hindered its success.

By contrast to Harnack's film, Baier eschews such contextualization. The first part of the film focuses on Stauffenberg as an individual; it narrates his personal journey from initial support of National Socialism to active resistance. While the first scene provides a frame by showing the execution of Stauffenberg, Olbricht, von Quirnheim and von Haeften in the courtyard of the Bendlerblock, from the second scene onwards the film adopts a chronological perspective. Starting in 1933, we see Stauffenberg and his fiancée Nina arrive late at the Opera where Wagner is being performed in the presence of Hitler. Persuading the doorman to let them slip in, the couple casts an admiring eye on Hitler who is seated opposite. The presence of the Leader inspires Stauffenberg to propose to Nina. In this way, the television drama makes the libidinal investment in the Leader a dominant leitmotif, which knits together Stauffenberg's personal life with the political. Throughout the film Stauffenberg's probing gaze at Hitler's image charts his growing rage towards this disappointing national father figure. For example, a scene in North Africa shows how Stauffenberg smashes a picture of Hitler after an air attack in which a young, likeable soldier from his home district is killed. During the coup in the Bendlerblock, his gaze falls again on Hitler's picture when it becomes increasingly apparent that the plot is going to be defeated. The events of the 20th July are thus given a psychoanalytical interpretation, according to which the military plot against Hitler re-enacts an archaic father–son conflict. This privatization of the political is further underlined by the way in which the film filters Stauffenberg's changing ideological convictions back to his wife Nina: for example, after the start of the war, Stauffenberg writes a letter to her from Poland, describing the Polish population in racist terms as a mongrel people with too many Jews. The following scene dramatizes his change of conviction in a conversation with Henning von Tresckow in Belorussia in 1942. Von Tresckow, a central player in the military resistance, remains, however, a marginalized figure in Baier's script: his own attempt to assassinate Hitler with a bomb that he placed in Hitler's plane on 13 March 1943 is not mentioned.[59] Instead of showing the resisters' wide-reaching network within the military, Baier depicts Stauffenberg as a singular individual: after his conversation with von Tresckow, he is shown writing a sort of conversion letter to Nina, expressing his growing doubts about his profession and life. The camera zooms in on Stauffenberg's illuminated face against a black background, lending him the aura of a martyr in a post-sacred world.

The privatization of the political is further underlined after Stauffenberg's injuries in Africa: waking up in a Munich hospital, he learns that he has lost an eye and his right hand. When he asks about the whereabouts of his wedding ring, his wife Nina tells him that the hand and the ring were thrown away by the doctors. The disregard for the ring symbolizes in this scene paradigmatically the dictator's lack of care for the nation. Family life and national life are aligned to such an extent that the nation appears as a family that is led by a father who turns out to be an ogre. The son's disaffection with the ogre-father is once more given symbolic expression by Stauffenberg's gaze at Hitler's image which is hanging on the wall of the hospital ward.

The domestification of the political culminates in a scene that precedes the actual execution of the 20th July plot and which shows Stauffenberg in his family environment. We watch how, after blessing his four children, Stauffenberg takes leave of his wife who suspects that he is involved in some dangerous enterprise. While Stauffenberg emphasizes his duty to the nation, Nina insists on the separation of nation and family: "Du bist mein Mann, du bist mit mir verheiratet, nicht mit dem Reich" (you are my husband, you are married to me, not to the Reich). But this separation of family and nation has already been undermined by the film's allegorization of the plot in terms of a father – son conflict: Stauffenberg is the courageous son who sacrifices his life on the altar of the nation-family. For this reason, the second part of the drama symbolizes Stauffenberg's failure to assassinate Hitler in terms of his failure to make contact with Nina. Neither nation nor family can be protected from the ogre-father. The privatization of history in Baier's film thus depoliticizes resistance, recoding it in terms of a drama of failed protection in a father – son battle. By mythologizing resistance in this way, the film also seeks to remove from the spectator's mind any awareness of the historical gulf that separates our world from the beliefs of the men of July 1944. The television drama results in an uprooting of history and thus obliterates the fact that the men of July 1944 were not the founders of the post-1945 Germany but the heirs of beliefs that originated in the first half of the 20th century. According to Hans Mommsen, the plot of 1944 must be assigned to an historical epoch which came to an end with the collapse in May 1945.[60] Baier's privatization of history erases the rift that separates us from the strange world of duty, honour and fatherland, inhabited by Stauffenberg and his class.

Resistance *in extremis*: Marc Rothemund's *Sophie Scholl. Die letzten Tage*

The second cornerstone of West German remembrance of resistance is The White Rose, a group of Munich students who had started distributing anti-Hitler leaflets in summer 1942. In West German discourse, it was this group, above all the siblings Hans and Sophie Scholl, which gained iconic status in the post-war resistance narrative: with their educated middle-class and Christian background, the group members symbolized principled opposition to the Third Reich based on one's individual conscience rather than on ideology. The group had such a wide public appeal precisely because its youthfulness went hand in hand with humanistic values which seemed to embody a purity of motivation, transcending the dirty realm of politics. In order to illuminate the constructed nature of this largely depoliticized image, a brief outline of the group's activities is necessary. This will provide the context for a reading of Marc Rothemund's acclaimed film *Sophie Scholl. Die letzten Tage* (Sophie Scholl. The final Days), which was released in German cinemas in 2005.

At the centre of the group were Hans Scholl and Alexander Schmorell, two medical students who – along with Hans's sister Sophie Scholl, their friends Christoph Probst and Willi Graf and with the support of Kurt Huber, a Munich Professor of Philosophy – wrote and distributed leaflets in a range of cities, including Munich, Stuttgart, Vienna, Linz and Salzburg. The first four leaflets were sent by post primarily to middle-class professionals; they appealed to those humanistic and Christian ideals which had underpinned the bourgeois belief system since the late 18th century. Authored by Alexander Schmorell and Hans Scholl, these leaflets proposed passive resistance to the Third Reich; linguistically they peppered a biblical language with quotations from Schiller and Goethe and ancient sources to legitimize the idea of resistance. By contrast, the style and content of the last two leaflets are far more direct and political: in the context of the decisive defeat of the Wehrmacht in Stalingrad in 1943, these leaflets now address the entire population, asking all Germans to rise up against Hitler. The authors formulate concrete ideas about a new post-war order based on a federal German state and European co-operation. The sharpened tone of the leaflets thus reflects the radicalization of the group which had become increasingly impatient with the lack of resistance to the system.[61] A decisive turning point for the male group members had been a stint at the eastern front, where they served as medical staff behind the lines from the end of July 1942 to the beginning of November of the same year. Dealing with huge loss of life on a daily basis, the medical students also witnessed atrocities against Jews and the civilian Russian population.[62] After their return to Munich they therefore attempted to intensify their activities by, for example, seeking contact with other resistance groups in or around Berlin, such as Bonhoeffer's *Bekennende Kirche*. Unlike many conservative resisters, Hans Scholl rejected the idea that a new post-war Germany had to be led by an unelected elite; he embraced the idea of parliamentary democracy.

On the night of the 15 February 1943, the group had printed between 2000 and 3000 copies of the final leaflet which was addressed to their fellow students. Approximately 1200 leaflets were posted to students in Munich; on 18 February 1943, Hans and Sophie Scholl attempted to distribute the remaining batch in the University, a high-risk undertaking which ended with their immediate arrest. When Sophie Scholl threw a pile of leaflets into the courtyard, they were observed by the caretaker. Unfortunately, Hans Scholl was carrying a hand-written draft that was quickly traced back to Christoph Probst, who was later arrested in Innsbruck. All three were interrogated by the Gestapo and tried before the People's Court on 22 February 1943 in a high-profile show trial. After only three-and-a-half hours, this trial, where none of the assigned defence lawyers spoke for the accused, finished with Roland Freisler, the fanatical President of the People's Court, pronouncing the death sentences against all three. The People's Court, a Nazi institution set up to terrorize the population, allowed no right to appeal, and the Scholl parents' petition for mercy was immediately turned down. Christoph Probst, Hans and Sophie Scholl were guillotined only 4 hours later. A second wave of arrests followed with more show trials: Willi Graf, Alexander Schmorell and Kurt Huber were also sentenced to death and executed a few months later after the Gestapo had interviewed them in detail about the activities and networks of the group. Others were sentenced to terms of imprisonment.[63]

Released in February 2005, *Sophie Scholl. Die letzten Tage* was nominated for an Oscar and has won a number of prestigious film prizes, amongst them the prize for best director and best actress at the

Berlinale, the Berlin Film Festival. Directed by Marc Rothemund, the script was by Fred Breinersdorfer; Julia Jentsch played the lead role of Sophie Scholl, and Alexander Held the Gestapo investigator Robert Mohr.[64] As some reviewers pointed out, Rothemund's was not the first film about the topic. His film had been preceded in the early 1980s by Michael Verhoeven's *Die Weiße Rose* (The White Rose, 1982), which drew a compelling and comprehensive picture of the activities and aims of the group based on historical documents, reports by eye-witnesses and the diaries of the Scholl siblings. In 1982, Percy Adlon's *Fünf letzte Tage* (The Five Last Days) was shown on Bavarian television, dramatizing the last days of Sophie Scholl's life from the perspective of her fellow inmate in prison. While Verhoeven covered the wider context of the group, Adlon homed in behind the prison walls. The two films thus helped to underpin the iconic status that The White Rose and, above all, Hans and Sophie Scholl had gained steadily after Inge Scholl, a surviving sister, had published her groundbreaking, if controversial, account *Die Weiße Rose* in 1955.

Against the backdrop of such a highly public image of Sophie Scholl, Rothemund and Breinersdorfer injected new life into this story by basing the script on the Gestapo records which, after unification, were found in Stasi archives. Their film is a successful example of a postmemorial engagement with resistance because it manages to keep a fine balance between historical veracity and postmemorial licence. In spite of its focus on Sophie Scholl, the film eschews a renewal of resistance myths. Instead it offers a psychological analysis of resistance *in extremis*, that is resistance to the Gestapo interviewer after the arrest has occurred. However, by drawing a psychological portrait of Sophie Scholl, the film does not privatize the political along the lines of Jo Baier's *Stauffenberg*; rather it traces how Sophie Scholl attempted to safeguard minimal spaces of agency in the face of absolute oppression. Rothemund's focus on the individual also illuminates how the representatives of the totalitarian regime felt threatened by this small group of students. In this way, the film brings to light the utter disproportion between the limited capabilities of The White Rose and the state apparatus for which the smallest sign of personal revolt required a totally crushing response. While the film has a documentary appeal, it is also characterized by what I shall call a postmemorial filter which locates it in our times.

The action begins on the 17 February 1943 with Sophie and her friend Gisela listening secretly to Billy Holliday on the radio. After this opening which gives a glimpse of Sophie as a typical student who is interested in modern music and fun, the following scenes adopt a documentary perspective. They reconstruct the production of the final leaflet in the cellar of a friends's studio, Hans's and Sophie's decision to distribute the remaining leaflets in the university, and the events on 18 February 1943 that lead to their arrest. The dynamic development of the plot is slowed down by one further domestic scene which shows Sophie and Hans in their apartment on the night before the leaflet campaign. While Hans is shown drinking tea and stowing away a large quantity of stamps (evidence which will be used against them later on), Sophie writes a letter to a friend with Schubert's "Trout Quintet" in the background. With a few brushstrokes, the film thus evokes the emotional and intellectual world of a young female student in the early 1940s who is attracted to German middle-class culture and simultaneously to the forbidden world of American Jazz. In this way, the film demythologizes Sophie, turning her from a saintly icon into a modern young woman.

However, at this point in the narrative, Sophie exudes a certain degree of naiveté, for her involvement with The White Rose appears to be the product of both her admiration for her brother and the sheer titillation of underground work. This impression changes after the arrest. Focusing on the Gestapo interviews, the film now adopts the perspective of a small stage production that revolves around an intellectual and emotional battle between Robert Mohr, the Gestapo investigator, and Sophie who, in the first interview, produces a series of persuasive lies in response to Mohr's questions. Julia Jentsch's subtle expressions manage to communicate both Sophie Scholl's ingenuity and a sense of fear. For example, during the first interview, Sophie speaks with a self-confident and even jokey voice: denying the authorship and distribution of the leaflets, she says that the leaflets had already been there when she arrived at the university with her brother. Admitting that she tossed a pile of leaflets from the banister into the courtyard of the stairwell, she adds tongue-in-cheek: "Solche Späße liegen in meiner Natur"(such jokes are in my nature). By contrast the Gestapo transcript reads, "Ich sehe nun ein, dass ich durch mein Verhalten eine Dummheit gemacht habe, die ich aber nicht mehr ändern kann" (I now know that this was a foolish act on my part, but one I cannot now undo). By translating what amounted to Sophie's admission of a regrettable mistake into a playful prank, Rothemund and Breiersdorfer accentuate the element of performance in front of the Gestapo inquisitor. This lends the film a Brechtian dimension, drawing attention to the gap between role-play and the person behind it. Periodically, the camera zooms in on Sophie clutching her hands in fear, which goes unnoticed by Mohr who is sitting behind his desk. The slippage between her defiant public performance on the one hand and her body language on the other thus charts the build-up of psychological pressure. As many critics have noticed, Sophie's recurring gaze through the window, a leitmotif throughout the film, can be read in terms of a Christian iconography symbolizing her faith.[65] However, it would be a mistake to read this in terms of Sophie's overall depiction as a martyr. Rothemund's character is a gutsy young woman who with intelligence, wit and quiet charm nearly beguiles her inquisitor. Mohr himself is depicted by Alex Held as a bureaucrat in the service of the Nazi state. Combining paternalistic attitudes with a criminological perspective, he is not the jackboot-wearing fanatical maniac but the convinced Nazi follower for whom Sophie is a misguided young woman from a privileged background. In the interview after Sophie's confession on 19 February, Mohr keeps pressing her hard for the names of other co-conspirators but Sophie refuses to comply. Some reviewers have read this in terms of too much poetic licence on the part of the filmmakers, since in reality Sophie and Hans Scholl did name their immediate co-conspirators.[66] However, a careful reading of the Gestapo records show that they attempted to downplay Schmorell's, Graf's and Probst's involvement as much as possible. Gestapo files are not objective records but the biased accounts of state-legitimized perpetrators whose interrogation methods ranged from psychological pressure and torture to brutal murder. Naturally, the records give no indication whether or not the Scholls were abused, threatened or beaten during the interrogations.

The film's study of resistance *in extremis* climaxes in a final interrogation scene which concerns the group's belief system. While Mohr shows himself here to be a staunch supporter of NS ideology, especially of the dream of a Germanified Europe, Sophie refutes his vision with reference to the reality of war, destruction and atrocities, ranging from the euthanasia of mentally handicapped people to the extermination of Jews in the concentration camps. While this debate may appear to be slightly anachronistic in that it ticks off the main boxes of post-war German memory debates, it again accentuates the fundamental conflict between the idea of individual conscience as opposed to blind allegiance. Rejecting Mohr's offer to save her own neck by distancing herself from the White Rose and shifting all responsibility onto her brother, Sophie concludes, "Ich bin nach wie vor der Meinung, dass ich das Beste für mein Volk getan habe. Ich bereue das nicht und ich will die Folgen dafür auf mich nehmen"[67] (I am still of the opinion that what I did was best for the German people. I do not regret it and will accept the consequences). In their disarming simplicity, these words sum up the idea of principled resistance to the total penetration of society which the Nazi State sought. The film's postmemorial dimension is perhaps most evident in these scenes: as time passes, Mohr increasingly looks at Sophie in terms of an iconic figure of the future. His Pilatus-like washing of hands at the end of the final interrogation scene communicates symbolically a knowledge of defeat.

However, unlike Jo Baier's *Stauffenberg*, Rothemund's postmemorial representation of this scene avoids a straightforward recreation of a specific myth of resistance. With its focus on resistance during the Gestapo interrogations, the film draws a psychological portrait of a young woman who, by all accounts, managed to maintain her principled opposition to the Nazi system. The film carefully avoids an overstatement in Sophie's Christianity: her motivation is shown to be derived from the idea of basic human rights. The film also offers an anatomy of the mechanisms of the fascist state in which the juridico-legal limitations of constitutional state power had been replaced by what, following Giorgio Agamben, one might call a permanent state of exception.[68] With their overt air of legalized proceedings, the interrogation scenes and the later court scenes highlight the rationalization of terror under NS rule. In her study *On Violence*, Hannah Arendt observes that terror "is the form of government that comes into being when violence, having destroyed all power, does not abdicate but, on the contrary, remains in full control".[69] Arendt argues that "violence appears where power is in jeopardy",[70] which explains the NS state's vicious reaction to the slightest sign of opposition and individual agency. With its focus on the state's total response to this small group of resisters, Rothemund's film thus highlights the rationalization of violence in the state of exception, while at the same time pointing to a sphere of independent action that lies beyond the state's control. Sophie's conscience is the film's metaphor for this basic idea of individual liberty.

Historical narrative or postmemorial drama? Margarethe von Trotta's *Rosenstraße*

The rediscovery of resistance in post-Wall cinema is also manifest in recent retro-films about the Holocaust. While Michael Verhoeven's *Mutters Courage* (Mother's Courage, 1995) and Agnieszka Holland's *Hitlerjunge Salomon* (Hitler Boy Salomon, 1990) focus on successful survival strategies by individual Jews against all odds, Margarethe von Trotta's *Rosenstraße* (2003) features public resistance by a group of so-called "intermarried" German women in Berlin.[71] The historical episode featured in the film can be summarized as follows: on 27 February 1943, the SS and Gestapo seized thousands of Jewish factory workers who, until that point, had survived the deportations as enforced labourers in the German armament industry. When it became known that this round-up also included some 2000 intermarried Jews, their gentile wives began to assemble outside the former Jewish community building in Berlin's Rosenstraße 2–4, where the men were held. At first this assembly was an unorganized coming together of worried wives and relatives; however, the protest gathered such momentum that the women felt empowered to demand back their husbands, since mixed marriages were supposed to be exempt from the deportations. Irrespective of the actual numbers participating in this week-long protest – the figures range from a couple of hundred women to a few thousand – the events in the Rosenstraße protest stand for a singular act of resistance: they involved a public group demonstration by ordinary unarmed women who, without leadership and plan, stood up to the most brutal forces of the Third Reich, the Gestapo and the SS.

However, historians disagree sharply over the question whether or not the women's courageous protest had a direct impact on the discharge of their husbands. In his ground-breaking study, *Resistance of the Heart*, Nathan Stoltzfus attributes the release of the men to the women's courage at a perilous time for the regime.[72] He argues that, intent on having Berlin racially cleansed, the leadership was nevertheless worried about the possible repercussions of shooting German women in the streets. According to Stoltzfus, Goebbels, who was *Gauleiter* of Berlin, therefore released the Rosenstraße prisoners and also ordered the return of the 25 men who had already been sent to Auschwitz. By contrast, Wolf Gruner and Beate Meyer deny the effectiveness of the Rosenstraße protest.[73] Their research suggests that the intermarried Jews were not actually herded up for deportation at this point but only for registration purposes. The argument over the Rosenstraße protests concerns fundamental principles of the historiography of German resistance and, in particular, it implies the wider issue of human agency: while Gruner's and Meyer's focus on the deportation machinery and Nazi bureaucracy de-emphasizes individual historical agency, Stoltzfus highlights agency by way of the undeniable courage and solidarity of a group of women, who had already withstood the regime by refusing to divorce their husbands in spite of the severe and endless harassment this entailed in everyday life.

However, while the historical essence of the film's plot is undoubtedly relevant, it is important to emphasize that von Trotta's film is not a documentary that sets out to settle this dispute. Rather it is a

fictionalized account based on an historical instance which, in dram-
aturgical terms, represents a unique and unprecedented event, inviting
artistic representation. This simple point was missed by many critics
after the film's release in 2003. A rather hostile tone was set by the
historian Wolfgang Benz who attacked the film for its alleged trivialization of history in an article for *Die Süddeutsche Zeitung*.[74] Highly polemical, Benz's review is important because it unleashed a public debate
which, prior to the film's release, had been confined to rarefied academic
circles. When Nathan Stoltzfus attempted to refute Benz, Gruner and
Meyer in *Die Zeit*, another memory contest ignited that preoccupied the
German public for some time.[75]

From a cinematographic perspective, however, the ensuing debate was
based on a fundamental misreading of the film's genre. Benz read a
title sequence which prefaced the film's opening scene as evidence of
the film's claim to documentary authenticity and he then attacked its
countless historical inaccuracies. However, while the film's brief preface
does state that the events in the Rosenstraße did take place, it does not
claim that the events had actually occurred *in the way* depicted by the
film. The argument over the film's lack of documentary authenticity was
thus the product of a rather wilful mis-quotation by a renowned German
historian, who launched historical arguments against a heritage film
which combines a melodramatic register with a postmemorial narrative
structure to dramatize the transgenerational remembering process.

In my view, the question is thus not whether the film is historically accurate or inaccurate but rather whether its melodramatic register
glorifies rare moments of German–Jewish solidarity. Heritage films can
be used to very different effect: as Lutz Koepnick argues, although
the heritage genre runs the risk of subjecting "different traumas to
self-assured and unified historical narratives", it may also be used to
reinterpret the past according to changing views of history which, in
turn, are influenced by changing attitudes to memory, gender and
ethnicity.[76] Following Koepnitz's analysis of the heritage genre, Daniela
Berghahn draws the conclusion that *Rosenstraße* underlines the worrying
trend to assimilate Germans "into a general sense of victimhood by
suggesting that the trauma of loss [...] affected Germans and Jews in
equal measure".[77] In her view the film "scales down German–Jewish
history by domesticating it in line with the narrative conventions of
a family saga".[78] Indeed, the film does enlist a range of postmemorial
devices which create a positive legacy, reaching out to both Germans
and Jews. However, rather than simply domesticating German–Jewish
history, the film raises subtle questions about intermarriage, both from

an historical and a contemporary perspective, while also exploring the productiveness of transgenerational memory work as a way of overcoming hardened binary divisions.

The plot follows Hannah, a young Jewish woman from New York, who embarks on a reconstruction of her mother Ruth's repressed history that only surfaces after the death of Ruth's husband. Although she never was a devout Jewess, Ruth suddenly embraces the orthodox ritual, insisting that the seven-day shiva be observed for her dead husband. This turn to orthodoxy is accompanied by Ruth's sudden, and for the rest of the family perplexing, rejection of Hannah's gentile partner Luis, who is of Latin-American extraction and who had been embraced by the entire family prior to the father's death. While Ruth's behaviour is inexplicable to her daughter Hannah, the viewer is given access to a series of flashbacks which Ruth experiences during the shiva and which reveal a hidden childhood trauma. Triggered by her husband's death, Ruth now remembers the traumatic loss of her own mother who was deported from Berlin in 1943 because her gentile German husband had divorced her. However, Hannah is unaware of her mother's trauma until a cousin called Rachel reveals Ruth's story to her: it turns out that Ruth's life was saved by Lena Fischer, a German woman married to a Jewish musician, who took Ruth in after her mother was arrested, taken to the Rosenstraße and later deported. Rachel also reveals that, after the war, Ruth was sent to the United States at the request of her Jewish American relatives, a second traumatic separation for which Ruth blamed Lena. As Ruth refuses to speak about her childhood, Hannah travels to Berlin where she tracks down Lena Fischer. Posing as an historian, Hannah begins to visit Lena who was one of the Rosenstraße protesters.

Hannah's interviews with Lena create a narrative frame that enables von Trotta to film the events of 1943 as a series of flashbacks which are informed by the remembering process itself. While the postmemorial device of using a member of the third generation as prime investigator of the past draws attention to the painfulness of recall by the first generation actor, it also highlights the historical distance that separates us from these events. The historical scenes are therefore interrupted by scenes set in the present: regular cuts ensure that we either see Hannah and Lena in Lena's apartment or Hannah in her hotel room where she struggles to relate her conflicting emotions to Luis as she is increasingly absorbed by the past. She is also shown walking through Berlin, visiting various memorial sites dedicated to the Holocaust. These present-day scenes ensure that the fragmentary nature of the process of remembering remains present in the viewer's mind. Although the transgenerational memory that emerges in the course of the film is marked by deep personal connection, the film accentuates the mediated nature of this collaborative memory: Lena's ability to relate her story and Hannah's willingness to engage with it create a dialogic setting in which a fragmentary and ultimately indeterminate story about the past can be told. None of the critics who faulted von Trotta for her historical "inaccuracies" seemed to notice that the historical scenes set in the 1940s deliberately eschew a documentary appeal; on the contrary, the cinematic techniques employed are clearly aimed at evoking Lena's subjective memories. For example, although the historical scenes were shot in colour, a complex technique of bleaching the colour reels was applied to give them a patina that separates them from the present. Furthermore, the volume level of certain sounds was increased, such as banging doors in the Rosenstraße, in order to reproduce the prominence of aural memories.

As Lena engages with her memories of the past, it becomes apparent that she too was traumatized by the post-war separation from Ruth. The melodramatic doubling of trauma allows von Trotta to cross-knit the German and the Jewish experiences of loss. In the end, the film resolves this dramaturgy of mutual loss by way of a transgenerational reconciliation between Lena and Hannah that also prepares Hannah's union with her partner Luis. One may argue that with this resolution von Trotta's *Rosenstraße* illustrates the tendency of the heritage genre to convert "bad history into a good story", as Koepnick put it so memorably. However, it is also possible to see the film as an understated representation of the Rosenstraße protests, a reading that has been put forward by Evelyn Wilcock.[79] As Wilcock points out, von Trotta excises any historical detail which might shift attention from the persecution of the Jews. The death of Ruth's mother alongside the suicide of another woman whose husband was deported underlines that the Rosenstraße protest only saved a small number of Jews. According to Wilcock, von Trotta does not idealize German resistance either: for when von Trotta lets Lena – a German woman married to a Jew – rescue Ruth, she is guided by the historical fact that persecuted Jews were often helped by non-Jews who had personal ties with Jews.

In spite of the melodramatic treatment of the plot, von Trotta employs the heritage genre in marked contrast to Baier and Rothemund: whereas the latter represent iconic resistance figures, who stand for individual heroism, von Trotta transforms an overlooked aspect of social history into a powerful symbol of genderized group protest. Clearly, the idea of a public group protest by ordinary women during the Third Reich interested her as a feminist film-maker. To my knowledge, none of the critics noticed that von Trotta accentuated her own postmemorial investment in the story cinematographically in the actual protest scenes that are set in the Rosenstraße. A central scene begins with a high-angle view of the street protest from a position half-way behind the women; the camera then moves to a frontal position that shows the women in full-shot. As the camera adopts a mid-shot perspective, panning the women who stand in front of the Rosenstraße building, we eavesdrop on bits of their conversation, until young Ruth spots a prisoner behind one of the windows. The camera zooms in on the women's sense of surprise, until one of them identifies the man as her husband Hans. As other women begin to call out the names of their husbands, the camera pans on a horizontal axis, capturing their emotions through a range of close-ups. After an SS officer has dragged Hans away from the window, there is a moment of silent disillusionment which von Trotta films frontally as a group shot. Eventually, one of the women begins to call out "I want to have my husband back", which is followed by a moment of charged silence. When another woman calls for her husband, more women join in, repeating the call "I want to have my husband back", which eventually turns into the collective "we want to have our husbands back". The point of this and other protest scenes, such as the one in which the women shout "murderers, murderers" at the guards – as Beate Meyer points out, quite an unthinkable occurrence in 1940s Germany[80] – is not to give a documentary representation of what really happened in the Rosenstraße but rather to offer a transhistorical reading of the symbolism of the protest. The powerful choreography of this scene transforms what began as the coincidental gathering of women into a Greek chorus in which the individual voice is absorbed by a meaningful collective, giving expression to those events and fears that cannot be articulated by the individual. By employing the register of Greek tragedy, von Trotta elevates the significance of her story, while at the same time signalling her own artistic investment in its postmemorial recreation.

Conclusion

The examples discussed in this chapter all point to the pluralization of cultural memory in Germany today. Although the annual commemorations of key resistance dates, such as the 20 July 1944, still draw upon the generic features of the normative resistance discourse that was established in the post-war era, the idea of resistance has become increasingly self-conscious and differentiated. A first example of the nuanced understanding of resistance is, as we have seen, the *Gedenkstätte Deutscher Widerstand*. The GDW's historical representation of resistance highlights, on the one hand, the contradictory beliefs of some of the resisters, while, on the other, it also communicates the historical obstacles on the road to resistance. Abstaining from a naturalistic representation with stage props and fake historical artefacts, the exhibition adopts a quiet language of symbols that evokes the historical distance that separates the contemporary visitor invariably from the worlds of the different resistance groupings. The curators of the GDW thus draw attention to the otherness of the past, resisting the type of instrumentalization which is part and parcel of the officially enshrined memory of resistance.

The mutation of resistance discourse which is evident in the GDW's critical appraisal is further underlined by the majority of literary examples discussed in this chapter: Wibke Bruhns's autobiographical narrative *Meines Vaters Land*, Friedrich Christian Delius's *Mein Jahr als Mörder* and Sibylle Mulot's *Nachbarn* all challenge the public remembrance of resistance from the point of view of family history. The privatization of history in these texts makes literature an instrument of critical analysis, illuminating the deficits of official cultural memory from a transgenerational perspective. Bruhns's critical engagement with conservative resistance questions the legacy of the men of the 20 July 1944, and the prevalent idea that the notion of "das andere Deutschland" represents a viable tradition for later generations. Delius telescopes a forgotten story of left-wing resistance through the eyes of a former member of 1968, adding an important building block to the fragmented story of resistance. Furthermore, this double perspective allows Delius to examine the transgenerational disturbance of tradition. For in Delius's view, the ideological antagonism between the "guilty" parental generation and their offspring only masked a defensiveness that was shared by both generations. Exposing the crude instrumentalization of the cultural memory of resistance during the Cold War period, the novel also lays bare the lasting impairment of the German language. In this way, the novel shows that, after the Second World War, tradition can only be thought of in terms of an agitated heritage that is a fragile and uncertain one. Full of symbolic nodes that point to the presence of unmastered phantoms of the past, this heritage, however, ought not be dismissed as the 1968 generation suggested. Instead, the novel proposes a symptomatic analysis that combines critical inquiry with empathy for the participants of the vagaries of history. Similarly, Sibylle Mulot's anatomy of the memory of French *Résistance* in a small community shows that this prime *lieu de mémoire* of French national consciousness is shadowed by repressed counter-narratives that undermine the reified nature of cultural memory. The ethnographic perspective on the highly ambivalent memory of resistance in a provincial French town also illuminates that, as the subject of self-conscious discourse, the idea of community has lost its binding force. Applied to German resistance this means that all attempts to reify the memory of resistance are unsettled by the subliminal awareness that the idea of an unbroken tradition has been fundamentally impaired. The impairment of tradition thus emerges as the productive shadow of the cultural memory of resistance in Germany today. However, where this self-consciousness is abandoned, one is faced with outright fantasy as, for example, in Michael Wallner's *April in Paris*. This novel exemplifies the type of postmemorial discourse that replaces historical reflection with a highly tendentious appropriation of the past that abandons the ethical distinction between perpetrator and victim. Examined from a wider angle, the trivialization of resistance discourse in this narrative underlines once more the inevitable shift from a memory culture to a postmemorial culture that takes increasing liberties in terms of its representational choices.

As one of the most powerful phenomena of popular mass culture, cinematic depictions of resistance deserve the critic's special attention. With their high production values and linear narratives that concentrate on character, these films belong to the genre of "heritage films" which are defined by a postmemorial perspective that "address[es] viewers whose entire knowledge of these events is based on various media of cultural transmission".[81] As Matthias Fiedler argues, as a cultural institution, cinema "reflects the tension between public and private, the public act of going to the cinema and watching a movie with strangers while still isolated in the darkness of the theater and in one's private, individual reception of the film".[82] My analysis of three cinematic representations of resistance shows that the popularization of resistance narratives through film does not inevitably result in trivialization. While both Jo Baier's *Stauffenberg. Der 20. Juli 1944* and Marc Rothemund's *Sophie Scholl. Die letzten Tage* focus on the heroic individual, they employ a comparable cinematic language to very different effect. Baier's allegorization of the events of the 20th July plot as an archaic father – son conflict ultimately transforms resistance back into myth by dislodging it from its historical context. Rothemund, however, avoids such mythologization by means of a subtle postmemorial iconography that shows the protagonist as a modern young woman in a bygone era. Although both films reanimate some of the generic features of the resistance discourse in that they both appeal to the idea of a moral legacy, they also indicate the historical distance that separates the contemporary viewer from the world depicted. Von Trotta's *Rosenstraße* popularizes a collective story of resistance from a feminist perspective. While the film employs melodrama, it undermines straightforward identification by way of a postmemorial structure that focuses on remembrance as a collaborative project between a first-generation eye-witness and a third-generation investigator. Accentuating its representational choices, the film clearly signals its concern for a previously largely forgotten aspect of social history.

The mutation of the German resistance narratives thus underlines the diversification of cultural memory. Instead of the pious remembrance of resistance, a range of competing narratives has emerged that provides evidence of a new historical consciousness in Germany today. While this new consciousness is characterized by the privatization of history, the majority of examples discussed here suggest that this takes place within a framework of historical reflection. Probing the moral legacy of the resistance, the contemporary resistance narrative understands resistance as a mode of critical and empathetic inquiry into the contested meanings of tradition.

6
Hitler Youth Autobiographies: Günter Grass's *Beim Häuten der Zwiebel* and Joachim Fest's *Ich nicht*

Autobiography and identity discourses

Until the arrival of post-structuralism in the 1980s, the debate on autobiography was largely genre-driven, focusing on attempts to distinguish autobiography from memoir, diary and biography and also from fiction. However, the project to establish clear genre criteria encountered a number of insurmountable epistemological problems. Not only were the boundaries between autobiography and other testimonial genres fluid in the extreme, but, more importantly, autobiography could not be identified as non-fiction because, on the one hand, fiction often employs autobiographical modes of self-expression and, likewise, autobiography frequently relies on fictionalizing strategies.

As a result of the busy traffic between autobiography and fiction, genre debates have largely been replaced by discursive approaches which focus on the conventions that guide our understanding of autobiography. Philippe Lejeune coined the helpful notion of an "autobiographical pact"; this presupposes that the reader believes in the identity of the author and protagonist of the autobiography.[1] While this identification of the author with the voice in the text itself reflects our strong desire for a "reality effect" in Roland Barthes's sense of the term[2], it is important to remember that autobiography is never the natural product of the author's lived life. As Paul de Man argues, autobiography is the effect of a textual rhetoric that influences the autobiographer's choices.[3] To put it differently, while autobiography has a strong mimetic appeal, it should not be defined by its enhanced referentiality, but rather by its preoccupation with modern identity discourses. In recent debates, the notion of "life writing" has established itself as a discursive category that captures a wide range of ego-documents, including autobiography, biography, oral history or even reality television programmes. The notion of life writing emphasizes the performance of identity through story-telling.[4]

From the early modern period to the 18th century, autobiography established itself as a dominant discourse precisely because it explores the complex relationship between the self and its social environment while simultaneously celebrating modernity's central ideas of autonomy and individuality. Jean-Jacques Rousseau is paradigmatic of this trend. In his *Confessions*, published in 1782, Rousseau secularized and radicalized the Augustinian model of autobiographical confession.[5] As has been noted by many critics, Rousseau mobilizes a fleet of metaphors of transparency in order to authenticate a subjectivity which, in its fragile vulnerability, nevertheless manages to assert itself in opposition to a damaging social order.[6] His gesture of total self-revelation promised to paint the unique and exact picture of a human being in all his veracity.[7] Such uncompromising transparency becomes an important precondition of modern subjectivity.[8]

For Rousseau the uniqueness of his subjectivity was founded in the totality of self-inquiry. However, Goethe overturned this premise later with the programmatically entitled autobiography *Dichtung und Wahrheit* (Poetry and Truth).[9] As Goethe explained in a much-cited letter to King Ludwig of Bavaria, dated 12 January 1830, he was concerned with the representation of a "foundational truth in his life" insofar "as he could access it".[10] While this caveat already delimits the subject's ability of recall, Goethe went beyond merely disclaiming a naively conceived idea of veracity. For Goethe, the construction of autobiographical truthfulness inevitably involved the power of imagination and poetry. In this way, he undermined the false opposition between fiction and truth in favour of the notion of a retrospective truthfulness that does not reflect the past as it happened but rather the autobiographer's engagement with the past in the present.

Rousseau's and Goethe's opposite positions mark two key moments in the history of modern autobiography. Other models have since emerged, dispelling the unity of life and work that characterizes both autobiographies. Nevertheless, the issue of how to conceptualize autobiographical truthfulness continues to accompany autobiographical discourse to this day. Autobiography has remained a deeply introspective mode of self-expression which highlights the fact that identity does not emerge naturally from one's experiences. As Anthony Giddens observes, identity discourses are themselves the product of a modernity that uproots and distances individuals from their communities.[11] Globalization has aggravated this crisis of belonging by undermining precisely those powerful national topographies of identity that, from the late 18th until the 20th century, bridged the gap between the self and the social environment by means of the notion of a national identity through birth. In the words of Zygmunt Bauman, the "naturalness" of the assumption that "belonging-through-birth" meant, automatically and unequivocally, belonging to a nation was a laboriously construed convention; the appearance of "naturalness" could be anything but "natural". Unlike the mini-societies of mutual familiarity, where most men and women in premodern times spent their lives from cradle to grave, "nation" was an imagined entity that could enter the *Lebenswelt* only if mediated by the artifice of a concept.[12]

Although the rhetoric of belonging disguised the artificiality of national identity, the phenomenon of naturalness helped to promote the idea of a non-negotiable rootedness based on birth. By contrast, in our transnational era of large-scale migration, nationhood and nationality have been hollowed out as reliable guarantors of identity. Nevertheless, the longing to belong and to own a personal history remains a driving force in contemporary identity discourses which, in the political arena, are increasingly voiced through ethnic, religious and even racial assertions of identity. The resurgence of these modern and all-too-often xenophobic categories in our postmodern age shows that, in spite of the erosion of traditional concepts of identity, individual selves are "locative systems" which, in the words of the cultural psychologist Ciarán Benson, remain defined by the need for anchorage in places.[13]

The Hitler Youth generation in post-war Germany

The analysis of contemporary family narratives in this study focuses on the emergence of a transgenerational dialogue in unified Germany against the backdrop of a public awareness that the last eye-witnesses of the Third Reich are passing away. As we saw in previous chapters, the move away from the sharp inter-generational antagonisms that characterized the 1960s and 1970s towards a new era of transgenerational understanding gives expression to a desire for historical and genealogical continuity in a time of massive technological, social and geopolitical change. Autobiographies by members of the so-called Hitler Youth generation should be placed in this context. From the mid-1990s, a range of autobiographical texts appeared that scrutinized the connections between personal historical experience, on the one hand, and this generation's ideological outlook after the war, on the other. Suddenly, the privatization of the historical became a main concern for the aging members of the Hitler Youth generation who began to reassess the long-term effects of the Third Reich through autobiography. As this chapter argues, this project also entailed a revaluation of their own cultural and political engagement in post-war German affairs.

Born around 1930, this generation was brought up in the age of ideologies to believe blindly in National Socialism and in the *Führer*; after 1945, these young men and women had to come to terms with the experience of Germany's total defeat and with a biographical caesura that divided their lives into a delegitimized past, on the one hand, and a legitimate concern for a radically different present, on the other. Also known as the "sceptical" generation[14], its members were the first to reject the apologist victim discourse in the Germany of the 1950s. They became the prime advocates of a critical engagement with Germany's National Socialist past, criticizing, in particular, the political continuities in the post-war period.[15] However, in recent years the long cultural and political dominance of this generation in post-war Germany has become a matter of public and academic debate. For example, Sigrid Weigel has argued that the Hitler Youth generation only managed to assume such an authoritative role because its members based their biographies on the "paradoxical construct of knowledge without guilt".[16] Due to their age, they carried no legal responsibility as perpetrators but they shared in the first-hand knowledge of the Hitler era.[17] Weigel specifically singled out Martin Walser, Peter Rühmkorf, Günter Grass and Hans Magnus Enzensberger as prime instigators of a gender-specific normative style that circulated the notion of an innocent birth, which – ironically – the German catastrophe had made possible.

Weigel's criticism raises a number of issues: first, her argument about the cultural dominance of the Hitler Youth generation in post-war West Germany sidelines the important role of those post-war writers who were at least one generation older than the Hitler Youth, such as Alfred Andersch (born in 1914), Heinrich Böll (born in 1917), Günter Eich (born in 1907) or Hans-Werner Richter (born in 1908). Secondly, she presents a far too unifying view of the sceptical generation's intellectual and ideological outlook. The first-hand experience of the Third Reich does indeed mark common biographical ground; however, the members of the Hitler Youth generation have drawn very diverse conclusions about the long-term effects of the Third Reich, on the post-war order and on German cultural memory. The following pages briefly illustrate this diversity with reference to three autobiographies by members of the Hitler Youth generation: Martin Walser, Ludwig Harig and Christa Wolf. We will see that the three writers address the question of guilt in very different ways: while Walser does indeed attempt to write his autobiographical novel from the point of view of the innocent child, Harig and Wolf use autobiography for a form of critical self-analysis that leaves little room for innocence.

In his autobiographical novel *Ein springender Brunnen*, Martin Walser insisted on his inalienable right to remember his childhood in terms of total historical innocence. Set in Wasserburg on Lake Constance, the novel anchors a childhood idyll in a local community which, in spite of its participation in National Socialism, remained attached to notions of regional identity. Walser deliberately taps into *Heimat* discourse to evoke Proustian childhood memories that refuse to obey the conventions of contritional writing. Pitching the idea of an authentic recall of the past against political correctness, Walser formulates what he calls "the illusory aim" of an "interesseloses Interesse an der Vergangenheit" (disinterested interest in the past).[18] Helmut Schmitz has rightly argued that in Walser's novel the past appears "as under glass, an irretrievably lost continent from which no road but the immediacy of memory leads to the present persona".[19] Walser represses the inevitable mediation of all our memories through the portrayal of a childhood idyll which is sealed off from the author's later historical knowledge. Defending the immediacy of experience against what Walser perceives as the destructive onslaught of historical reflection, the narrative refuses to contextualize history. As Schmitz argues, the "motor of its narrative energy is the unspoken fear of the invalidation of his childhood memories by any form of posterior awareness. It is this assumed, rather than real, invalidation by the perspective of Nazi victims against which the narrative mobilises its energies."[20]

By contrast to Walser's denial of the historicization of the past, Ludwig Harig, an experimental post-war poet and writer, adopts a much more self-reflexive stance in his three-part autobiography, which takes the reader from the Weimar Republic into post-war West Germany.[21] For Harig, who was born in 1927, the caesura of 1945 and the biographical discontinuity between his younger Nazi self and his post-war self requires a mode of expression that gives voice to the fragmentation of autobiographical experience. *Weh dem, der aus der Reihe tanzt* (Woe to him who steps out of line, 1990) highlights not only the indoctrination of the Hitler Youth generation during the 1930s and early 1940s, but it also shows that the normality of family life which Walser had tried to reclaim cannot be detached from Nazi policies because these had tangible effects on the local community.[22] Likewise, the third part of Harig's trilogy, *Wer mit den Wölfen heult, wird Wolf* (Whoever Runs with the Pack Becomes a Wolf, 1996), recreates the historical rupture of 1945 on a personal and collective level. Here Harig employs the metaphor of the kaleidoscope to capture the succession of splintered images that cannot be synthesized in the manner which Walser later advocated. While the autobiographer explores the multiple gaps between his former and present selves, he does not abdicate historical responsibility for his younger alter ego. Rather, he adopts a critical perspective that turns the project of autobiographical self-inquiry into a case study of the Hitler Youth generation itself. In this way, Harig embraces the project of symptomatic self-analysis that had already underpinned Christa Wolf's autobiographical novel *Kindheitsmuster* (1976; Engl. transl. *A Model Childhood*, 1982).

Also born in 1927, the GDR writer Christa Wolf was one of the first members of the Hitler Youth generation to embark on a project of working through the Nazi past from a deeply personal point of view.[23] Her poetic subjectivism defied the official interpretation of National Socialism in the GDR, according to which Nazism was a bourgeois imperialist phenomenon which had been objectively overcome by the socialist state. According to Wolf, the positing of a complete ideological rupture between Nazi Germany and the GDR had created a moral vacuum which dissociated GDR citizens from their personal history and, by implication, from the idea of historical responsibility. Wolf attempts to fill this vacuum by means of an autobiographical discourse which makes personal history a paradigmatic case study of a collective complicity that is already alluded to in the German title "childhood pattern". Like Walser, Wolf employs the third person for her autobiographical alter ego, but she uses this device to very different effect: while, in Walser's narrative, the third person detaches Johann from the autobiographer, Wolf self-consciously explores the relationship between the remembering self and Nelly, the child. She adopts a method of subjective authenticity which, while recognizing the pastness of the past, attempts to retrieve it by means of a carefully orchestrated process of mediation.[24] By contrast to Walser, Wolf sees mediation as indispensable for the construction of authenticity.[25]

The brief comparison of Walser, Harig and Wolf highlights widely differing attitudes to autobiographical discourse and memory. Furthermore, these examples underline that all autobiographical discourse is inevitably caught up in a paradoxical self-inquiry that sets fictionalizing self-inventions in motion. However, this paradox gains an even greater historical dimension in the case of Hitler Youth autobiographies which negotiate the human need for biographical continuity[26] against the backdrop of massive historical discontinuities. The three examples mentioned above already indicate that these narratives inevitably imply questions of historical responsibility, in terms of both a responsible treatment of their subject matter and a responsibility towards the victims of National Socialism. It is clear that in the case of Hitler Youth autobiographies, the question of truthfulness cannot be dealt with satisfactorily from a merely poststructuralist perspective which emphasizes the rhetorical nature of truth in all autobiographical writing. Rather, it is necessary to reconfigure the question of truthfulness in terms of an ethics of remembering which recognizes the need for objective historical documentation, on the one hand, and an affective engagement with the past, on the other. Writing on the subject of Holocaust historiography, Dominick LaCapra has suggested that historians can negotiate this difficult terrain by what he terms "empathic unsettlement". By this he means a mode of inquiry that "poses a barrier to closure in discourse and places in jeopardy harmonizing or spiritually uplifting accounts of extreme events from which we attempt to derive reassurance or a benefit".[27] Applied to Hitler Youth autobiographies, this does not mean that the Holocaust must feature prominently in these narratives, but rather that the autobiographer should recognize an ethical obligation towards history. While the testimonial nature of autobiography reflects the experiential dimension of history, which is often absent from standard historical narratives, its best examples resist the type of ahistorical identification with the past that Walser advocates. As Peter Sloterdijk has argued, in the 20th century autobiography inevitably focuses on disruptive experiences, which cannot be integrated into a harmonious life-story.[28] Where this is not the case, autobiography becomes tendentious, subscribing either to a mythical past or to a particular ideology which wilfully erases history's multiple fractures from a would-be unifying point of view.

In order to elucidate this further, the following sections compare and contrast two autobiographies by two prominent post-war figures who were life-long political opponents: Günter Grass's *Beim Häuten der Zwiebel* (Peeling the Onion) and Joachim Fest's *Ich nicht. Erinnerungen an eine Kindheit und Jugend* (Not I. Memories of a Childhood and Youth), both published in 2006. This analysis focuses on their management of the process of autobiographical recall. Although, conformism and resistance emerge as key tropes that guide autobiographical self-inquiry in both the texts, the two authors employ the confessional paradigm to very different effects.

Grass's confession and the public debate

The annual silly season in the German media came to an abrupt end on 12 August 2006 when the *Frankfurter Allgemeine Zeitung* published an interview with Günter Grass about his forthcoming autobiography *Beim Häuten der Zwiebel*.[29] Although large sections of this interview focused on literary issues, primarily on the difficulty of finding an appropriate autobiographical form and on the manifold interconnections between Grass's life and his work, a storm broke loose in the German media over Grass's revelation that he had served in the 10th tank division of the Waffen-SS for a few months at the very end of the war. In the course of the interview, Grass revealed that a personal sense of guilt about his membership of the SS only arose after the end of the war when he had to face the question of German collective guilt. When asked whether the post-war period had failed to present an appropriate moment for him to admit his SS membership, Grass stated,

> I don't know. I may have believed that my writing would have been enough. I went through my learning curve and I have drawn my conclusions from that. But a residual blemish remained. Because of this, it was always clear to me that this residue would have to find its own space, should I ever decide to write something auto-biographical.[30]

In what, at first, appears to be a rather evasive answer, Grass makes an interesting point about the role of autobiography: although his fictional works, above all the Danzig trilogy, tackled the issues of widespread support for Hitler and petit-bourgeois conformism head-on, his former SS membership remained an indelible blemish in his life until he found the right autobiographical form. At the beginning of the same interview, Grass highlighted the unreliability of autobiographical truth, arguing that it is subject to the distorting tricks of memory.[31] Here, however, he implies a subtle but important epistemological difference between autobiography and fiction: although his fictional works were closely linked to his life story, a point to which I return later, he needed to write an autobiography to deal with the fundamental question of personal responsibility. Grass seems to suggest that, although autobiography itself is a literary construct, its enhanced mimetic appeal makes it the ideal playing field for addressing the transformation of historical experience through the prism of the writer's imagination. The issue is thus not autobiography's enhanced referentiality, but rather the fruitful traffic between biography and fiction. In the following, I wish to demonstrate that this trade-off between biography and fiction is a major concern of Grass's confessional autobiography. I argue that the confession of shame and guilt, which characterizes the first part of the autobiography, is counter-balanced by an exploration of the role of imagination, which is shown to be ahead of the discursive understanding of history. The notion of belatedness emerges in this narrative as a key trope of auto-biographical discourse, which allows Grass to trace how a range of biographical episodes, including his stint as an SS soldier, resurfaced in his literary writings. In this way, Grass highlights the cultural product-iveness of deferral and he assigns literary imagination a key role in the complex task of dealing with the NS past. However, the urgent confes-sional tone of the narrative also emphasizes the inadequacies of a solely literary encounter with the past. The autobiographer suggests that at the end of his life he needed to complement his literary imagination with a final gesture of owning-up in order to overcome the gap between his public persona and his intimate self-knowledge. This transmutation of confession makes *Beim Häuten der Zwiebel* a true "Alterswerk" (work of old age) in the tradition of Goethe's *Dichtung und Wahrheit*. Before analyzing the interrelationship between confession and imagination, it is necessary to deal with the media's response to Grass's confession, as this illuminates the ongoing transformation of Germany's memory culture.

Rather than focusing on the issue of his SS membership, the debate which followed Grass's admission revolved primarily around the belatedness of his confession, effectively brushing aside his insightful reflections on the difficulty of writing autobiography. Frank Schirrmacher opened this German memory contest with a lead article in the *FAZ* which argued that Grass's intervention in the 1985 Bitburg debate, a debate which centred on Kohl's and Reagan's visit to the war cemetery in Bitburg, would have been more honest if the public had known that "out of an enraptured member of the Waffen-SS, one of the youths lying buried there, could have become someone like him – not just a defender but a protagonist of freedom and democracy".[32] For Schirrmacher, Grass's revelation is the final chapter in the long German post-war narrative about guilt and redemption. Similarly, Gustav Seibt of *Die Süddeutsche Zeitung* made the point that from an historical perspective one could hardly blame Grass for a brief stint as an SS soldier at the very end of the war. After all, he had been drafted into the SS with the mental condition of what Seibt calls "a moderately intelligent, rather narrow-minded little 'Pimpf'. His soldierly commitment was limited to running away and getting wounded".[33] According to Seibt, however, one should blame Grass for his uncompromising denial of doubt in his many public interventions in Germany's post-war politics. He concludes that one should distinguish Günter Grass's public persona from the writer whose works are far more intelligent than the public voice of their author. By contrast, Jens Jessen in *Die Zeit* was less moderate in his judgement: expressing disgust at the calculated manner in which Grass had staged his public confession shortly before the appearance of his autobiography, he suggested that Grass had cunningly converted his public confession into a publicity stunt.[34] In other words, Jessen queried not just the belatedness of the admission but also the sincerity of Grass's motivation for revealing his buried past. Stephan Speicher in the *taz* echoes this charge and adds that Grass's admission was not just simply too late but also too vague.[35] Similarly, writing for the *Frankfurter Rundschau*, Christian Thomas notes a monstrously mono-syllabic tone and moral taciturnity in Grass's interview, which is in marked contrast to the verbosity of his literary writings. Returning to the issue of the belatedness of Grass's admission, he asks "who would have reproached him?".[36]

Thomas's question entirely misses the significance of the Grass debate, which points to a steady shift in German memory politics since unifica-tion. Arguably, in the 1980s, Grass's admission would have met a much more ferocious response as historical research at the time concentrated on the extent and on the systemic nature of SS crimes committed on the eastern front. In all likelihood, an earlier debate on Grass's SS member-ship would have seriously damaged his reputation. While this is open to speculation, it is evident that, 20 years later, the focus of the debate has shifted away from historical facts and on to the mediation of these facts in the public domain. In this way, the Grass debate highlights the ongoing transformation of Germany's discourse of contrition since unification. Interestingly, the sense of outrage evident in some of the media coverage stands in marked contrast to the public perception of the debate: while certain participants in this latest memory contest were all too eager to censor Grass for what they interpreted as his hypocritical public persona, the general public did not share this sentiment. In an Infratest survey carried out for the *Spiegel* which questioned whether Grass's opinion on political or moral issues would continue to matter after his admission, 65 per cent of those interviewed answered this ques-tion positively.[37] While the wider public thus gave expression to a sense of exhaustion with the culture of accusation, the media continued to fuel the debate, recycling the same arguments about the belatedness of Grass's admission. Therefore, the question is raised as to what this particular memory contest tells us about the German public management of the past.

Above all, the Grass debate emphasized the centrality of generation in contemporary German identity debates. Some participants saw the controversy as an opportunity to dismantle the political and intellectual authority of the Hitler Youth generation, which had dominated post-war affairs for more than 40 years. The *Spiegel* launched a sweeping attack on Grass as an icon of the post-war German intellectual scene.[38] Its cover issue on 21 August 2006 showed Grass as an Oskar Matzerath, drumming an SS helmet. Entitled *Der Blechtrommler* (The Tin Drummer), with the word "Blech" highlighted, the cartoon implied that Grass's belated confession turned his many interventions in Germany's post-war politics into a heap of rubbish. Unsurprisingly, the lead article denounced Grass as a "moralistic executioner",[39] hammering him for his alleged black-and-white thinking in an article that in style and argument reiterates the Manichean categories that it purports to diagnose as a characteristic of Grass's political thinking.[40] Interestingly, the *Spiegel*'s indictment of Grass's public persona largely ignored Grass, the author. Detailed references to Grass's published essays or works would have got in the way of the magazine's deliberate representation of Grass as a self-righteous simpleton with an inflated public profile. The iconoclastic desire to topple a living monument explains perhaps the astonishing ignorance of the statement: "his memoir *Peeling the Onion* is not exactly a document of clarity".[41] Indeed, autobiographies are not documents that archive an individual's life in the manner of a birth and death register.

However, there were other voices from a younger generation that also took issue with the long dominance of the Hitler Youth generation in Germany's intellectual life. The generational argument was openly introduced by Georg Klein who read the entire controversy as Grass's failed attempt to force the hand of history by orchestrating the continued standing and growth of his works as well as his own public appearances in the media.[42] Other interventions by a range of younger writers and commentators gave expression to a deep-seated sense of tiredness with this type of German memory contest that continues to make the NS past a prime concern of the present at the expense of other more contemporary and pressing issues.

The controversy over Grass's hypocrisy seems to mark the end of the Hitler Youth generation's intellectual prominence. The public discussion of when it would have been appropriate for Grass to have made this confession – there was consensus that 1985 would have been the right moment – was underpinned by the idea that the moral and political authority of post-war German intellectuals depends not so much on the quality of their argument but on the public transparency of their inner selves. According to this logic, the modern subject is not so much a fragmented and split self, governed by subconscious and contradictory impulses, but it is viewed as an authoritative archivist of a personal past that can be accessed and made public at any given point in time. In this way, the figure of the writer as archivist upholds the false dichotomy between forgetting and remembrance, between repression and mastery that had marked the West German discourse of contrition since the late 1960s. For Grass, the writer, it made sense to deal with the important question "why only now?" in his autobiography, a question that he had already approached indirectly in his previous book *Im Krebsgang*. Some of his censorious critics were eager to use this open question to settle old scores and to demolish the lasting influence of centre-left intellectuals in the public domain.[43]

Constructing autobiographical truthfulness: Grass's *Beim Häuten der Zwiebel*

The question remains: how does Grass handle the issue of autobiographical truthfulness in *Beim Häuten der Zwiebel*? Written in a highly self-conscious manner, the book does not begin with Grass's birth and early childhood memories but rather with the outbreak of the Second World War on 1 September 1939, which for Grass marks the abrupt end of his childhood; and it ends with the publication of *Die Blechtrommel* in 1959. The first 180 pages cover Grass's experiences as an adolescent during National Socialism, including his attempt to sign up for the submarine corps as a 15-year-old, the "Flakhelfer" (anti-aircraft auxiliary) training he received and his brief service as an SS soldier in 1945. The following 300 pages deal with the immediate post-war era and his development as a sculptor, an artist and a writer. In the following, I shall analyze how the book moves from a confessional account of Grass's youthful errors to a picaresque rendition of the immediate post-war period and, finally, to an intellectual autobiography that traces the cultural influences that helped to liberate German intellectual life from the parochial atmosphere of the NS period.

The chapters dealing with Grass's NS youth are punctuated by highly self-conscious reflections on the malleability and cunning tricks of human memory that, as Grass writes, tend to play the hide-and-seek games of children: "Sie verkriecht sich. Zum Schönreden neigt sie und schmückt, oft ohne Not. Sie widerspricht dem Gedächtnis, das sich pedantisch gibt und zänkisch rechthaben will" (*BH*, 8; It hides away. It tends to enhance things and often embellishes without need. It contradicts memory, which is pedantic and which churlishly wants to be right). Here, Grass sets up the well-known opposition between "Erinnerung" (remembering) and "Gedächtnis" (memory), between our subjective acts of remembrance, on the one hand, and a more objective archival memory, on the other. In the course of the narrative this difference is further elaborated through two complementary tropes that guide the autobiographer's self-inquiry: the typically Grassian title metaphor of peeling onions and the image of studying objects encased in a piece of amber. The organic image of peeling onions emphasizes the layered dimension of autobiographical remembrance which disguises those biographical facts that are incompatible with the autobiographer's self-image:

> Wenn ihr mit Fragen zugesetzt wird, gleicht die Erinnerung einer Zwiebel, die gehäutet sein möchte, damit freigelegt werden kann, was Buchstab nach Buchstab ablesbar steht: selten eindeutig, oft in Spiegelschrift oder sonstwie verrätselt.
> Unter der ersten, noch trockenen Haut findet sich die nächste, die kaum gelöst, feucht eine dritte freigibt, unter der die vierte, fünfte warten und flüstern. Und jede weitere schwitzt zu lange gemiedene Wörter aus, auch schnörkelige Zeichen, als habe sich ein Geheimniskrämer von jung an, als die Zwiebel noch keimte, verschlüsseln wollen. (*BH*, 9)

> [If harassed with questions, memory is like an onion which needs to be peeled in order to reveal that which can be read letter by letter: seldom clear-cut, often in mirror writing or codified in some way.
> Beneath the first dry layer there is another one which, hardly has it been removed in its moistness, uncovers a third skin, under which the fourth and fifth are waiting and whispering. And each further one sweats out words which were avoided for too long, squiggly characters, as if a mystery monger had been trying to encode them from early on, while the onion was still germinating.]

It is important to note that the title metaphor is as ambiguous as the activity of autobiographical recall. While, on the one hand, it implies that the autobiographer must peel back a multitude of biographical layers in search of his bygone selves, on the other hand, it also suggests that this method cannot ultimately break through the distorting effects of autobiographical remembrance. For the self remains a construct that disappears in the thick undergrowth of fiction (*BH*, 39). According to this image, the writer's imagination produces a camouflage of anecdotes that disguises the autobiographer's deeply ingrained sense of shame about his youthful conformism. The notion of shame is introduced early on when Grass relates various episodes in which his youthful alter ego failed to ask obvious questions about the disturbing disappearance of people in his immediate environment, such as his uncle Franz, who was executed by the National Socialists for fighting on the Polish side. The reader learns that the uncle's death was never talked about in the Grass family. Reflecting on the possible reasons for his own cowardice, Grass suggests that his awareness of a moral blemish hindered him from addressing his silence earlier: "Also schreibe ich über die Schande und die ihr nach-hinkende Scham. Selten genutzte Wörter, gesetzt im Nachholverfahren" (*BH*, 17; thus I write about the disgrace and the sense of shame which stumbles behind it. Words seldom used, put down as a belated admis-sion). Here, Grass introduces the well-known anthropological distinc-tion between "Schande" (disgrace) and "Scham" (shame) that, according to Ruth Benedict, regulates social activity: while "Schande" refers to the violation of cultural or social values and the loss of face in the public domain, "Scham" captures a fundamental disturbance of one's internalized norms.[44] Interestingly, in the above passage, Grass invokes both ideas and moves from the collective norms that censor behaviour to the individual's conscience. In this way, he shows how these two expressions of social control reinforced each other mutually, guiding his behaviour in the post-war period. While, after the war, his sense of disgrace and shame resulted in denial, the autobiographer can now mobilize these moral sentiments for his confessional narrative.

There is, however, a further implication: what appears as a straight-forward confession of an earlier omission carries with it a complex justification of the idea of belatedness. For the belated admission that Grass talks about makes autobiography the very site where a Freudian deferral of remembrance can gain literary shape. But if deferral is the prime trope of autobiographical discourse, then it makes little sense to blame the autobiographer for his belated confession. To put it differ-ently, if the confession of an omission is the quintessential speech act of modern autobiography, then omission is the very signature of the autobiographical imagination.

Based on the inevitable ambiguity of confession, Grass relates other examples of his conformism. He exemplifies his failure by including counter-narratives that represent individual resistance to the system. One of the most prominent examples in this respect is the story of an anonymous young man whom Grass calls "Wirtunsowasnicht" (Wedontdosuchthings): a member of Jehovah's Witnesses, this young man refused to hold or even touch a gun during his military training.[45] In spite of various strategies employed by his superiors and his fellow soldiers to coax, punish, bully and beat him into submission, he stands by his refusal which he reiterates with the same simple words: "We don't do such things". The simplicity and conviction of this refusal unsettle the other trainee warriors considerably: "Seine Haltung veränderte uns. Von Tag zu Tag bröckelte ab, was verfestigt zu sein schien. In unseren Haß mischte sich Staunen, schließlich in Fragen gekleidete Bewunderung" (*BH*, 100; his behaviour changed us. From day to day that which appeared rooted broke away. Astonishment was mixed in our hatred, wonder disguised as questions). A real threat to the NS ethos of group behaviour, the young man disappears one day from the military training camp, and the autobiographer speculates that he probably ended up in Stutthof, the concentration camp just outside Danzig. On the overt narrative level, such counter-narratives exemplify the idea of resistance to the system, demonstrating that alternative non-conformist behaviour would have been possible. However, by highlighting the repressiveness of the NS State, they justify, in an underhand way, the widespread conformism that is the subject of Grass's confessional narrative. It becomes clear that autobiographical confession is a dialectical process in which each act of self-accusation triggers moments of self-exoneration. This dialectic also explains why the autobiographer reiterates his confession through a series of similarly structured episodes. For example, a further story of individual resistance involves Grass's Latin teacher, Monsignor Stachnik, who was also imprisoned in Stutthof. Once again the autobiographer reproaches his youthful self in a demonstrative gesture for not having asked the right questions although everyone was talking about the camp (*BH*, 45). A few paragraphs later, he reports that when he visited his old teacher in the 1970s, he brought up his sense of persistent guilt, a confession that the old Monsignor declines smilingly, apparently absolving the writer from his guilt (*BH*, 48). This mock-confession underlines once again the dialectic of self-accusation and self-exoneration that propels Grass's confessional narrative. Even a layer of the onion whispers a range of convenient excuses into the autobiographer's ear: "du bist doch fein raus, warst nur ein dummer

Junge, hast nichts Schlimmes getan, hast niemanden, keinen Nachbarn denunziert [...]" (*BH*, 44; you are well out of it, you were just a silly boy, you didn't do anything bad, you never denounced anyone, none of the neighbours). On the one hand, the metaphor of the onion gives expression to the idea that the peeling back of different layers of bygone selves stresses the autobiographer's vulnerability; on the other, the onion is a basic ingredient in a concoction that services his desire for exculpation.

Notwithstanding the inevitable compromises of human memory, Grass insists, however, that the work of imagination is bounded by historically verifiable truth. Working through his deep sense of shame by means of the confessional narrative, the autobiographer claims that he can make glimpses of his former self visible that have been unaffected by distortion. In order to create a metaphor for the referential boundaries of autobiographical memory, Grass introduces the image of looking at an insect encased in a piece of amber (*BH*, 65).

This image suggests that some autobiographical memories are more knowing than others, a claim that the autobiographer exemplifies with reference to his awakening sexuality during adolescence. In the first instance, the amber metaphor is used to reveal the fairly innocuous sexual desire of the adolescent Grass; later, however, it exposes his continued belief in National Socialism at a time when the cracks in the façade of the regime had become ever more visible. Laying bare the strategies of exculpation and displacement that underpin his more anecdotal memories of the war period, the autobiographer depicts himself as grabbing a piece of amber which he keeps on a shelf above his writing lectern as a memento of the notion of an unalterable historical truth. In this way, studying the piece of amber helps him to find out "wie unbeschadet sich mein Glaube an den Führer trotz überprüfbarer Fassadenrisse, zunehmender Flüsterparolen und des überall, nun auch in Frankreich rückgängigen Frontverlaufs konserviert hatte" (*BH*, 106; how my belief in Hitler had been conserved in spite of the verifiable cracks in the façade, the increasing whispered messages and the retreating frontlines far and wide, now even in France). Accordingly, when Grass addresses his conscription into the SS, he notes that he can find no evidence that his younger self was shocked or revolted by the emblem of the SS (*BH*, 126). Reflecting that he probably saw the SS as an elite military force, Grass speculates that the 10th SS tank division might have exuded a sense of liberation for his younger self because it was named after Jörg von Frundsberg, a leader in the peasants' war of the early 16th century. He also draws attention to the cosmopolitan composition of some SS divisions, in which Norwegians, Danes, Dutch and French soldiers fought alongside Germans in order to stem the so-called "Bolshevist flood" (*BH*, 126–7). However, in the end he brushes aside such possible explanations as "Ausreden" (excuses) that failed to repress the emerging sense of guilt (*BH*, 127). Again, Grass demonstrates that the burden of an unshared secret both legitimates and necessitates the confessional narrative. Once more belatedness emerges as the prime motor of the autobiographical imaginary.

In this way, Grass's *Beim Häuten der Zwiebel* sets a contemporary version of the Goethean dialectic of *Dichtung und Wahrheit* in motion, which gives shape to the idea of a retrospective truthfulness that concerns not the past as such but the autobiographer's present engagement with this past. Since, in this text, the idea of truthfulness depends on demonstrative gestures of autobiographical self-consciousness, the autobiographer must continuously work over his key tropes. The act of autobiographical confession no longer aims to achieve total transparency of the autobiographer's selfhood, a claim that had underpinned Rousseau's seminal conception of modern subjectivity in the 18th century. Instead, it turns Rousseau's confident self-proclamation on its head by making the autobiographer's partial blindness a touchstone of autobiographical authenticity. This is particularly evident in the passages that deal with Grass's time at the front. Addressing the darker part of his biography, Grass now introduces a visual metaphor that recasts the dialectic between remembering and forgetting as a damaged film reel:

Ab dann reißt der Film. Sooft ich ihn flicke und wieder anlaufen lasse, bietet er Bildsalat. Irgendwo kann ich meine vergammelten Fußlappen wegwerfen und durch wollene Strümpfe ersetzen, die wir in einer geräumten Heereskammer finden, auch Unterhemden und Zeltplanen gegen Regen liegen in Stapeln dort. Bei einem Halt in der Flußniederung berühre ich blühende Weidenkätzchen.

Rief ein Kuckuck verfrüht? Zählte ich seine Rufe?

Und dann sehe ich die ersten Toten. Junge und alte Soldaten in Uniformen der Wehrmacht. An noch kahlen Chauseebäumen und Linden auf Marktplätzen hängen sie. Mit Pappschildern vor der Brust sind die Erhängten als "wehrkraftzersetzende Feiglinge" ausgewiesen. Ein Junge meines Alters, der zudem wie ich links gescheitelt ist, hängt neben einem betagten Offizier unbestimmten Ranges, den das Feldgericht vor dem Erhängen degradiert hat. Ein Leichenspalier, an

dem wir mit alles übertönendem Panzerkettengeräusch vorbeirattern.
Keine Gedanken, nur Bilder. (*BH*, 138–39)

[From there, the film is torn. No matter how often I stick it together
and let it run again, it simply offers chopped-up images. Somewhere
I throw away the rotting cloths swaddling my feet and replace them
with woollen socks, which we found in a cleared army depot, there
were also vests and water resistant tarpaulin lying there stacked in
piles. During a stop in the low areas of the river, I touch blossoming
catkin.

Did a cuckoo call early? Did I count its calls?

And then I see the first casualties. Young and old in *Wehrmacht*
army uniforms. They are hanging from bare trees along country roads
and from lime trees on market squares. With cardboard signs on their
chests, the hanged are marked out as "demoralizing cowards". A boy
my age, who, like me, wears a parting on the left side, dangles beside
an old officer of an unknown rank, whom the military tribunal had
degraded before hanging. A row of corpses past which we rattled, the
chains of the tank drowning out all noise. No thoughts, just images.]

The passage is somewhat reminiscent of anti-war films, such as Lewis
Milestone's adaptation of Remarque's *All Quiet on the Western Front*
(1930), which dramatized the experience of the so-called "lost generation" of the First World War in understated language. In a cinematic
motion, Grass zooms in here on the rags of military equipment before
focusing on the stark images of hanged *Wehrmacht* deserters. The small
iconographic incongruity between the peaceful image of the catkins
and the hanging soldiers authenticates this memory by drawing attention to nature's indifference to the scale of human destruction. The
scene thus overwrites the propagandist representations of the war in the
Wochenschau (weekly news reels) and in films such as *Kolberg*, which, as
the autobiographer emphasizes, had shaped the young Grass's outlook
on the war (*BH*, 123). However, although the cinematic rendition of the
discovery of the hanged soldiers authenticates this memory, the film
metaphor also draws attention to a range of editorial devices, including
blurred edges, cutting and lighting techniques. While, as illustrated in
the above episode, Grass employs such cinematic scenes for a realistic
representation of the cruelty of war, he also shows that they can be used
in the production of screen memories. Addressing the limits of all tropes
of autobiographical recall, Grass cautions his readers that they ought to
question the veracity of every episode, including those that appear to

be based on the most iconic detail (*BH*, 145). Later on, the narrative foregrounds the irresolvable ambiguity of autobiographical recall once more in the context of Grass's claim that he played dice with Joseph Ratzinger when he was a PoW in June 1945. His sister's exclamation, "Ehrlich, du lügst wie gedruckt!" (*BH*, 422; "really, you are lying your head off!"), reminds the reader of the constant trade-off between fact and fiction which underpins Grass's autobiography as a whole.

The at-times tortured acts of self-examination that interrupt the narrative proper are thus not just the vain poses of the author, as some critics have suggested, instead, they are indispensable speech acts in the attempt to make visible an irreconcilable rupture between the autobiographer's present self and his youthful counterpart. Thus, the autobiographer's blindness is as constitutive for this self-confession as that which he can see. For example, when dealing with the key moment of his conscription into the SS, the autobiographer claims that his memory produced nothing but an empty leaf, before he explores the delegation of biographical recall to fiction. In this context, Grass mentions *Hundejahre* (1963, Engl. transl. *Dog Years*, 1965) in which Harry Liebenau writes to Tulla Pokriefke about his experiences at the eastern front (*BH*, 114). Interestingly, Grass frames the quotation of a passage from the novel with a reflection on what one might call "fictional insufficiency". Although the novel is a fat tome – "über siebenhundert Seiten lang wälzen sich die *Hundejahre* dahin" (*BH*, 114; the *Dog Years* churn their way through over seven hundred pages) – it is ultimately an insufficient receptacle for the story of the autobiographer's life. The delegation of his SS past to fiction makes the writer complicit in the widespread denial of personal responsibility that had been popular in the post-war era. From a literary-historical point of view, the Danzig trilogy was a milestone on the road to illuminating the issue of widespread conformism during the NS era; from the point of view of the confessional narrative, it now appears as a screen narrative that helped to divorce the writer from his own past. As for *Beim Häuten der Zwiebel*, the sister's exclamation, "Ehrlich, du lügst wie gedruckt", is an ironic acknowledgement of the transfer of inassimilable biographical facts into his fictional works. In this way, the autobiographer admits that his lies went into print, while simultaneously winking conspiratorially at his knowing reader that this had been an advantageous endeavour. It should not be forgotten that, in this context, *Beim Häuten der Zwiebel* also shows that the irreconcilable split between Grass's former Nazi self and his post-war selves was the source of astonishing productivity. Tracing the genesis of works such as *Die Blechtrommel* (1959; Engl. transl. *The Tin Drum*, 1962), *Katz und*

Maus (1961; Engl. transl. *Cat and Mouse*, 1963), *Hundejahre* and others back to key autobiographical moments during the NS period, the auto-biographer explores the power of the literary imagination, which was ahead of his discursive analysis of history.

In the end, the confessional gesture of the first part of the text is superseded by the picaresque rendition of the immediate post-war era. After the war, the reader encounters a stray self who lives a vagabond-like existence in search of food, women and entertainment that is modelled on Grimmelshausen's *Simplicissimus*. For example, the chapters that cover his time as a PoW contain the amusing story of a cookery course that, according to Grass, was offered by a fellow PoW, a former chef from south-eastern Europe. Equipped with no real ingredients, the chef covered the preparation of "Hausmannskost" or plain fare in an entirely imaginary course that was attended by a group of hungry PoWs (*BH*, 205). Dramatizing the chef's evocative concoctions of mouth-watering dishes, Grass underlines the resilience of the human imagination against the backdrop of the reality of Germany's total defeat. The hunger for food is aggravated by carnal desires which Grass's inexperienced hero satisfies (temporarily) in the proverbial haystack, guided by a more experienced Inge from the Hunsrück (*BH*, 240). From a Freudian angle, such comical renditions may appear a defensive mechanism that could serve the repression of a more unpalatable truth about the moral ruin-ation of post-war Germans. However, as Wolfgang Preisendanz has pointed out, humour is a prime mode of articulating the incongruity of historical experience. Unlike historical discourse, which is guided by principles of historical relevance and exemplariness, comic renditions of history set aside all such criteria. Instead they articulate heterogene-ous and disparate stories that escape the historian's standard attribu-tions of meaning.[46] By homing in on the immediacy of the individual's situational historical experience, these stories undermine notions of historical relevance, intelligibility and coherence. In this way, Grass's grotesque rendition of the picaresque self in the immediate post-war period converts the moralizing self-consciousness of the first part of the autobiography into a comic representation of history's incongruities which articulates its own ambivalence.

The Grass in this part of the narrative appears a stray self without real orientation until his desire to become a sculptor emerges as a directing force. Once his young alter ego has managed to enrol for the art academy in Düsseldorf, the autobiography reads like a cultural history of Germany in the 1950s, where political restoration went hand in hand with a drive towards internationalization and liberalization in intellectual and cultural circles. Comparable to Ludwig Harig's, *Wer mit den Wölfen heult, wird Wolf* (1996), Grass's account of 1950s Germany emphasizes the disjunction between the personal and the political. For example, evoking the dance fever of the 1950s, including his own passion for dancing, Grass presents a collective celebration of survival against the backdrop of the horrors of war (*BH*, 304). Instead of condemning the much-debated "inability to mourn" in the manner of Sebald, the autobiographer implies that repression was an indispensable psychological defence mechanism that made room for collective and individual reorientation in the post-war era. One poignant example in this respect is a conversation between mother and son about the mother's and daughter's experience of multiple rape at the end of the war. Pressed by the son on this matter, the mother fends off his questions (*BH*, 321). It is only after her death that his sister reveals that their mother had tried to protect her by offering herself up to the Russian soldiers. Grass diagnoses a universal speechlessness here as a signature of a period that dealt with defeat by channelling all its energy into building the future. Grass recognizes that this psychological taboo was produced by the experience of total defeat which defied emotional and cognitive assimilation (*BH*, 272).

Although the final part of the narrative reiterates Grass's criticism of the stuffiness of the Adenauer era, the actual account of his own experiences of the 1950s undermines his claim that it was, above all, a period that reinstated conservative values. 1950s West Germany appears a multi-faceted era characterized by the birth of consumer culture as well as by an existentialist style, which, according to Grass, allowed his generation to translate the experience of defeat into the tragic register of a universally available philosophical code (*BH*, 330). As Andrew Plowman has shown in his analysis of 1950s Germany, literary accounts of the period emphasize "an acute sense of the contradictoriness of the decade".[47] This is precisely the point of the concluding part of Grass's autobiography, in which the critical account of the so-called "economic miracle" and the establishment of the conservative political culture of the Adenauer years is punctured by the image of a lively counter-culture that finds expression through art, Jazz and sexual experimentation.

However, the book finishes with the invocation of Paris as the site of a bohemian lifestyle which allows Grass to suspend the image of a drab and ruined Berlin. According to Grass, Paris is also the location where he managed to overcome the disabling disjunction between the political and the personal. After finding the famous first sentence of *Die Blechtrommel*, the writer is engulfed by a flood of words (*BH*, 475).

With the image of the unleashing of an unbounded creativity, Grass completes his *Bildungsroman*, switching from a moralizing discourse on disgrace and guilt to an exploration of the role of the imagination. It is precisely this transmutation of the discourse on guilt that makes *Beim Häuten der Zwiebel* such a compelling intellectual autobiography.

Fest, Grass and the politics of memory in unified Germany

The controversy over Grass's autobiography had not yet abated when the publication of Joachim Fest's *Ich nicht* in September 2006 rekindled the debate about Germany's management of the past. Fest, who died on 11 September shortly before his book appeared, had been a key player in West Germany's cultural establishment for more than 30 years. Born into an educated middle-class family in Berlin in 1926, his life and career exemplify the outlook of the West German conservative bourgeoisie in the post-war era. After the war, he began his career as a radio journalist for RIAS in Berlin, where he headed the contemporary history section; he then moved to the *Norddeutscher Rundfunk* (North German Radio) in Hamburg as editor-in-chief. From 1973 to 1993 he was co-editor of the conservative *Frankfurter Allgemeine Zeitung* and head of its influential culture section, which continues to shape public debates in Germany to the present day. His international fame was established with the publication of *Hitler* in 1973, which appeared in English in 1974.[48] In this biography, which adopts an Anglo-Saxon narrative flair, Fest probed the pathological psyche and self-serving delusions of Hitler and of the NS elite. It was considered a watershed publication precisely because it shifted focus from an economic explanation of Hitler's rise to power to a psychological analysis of German middle-class mentality after the First World War. In his eyes, the fear of Bolshevism and of modernization, and the experience of dislocation fuelled a romantic longing for the past, which made Germans peculiarly susceptible to Hitler. More controversial than his Hitler biography was his engagement with Albert Speer, Hitler's chief architect and armament minister, who was sentenced at Nuremberg and imprisoned in Spandau for 20 years. After his release, Fest helped to promote him by publishing Speer's *Spandauer Tagebücher* (Spandau Diaries, 1975). In 1999 he returned to this figure once more in *Speer. Eine Biographie* (Speer. A Biography) after it had become public knowledge that Speer was far more than the apolitical technocrat and aesthete who had been taken in by Hitler.[49] Although historical research had implicated Speer in the knowledge and execution of the Holocaust – he was responsible for the deportation of the Jews in Berlin and for enlarging the camp at Auschwitz – Speer continued to be remembered as the "good Nazi", an image that had been popularized by Fest too.[50] Fest also played a key role in the Historians' Debate of 1986 by publishing an article by the historian Ernst Nolte, who compared the Holocaust with Stalin's mass murder and suggested that Hitler's aggressive-expansionist war was a response to the threat of Bolshevism. Other well-known publications include his account of German conservative resistance in *Staatsstreich. Der lange Weg zum 20. Juli* (1994, Engl. transl. *Plotting Hitler's Death*, 1996) and *Der Untergang. Hitler und das Ende des Dritten Reiches* (2003, The Downfall. Hitler and the End of the Third Reich), which together with the account by Traudl Junge, Hitler's secretary, provided the basis for Oliver Hirschbiegel's and Bernd Eichinger's blockbuster film, *Der Untergang*.[51]

Clearly, in the light of such a prolific biography, Fest was a formidable personality in Germany's intellectual scene. Unsurprisingly, his autobiography was received in terms of another milestone publication precisely because it offered a personal account of conservative resistance and integrity. For example, Robert Leicht appraised *Ich nicht* in *Die Zeit* as a narrative at the centre of which is Fest's father, who was sacked as headmaster in the 1930s because of his staunch opposition to Hitler.[52] Similarly, the *Stuttgarter Zeitung* hailed the book as the author's great bow to his father, and *Die Welt* emphasized the "the shining paternal example which exemplifies an almost supra-human integrity and uprightness".[53] Even the left-wing *taz* joined in the universally enthusiastic reception, classifying Fest's autobiography alongside Sebastian Haffner's *Geschichte eines Deutschen* (Story of a German, 2000) as one of the two most important German moral narratives of the 20th century.[54] The publication of Grass's *Beim Häuten der Zwiebel* and Fest's *Ich nicht* within weeks of each other invited comparisons that focused on the question whether the centre-right or the left had the upper moral hand in Germany's memory culture. Fest had also helped to ignite this debate shortly before his death by denouncing Grass for his belated admission of his SS membership. For centre-right critics, the Grass controversy seemed to provide further evidence that the left's moral superiority – as far as Grass's generation was concerned – was tainted by greater complicity with National Socialism than they were possibly willing to admit. In this way, the comparison of Fest's and Grass's respective autobiographies re-ignited the debate about the alleged cultural hegemony of the left in post-war Germany which had taken place during the 1990s.[55]

In order to understand the political implications of the reception of Fest's autobiography, one must place it in the context of German memory politics. After 1968, West German discourse was dominated by the centre-left, which promoted an open confrontation with the Nazi past and an unqualified rejection of narrow forms of German patriotism. By contrast, after unification, Germany's regaining of full national sovereignty seemed to legitimate or even necessitate a revival of a more conventional German patriotism.[56]

Conservative commentators felt that at last the time had come to demolish the left's guardianship of a negative national identity that was primarily based on the remembrance of Auschwitz. The neo-right author, Botho Strauß, led the attack on the left's alleged cultural hegemony in his 1993 essay "Anschwellender Bocksgesang" (The Rising Song of the Goat), in which he claimed that the liberal media had put in place an effective moral dictatorship.[57] This was echoed five years later in Martin Walser's controversial and much-debated speech "Erfahrungen beim Verfassen einer Sonntagsrede" (Experiences When Writing a Sunday Speech) on the occasion of his acceptance of the Peace Prize of the German Book Traders Association on 11 October 1998 in the historic surroundings of Frankfurt's Paulskirche. Walser's highly polemical attack on political correctness resulted in one of the most ferocious memory contests of the post-war period.[58]

However, it is important to emphasize that this resurgence of cultural nationalism in the 1990s was punctured by the election of an SPD–Green parliamentary coalition in 1998 that, under Chancellor Gerhard Schröder and Minister for Foreign Affairs Joschka Fischer, ran the country until 2005. The media were quick to note that the election of the Red–Green government signalled the end of the post-war era. For the first time since 1945, Germany was run by a generation of politicians who had been born after the war. Furthermore, the electoral victory of the Red–Green coalition also marked the arrival of the generation of 1968 in the Berlin Republic and their adoption of mainstream *Realpolitik*.[59] Notwithstanding this new pragmatism, the Red–Green coalition continued to place German guilt and Jewish victimhood at the centre of Germany's official memory politics. In practical terms, this commitment found expression in the year 2000, when the government passed a law that regulated the compensation of former forced labourers. In co-operation with those firms that had profited from slave workers during National Socialism, the government set up the foundation *Erinnerung, Verantwortung und Zukunft* (Memory, Responsibility and Future), which received 10,000 million DM for this purpose. Furthermore, the Red–Green coalition initiated one of the most profound legislative changes by breaking with the notion of ethnic nationhood in its reform of the citizenship laws in 2000. The new government replaced the old *ius sanguinis*, which made German citizenship dependent on ethnic membership, with the *ius soli* and the so-called "Geburtsrecht", according to which all children of foreign nationals born in Germany would be automatically entitled to German citizenship.[60] In this way, the law recognized that Germany had become an immigration country. Arguably, under the Red–Green government, Germany became more pluralist, diverse and more self-confident in the international arena. Notwithstanding this new German multi-culturalism, the attack on the generation of 1968 and the left gathered pace in the centre-right media, which, for example, attempted to demolish Joschka Fischer's public image as a politician of unsurpassed integrity. However, the outing of Fischer as a radical member of 1968 with a militant past, who had participated in violent demonstrations in the 1960s, achieved little as Fischer's popularity ratings remained high.[61]

Against the backdrop of the ongoing debate about German national identity, the publication of Fest's *Ich nicht* appeared, for some commentators, to put the nail in the coffin of the left's perceived cultural hegemony. A case in point is Matthias Matussek's review in the *Spiegel*, which celebrated Fest's book as the story of an upright citizen whose conservative-bourgeois background had enabled him to become a proud loner, who heroically opposed the mainstream thinking of the left in the post-war period. For Matussek, Fest's account of his father's life demonstrates not only that opposition to National Socialism was possible, but, more importantly, that a good upbringing – "a bourgeois, Catholic and Prussian upbringing" – was the most fundamental aspect.[62] With this breath-taking statement, Matussek attempted to make precisely those values the cornerstone of principled opposition to National Socialism that had come under attack in 1968: Prussianism, Christianity – in this case Catholicism and not Protestantism – and a bourgeois background are reconfigured in terms of promoting non-conformist principles. By contrast to the critical father literature discussed in Chapter 2 and the critical discourse on conservative resistance, as exemplified by Wibke Bruhns's book (see Chapter 5), Matussek appeals to a conservative notion of tradition unaffected by National Socialism. Championing the idea of an uninterrupted cultural tradition, he implies that National Socialism was not supported by the educated elite. He therefore bases his revisionist interpretation on the central image of Fest's uprightness, which he contrasts with Grass's alleged crookedness. The orientalist connotations of this chauvinistic imagery become even more notorious a few passages later, where he compares Fest's stylistic plainness with

Grass's ornamental orientalism, by which he means Grass's exaggerated linguistic acrobatics: "Fest kommt schnörkellos zur Sache, Grass weicht orientalisch aus" (Fest gets straight to the matter, Grass evades this in oriental fashion). The startling bile of this review does not shy away from employing ancient prejudices about the "wily oriental". Matussek's review is thus an example of the right's attempt to posit a viable tradition that ignores the reality of mass support for National Socialism after 1933.

In contrast to Matussek's celebration of a particular type of Germanness based on historical continuity, others were more guarded in their appraisal of Fest's autobiography. For example, although Robert Leicht was, on the whole, impressed by the book, he did raise the question whether Joachim Fest really had the right to apply his father's oppositional attitude to his own life. In other words, Leicht drew attention to the problematic construction of historical continuity based on familial lineage. The following section explores this question by analyzing the construction of tradition in Fest's autobiography.

Reclaiming Prussianism, catholicism and the bourgeois education: Joachim Fest's *Ich Nicht*

No autobiographer can ignore the fact that the mental time journeys of autobiography are based on the conscious effort to reconstruct a version of the past that is compatible with his or her self-image. This does not imply that autobiographies are narratives that leave no room for the experience of a discontinuous self; rather it suggests that, where the experience of biographical discontinuity is of central importance, it tends to be narrated from the point of view of some kind of biographical "conversion". Augustine provided the model for this practice in his *Confessions*. In that seminal work, Augustine gave expression to the foundational moment of Christian conversion, privileging interiority as a way of recovering knowledge of selfhood.[63] Accordingly, the modern reception of Augustine's work emphasized the self-conscious exploration of the dichotomy between two irreconcilable selves. This moment became paradigmatic for the modern confessional autobiography.

In the previous section, I argued that Grass's autobiography is just such a confessional narrative that articulates the difficulty of coming to terms with his former Nazi and SS past. In Grass's case, the biographical rift between his present and former selves motivates the autobiographer's self-conscious exploration of the distorting tricks of human recall. The enterprise of writing autobiography is fraught with pitfalls precisely because we are socially constituted beings who adapt our life stories to changing social pressures. In contrast to Grass, whose self-conscious use of metaphor deliberately obstructs straightforward narrative, Joachim Fest adopts the tone of the confident historian who can place his family history authoritatively in the wider context of German history.

Fest's authorial confidence manifests itself in his treatment of the issue of autobiographical truthfulness. Like most modern autobiographers, Fest addresses the malleability of our memory from the outset. At the beginning of Chapter 1, he reflects that we tend to forget the majority of our experiences as our memory constantly edits our life stories according to present demands and new insights. Looking back on his life, the auto-biographer is faced with a flood of images that for a long time appeared confused and arbitrary before he managed to read "die verborgenen Wasserzeichen in den Lebenspapieren" (the hidden water marks in the book of my life).[64] The metaphor of the hidden watermark in the book of life suggests that writing autobiography involves the discovery of a meaning that is already inherent in one's lived life. In other words: the autobiographer does not construct meaning through narrative but he discovers it like the watermark imprinted on each sheet of paper as a mark of quality.

Chapter 1 is the only chapter that begins with a reflection on the nature of autobiography. While Grass addresses this question throughout his narrative proper, Fest delegates such meta-discursive interventions to the Preface and Afterword, which offer a brief account of his methodological difficulties and solutions. The Preface makes clear that Fest's main problem was not the integration of a discontinuous former self into his overall life story, but rather the lack of a family archive that could fill the gaps in his own memory (*IN*, 9–10). Faced with the absence of an historical archive, Fest explains that he only managed to overcome his methodological difficulties by means of the historical research that he had carried out after the war for the radio station RIAS in Berlin. Apparently, his notes on conversations, which he conducted in the early 1950s with various historical eye-witnesses, including his father, form the backbone of his narrative. In other words, the narrative is at least twice removed from the event: it synthesizes and mediates the 1950s interpretation of history from the point of view of the present. However, Fest gives us no indication that such a methodology leaves little room for the exploration of conflicting memories.

The problematic nature of this way of writing autobiography will be the subject of the following pages that focus on Fest's handling of the paternal voice. I argue that Fest adopts the role of a ventriloquist who speaks on behalf of his dead father. In this way, he re-establishes those notions of lineage and tradition that were the target of the father discourse of the late 1960s and 1970s. Chapter 2 of this book showed that, in the late 1970s, the German genre of fathers' literature became the literary battlefield for a conflict that centred on the legacy of the Hitler generation in the post-war era. The vehement attack by the members of 1968 on their parents' generation, whom they held collectively responsible for the war, challenged a set of values that had underpinned the German *völkisch* dream. Prussianism, Protestantism, the culture of shame of the inter-war period, as well as the cult of the cold persona emerged as a value system that had survived the war. However, the need for tradition remained an unresolved issue in the fathers' literature of the late 1970s; it therefore resurfaced in 1990s Germany at a time when family history was rediscovered as an untapped source for the enhanced understanding of how ordinary people experience history's vagaries. As the examples of Timm and Leupold demonstrate, such privatization of history does not automatically affirm the triumph of personal memory over historical analysis. Both narratives dismantle those family legends that have produced negative legacies that haunt the sons and daughters; both maintain the dialectic between continuity and rupture, between the desire for a generational break and for generational affiliation, between historical analysis and subjective memory. In contrast to such careful handling of the issues of generational rupture and continuity, Fest resolves this tension in favour of an enforced harmonization that represses almost all signs of inter-generational dissonance. The self in this narrative has no difficulty with the idea of being his father's son; on the contrary, by adopting his father's voice, the son appears as the father's true heir who managed to transfer paternal resistance to Hitler's Germany to the post-war era. The implied equation of the father's resistance to Hitler's dictatorship with the son's criticism of the left-wing political and cultural scene in West Germany is one of the most problematic aspects of this narrative; it is part of the wider project of the new right to posit a cultural tradition based on continuity and lineage. In the light of this, the question arises how Fest introduces the role of ventriloquist, which is crucial for the staging of his autobiographical self as a resister.

In order to answer this question, one must return to the Preface, where Fest explains that the notes on his conversations with his father after the end of war consisted primarily of key words whose context and meaning he could often not reconstruct. The autobiographer also mentions that, although he does not agree with some of the father's historical judgements, he did not edit them in any way in order to reproduce the perceptions, worries and disappointments of an eye-witness (*IN*, 10). Clearly, this explanation lends the book the objectivity of the experienced historian who reproduces his source material faithfully before submitting it to historical interpretation. However, Fest then explains that, in order to make his book more readable, he cited some of these notes in direct speech, a method – he emphasizes – the historian could never adopt. One sentence later, the rendition of notes in direct speech is reconfigured as "dialogische Erweiterungen" (dialogic extensions), which attempt to reproduce both the content and the tone of the father's historical explanations. Fest concludes his methodological explanation as follows: "Wo einzelne Bemerkungen in Anführungszeichen gesetzt sind, geben sie eine Äußerung, dem *Gedächtnis entprechend, wortgetreu* wieder" (*IN*, 11; my emphasis AF; where quotations marks frame individual remarks, they reproduce an utterance *literally in accordance with my memory*).

This is an extraordinarily muddled passage: Fest began with the admission that he had to elaborate the key words that provide the historical backbone of his narrative about his father. In this way, he seems to acknowledge the inevitable epistemological gap between his source material, on the one hand, and the representation of this material in the autobiographical narrative, on the other. However, this gap, which invites the kind of self-conscious discourse that is typical of modern autobiography, is closed up only one sentence later when Fest explains that he inserted quotation marks around his dialogic representations of the father's remarks. It appears that the autobiographer is extremely anxious to repress the distance that separates him from his father. That such editorial practice is a rather forced affair becomes evident in the final sentence where Fest refers to a literal citation of the paternal words from memory. Arguably, this contradiction is not just a naive slip but the central construction that underpins the logic of this autobiography as a whole: it makes the son the ventriloquist for his father's words. Because the father speaks through his son, the difference between memory and history disappears. Furthermore, as a ventriloquist of the paternal legacy, the son can bypass the issue of inter-generational differences and the need for rupture in the post-war period.

Fest returns to the issue of writing autobiography once more in a brief postscript. Addressing the manifold gaps in his narrative, the autobiographer refers to the past in these final passages as an "imaginary museum", which does not represent our real experiences in the past but what "die Zeit, die wachsende Verschiebung sowie der eigene Form-wille im Chaos halbverschütteter Erlebnisse daraus gemacht haben. Im ganzen hält man weniger fest, wie es eigentlich gewesen, sondern wie man wurde, wer man ist" (*IN*, 366; time, the growing perspectival shift and the desire for shape have made out of them in the chaos of half-buried experiences. All in all, one does not capture the story of how it was, but rather how one developed into oneself). Fest's concession that all representations of selfhood have an imaginary quality was barely noticed by those reviewers who celebrated his book as evidence of the viability of the bourgeois German tradition. Although Fest is undoubtedly far more knowing than some of his reviewers, this reception was helped by the hagiographic representation of the paternal figure in the narrative proper, a topic that deserves closer analysis.

From autobiography to hagiography

As we could see in Chapter 2 of this book, fathers did not receive a good press in post-war literary discourse. From the early father texts by Christoph Meckel, Elisabeth Plessen, Ruth Rehmann and Hermann Kinder to recent narratives by Uwe Timm, Dagmar Leupold, Friedrich Christian Delius and Stephan Wackwitz, fathers or grandfathers are held responsible for a deep-seated form of resentment which found expression in the formulaic notion of the "Schmach von Versailles" (the disgrace of Versailles).[65] For the generation of men born around 1900, the Treaty of Versailles, which blamed Germany single-handedly for the First World War, amounted to a massive national humiliation, which was further aggravated by the democracy of the Weimar Republic.[66] As a response to this perceived degradation, the cult of the cold persona (exemplified by Ernst Jünger's steel warrior) emerged in the inter-war period, advocating the masking of pain and emotion behind a protective shield of masculine honour, duty and hardness. After the Second World War, the authors of father texts suggested that it was this code and the *völkisch* dream of a Germanified Europe that prepared the ground for the older generation's involvement with National Socialism. Meckel's narrative, for example, highlights that, while the father's subscription to Prussian military values set him initially in opposition to the perceived vulgarity of National Socialism, the father ended up colluding with NS policies after the beginning of the Second World War. Meckel's portrayal of his father's cold persona is in line with other generational narratives, such as Dagmar Leupold's, Uwe Timm's or Stephan Wackwitz's, which also diagnose a gender-specific authoritarian value system as a condition that prevented this generation from taking responsibility for their actions after the Second World War. In all these texts, the *pater familias* (or the grandfather) registers the defeat in two world wars as a dethroned, helpless despot who evades the question of individual responsibility. By contrast to this critical investigation of the belief system of the paternal generation, Joachim Fest constructs a narrative of heroic resistance that derives its integrity from some of the very values that the above-mentioned authors hold responsible for the German malaise. In Fest's narrative, the father's bourgeois education, which he had to struggle to obtain, combines with his belief in Prussianism, Catholicism and his principled support of the Weimar Republic. A miller's son, Johannes Fest is introduced as a highly gifted student who decided not to follow his inclination to study mathematics or theology but to remain grounded in reality by opting for the more socially practical career of teaching (*IN*, 27). He served briefly in the First World War, but was seriously wounded early on and resumed his teaching during the war period. After the demise of the *Kaiserreich*, he quickly accepted the reality of the new Weimar Republic and became a staunch supporter of the Catholic *Zentrumspartei* (Centre Party) in Berlin. Later on, he joined the *Reichsbanner*[67] in order to defend the fragile democratic order against increasingly militant attacks from the left and the right. Fest reports how, in 1932, his father returned home injured because, as a member of the *Reichsbanner*, he had defended a local SPD meeting against a communist attack (*IN*, 43). After the Nazi's rise to power, the father was first suspended and then sacked as headmaster for refusing to join the NSDAP. In spite of various attempts to persuade him to accept the new reality of Nazi Germany, Johannes Fest stood by his principled opposition, thus remaining unemployed through the entire NS period. Clearly, Johannes Fest's continued support of the democratic and constitutional principles of the Weimar Republic set him objectively apart from the fathers who feature in the above-mentioned narratives as authoritarian ogres who channelled their Prussianism into National Socialism.

The father's Catholicism was a further ingredient in his belief system; this was politically embedded in the *Zentrumspartei* and, in particular, in the figure of Reichskanzler Brüning, who was Chancellor of the fragile Weimar Republic from 30 March 1930 to 7 October 1931. According to his son, Joachim, the father believed that if Heinrich Brüning had managed to reconcile Prussianism and Catholicism, history might have taken a different turn (*IN*, 31). While all these traits build up the image of an upright individual who based his life on sound political and moral principles, it is, above all, the father's membership of the educated bourgeoisie, the so-called *Bildungsbürgertum*, that makes him an exemplary figure of a better German tradition. Describing his father as a committed member of the educated bourgeoisie, Fest argues that after the war this class was held responsible for National Socialism. He attributes this misleading accusation to the resentment of "spoiled children" who were trying to elevate themselves morally over their parents, denouncing education as a useless endeavour (*IN*, 31–3). Through such comments, the autobiographer articulates his ideological outlook: by making a bourgeois *Bildung* the very foundation of the father's staunch opposition to Hitler, Fest implies that the educated bourgeoisie had largely opposed Hitler. Right from the start, *Bildung* is presented as a panacea against the malaise of National Socialism.[68] In Fest's eyes, *Bildung* was wrongly targeted by the resentful 1968 generation that was ultimately too lazy to study and learn. This is a startling claim for a historian, given the overall evidence of widespread support for Hitler after his rise to power: the *Gleichschaltung*, or co-ordination, of bourgeois professions in medicine, law and education after 1933 was not just a top-down process that was met by the silent opposition of the educated class, but it was perceived by many as a career path that accelerated promotion. For example, historical research on the *Gleichschaltung* of the humanities in the 1930s shows that in the last phase of National Socialism two-thirds of all academic personnel were members of the NSDAP, and many of those who were not official members were involved with other NS organizations.[69] Vice versa, the example of left-wing and communist resistance demonstrates that resistance cannot be attributed to a particular educational or class background. Resistance to the system was enacted by a minority of people who were motivated by diverse ideologies and attitudes. Fest also ignores the fact that the generation of 1968 reacted against the swift integration of many of Hitler's elite into the new Federal Republic in spite of the initial Allied de-nazification programme in the 1940s.[70] So the question arises how Fest, the historian, can advance the idea of the *Bildungsbürger*'s resistance?

The autobiographer answers this question one sentence later, where he explains that, in reality, only one per cent of the population belonged to the *Bildungsbürgertum*. In this way, membership of the *Bildungsbürgertum* shifts ground from the educated middle-class to a tiny minority, the composition of which remains unspecified. The ensuing narrative wavers between advancing the notion of a middle-class *Bildungsbürgertum*, on the one hand, and the elitist character of *Bildung*, on the other: for example, recalling the regular political conversations at home, Fest describes them in terms of a counter-culture to the anti-bourgeois orientation of National Socialism. Interpreting his story as a "bürgerliche Entwicklungsgeschichte in unbürgerlicher Zeit" (*IN*, 103; bourgeois narrative of education in an anti-bourgeois era), he proceeds to cite the father's educational principles, which assert a shared decency based on Christian morality and the great European philosophical and literary tradition (*IN*, 103). The father's value system evokes here, in very general terms, the value system of the German bourgeoisie for which German idealism and the unification of Germany in 1871 were important markers of cultural identity. In other words, the father is seen here as a typical representative of a belief system that, for his son, has a timeless appeal precisely because it claims to be based on universal notions of decency. In the past few decades, such claims about a universal morality have come under attack: post-colonial discourse and deconstruction have both exposed such beliefs as an example of a Eurocentric world view that applied its outlook to the colonial enterprise. Fest ignores this criticism, subscribing to the idea that true *Bildung* immunized him and others against the disease of extremist ideologies. In his narrative, the representatives of the centre hold the moral upper hand. These range from his father to his inner circle of friends or the 2 000 people who attended the funeral of the former leader of the Social Democratic Party in Berlin, Franz Künstler, who died in 1942 after persecution by the Nazi state. According to Fest's father, this funeral was the last mass demonstration against Hitler's dictatorship (*IN*, 83).

Such examples exemplify a decency that was shared by a sizeable minority. On the other hand, Fest represents the *Bildung* he experienced at home as exceptional. This is most evident in the conspiratorial scene that gives the book its title. Fest relates how, around New Year's Eve in 1936, the father explained to his two older sons, Wolfgang and Joachim, that the family was going to take their evening meals in two sittings: a first sitting for the younger children was to be followed by a later sitting that the parents and older brothers would attend. This arrangement alone would allow the father to air his anti-Nazi views openly (*IN*, 74). The father asked his sons to be extra vigilant and not to relay any of the political conversations outside the home as anybody could be a traitor. He concluded this announcement of regular conspiratorial gatherings around the dinner table with the citation of a Latin sentence that the boys were admonished never to forget:

Er wolle uns dafür einen lateinischen Satz aufgeben, den wir nie vergessen sollten; am besten wäre es, ihn aufzuschreiben, dann ins Gedächtnis sozusagen einzubrennen und die Notiz wegzuwerfen. Ihm jedenfalls hätte dieser Satz geholfen und sogar manche Fehlentscheidung erspart. Denn am seltensten habe er geirrt, wenn er einzig dem eigenen Urteil gefolgt sei. Er legte jedem von uns einen Zettel hin und diktierte: "Etiam si omnes – ego non! Ist aus 'Matthäus' ", erläuterte er, " 'Ölbergszene'." (*IN*, 75)

[He wanted to give us a Latin sentence which we should never forget; it would be best to write it down, then engrave it in our memories, and then to throw away the paper. This sentence had helped him and had even spared him from making some wrong decisions. Because he had erred least when he had exclusively followed his own judgement. He placed a piece of paper in front of us and dictated "Etiam si omnes – ego non! It is from 'Matthew' ", he explained, "the 'Mount of Olives scene'."]

With this theatrical presentation, Fest turns his autobiography into a sort of hagiography, at the centre of which is the biblical act of supporting Christ against his opponents. "If all others – not I" is what the father dictates to his sons, placing them in a tradition of Christian martyrdom that prioritizes faith and loyalty to God above and beyond everything else, including one's own life. This scene is foundational for the narrative as a whole in that it posits a rite of initiation into principled opposition against the system; accordingly, both children experience this moment as a conspiratorial baptism: while Wolfgang, the older brother, excitingly exclaims "Wir gegen die Welt!" (we stand against the world), the younger brother Joachim feels "auf unbestimmte Weise ausgezeichnet" (elevated in an unspecified way). However, this rite of passage is based on an error: the Book of Matthew (Chapter 26, verses 31–3) relates how, after the last supper, Jesus predicts Peter's denial of Christ. Peter replies, "Though all men shall be offended because of thee, yet will I never be offended. Jesus said unto him, Verily I say unto thee, that this night, before the cock crow, thou shalt deny me thrice."[71] In other words, the quotation goes back to the very disciple who denied Christ; it is, as such, hardly a suitable motto for resistance. Furthermore, the Latin version that is cited by Fest does not appear in the Book of Matthew in the *Biblia Sacra Vulgata*, where the Latin of Peter's reply to Christ's announcement is as follows: "si omnes scandalizati fuerint in te ego numquam scandalizabor" (if all are aggrieved/offended by you, I will not be offended).[72] The biblical phrase "etiam si omnes – ego non" does not exist. With a few notable exceptions, the majority of reviewers did not check the Bible and simply accepted Fest's invocation of a biblical tradition of resistance at face value.[73]

This is more than a slip: the scene is central for the narrative representation of the Fest family as both exemplary and exceptional *Bildungsbürger*. The paradoxical construction of an exemplary exceptionality or, vice versa, an exceptional exemplariness enables the autobiographer to posit the existence of a viable German tradition. Although this tradition was only adhered to by an exceptional minority during National Socialism, for the autobiographer it represents the conservative middle ground.

This implied appeal to a form of German patriotism that is nevertheless embedded in the European philosophical and cultural tradition helps to mask some of the father's more worrying ideological beliefs. For example, when dealing with the annexation of Austria in 1938, Fest emphasizes that his father viewed that event as yet another disheartening example of Hitler's success in the international arena. However, he also mentions in passing that, like the majority of Germans and Austrians at the time, his father thought in pan-Germanic terms (*IN*, 114). Although these pan-Germanic views show that the father was not completely immunized against *völkisch* ideology, his son does not provide any critical commentary on this issue. Likewise, the autobiographer reports that although his father was disgusted by Hitler's triumph after Germany's invasion of France in May 1940, he was nevertheless happy that the French were defeated (*IN*, 155). Clearly, like many men of his generation, Johannes Fest believed in the "Schmach von Versailles" and appears to have channelled his resentment into an anti-French revanchist mentality that the authors of the critical father literature identified as a major factor in Hitler's rise to power. Of course, I do not wish to diminish Johannes Fest's integrity and the hardship that his family experienced as a result of his principled opposition to Hitler. What is at stake here is not the father's resistance, but rather the son's unquestioning representation of this resistance in terms of a better German tradition that transcends both National Socialism and the left-wing extremism in the Federal Republic of the 1960s and 1970s.

The programmatic pathos of the title "Not I" creates a transgenerational legacy of an oppositional attitude that finds further expression in an episode that results in the brothers' expulsion from their school. Fest relates how one day in school he scratched a caricature of Hitler into his desk, undoubtedly a very dangerous act in the Germany of the 1940s. Although his friend attempted to quickly erase the cartoon, Joachim was caught, interviewed by the Gestapo and asked to leave the school together with his brothers (*IN*, 158–9). Subsequently, Joachim and his older brother Wolfgang were sent to a Catholic boarding school in Freiburg, where, after some time, they were, however, forced to join the Hitler Youth (*IN*, 185). This is a surprising admission given the title's emphatic assertion of an absolute moral distinction between the Fests and the conformist majority. The transgenerational applicability of the "not I!" is further eroded a little later when we are told that, after his obligatory *Flakhelfer* training and service in the *Reichsarbeitsdienst* (National Labour Service), Joachim signed up for the *Luftwaffe* (air force). In a letter to his father, the son explains that he did this in order to avoid being drafted into the SS. The son's decision results in a major argument with his father, who insists that "zu dem 'Verbrecherkrieg Hitlers' melde man sich nicht freiwillig" (*IN*, 225; one does not sign up voluntarily for Hitler's criminal war). This is one of the rare instances where an inter-generational conflict is openly articulated in this narrative. The episode creates the impression that Joachim's enlistment in the *Luftwaffe* is an example of the type of pragmatic conformism that was shared by many members of his generation – a position that is perfectly understandable but that nevertheless undermines the totality of his opposition to the Nazi state. Joachim Fest explains a little later that, after the war, he had one more conversation about his *Luftwaffe* service with his father: " 'Du hast', bemerkte er, 'bei diesem einzigen ernsten Streit, den wir während der Nazijahre hatten, nicht unrecht gehabt. Aber recht gehabt habe ich!' " (*IN*, 225; "you were", he noted, "not wrong in that first serious argument which we had during the Nazi years. But I was right!"). The father's witty conversion of the double negation "nicht unrecht haben", being not wrong, into a higher positive "recht haben", being right, eradicates the difference between the two men and reaffirms the son's membership of the oppositional elite.

After the war, Fest found his topic, contemporary German history. In the eyes of his father, he would have been better off writing about the Renaissance, since contemporary history was nothing but a "Gossen-thema", a theme from the gutter, which did not deserve the historian's closer attention because such engagement would ultimately attribute "historische Würde", historical dignity, to the Nazis (*IN*, 351). Fest explains that the label "Gossenthema" continued to be on his mind when he wrote his Hitler biography. The question of the German *Bürgertum*'s role during the Hitler era resurfaces once more when the autobiographer summarizes his historical insight. Looking at the bigger picture, Fest now states that he witnessed the collapse of the bourgeois world. In his view, its demise had already been foreseeable before Hitler entered the scene. Describing Hitler as a revolutionary, he argues that

Hitler simply cleared away the crumbling remnants of the bourgeoisie. However, as Hitler gave himself the veneer of bourgeois values, he managed to destroy the hollow façade of the bourgeoisie with their help (*IN*, 343). Fest concludes that, although he was brought up according to the principles of a dying class, its rules and traditions nevertheless distanced him from his own times, and thus afforded him a piece of *terra firma* (*IN*, 344).

Fest's evaluation of the notion of the *Bürgertum* remains contradictory: on the one hand, the historian analyzes it in terms of hollow pretensions that were no longer underpinned by the value of true *Bildung*; on the other, he claims that, in his own life, the rules of this obsolete class provided him with an anchor in a rapidly changing post-war world. In this way, Fest manages to turn that which he first designated as an obsolete *Bildung* into a transhistorical perspective that is supposed to legitimate his own political outlook on post-war affairs. It is in line with this that the autobiographer now transfers the programmatic "ego non!" from the Third Reich to the political divisions in post-war Germany. In a conversation with his brother, Fest represents his staunch opposition to the left-wing liberalism of the 1970s, which had sought, and achieved, rapprochement with the GDR, as an act of resistance in the paternal spirit. He goes on to explain that the "ego non" enabled him to go against popular thinking and to resist the allure of communism (*IN*, 360). The example of some of his friends who had remained in the East taught him that the GDR system was often more deceptive and impermeable than "die braune Herrschaft" (*IN*, 360; brown rule).

Fest argues that the state surveillance of everyday life in the GDR was often more harsh than the brutal repression exerted by the National Socialists: this is an astonishing claim for an historian of the Hitler era. It reveals a blind spot in an autobiography that squarely places this self in a better German tradition, based on Prussianism, Catholicism and *Bildung*. Although Fest concedes that this conservative tradition is obsolete, the entire tenor of his autobiography suggests that this is Germany's only viable tradition.

Conclusion

Günter Grass's *Beim Häuten der Zwiebel* is a confessional narrative that combines the admission of personal guilt and shame with an exploration of the role of the imagination in coming to terms with the past. On the one hand, Grass the writer assigns the literary imagination a key role in the management of the NS past. However, on the other hand, the autobiographer's demonstrative gestures of owning-up highlight the deficit of a solely literary encounter with the Nazi past. Autobiographical discourse allows Grass to finally acknowledge that the delegation of his previously hidden SS past to fiction made his writing complicit in the widespread denial of personal responsibility that characterized the post-war period. However, Grass not only illuminates the dialectic between self-accusation and self-exoneration that propels his confessional narrative, but through this process he also makes partial blindness the touchstone of autobiographical authenticity. This rejection of the notion of total recall goes hand in hand with an ongoing reflection on the belatedness of his confession: while Grass admits a deep-seated and, in my opinion, genuine sense of shame about his membership of the SS, he also shows in the same breath that the confession of an earlier omission is a foundational speech-act of the confessional autobiography. A highly self-conscious narrative, *Beim Häuten der Zwiebel* manages to both identify a moral blemish and to explore the culturally productive force of this blemish in Grass's post-war career as a writer. However, Grass's handling of the fruitful traffic between biography and fiction is not exculpatory; it is, as I have argued, bounded by his recognition of an ethical obligation towards history. By probing the irreconcilable split between his former and present selves, the autobiographer rejects closure and harmonizing interpretations of the historical discontinuities that have marked German history throughout the 20th century.

In sharp contrast to Grass's urgent confessional narrative, Fest's autobiography deliberately represses all signs of biographical rupture in favour of biographical continuity based on resistance. Here self-consciousness is replaced by an authorial historical confidence that renders the past accessible in the act of narration. Relating the father's story of heroic resistance to the Third Reich, Fest represents himself as true heir of a better German tradition that survived the Nazi period intact. Ironically, according to Fest's analysis, this better Germany was only destroyed in the post-war period when left-wing trends and the student movement of the late 1960s combined to topple the cherished values of the *Bildungsbürgertum*. Fest's celebration of his *Bildung* in terms of an exceptional exemplariness posits that the conservative middle ground has always represented the better Germany. The theatricality of the conspiratorial *Urszene* (primal scene), in which the father and his older sons enter a pact of resistance to the system underlines the mythologizing dimension of a narrative that attempts to erase most traces of biographical discontinuity. The episode where Fest represents his enrolment in the *Luftwaffe* as yet another act of resistance is further evidence of this. The repeated demonstration of a transgenerational legacy of principled opposition leaves little room for the kind of self-doubt that is the dominant feature of modern autobiography. Arguably, the tendentious nature of *Ich nicht* appeals to those critics who wish to recover traditional notions of an anchorage in a heritage that denies that National Socialism has impaired the idea of an uninterrupted German tradition.

7
Epilogue: Germany as a Threshold Culture

The issues involved in the Grass/Fest controversy surfaced once more in the autumn of 2006, when the conservative right launched another attack on the left over the guardianship of the past. This time, Jürgen Busche, a former journalist of the *Frankfurter Allgemeine Zeitung*, targeted the philosopher Jürgen Habermas in the November issue of the political magazine *Cicero* in an article entitled "Hat Habermas die Wahrheit verschluckt?" (Did Habermas swallow the Truth?).[1] Busche's piece recycled an anecdote about the philosopher's alleged past as a member of the Hitler Youth that had circulated in philosophical circles for some time and that, as we will see below, was also a feature of Fest's autobiography. According to this story, the historian Hans-Ulrich Wehler found a formal reprimand from the young Habermas for not attending the obligatory Hitler Youth training sessions amongst his possessions years after the war. When Wehler handed this form to Habermas decades later, the latter was so shocked that he instantly swallowed it.

However, the facts behind this tendentious anecdote had already been the subject of discussion. In 2004, Gereon Wolters revealed that, as a 14-year-old, Habermas had indeed served as a medical attendant in the same branch of the Hitler Youth as Wehler.[2] Both men came from the same area and ended up in the same branch of the Hitler Youth. As Habermas was the medical trainer of his unit, he was required to fill out and sign a standard form of reprimand whenever a trainee failed to turn up for the obligatory training sessions. One such recipient was Wehler, who, after discovering the form decades after the war, sent it to his friend Habermas by post. When the subject came up casually in a conversation between the Habermas and Wehler families, Habermas's wife jokingly said that her husband had "swallowed" the form after receiving it. What was at first nothing but a witty *bon mot* coined by

Habermas's wife was later traded in philosophical circles as an anecdote. Others, however, manipulated the narrative, most prominently Joachim Fest, who, in the first edition of *Ich nicht*, related the anecdote with a tendentious twist that implied the philosopher's inability to come to terms with his own Nazi past. Instead of eating humble pie, according to Fest's punch-line, the left-wing philosopher devoured a written piece of evidence concerning his embroilment in National Socialism. But Fest went further than simply rehashing the anecdotal swallowing of a form: in the first edition of *Ich nicht*, he claimed that the episode referred to one of the leading intellectuals in post-war Germany who was in reality "ein dem Regime in allen Fasern seiner Existenz verbundener HJ-Führer" (a leader of the Hitler Youth attached to the system with every fibre of his being). Although Fest did not name Habermas, it was all too easy for the informed reader to identify Habermas as the target of this malicious attack since Fest suggested that the intellectual in question was involved in "eine Art Schadensabwicklung" (a type of damage limitation exercise), the title of Habermas's essay of 1986 that had ignited the Historians Debate.³ Even if one were to ignore the blatant absurdity of labelling a 14-year-old boy a fanatical Nazi, the vindictive motivation of this slanderous charge is breathtaking. The *Süddeutsche Zeitung* pointed out that Fest wrote this passage despite the fact that Wehler had already informed him about the real background of the story.⁴

Unsurprisingly, after the publication of *Ich nicht* in September 2006, Habermas was granted an injunction against the publishing house which then had to remove the passage from Fest's autobiography. Although no evidence emerged to support the claim that Habermas had ever been a fervent Nazi Youth – as Habermas pointed out, his physical impairment alone would have made it impossible for him to become a leader in the Hitler Youth – the story was regurgitated once more in Jürgen Busche's aforementioned article in *Cicero*. Arguably, Busche's piece was even more invidious because the journalist relayed the real facts of the Wehler/Habermas story before insinuating that the story had only resurfaced because Wehler, "the busy professor" of history, would not have sent the signed form to Habermas unless it contained more than merely the 14-year-old's signature on a standard form of reprimand. Busche concludes his perfidious game of suggesting a buried truth in the philosopher's life by citing once more Joachim Fest: "Wenn eine Geschichte sich schon falsch ereignet hat, sollte man sie wenigstens richtig erzählen" (if a story has already happened in the wrong way, one should at least relate it in the right manner). In an open letter to the magazine's editor, Jürgen Habermas called Busche a slanderer who had used long refuted rumours to insinuate lies. He interpreted this episode as the resurgence of a political campaign unleashed by the *Frankfurter Allgemeine Zeitung* in the 1970s and continued well into the 1980s:

> Wie wehrt man sich gegen eine Denunziation, die das durchsichtige Ziel verfolgt, zusammen mit Grass eine unbequeme Generation von Intellektuellen abzuräumen, die sich für die selbstkritische Vergewisserung des Traditionshintergrundes der – auch und vor allem – in akademischen Schichten verbreiteten Zustimmung zur NS-Herrschaft eingesetzt hat?[5]

> [How does one defend oneself against a slander which pursues the transparent aim of denouncing an awkward generation of intellectuals alongside Grass? A generation that put forward the idea of a self-critical engagement with the traditions manifest in the far-reaching support of the NS regime above all in academic circles?]

In the end, even the conservative *Frankfurter Allgemeine Zeitung* had to concede that Busche's suggestion was a cheap and tasteless way of contorting the historical truth, as there was not a single shred of evidence to support his suggestion.[6] However, this story is more than a scandal about the abandonment of standard ethical criteria by Busche and Fest. It is a story that highlights once more that the question of responsibility for National Socialism remains a tinderbox of memory that continues to ignite ferocious memory contests in the public domain.

Günther Oettinger's unfortunate oration on the occasion of the state funeral of Hans Filbinger, the former *Ministerpräsident* of the state of Baden-Württemberg, who had to resign from his post in 1979 after Rolf Hochhuth had exposed him as a Nazi judge, is a case in point.[7] When Oettinger, the current *Ministerpräsident* of Baden-Württemberg, praised Filbinger, a member of the NSDAP and member of the Sturmabteilung (SA), as having actually been an opponent of the regime, another storm broke loose in the media that only abated when Angela Merkel reprimanded Oettinger, who in the end was forced to withdraw his remarks.[8] Both the Fest/Busche and the Oettinger cases involved counter-narratives that challenged Germany's official memory politics: while the attacks by Fest and Busche on Habermas's alleged youthful errors attempted (but failed) to unmask the philosopher as yet another left-wing intellectual with doubtful credentials, Oettinger's attempt to rehabilitate Filbinger tried to redraw the topography of

Germany's memory culture by reinstating the notion of a widespread inner opposition to Hitler, an idea that was already prevalent in the post-war period. In the end, both cases and the attendant debate in the media showed that such memory contests do not simply feed into a revisionist interpretation of the legacy of National Socialism. For, in both cases, the media responded with a critical and rather careful evaluation of the issues involved.

On the other hand, the regular occurrence of such debates in contemporary Germany suggests that the legacy of National Socialism cannot be put to rest so easily. Although this topic has preoccupied the public domain in West Germany for more than 50 years, the regular eruption of such memory contests points to a transgenerational legacy that has been the subject of this study. In many of the literary and autobiographical narratives discussed here, the *longue durée* of National Socialism is subject to more subtle and, arguably, more productive analyses than the public controversies outlined above. As a self-reflexive medium that scrutinizes language itself, literature has the ability to bring to the fore both the agitated nature of such memory contests and the silences and gaps that have punctuated these debates about Germany's National Socialist past. Similarly, the films included in this book probe the contested issue of Germany's cultural heritage by representing resistance from a postmemorial position. By tuning into the *sous-entendues* that have accompanied the discourse about National Socialism, these narratives – filmic, fictional or autobiographical – highlight the function of transference and deferral in post-war family narratives. While this preoccupation with psychological issues places them squarely in the framework of contemporary trauma theory and the attendant victim discourse, my study makes the case that the best examples of the contemporary family narrative offer a meta-critical perspective on the very categories that underpin this discourse itself. As we have seen throughout this book, many family narratives undertake a critical evaluation of the currently fashionable concepts of postmemory, victimhood, trauma and generation. However, this critical impetus is often accompanied by moments of nostalgic longing. The contemporary German family narrative is characterized by a sorrowful acknowledgement of the havoc wrought by a violent history that could have gone the other way if only the historical actors had played a different part. By investigating the historical choices of the previous generations, these stories point to an alternative history that, unfortunately, did not happen. The idea of a retrospective historical agency is thus their prime trope. Their nostalgic tenor is the product of an historical consciousness that has internalized the disturbance of tradition. The family narrative represents the shattered or damaged post-war German family as a symptom of the impairment of the nation as a whole, a condition that cannot simply be mastered through acts of patriotic self-proclamation à la Joachim Fest, Martin Walser or Botho Strauß. By contrast to such neo-conservative attempts to reinstate traditional notions of patriotism, the family narrative discussed here probes the idea of tradition in terms of a haunting phantom that irritates and beguiles at the same time. As "the residue of historical disaster",[9] the ghosts from the past unsettle the present whenever it promotes a form of self-authorization that aims to erase the relevance of the past. Arguably, the idea that tradition after the Holocaust and National Socialism is a phantom has been a powerful and highly productive cultural force in German identity debates to the present day. However, one must not lose sight of the fact that the material discussed in this book also explores the idea of a generational renewal. Arguably, the current fashion for books and films about the long afterlife of National Socialism, given particular impetus by unification, marks the transitional discourse of a threshold culture that is about to redefine its cultural identity. Germany today presents itself as a pluralist culture that has now made room for competing concerns and interests by later generations for whom National Socialism is an important, albeit a less agitated lesson from history.

Notes

1 Introduction: Family narratives between vernacular and official memory

1. See Günter Grass, "Schreiben nach Auschwitz. Frankfurter Poetik-Vorlesung", in *Der Autor als fragwürdiger Zeuge*, ed. Daniela Hermes (Munich: dtv, 1997), pp. 195–222. Fest was instrumental in igniting the Historians' Debate as he published Nolte's controversial essay "Vergangenheit, die nicht vergehen will" in the *Frankfurter Allgemeine Zeitung*, 6 June 1986. On the Historians' Debate, see Wolfgang Wippermann, *Wessen Schuld? Vom Historikerstreit zur Goldhagenkontroverse* (Berlin: Elefanten Press, 1997); Jürgen Peter, *Der Historikerstreit und die Suche nach einer nationalen Identität der achtziger Jahre* (Frankfurt a. M.: Peter Lang, 1995).

2. Among the most prominent examples are the much-cited Walser-Bubis debate (see Note 5), the debate about the Wehrmacht exhibition, the protracted discussion about the building of the Holocaust memorial in Berlin, the controversy about the relevance of 1968, and, with reference to the GDR past, the debates about the Stasi past, the legacy of Socialism, or – from an eastern perspective – the question of West German cultural hegemony.

3. Mary Cosgrove and Anne Fuchs, "Introduction", *German Life & Letters* 59 (2006), Special Issue: Anne Fuchs and Mary Cosgrove (eds), *Memory Contests*, 3–10; here, 4.

4. The town of Weimar, as the seat of 18th-century literature, philosophy and art, had been the very embodiment of Germany's heritage as a *Kulturnation*. The idea of *Kulturnation* was defined, on the one hand, by concepts specific to the German culture, such as Herder's notion of the German language and, on the other, by ideas that transcend German culture, such as Goethe's notion of "Weltliteratur" (world literature). After the war, the cultural leadership of the two Germanys tried to reconnect with this heritage pedagogically: East Germany claimed that the great German classics were the real precursors of the socialist state and could be used for re-educating the people for the emerging socialist order. In the West, the historian Friedrich Meinecke proposed a cultural reorientation through the foundation of Goethe societies. Friedrich Meinecke, *Die deutsche Katastrophe: Betrachtungen und Erinnerungen* (Wiesbaden: Brockhaus, 1946).

5. See Botho Strauß, "Anschwellender Bocksgesang", in *Der Aufstand gegen die sekundäre Welt* (Munich: Hanser, 1999), pp. 55–79; Martin Walser, "Erfahrungen beim Verfassen einer Sonntagsrede", in *Die Walser-Bubis-Debatte. Eine Dokumentation*, ed. Frank Schirrmacher (Frankfurt a. M.: Suhrkamp, 1999), pp. 7–29; Rainer Zitelmann, "Position und Begriff", in *Vereinigungskrise. Zur Geschichte der Gegenwart*, ed. Jürgen Kocka (Göttingen: Vandenhoeck & Ruprecht, 1995), pp. 9–32.

6. For a discussion of these conceptual distinctions, see Aleida Assmann, *Der lange Schatten der Vergangenheit. Erinnerungskultur und Geschichtspolitik* (Munich: Beck, 2006), pp. 205–17.

7. Alon Confino, *Germany as a Culture of Remembrance. Promises and Limits of Writing History* (Chapel Hill: The University of North Carolina Press, 2006), p. 200.

8. Maurice Halbwachs, *On Collective Memory*, ed. and transl. Lewis A. Coser (Chicago: Chicago University Press, 1992).

9. Jeffrey Prager, *Presenting the Past. Psychoanalysis and the Sociology of Misremembering* (Cambridge, MA: Harvard University Press, 1998), p. 70.

10. Confino, *Germany as a Culture of Remembrance*, p. 183.

11. Ibid., p. 211.

12. Assmann, *Der lange Schatten*, p. 121. Although Assmann does not discuss the family in terms of a *lieu de souvenir*, it is evident that it is a prime example of a subjective site of remembrance where relationships are not just defined by anthropological, social or biological ties between family members but also by the subjective experience of family life.

13. Jan Assmann, *Das kulturelle Gedächtnis. Schrift, Erinnerung und politische Identität in den frühen Hochkulturen* (Munich: Beck, 2000), p. 50.

14. Jan Assmann, "Collective Memory and Cultural Identity", *New German Critique* 65 (1995), 125–33; here, 129.

15. Harald Welzer, "Schön unscharf: Über die Konjunktur der Familien- und Generationenromane", *Mittelweg* 36 (2004), 53–64; here, 53.

16. Harald Welzer, Sabine Moller and Karoline Tschugnall, *"Opa war kein Nazi" – Nationalsozialismus und Holocaust im Familiengedächtnis* (Frankfurt a. M.: Fischer, 2003).

17. Ibid., p. 10.

18. Ibid., p. 79.

19. Bill Niven (ed.), "Introduction", *Germans as Victims. Remembering the Past in Contemporary Germany* (Houndsmills: Palgrave, Macmillan, 2006), pp. 1–25; here, p. 20.

20. On family memory and kinship, see Halbwachs, *On Collective Memory*, pp. 54–83.

21. This argument was put forward by Aleida Assmann, "Grenzen des Verstehens. Generationsidentitäten in der neuen deutschen Erinnerungsliteratur", *Familiendynamik. Interdisziplinäre Zeitschrift für systemtorientierte Praxis und Forschung* 30 (2005), 370–89; here, 375.

22. Friederike Eigler, *Gedächtnis und Geschichte in Generationenromanen seit der Wende* (Berlin: Erich Schmidt, 2005), p. 29.

23. Matthias Fiedler, "German Crossroads: Visions of the Past in German Cinema after Reunification", in *German Memory Contests. The Quest for Identity in Literature, Film and Discourse Since 1990*, ed. Anne Fuchs, Mary Cosgrove and Georg Grote (Rochester: Camden House, 2006), pp. 127–45; here, pp. 128–30.

24. Peter Reichel, *Erfundene Erinnerung: Weltkrieg und Judenmord in Film und Theater* (Munich: Hanser, 2004), pp. 13–4.

25. Wilhelm Dilthey, "Über das Studium der Geschichte der Wissenschaften vom Menschen, der Geschichte und dem Staat", in *Die geistige Welt, Einleitung in die Philosophie des Lebens. Erste Hälfte: Abhandlungen zur Grundlegung*

der Geisteswissenschaften. Gesammelte Schriften V, ed. Georg Misch (Leipzig, Berlin: B. G. Teubner, 1924), pp. 31–73.

26. Karl Mannheim, "Das Problem der Generationen", in *Wissenssoziologie*, ed. Kurt H. Wolff (Soziologische Texte 28) (Berlin, Neuwied: Luchterhand, 1964), pp. 509–65. For an English translation see K. Mannheim, "The Problem of Generations", in *Essays on the Sociology of Knowledge*, ed. Paul Kecskemeti (London: Routledge, 1964), pp. 276–322.

27. Wilhelm Pinder, *Das Problem der Generation in der Kunstgeschichte Europas* (Cologne: E. A Seemann, 1949, 1st ed. 1926), p. 35; see Richard Alewyn for a critical evaluation of the generational debate: "Das Problem der Generation in der Geschichte", *Zeitschrift für deutsche Bildung* 5 (1929), 519–27.

28. Pinder, *Das Problem der Generation*, p. 57.

29. On this issue, see Alexander Honold, " 'Verlorene Generation': Die Suggestivität eines Deutungsmusters zwischen Fin de siècle und Erstem Weltkrieg", in *Generation: Zur Genealogie des Konzepts – Konzepte von Genealogie*, ed. Sigrid Weigel, Ohad Parnes, Ulrike Vedder, Stefan Willer (Munich: Fink, 2005), pp. 31–56.

30. W. G. Sebald, *Luftkrieg und Literatur. Mit einem Essay über Alfred Andersch* (Frankfurt a. M.: Fischer, 2003).

31. Jörg Friedrich, *Der Brand. Deutschland im Bombenkrieg 1940–1945* (Munich: Propyläen, 2002); Jörg Friedrich, *Brandstätten. Der Anblick des Bombenkrieges* (Munich: Propyläen, 2003); Christoph Kucklick, *Feuersturm. Der Bombenkrieg gegen Deutschland* (Hamburg: Ellert & Richter, 2003); Guido Knopp, *Die große Flucht* (Universum Film, 2002); K. E. Franzen and Hans Lemberg, *Die Vertriebenen. Hitlers letzte Opfer* (Munich: Propyläen, 2001). The book accompanied the three-part ARD documentary of the same title.

32. On this issue, see William Collins Donahue, "Illusions of Subtlety: Bernhard Schlink's *Der Vorleser* and the Moral Limits of Holocaust Fiction", *German Life & Letters* 54 (2001), 60–81; Omer Bartov, "Germany as Victim", *New German Critique* 80 (2000), 29–40; Bill Niven, "Bernhard Schlink's *Der Vorleser* and the Problem of Shame", *MLR* 98 (2003), 381–96.

33. For a critical analysis of Jörg Friedrich's position, see Aleida Assmann, "On the (In)compatibility of Guilt and Suffering in German Memory", *German Life & Letters* 59 (2006), 187–200. See also Lothar Kettenacker (ed.), *Ein Volk von Opfern? Die neue Debatte um den Bombenkrieg 1940–1945* (Berlin: Rowohlt, 2003); Bernd Greiner, " 'Overbombed': Warum die Diskussion über die alliierten Luftangriffe nicht mit dem Hinweis auf die deutsche Schuld beendet werden darf", *Literaturen* 3 (2003) 42–44; Klaus Naumann, "Bombenkrieg – Totaler Krieg – Massaker. Jörg Friedrichs Buch *Der Brand* in der Diskussion", *Mittelweg* 36 (2003), 40–60.

34. See Andreas Huyssen, "Monuments and Holocaust Memory in a Media Age", in *Twilight Memories. Marking Time in a Culture of Amnesia* (New York, London: Routledge, 1995), pp. 249–60; here, p. 253; Daniel Levy and Natan Sznaider, *Erinnerung im globalen Zeitalter: Der Holocaust* (Frankfurt a. M.: Suhrkamp, 2001).

35. Attempting to make more plausible this unlikely relationship between a British bomber pilot and a German nurse in February 1945, the script makes Robert the son of a German woman and an English man.

36. On Dresden as an icon from a GDR perspective, see Bill Niven (ed.), "The GDR and Memory of the Bombing of Dresden", *Germans as Victims*, pp. 109–29; in the same volume, Andreas Huyssen, "Air War Legacies: From Dresden to Baghdad", pp. 181–93.

37. For a positive appraisal of *Dresden*, see Michael Hanfeld, "In der Wut des Feuersturms. Dresden im Fernsehen", *Frankfurter Allgemeine Zeitung*, 20 February 2006; Hannah Pilarczyk, "Dresden, 13. Februar 1945: Ohne Anlass zu Opferdiskursen", *die tageszeitung*, 4 March 2006; for scathing critiques, see Joachim Günter, "Bomben-Kitsch. Dresdens Untergang im Fernsehen", *Neue Zürcher Zeitung*, 8 March 2006; Peter von Becker, "Schmalzbomben auf Dresden", *Der Tagesspiegel*, 7 March 2006; Oliver Storz, "Ärzte, Flammen, Sensationen", *Süddeutsche Zeitung*, 7 March 2006; On *Die Flucht*, see Peter von Becker, "Vertreibung als Drama. Die Flucht von uns selbst", *Tagesspiegel*, 6 March 2007; Gustav Seibt, "Fette Torte. Im Fernsehen: Maria Furtwängler in *Die Flucht*", *Die Süddeutsche Zeitung*, 1 March 2007; Christian Buß, "Go West, Gräfin", *Spiegel Online*, 2 March 2007 (http://www.spiegel.de/kultur/gesellschaft/o,1518,469480,00.html,accessed 2 March 2007).

38. Evelyn Finger, "Die Ohnmacht der Bilder", *Die Zeit*, 1 March 2007. See her critical review of *Die Flucht*: Evelyn Finger, "Quotenopfer", *Die Zeit*, 8 March 2007.

39. Niven, "Introduction", *Germans as Victims*, here, p. 18.

40. Alexander and Margarete Mitscherlich, *Die Unfähigkeit zu trauern. Grundlagen kollektiven Verhaltens* (Munich: Piper, 1967).

41. On Sebald's "Luftkrieg" essay, see Andreas Huyssen, "On Writings and New Beginnings: W. G. Sebald and the Literature about the Luftkrieg", *Zeitschrift für Literaturwissenschaft und Linguistik* 31 (2001), 72–90; Wilfried Wilms, "Taboo and Repression", in W. G. Sebald's *On the Natural History of Destruction*, in *W. G. Sebald – A Critical Companion*, ed. J. J. Long and Anne Whitehead (Edinburgh: Edinburgh UP, 2004), pp. 175–89; Anne Fuchs, "A Heimat in Ruins and the Ruins as Heimat: W. G. Sebald's *Luftkrieg und Literatur*", in *German Memory Contests: The Quest for Identity in Literature, Film and Discourse*, ed. Anne Fuchs, Mary Cosgrove and Georg Grote (Rochester: Camden House, 2006), pp. 287–302; Carolin Duttlinger, "A Lineage of Destruction? Rethinking Photography in Luftkrieg und Literatur", in *W. G. Sebald and the Writing of History*, ed. Anne Fuchs and J. J. Long (Würzburg: Königshausen & Neumann, 2007), pp. 167–81.

42. Hermann Lübbe, "Der Nationalsozialismus im politischen Bewußtsein der Gegenwart", in *Deutschlands Weg in die Diktatur*, ed. Martin Broszat (Berlin: Siedler, 1983), pp. 329–49; here, p. 335.

43. On this issue, see Anne Fuchs, "From Vergangenheitsbewältigung to Generational Memory Contests in Günter Grass, Monika Maron and Uwe Timm", *German Life & Letters* 59 (2006), 169–86; here, 176–79.

44. Confino, *Germany as a Culture of Remembrance*, p. 237.

45. Robert G. Moeller, *War Stories. The Search for a Usable Past in the Federal Republic of Germany* (Berkeley, Los Angeles, London: University of California Press, 2001). On *Heimat* films, see Elizabeth Boa and Rachel Palfreyman, *Heimat – A German Dream. Regional Loyalties and National Identity in German Culture 1890–1990* (Oxford: Oxford UP, 2000), pp. 86–129.

46. Moeller, *War Stories*, pp. 123–70.

47. Ibid., p. 182.
48. On this distinction, see John Bodnar, *Remaking America. Public Memory, Commemoration and Patriotism in the Twentieth Century* (Princeton: Princeton UP, 1992), pp. 13–14.

2   Generational conflict and masculinity in *Väterliteratur* by Christoph Meckel, Uwe Timm, Dagmar Leupold and Ulla Hahn

1. Prominent examples of *Väterliteratur* are Elisabeth Plessen's *Mitteilung an den Adel* (Message for the Nobility, 1976); Hermann Kinder's *Im Schleiftrog* (The Grinding Trough, 1977); Ruth Rehmann's *Der Mann auf der Kanzel. Fragen an einen Vater* (The Man in the Pulpit. Questions for a Father, 1979); Bernward Vesper's *Die Reise* (The Trip, 1977); Peter Härtling's *Nachgetragene Liebe* (Belated Love, 1980). A late example of this first wave of father books is Peter Schneider's novella *Vati* (Daddy, 1989), which relates the one and only encounter between the concentration-camp doctor Josef Mengele and his son Rolf.
2. Ernestine Schlant, *The Language of Silence. West German Literature and the Holocaust* (New York: Routledge, 1999), pp. 80–98; here, p. 85. Also see Jochen Vogt's more sympathetic reading of the genre: "Er fehlt, er fehlte, er hat gefehlt... Ein Rückblick auf die sogenannten Väterbücher", in *Deutsche Nachkriegsliteratur und der Holocaust*, ed. Stephan Braese, Holger Gehle, Doron Kiesel, Hanno Lowey (Frankfurt a. M., NY: Campus, 1998), pp. 385–99; Claudia Mauelshagen, *Der Schatten des Vaters: deutschsprachige Väterliteratur der siebziger und achtziger Jahre* (Frankfurt a. M., Berlin: Lang, 1995).
3. Schlant, *The Language of Silence*, pp. 92–93.
4. Pierre Nora, "Generation", in *Realms of Memory: Rethinking the French Past. Vol. 1: Conflicts and Divisions*, translated from the French by Arthur Goldhammer (New York: Columbia UP, 1996), pp. 499–531; here, p. 499.
5. Two prominent examples stand out in this respect: Uwe Timm's novel *Rot* (Red, 2001) and Friedrich Christian Delius's *Mein Jahr als Mörder* (My Year as an Assassin, 2004). Both novels attempt a retrospective and personal evaluation of 1968.
6. Norbert Frei, *1945 und Wir. Das Dritte Reich im Bewußtsein der Deutschen* (Munich: Beck, 2005), p. 12 and p. 37 [my translations].
7. One has to caution, however, that the counting of generations and the attempt to map generational affiliation onto a history of mentality is fraught with pitfalls: while Frei's model implies that the generation born around 1900 also made up the first generation after the Second World War with many of its members shaping policy in education, politics and the judiciary, Sigrid Weigel views the "Flakhelfer" generation as the first, albeit concealed post-war generation. See Sigrid Weigel, " 'Generation' as a Symbolic Form: On the Genealogical Discourse of Memory Since 1945", *The Germanic Review* 77 (2002), 264–77; here, 273. Also see Norbert Frei (ed.), *Hitlers Eliten nach 1945* (Munich: dtv, 2003). Heinrich Böll, a key actor in the post-war period, fits neither model: born in 1917, he was neither a member of the generation born around 1900 nor did he qualify for membership of the "Flakhelfer"

generation. His critical engagement with Germany's moral responsibility shows that the notion of generation must not be viewed in a deterministic manner.

8. Weigel, "'Generation' as a Symbolic Form", 163. For a comprehensive analysis of the genealogy of the concept, see the essays in Sigrid Weigel, Ohad Parmes, Ulrike Vedder, and Stefan Willer (eds), *Generation. Zur Genealogie des Konzepts – Konzepte von Genealogie* (Munich: Fink, 2005).
9. Quoted in Nora, "Generation", p. 502.
10. Ibid.
11. Ibid., pp. 503–4.
12. Ibid., p. 528.
13. This is in contrast to Nora's claim that generation as a *lieu de mémoire* is a particularly French phenomenon. Nora writes, "There are indeed 'French' generations. If, moreover, a generation is a *lieu de mémoire*, it is not at all in the simple sense that shared experiences imply shared memories. It is rather as a result of the simple yet subtle interplay of memory and history, of the eternally re-emerging dialectic of a past that remains present, of actors who become their own witnesses and of new witnesses in turn transformed into actors. When all three elements are present, a mere spark can ignite a blaze. It is their presence in today's France, that tinderbox of memory, that fuels the 'generational' blaze." Nora, "Generation", pp. 530–31.
14. Christoph Meckel, *Suchbild. Über meinen Vater* (Frankfurt a. M.: Fischer, 1983). Further references appear in the text as *S* followed by the page number.
15. All translations are mine unless otherwise indicated.
16. Helmut Lethen, *Verhaltenslehre der Kälte. Lebensversuche zwischen den Kriegen* (Frankfurt a. M.: Suhrkamp, 1994), p. 35.
17. Ibid., p. 36.
18. Quoted in Lethen, *Verhaltenslehre der Kälte*, p. 85 [my translation].
19. A poignant example of the creature are the soldiers who returned from the war so badly injured and disfigured that they were locked up in special institutions since their appearance in the public was deemed not to be acceptable.
20. Lethen, *Verhaltenslehre der Kälte*, p. 256.
21. See Giorgio Agamben, *Homo Sacer. Sovereign Power and Bare Life*, translated from the Italian by Daniel Heller-Rozen (Stanford: Stanford UP, 1998).
22. Lethen, *Verhaltenslehre der Kälte*, p. 94.
23. Meckel uses capitals whenever he wants to emphasize the father's insistent tone of voice.
24. Uwe Timm, *Am Beispiel meines Bruders* (Cologne: Kiepenheuer & Witsch, 2003). All subsequent references appear in the text as *AB* followed by the page number.
25. In 2002 Meckel published a complementary and equally scathing portrait of his mother, entitled *Suchbild. Meine Mutter* (Munich, Vienna: Hanser, 2002).
26. All English quotations follow the translation by Anthea Bell. See Uwe Timm, *In My Brother's Shadow*, translated from the German by Anthea Bell (London: Bloomsbury, 2005). Cited as *MB* followed by page number; here, p. 10.
27. Lethen, *Verhaltenslehre der Kälte*, p. 215.
28. See Carl Schmitt, *Ex Captivitate Salus. Erfahrungen der Zeit 1945/47* (Berlin: Duncker & Humblot, 1950), p. 79. On Schmitt's culture of shame, see Lethen, *Verhaltenslehre der Kälte*, pp. 219–31.

29. On this issue, see Chloe Paver's article, " 'Ein Stück langweiliger als die Wehrmachtsausstellung, aber dafür repräsentativer': The Exhibition *Fotofeldpost* as Riposte to the Wehrmacht Exhibition", in Anne Fuchs, Mary Cosgrove and Georg Grote (eds), *German Memory Contests*, pp. 107–25, and the account by Hannes Heer, historian and former curator of the first Wehrmacht exhibition: Hannes Heer, *Vom Verschwinden der Täter. Der Vernichtungskrieg fand statt, aber keiner war dabei* (Berlin: Aufbau, 2005), pp. 12–66.
30. Ulla Hahn, *Unscharfe Bilder. Roman* (Munich: dtv, 2005). All further references appear in the text as *UB* followed by the page number.
31. Helmut Schmitz, "Reconciliation between the Generations: The Image of the Ordinary Soldier in Dieter Wellershoff's *Der Ernstfall* and Ulla Hahn's *Unscharfe Bilder*", in *German Culture, Politics and Literature into the Twenty-First Century*, ed. Stuart Taberner and Paul Cooke (Rochester, NY: Camden House, 2006), pp. 151–65; here, p. 157.
32. See Sigmund Freud, "Über die Deckerinnerung", in Freud, *Gesammelte Werke*, ed. Anna Freud et al. (Frankfurt a. M.: Fischer, 1999), vol. 1, pp. 529–54.
33. Welzer, "Schön unscharf", 56.
34. Ibid., 57.
35. Dagmar Leupold, *Nach den Kriegen* (Munich: Beck, 2004). All subsequent references appear in the text as *NK* followed by the page number.
36. Friedrich Christian Delius, *Mein Jahr als Mörder* (Berlin: Rowohlt, 2004), p. 126.
37. See Lethen on this, *Verhaltenslehre der Kälte*, pp. 198–215.
38. Ernst Jünger, *In Stahlgewittern* (Stuttgart: Klett-Cotta, 1978), p. 104.
39. Lethen, *Verhaltenslehre der Kälte*, p. 206.
40. Ernst Jünger, *Strahlungen I* (Stuttgart: Klett-Cotta, 1988), p. 242. Leupold cites a slightly different version: "Auch will ich mir gestehen, daß ein Akt höherer Neugier den Ausschlag gab" (*NK*, 170).

3 Family narratives and postmemory: Günter Grass's *Im Krebsgang*, Tanja Dückers's *Himmelskörper* and Marcel Beyer's *Spione*

1. On contemporary family narratives, see Stuart Taberner, "Representations of German Wartime Suffering", in Bill Niven (ed.), *Germans as Victims*, pp. 164–80. For a critical evaluation of family narratives by Sabine Schiffner, Arno Orzessek, Eva Menasse and Arno Geiger, see Bernhard Jahn, "Familienkonstruktionen 2005. Zum Problem des Zusammenhangs der Generationen im aktuellen Familienroman", *Zeitschrift für Germanistik* 3 (2006), 581–96.
2. Sigrid Weigel, *Genea-Logik. Generation, Tradition und Evolution zwischen Kultur- und Naturwissenschaften* (Munich: Fink, 2006), pp. 87–103.
3. Ibid., p. 90.
4. Marianne Hirsch, *Family Frames. Photography, Narrative and Postmemory* (Cambridge, MA: Harvard UP, 1997), p. 22.
5. J. J. Long, "Monika Maron's Pawels Briefe: Photography, Narrative and the Claims of Postmemory", in Anne Fuchs, Mary Cosgrove and Georg Grote (eds), *German Memory Contests*, pp. 147–65; here, p. 149.
6. Hirsch, *Family Frames*, p. 28.
7. J. J. Long, "Monika Maron's Pawels Briefe", pp. 149–50.

8. Ibid., p. 150.
9. Cathy Caruth, *Unclaimed Experience. Trauma, Narrative and History* (Baltimore, London: John Hopkins UP, 1996). See also Shoshana Felman and Cathy Caruth (eds), *Testimony. Crisis of Witnessing in Literature, Psychoanalysis and Art* (New York, London: Routledge, 1992).
10. Caruth, *Unclaimed Experience*, pp. 17–18.
11. See Ruth Leys, *Trauma. A Genealogy* (Chicago: Chicago UP, 2000), p. 267.
12. Ibid., p. 273.
13. Ibid.
14. For an incisive critique, see Dominick LaCapra's book, *Writing History, Writing Trauma* (Baltimore, London: The John Hopkins UP, 2001); Sigrid Weigel, "Téléscopage im Unbewußten: Zum Verhältnis von Trauma, Geschichtsbegriff und Literatur", in *Trauma: Zwischen Psychoanalyse und kulturellem Deutungsmuster*, ed. Elisabeth Bronfen, Birgit Erdle and Sigrid Weigel (Cologne, Weimar, Vienna: Böhlau, 1999), pp. 51–76.
15. However, the historian Jörn Rüsen suggests that historians too should respond to the challenge of what he calls the "catastrophic crisis" of the Holocaust by means of a historical discourse which achieves the effect of secondary traumatization in the reader. See Jörn Rüsen, *Zerbrechende Zeit. Über den Sinn der Geschichte* (Cologne, Weimar, Vienna: Böhlau, 2001), pp. 176–79. For a detailed discussion of various attempts by historians to integrate psychoanalysis and history, see Alfred Krovoza, "Psychoanalyse und Geschichtswissenschaft. Anmerkungen zu Stationen eines Projekts", *Psyche* 57 (2003), 904–37.
16. Caruth, *Unclaimed Experience*, pp. 17–8.
17. See Anne Fuchs, *Die Schmerzensspuren der Geschichte. Zur Poetik der Erinnerung in W. G. Sebalds Prosa* (Cologne, Weimar, Vienna: Böhlau, 2004). For further critical appraisal of Sebald's memory politics against the grain, see Mary Cosgrove, "Melancholy Competitions: W. G. Sebald reads Günter Grass and Wolfgang Hildesheimer", in *German Life & Letters* 59 (2006), Special Issue: Anne Fuchs and Mary Cosgrove (eds), *Memory Contests*, 217–32.
18. See Ingeborg Bachmann's programmatic lecture "Literatur als Utopie", in *Ingeborg Bachmann. Kritische Schriften*, ed. Monika Albrecht and Dirk Göttsche (Munich, Zurich: Piper, 2005), pp. 329–49. On Bachmann's critique of the political language of the post-war era, see Dirk Göttsche, "Politische Sprachkritik in Ingeborg Bachmanns Kritischen Schriften", in *Schreiben gegen Krieg und Gewalt. Ingeborg Bachmann und die deutschsprachige Literatur 1945–1980* [*Krieg und Literatur/War and Literature* vol. X], ed. Dirk Göttsche, Franziska Meyer et al. (Göttingen: V& R Unipress, 2006), pp. 49–64. For a succinct introduction to Anne Duden, see Elizabeth Boa, "Introduction: Notes from a Symposium – Notes Towards 'Hingegend'", in *Anne Duden: A Revolution of Words. Approaches to her Fiction, Poetry and Essays* [*German Monitor* 56.], ed. Heike Bartel and Elizabeth Boa (Amsterdam: Rodopi, 2003), pp. 1–18. In the same volume, see Dirk Göttsche, "Beobachtungen zu Anne Dudens Kurzprosa und Essayistik", pp. 19–42; Margaret Littler, "Trauma and Terrorism: The Problem of Violence in the Work of Anne Duden", pp. 43–62. Also see Teresa Ludden, "History, Memory, Montage in Anne Duden's *Das Judasschaf*", *German Life & Letters* 59 (2006), Special Issue: Anne Fuchs and Mary Cosgrove (eds), *Memory Contests*, 249–65.

19. W. G. Sebald, *Austerlitz* (Munich, Vienna: Hanser, 2001), p. 20.
20. Caruth, *Unclaimed Experience*, pp. 17–18.
21. Paul, a trained journalist, reflects on his narrative method in the following way: "Aber noch weiß ich nicht, ob, wie gelernt, erst das eine, dann das andere und danach dieser oder jener Lebenslauf abgespult werden soll oder ob ich der Zeit eher schrägläufig in die Quere kommen muß, etwa nach Art der Krebse, die den Rückwärtsgang seitlich ausscherend vortäuschen, doch ziemlich schnell vorankommen." Günter Grass, *Im Krebsgang. Eine Novelle* (Göttingen: Steidl, 2002), p. 8. ["But I'm still not sure how to go about this: should I do as I was taught and unpack one life at a time, in order, or do I have to sneak up on time in a crabwalk, seeming to go backward but actually scuttling sideways, and thereby working my way forward fairly rapidly?", Günter Grass, *Crabwalk*, transl. Krishna Winston (London: Faber & Faber, 2003), p. 3].
22. On the issue of German victim discourse, see Stuart Taberner, "Normalization and the New Consensus on the Nazi Past: Günter Grass's *Im Krebsgang* and the Problem of German Wartime Suffering", *Oxford German Studies* 31 (2002), 161–86.
23. Kirsten Prinz, " 'Mochte doch keiner was davon hören' – Günter Grass's *Im Krebsgang* und das Feuilleton im Kontext aktueller Erinnerungsverhandlungen", in *Medien des kulturellen Gedächtnisses: Konstruktivität – Historizität – Kulturspezifizität*, ed. Astrid Erll and Ansgar Nüning (Berlin, New York: Walter de Gruyter, 2004), pp. 179–94.
24. Ulrike Vedder, "Luftkrieg und Vertreibung. Zu ihrer Übertragung und Literarisierung in der Gegenwartsliteratur", in *Chiffre 2000 – Neue Paradigmen der Gegenwartsliteratur*, ed. Corinna Caduff and Ulrike Vedder (Munich: Fink, 2006), pp. 59–79.
25. Ibid., p. 73.
26. Tanja Dückers, *Spielzone* (Berlin: Aufbau, 1999), pp. 20–21.
27. "Der nüchterne Blick der Enkel. Wie begegnen junge Autoren der Kriegsgeneration? Ein Gespräch mit Tanja Dückers", *Die Zeit*, 30 April 2004, *Literatur*, p. 1 [my translation].
28. On this issue, see Hayden White, *The Content of the Form. Narrative Discourse and Historical Representation* (Baltimore, London: John Hopkins UP, 1987). On the complex relationship between history and memory, see Jacques Le Goff's seminal book, *History and Memory*, translated from the French by Steven Rendall and Elizabeth Claman (New York, Oxford: Columbia UP, 1992).
29. Tanja Dückers and Verena Carl (eds), *stadt land krieg. Autoren der Gegenwart erzählen von der deutschen Vergangenheit* (Berlin: Aufbau, 2004).
30. Ibid., p. 12.
31. Ibid., p. 13.
32. Nora, "Generation", p. 502.
33. Ibid., p. 528.
34. Tanja Dückers, *Himmelskörper* (Berlin: Aufbau, 2003). All subsequent references appear in the text as *HK* followed by the page number.
35. Freia reflects on this issue in the following way: "Plötzlich war ich Teil einer langen Kette, einer Verbindung, eines Konstrukts, das mir eigentlich immer suspekt gewesen war" [*HK*, 26; Suddenly, I became part of a long chain, a connection, a construct that had always seemed suspect to me].

36. By contrast, Ulrike Vedder distinguishes two types of memory discourse, representing the two generations: the grandparents' monologic victim stories and the grandchildren's alternative polyphonous retellings of this story. See Vedder, "Luftkrieg und Vertreibung", p. 75. However, this distinction only captures two of the three voices that make up family memory: Freia's mother Renate punctures the grandparents' stories with a counternarrative based on her historical background reading. It is highly questionable that the multiple interpretations of historical fragments in the grandchildren's narrative really offer a viable alternative to the other narrative modes. After all, the children's stories about the grandfather's lost leg are fantasies detached from historical fact. If it is anchored in critical discourse, polyphony can indeed contribute to a multiple interpretation of history; however, polyphony as such does not guarantee a critical perspective on history.

37. See Adolf Höfer, "Himmelskörper und andere Unscharfe Bilder. Romane zur Thematik der deutschen Kriegsopfer im Gefolge der Novelle *Im Krebsgang* von Günter Grass", *Literatur für Leser* 28 (2005), 147–61; here, 152.

38. Grass, *Im Krebsgang*, p. 140; ["They all skidded off the ship the wrong way round, head first. So there they was, floating in them bulky life jackets, their little legs poking up in the air...", Grass, *Crabwalk*, p. 149].

39. On the dilemmas of memorial culture, see James E. Young, *At Memory's Edge. After-Images of the Holocaust in Contemporary Art and Architecture* (New Haven, London: Yale UP, 2000). For a critique of Young, see Maeve Cooke, "The Ethics of Post-Holocaust Art: Reflections on Redemption and Representation", *German Life & Letters* 59 (2006), Special Issue: Anne Fuchs and Mary Cosgrove (eds), *Memory Contests*, 266–79.

40. Hartmut Böhme, *Fetischismus und Kultur. Eine andere Theorie der Moderne* (Hamburg: Rowohlt, 2006), p. 190.

41. Ibid., p. 257.

42. Ibid., p. 271.

43. Dan Brown, *The da Vinci Code* (London: Corgi Books, 2003).

44. In his "Theses on the Philosophy of History", Benjamin distinguishes between the empty homogenous time of historicism and a time filled with presence, the proper object of the counter-historiography of historical materialism: "History is the subject of a structure whose site is not homogeneous, empty time, but time filled by the presence of the now [*Jetztzeit*]. Thus, to Robespierre ancient Rome was a past charged with the time of the now which he blasted out of the continuum of history." Walter Benjamin, "Theses on the Philosophy of History", in *Illuminations*, ed. Hannah Arendt, transl. Harry Zorn (London: Pimlico, 1999), pp. 245–55; here, p. 253.

45. Nietzsche writes, "The antiquarian sense of a man, of an urban community, of a whole people always has an extremely limited field of vision; by far the most is not seen at all, and the little that is seen is seen too closely and in isolation; it cannot apply a standard and therefore takes everything to be equally important." Friedrich Nietzsche, *On the Advantage and Disadvantage of History for Life*, transl. Peter Heuss (Indianapolis, Cambridge: Hackett Publishing Company, Inc., 1980), p. 20.

46. Stuart McLean, *The Event and its Terrors. Ireland, Famine, Modernity* (Stanford: Stanford UP, 2004), p. 9.

47. Ibid., p. 10.
48. Literally the title means "Flying Dogs". The English translation appeared under the title *The Karnau Tapes*, transl. John Brownjohn (London: Secker & Warburg, 1997).
49. Although *Flughunde* is related from two narrative points of view, namely that of the sound technician Hermann Karnau and that of Helga Goebbels, the propaganda minister's eldest daughter, literary criticism has focused on Beyer's representation of sound technology as the Nazis' preferred propaganda tool and means of domination. See Ulrich Schönherr, "Topophony of Fascism: On Marcel Beyer's *The Karnau Tapes*", *The Germanic Review* 73 (1998), 328–48; Ulrich Baer, " 'Learning to Speak Like a Victim': Media and Authenticity in Marcel Beyer's *Flughunde*", *Gegenwartsliteratur. Ein germanistisches Jahrbuch* 2 (2003), 245–61; Helmut Schmitz, " 'Just erase it. Erase it all' – Marcel Beyer's *Flughunde*", *On their Own Terms. The Legacy of National Socialism in Post-1990s German Fiction* (Birmingham: Birmingham UP, 2004), pp. 125–50; Bernd Künzig, "Schreie und Flüstern – Marcel Beyers *Flughunde*", in *Baustelle Gegenwartsliteratur. Die neunziger Jahre*, ed. Andreas Erb (Opladen, Wiesbaden: Westdeutscher Verlag, 1998), pp. 122–53.
50. Marcel Beyer, *Spione* (Frankfurt a. M.: Fischer, 2002), p. 7. Further references appear as *S* followed by the page number in the main text.
51. All English quotations follow the translation by Breon Mitchell. See Marcel Beyer, *Spies*, transl. Breon Mitchell (Florida: Harcourt, 2005). Cited as *Sp* followed by page number, here, p. 1.
52. On this issue, see Roland Barthes' reading of a portrait of his mother in his classic essay *La chambre claire. Note sur la photographie* (Paris: Gallimard, 1980), p. 109; Jo Spence and Patricia Holland (eds), *Family Snaps. The Meaning of Domestic Photography* (London: Virago, 1991); Annette Kuhn, *Family Secrets. Acts of Memory and Imagination* (London, New York: Verso, 1995).
53. Later on for example, the grandmother ponders the absence of photographs in the grandfather's letters that he sent to her once he had assumed his secret mission in the Legion Condor. Again the absence of photographs has a ghosting effect which communicates a secret in the register of necromancy. Here the political secret of the grandfather's involvement in the Spanish Civil War causes a disturbance in communication between the two lovers which is only resolved by way of a new secret pact: when he eventually reveals the nature of his mission to her, they decide to keep this secret from their children (*S*, 180).
54. Hirsch, *Family Frames*, p. 11.
55. Kaja Silverman, *The Threshold of the Visible World* (London: Routledge, 1996), p. 221.
56. The humour is further heightened by the pun on the double meaning of the word "stepmother" in the German language: the evil witch from Grimm's fairy tales appears here as the innocent "Stiefmütterchen", that is the pansies in the picture.
57. This mass-produced tourist souvenir which the grandfather brings home from Spain as a gift for his wife is transmuted into a spectral prop by way of its sudden appearance in the various narrative strands.
58. A more accurate translation would be "he can hardly wait".
59. Sigmund Freud, "Der Familienroman der Neurotiker", in *Gesammelte Werke*, ed. Anna Freud et al. (Frankfurt a. M.: Fischer, 1999), vol. 7, pp. 227–31.

60. This is the main thesis of Andreas Huyssen's widely cited book *Twilight Memories. Marking Time in a Culture of Amnesia* (London, NY: Routledge, 1995).
61. Peter Fritzsche, *Stranded in the Present. Modern Time and the Melancholy of History* (Cambridge, MA: Harvard UP, 2004).

4   *Heimat* and Territory in Thomas Medicus's *In den Augen meines Großvaters* and Stephan Wackwitz's *Ein unsichtbares Land*

1. Thomas Medicus, *In den Augen meines Großvaters* (Munich: Deutsche Verlagsanstalt, 2004). All page references appear in the text preceded by *AG*. Stephan Wackwitz, *Ein unsichtbares Land. Familienroman* (Frankfurt a. M.: Fischer, 2003). Subsequent references appear in the text preceded by *UL*.
2. It is estimated that 500,000 refuges died on the treck. For up-to-date figures, see Rüdiger Overmans, *Deutsche militärische Verluste im Zweiten Weltkrieg* (Munich: Oldenburg, 1999), pp. 298–300.
3. On this issue, see Bill Niven, "Introduction: German Victimhood at the Turn of the Millenium", in Bill Niven (ed.), *Germans as Victims*, p. 3.
4. Formal recognition of the Oder-Neiße Line was achieved after the fall of the Wall in 1990, when the 2 + 4 Treaty also confirmed Poland's western border.
5. Ruth Wittlinger rightly argues that the discourse on victimhood never disappeared in West Germany as book publications and films continued to represent expellee interests. While it is important to acknowledge that this type of victim discourse continued to play a role, on the whole, the influence of the expellees on German policy and on official expressions of cultural memory decreased over time. See Ruth Wittlinger, "Taboo or Tradition: The 'German as Victims' Theme in the Federal Republic until the mid-1990s", in Bill Niven (ed.), *Germans as Victims*, pp. 62–75; here, pp. 72–73.
6. On landscape, see Joachim Ritter, "Landschaft. Zur Funktion des Ästhetischen in der modernen Gesellschaft", in *Subjektivität* (Frankfurt a. M.: Suhrkamp, 1980), pp. 141–63; Rainer Piepmeier, "Das Ende der ästhetischen Kategorie Landschaft. Zu einem Aspekt neuzeitlichen Naturverhältnisses", *Westfälische Forschungen* 30 (1980), 8–46; Rainer Piepmeier, "Landschaft", in *Historisches Wörterbuch der Philosophie*, ed. Joachim Ritter and Karlfried Gründer (Basel, Stuttgart: Schwabe & Coag, 1980), vol. 5, pp. 11–28; Manfred Smuda, "Natur als ästhetischer Gegenstand und als Gegenstand der Ästhetik," in *Landschaft*, ed. Manfred Smuda (Frankfurt a. M.: Suhrkamp, 1986), pp. 44–69.
7. Schiller's famous poem "Der Spaziergang" (The Walk) is paradigmatic expression of this double vision of landscape as a space of imaginary freedom and simultaneous domestication. On Schiller, see Wolfgang Riedel, *Der Spaziergang. Ästhetik der Landschaft* (Würzburg: Königshausen & Neumann, 1989).
8. On territory as an anthropological category, see Wolfgang Reinhard, *Lebensformen Europas. Eine historische Kulturanthropologie* (Munich: Beck, 2005), pp. 395–401.

9. See John Lennon and Malcolm Foley, *Dark Tourism: The Attraction of Death and Disaster* (London and New York: Continuum, 2000). Concerned with the popularity of sites of death and disaster in modern tourism, the authors analyze the processes of commemoration and representation that transform sites of horror into accessible commodities. Insofar as sites of dark tourism reflect on the role of technology, they offer critiques of modernity.

10. Georg Simmel, "Philosophie der Landschaft", in *Das Individuum und die Freiheit. Essais* (Berlin: Wagenbach, 1984), pp. 130–38; here, p. 131.

11. Simmel, "Philosophie der Landschaft", p. 136 [my translation].

12. On Sebald's widely debated use of photography, see Carolin Duttlinger, "Traumatic Photographs: Remembrance and the Technical Media in W. G. Sebald's *Austerlitz*", in *W. G. Sebald: A Critical Companion*, ed. J. J. Long and Anne Whitehead (Edinburgh: Edinburgh UP, 2003), pp. 155–71; J. J. Long, "History, Narrative and Photography in W. G. Sebald's *Die Ausgewanderten*", *MLR* 98 (2003), 117–37; Heiner Boehncke, "Clair obscur. W. G. Sebalds Bilder", *Text + Kritik* 158 (2003), 43–62; Stefanie Harris, "The Return of the Dead: Memory and Photography in W. G. Sebald's *Die Ausgewanderten*", *German Quarterly* 74 (2001), 370–92; On Sebald's landscape discourse, see Anne Fuchs, " 'Ein Hauptkapitel der Geschichte der Unterwerfung': Representations of Nature in W. G. Sebald's *Die Ringe des Saturn*", in *W. G. Sebald and the Writing of History*, ed. Anne Fuchs and J. J. Long (Würzburg: Königshausen & Neumann), pp. 121–38.

13. See Rupert Brooke, "The Soldier", in *The Poetical Works of Rupert Brooke*, ed. Geoffrey Keynes (London: Faber & Faber, 1951), p. 23.

14. Roland Barthes, *Camera Lucida. Reflections on Photography* (London: Jonathan Cape, 1982), p. 76.

15. Hirsch, *Family Frames*, p. 21.

16. Ibid., p. 23.

17. See John Chiene Sheperd, *Italian Gardens of the Renaissance* (London: Academy Editions, 1994). Torsten Olaf Enge, *Garden Architecture in Europe; 1450–1800. From the Villa Garden of the Italian Renaissance to the English Landscape Garden* (Cologne: Taschen, 1992).

18. Elizabeth Boa and Rachel Palfreyman, *Heimat. A German Dream*, p. 20. On *Heimat*, see also Celia Applegate, *A Nation of Provincials. The German Idea of Heimat* (Berkeley: University of California Press, 1990).

19. Thomas M. Lekan, *Imagining the Nation in Nature. Landscape Preservation and German Identity, 1885–1945* (Cambridge, MA., London: Harvard UP, 2004), p. 14.

20. Ibid., p. 17.

21. These plans included the planting of hedgerows to germanify the territory. See Lekan, *Imagining the Nation*, p. 244.

22. Erasure is a device which, by crossing things out, makes them even more visible. It thus operates like the uncanny, which is something that should have remained hidden but that has emerged. On "erasure", see Jacques Derrida, *De la grammatologie* (Paris: Minuit, 1967), p. 31. Also see Elizabeth Boa who argues that erasure is often a melodramatic device, "Telling It How It Wasn't: Familial Allegories of Wish-Fulfillment in Postunification Germany", in Anne Fuchs, Mary Cosgrove and Georg Grote (eds), *German Memory Contests*, pp. 67–83; here, p. 73.

23. See Sigmund Freud, "Das Unheimliche", in *Gesammelte Werke*, ed. Anna Freud (Frankfurt a. M.: Fischer, 1999), vol. 12, pp. 292–68. On Freud's overdetermined rhetoric, see Sarah Kofmann, *The Childhood of Art. An Interpretation of Freud's Aesthetics*, translated from the French by Winifred Woodhull (New York: Columbia UP, 1988).

24. Friederike Eigler analyzes four types of the uncanny: uncanny coincidences, uncanny origins, uncanny convergences and uncanny continuities. She argues that Wackwitz's critique of 1968 loses sight of the intra-generational differences amongst the various members of that generation who in no way shared an homogenous outlook on life. Eigler, *Gedächtnis und Geschichte*, p. 224.

25. On German colonialism, see Susanne Zantop, *Colonial Fantasies. Conquest, Family, and Nation in Precolonial Germany 1770–1870* (London, Durham NC: Duke UP, 1997); Matthias Fiedler, *Zwischen Abenteuer, Wissenschaft und Kolonialismus. Der deutsche Afrikadiskurs im 18. und 19. Jahrhundert* (Cologne, Weimar, Vienna: Böhlau, 2005); Dirk Göttsche, "Der neue historische Afrika-Roman. Kolonialismus aus postkolonialer Sicht", *German Life & Letters* 56 (2003), 261–80.

26. Dirk Göttsche, "Der koloniale Zusammenhang der Dinge in der deutschen Provinz. Wilhelm Raabe in postkolonialer Sicht", *Jahrbuch der Raabe-Gesellschaft* (2005), 53–73, here, 54.

27. Göttsche argues that this is not simply a question of analyzing Europe's literary perception of non-European worlds and their inhabitants; instead, it is a matter of adopting fundamentally new perspectives by bringing into focus the literary reflection of the prerequisites, omissions and the repercussions of colonialism in European society itself. For Göttsche this must include Germany where the memories of colonialism have been covered over by memories of National Socialism and the Holocaust. Göttsche, "Der koloniale Zusammengang", p. 55.

28. See Alfred Karasek-Langer and Elfriede Strzygowksi, *Sagen der Beskidendeutschen* (Plauen: Wolff, 1930). The book was published as volume 3 of *Ostdeutsche Heimatbücher* in 1930 and not in 1931 as Wackwitz suggests. Wackwitz's grandfather is mentioned in the introduction as one of the contributors; *Sagen der Beskidendeutschen*, p. 17.

29. In most cases the English quotations follow the translation by Stephen Lehmann. See Stephan Wackwitz, *An Invisible Country*, transl. Stephan Lehmann, with a foreword by Wendy Lesser (Philadelphia: Paul Dry Books, 2005), p. 18. Where I have used this edition, quotations are cited as *IC* followed by page number. Occasionally, however, I have opted for a more literal translation.

30. See Sigmund Freud, "Der Familienroman der Neurotiker", in *Gesammelte Werke*, ed. Anna Freud et al. (Frankfurt a. M.: Fischer, 1999), vol. 7, pp. 227–31.

31. Franz Kafka, "Eine kaiserliche Botschaft", in, *Die Erzählungen und andere ausgewählte Prosa. Originalfassung*, ed. Jürgen Born, Gerhard Neumann, Malcolm Paisley and Jost Schillemeit (Frankfurt a. M.: Fischer, 1996), pp. 305–6; here, p. 305.

32. See Elizabeth Boa, *Kafka. Gender, Class, and Race in the Letters and Fictions* (Oxford: Clarendon Press, 1996), p. 89.

33. Johann Gottlieb Fichte, *Reden an die deutsche Nation*, ed. Reinhard Lauth (Hamburg: Meiner, 1978). See for example, the opening of the seventh lecture where Fichte argues that German history proves that the Germans were the most primal and purest people. However, he continues to argue that German philosophy and thought had come under the influence of "Ausländerei" (foreign influences) which is defined by its "Nichtursprünglichkeit"(lack of an original naturalness). See the eighth and ninth lectures on this. Fichte, *Reden an die deutsche Nation*.

34. Eigler argues that Wackwitz does not adopt the so-called "Sonderwegthese", "the thesis of the special German path", according to which Germany's development took a different turn from other European countries in the 19th century. In her view, he draws a comparison between the political situation in early 19th century and in the early 20th century. By contrast, my analysis of the colonial narrative strand suggests that Wackwitz does indeed identify a strong ideological connection between the *völkisch* nationalism of the early 19th century, the colonial dream of the late 19th century and the National Socialist vision of "Lebensraum". See Eigler, *Gedächtnis und Geschichte*, p. 202.

35. See Friedrich Schleiermacher, *Hermeneutik und Kritik*, ed. and introduced by Manfred Frank (Frankfurt a. M.: Suhrkamp, 1977). See also Harald Schnur, *Schleiermachers Hermeneutik und ihre Vorgeschichte im 18. Jahrhundert: Studien zur Bibelauslegung zu Hamann, Herder und Friedrich Schlegel* (Stuttgart: Metzler: 1994).

36. On Raabe's representation of the German colonial imagination, see Peter J. Brenner, "Zur Entzauberung der Fremde und Verfremdung der Heimat in Raabes *Abu Telfan*", *Jahrbuch der Raabe-Gesellschaft* (1989), 45–62; Doris Bachmann, "Die Dritte Welt der Literatur. Eine ethnologische Methodenkritik literaturwissenschaftlichen Interpretierens am Beispiel von Wilhelm Raabes Roman *Abu Telfan oder die Heimkehr vom Mondgebirge*", *Jahrbuch der Raabe-Gesellschaft* (1979), 27–71; Göttsche, "Der koloniale Zusammenhang der Dinge", 53–73; Fiedler, *Zwischen Abenteuer, Wissenschaft und Kolonialismus*, pp. 178–98.

37. Wackwitz also mentions Hans Grimm's *Volk ohne Raum* (A People Without Space) and *Der Ölsucher von Duala* (The Oil Seeker of Duala) and *Lützeritzland* as other examples of the colonial fantasy: "es sind gustavfreytagartige, erschütternd schlechte und eigentlich fast unerträgliche Programmromane einer verspäteten kolonialen Wut und Sehnsucht, die schon 1933 politisch völlig illusionär gewesen ist (nachdem der nationale Erlöser sich mittlerweile auf 'den Osten' kapriziert hatte" (*UL*, 189; they are Gustav Freytag-like, shockingly bad and actually almost unbearably programmatic novels, throbbing with late colonial rage and a longing that by 1933 was completely delusional; *IC*, 159).

38. According to Friederike Eigler, this mix of personal recollection and cultural – historical analysis makes evident the overdetermined character of the snake story. See Eigler, *Gedächtnis und Geschichte*, p. 197.

39. Wackwitz addresses the figure of the father in *Neue Menschen. Bildungsroman* (Frankfurt a. M.: Firscher, 2005). This second generational narrative is, however, a far less cogent continuation of *Ein unsichtbares Land*. The narrator of *Neue Menschen* indulges in laboured philosophical and poetic excursions that lack thematic integration.

5   Narrating resistance to the Third Reich: Museum discourse, autobiography, fiction and film

1. For an excellent survey of the contemporary debate, see Gerd R. Ueber-schär (ed.), *Der 20. Juli. Das andere Deutschland in der Vergangenheitspolitik nach 1945* (Berlin: Elefanten Press, 1998). The title is a misnomer since the volume covers a wide range of resistance movements and activities beyond the 20 July 1944. See also Wolfgang Benz and Walter H. Pehle, *Lexikon des deutschen Widerstandes* (Frankfurt a. M.: Fischer, 2nd ed. 2004).

2. One extreme example of the widening of the term is the so-called *Bavaria Project* which, under the directorship of Peter Hüttenberger and Martin Broszat, understood resistance to include all acts which blocked Nazism's total claim to power. Broszat coined the term "Resistenz" to capture the immunity of individuals or groups to the Nazis' total penetration of society. Examples of such acts could include the refusal to say "Heil Hitler" or the continued trade by Bavarian farmers with Jews. See Martin Broszat, "Resistenz und Widerstand", *Bayern in der NS-Zeit* (Munich, Vienna: 1977–1983), vol. 4, pp. 691–709.

3. Ian Kershaw, "Resistance without the People?", in *The Nazi Dictatorship. Problems and Perspectives of Interpretation* (London, New York: Edward Arnold, 1985), pp. 150–79; here, p. 170.

4. Kershaw, "Resistance without the People?", pp. 168–69.

5. One should note, however, that this piece of legislation already reflected the impact of Cold War politics on resistance discourse; paragraph 6 I, 2, for example, denied compensation to those who were enemies of free parliamentary democracy and who supported totalitarian regimes elsewhere. This paragraph effectively meant that communist resisters were denied compensation in the West.

6. On the legal debate, see Rudolf Wassermann, "Widerstand als Rechtsproblem. Zur rechtlichen Rezeption des Widerstandes gegen das NS-Regime", in Gerd. R. Ueberschär (ed.), *Der 20. Juli*, pp. 254–67.

7. See Ulrich von Hassell, *Vom anderen Deutschland. Aus den nachgelassenen Tagebüchern 1938–1944* (Zurich: Atlantis, 1945); Fabian von Schlabrendorff, *Offiziere gegen Hitler*, ed. Gero v. Schulze Gaevernitz (Zurich: Europa Verlag, 1946); Hans Bernd Gisevius, *Bis zum bitteren Ende*. 2 vols (Zurich: Fretz & Wasmuth, 1946).

8. Norbert Frei argues that the notion of collective guilt was a product of the Germans' own defensiveness in the post-war period. Norbert Frei, "Von deutscher Erfindungskraft. Oder: Die Kollektivschuldthese in der Nach-kriegszeit", in *1945 und Wir: Das Dritte Reich im Bewußtsein der Deutschen* (Munich: Beck, 2005), pp. 145–55.

9. On the question of collective guilt, see the seminal essay by the philosopher Karl Jaspers, who in 1945 resumed his lecturing at Heidelberg University with a series on collective guilt. Karl Jaspers, *Die Schuldfrage* (Heidelberg: Lambert Schneider, 1946). For an analysis of Allied media policy to confront the Germans with their responsibility for National Socialism through photographic images and films about the concentration camps, see Dagmar Barnouw, *Germany 1945. Views of War and Violence* (Bloomington: Indiana UP, 1996).

10. In the second edition of his book *Offiziere gegen Hitler*, Fabian von Schlabrendorff claimed that the group had worked for an external power, thus denouncing the motivation of the group members as alien to German interests. See Fabian von Schlabrendorff, *Offiziere gegen Hitler* (Zurich: Europa Verlag, 2nd ed. 1951), pp. 96–97. In his biography on Carl Goerdeler, the conservative historian Gerhard Ritter labelled the group "Edelkommunisten" (champagne communists) who had been in the service of the enemy. See Gerhard Ritter, *Carl Goerdeler und die deutsche Widerstandsbewegung* (Stuttgart: Deutsche Verlagsanstalt, 1955), p. 106. The implication of Ritter's view is that resistance was illegitimate if it serviced the interests of the Soviet Union. The fear of the so-called "Bolshevik danger" outweighs for Ritter the idea of a principled opposition against Hitler, a line of argument which was often used to justify conformism.

11. For a critical evaluation of the group, see Johannes Tuchel, "Das Ende der Legenden. Die Rote Kapelle im Widerstand gegen den Nationalsozialismus", in Gerd. R. Ueberschär (ed.), *Der 20. Juli*, pp. 347–65.

12. See the reports in *Neues Deutschland*, 24 September 1946.

13. Anton Ackermann, "Legende und Wahrheit über den 20. Juli", *Einheit* 7 (1947), 1172–82. Quoted in Ines Reich und Kurt Finker, "Reaktionäre oder Patrioten? Zur Historiographie und Widerstandsforschung in der DDR bis 1990", in Gerd. R. Ueberschär (ed.), *Der 20. Juli*, pp. 158–78; here, pp. 159–60.

14. Reich und Finker, "Reaktionäre oder Patrioten?", p. 161.

15. See Walter Schmitthenner and Hans Buchheim (eds), *Der deutsche Widerstand gegen Hitler. Vier historisch-kritische Studien von Herrmann Graml, Hans Mommsen, Hans J. Reichardt und Ernst Wolff* (Cologne, Berlin: Kiepenheuer & Witsch, 1966).

16. Kurt Finker, *Stauffenberg und der 20. Juli 1944* (Berlin: Union-Verlag, 1967).

17. These features are the natural target of the type of critical historiography which has established itself since the 1960s. The reception of resistance discourse since the millenium shows, however, that the finer points of historical research do not necessarily infiltrate cultural memory. This will be the subject of later analysis.

18. An interesting case in point is the Red Army Faction which saw itself as a legitimate resistance movement against "imperialist" West German rule. While this view was neither shared by the legislator nor by the general public, many representatives of 1968 did advocate resistance to the "imperialist" system. However, while many student protesters did support the idea of legitimate violence against objects and institutions, dissent arose over the abduction and murder of people.

19. For details of this controversy, see Bill Niven's account: *Facing the Nazi Past. United Germany and the Legacy of the Third Reich* (London, New York: Routledge, 2002), pp. 77–84.

20. Niven, *Facing the Nazi Past*, p. 83.

21. Schröder's speech and all other speeches held in the courtyard of the Bendlerblock since 1952 can be accessed on the website of the *Gedenkstätte Deutscher Widerstand*: www.20-juli-44.de/reden.

22. Peter Steinbach, "Vermächtnis oder Verfälschung? Erfahrungen mit Ausstellungen über den deutschen Widerstand", in Gerd R. Ueberschär (ed.), *Der 20. Juli*, pp. 212–34; here, p. 230.

23. Steinbach, "Vermächtnis oder Verfälschung?", p. 219.
24. For more information, see the entry "Goerdeler-Kreis", in Wolfgang Benz and Walter H. Pehle (eds), *Lexikon des deutschen Widerstandes*, pp. 218–22.
25. On conservative resistance, see Hans Mommsen, *Alternatives to Hitler. German Resistance under the Third Reich*, translated and annotated by Angus McGeoch, with an introduction by Jeremy Noakes (London, New York: I. B. Tauris, 2003), p. 32 and p. 66.
26. Mommsen, *Alternatives to Hitler*, pp. 43–44.
27. Stauffenberg, Friedrich Olbricht, Albrecht Ritter Merz von Quirnheim and Werner von Haeften were executed on the 20th July plot in the courtyard of the Bendlerblock.
28. Wibke Bruhns, *Meines Vaters Land. Geschichte einer deutschen Familie* (Munich: Econ, 2004). All subsequent page references appear as *MV* followed by the page number in the main text.
29. For example, Sabine Vogel in *die tageszeitung* praises the book as a subtle family novel, offering an economic and social history of the German bourgeoisie from the 19th century onwards (*die tageszeitung*, 17 July 2004). Similarly, Elke Schubert in *Die Frankfurter Rundschau* appreciates the exemplariness with which Bruhns shows the pathway of the bourgeois family to National Socialism (*Frankfurter Rundschau*, 6 April 2004). Cathrin Kahlweit in the *Süddeutsche* also appreciates the privatization of history in Bruhns's book (*Süddeutsche Zeitung*, 22 March 2004). The reviewer of the *Frankfurter Allgemeine Zeitung* was equally positive (*FAZ*, 19 February 2004).
30. Volker Ullrich, "Gruppenbild mit Nazis", *Die Zeit*, 19 February 2004.
31. Justin Cartwright's recent novel *The Song Before it is Sung* (London: Bloomsbury, 2007) makes an interesting contribution to the resistance narrative by reconstructing the fallout between the Jewish philosopher Isaiah Berlin and Adam Trott von Solz, who had met and befriended Berlin in Cambridge when Adam Trott was a Rhodes Scholar.
32. On repression as a mnemonic technique, see Anne Fuchs, "From *Vergangenheitsbewältigung* to Generational Memory Contests", *GLL* 59(2006), 176–79.
33. Nicolas Abraham, "Aufzeichnungen über das Phantom. Ergänzungen zu Freuds Metapsychologie", *Psyche* 8 (1991), 691–98; here, 697.
34. Weigel, *Genea-Logik*, p. 74.
35. For Weigel literary history itself can be viewed in terms of a phantom. Weigel, *Genea-Logik*, p. 75. She argues that insofar as literary history subscribes to the idea of a secure national tradition anchored in an unquestionable heritage, it is itself a phantom of the repressed knowledge that the very idea of tradition is inherently unstable and shadowed by the uncanny. Or to put it differently, the eradication of all gaps in national traditions produces an inverse effect: tradition itself becomes a phantom haunted by that which it represses.
36. Although Bruhns does not explicitly refer to Peter Weiss, her depiction of the executions must be read against the backdrop of Weiss's seminal treatment of the subject in *Die Ästhetik des Widerstands*. Weiss describes in great detail the executions of the members of the Rote Kapelle from the point of view of various observers, such as the prison pastor at Plötzensee. See Peter Weiss, *Die Ästhetik des Widerstands* (Frankfurt a. M.: Suhrkamp, 1983), vol. III.2, pp. 210–20.

37. Friedrich Christian Delius, *Mein Jahr als Mörder. Roman* (Berlin: Rowohlt, 2004). All subsequent references appear as *MJ* followed by the page number in the main text.

38. On the 1 May 1951, the West Berlin *Tagesspiegel* published an article on p. 2 entitled "Kommunistenfiliale in Westberlin" (branch of communists in West Berlin) which opened the witchhunt against Anneliese Groscurth. Nine days later the paper titled "Rote Propagandistin entlassen" (Red propagandist sacked) when Anneliese Groscurth had lost her job in the public health service as a direct result of the paper's article. After the publication of Delius's acclaimed novel the paper made no reference to its own involvement in the Groscurth affair.

39. On the notion of agitated words, see Abraham, "Aufzeichnungen über das Phantom", 698.

40. According to Sigrid Weigel, insofar as the family romance of nations always goes back to dark origins and includes repressed events in its tradition, one has to assume that the phantom represents a regular way of forming traditions. Weigel, *Genea-Logik*, p. 76.

41. Other works by Mulot that are written in this vein are *Die unschuldigen Jahre* (The Innocent Years, 1999) and *Die Fabrikanten* (The Entrepreneurs, 2005).

42. Sibylle Mulot, *Nachbarn* (Zurich: Diogenes, 1995), p. 34. All subsequent page references appear in the main text as *N* followed by the page number.

43. For a comprehensive analysis of the French resistance narrative, see Christopher Lloyd, *Collaboration and Resistance in Occupied France. Representing Treason and Sacrifice* (Basingstoke: Palgrave, 2003).

44. Zygmunt Bauman, *Community. Seeking Safety in an Insecure World* (Cambridge: Polity Press, 2001), p. 11.

45. Michael Wallner, *April in Paris* (Munich: Luchterhand, 2006). Henceforth cited as *AP* in main body of text followed by page reference.

46. The list includes Australia, the United States, Great Britain, Brazil, Israel and many European countries. His previous novels are *Cliehms Begabung* (2000) and *Finale* (2003).

47. On this point, see Juliet John, *Dickens's Villains. Melodrama, Character, Popular Culture* (Oxford: Oxford UP, 2001), p. 49.

48. Robert Heilman, *Tragedy and Melodrama, Versions of Experience* (Seattle, London: University of Washington Press, 1968), p. 243.

49. Michael R. Booth, *English Melodrama* (London: Herbert Jenkins, 1965), p. 14.

50. John, *Dickens's Villains*, p. 56.

51. Peter Brooks, *The Melodramatic Imagination: Balzac, Henry James, Melodrama, and the Mode of Excess* (New York: Columbia UP, 1984), p. 43.

52. Frank Schirrmacher, "Stauffenberg: ein Geschichtsfilm ohne Geschichte", *FAZ*, 25 February 2004. See also Jens Jessen's review which similarly argues that the film is lacking an historical perspective, "Unternehmen Walküre", *Die Zeit*, 19 February 2004.

53. Sabine Hake, *German National Cinema* (London and New York: Routledge, 2002), p. 180.

54. Ibid., p. 187.

55. Lutz Koepnick, "Reframing the Past: Heritage Cinema and Holocaust in the 1990s", *New German Critique* 87 (2002), 47–82; here, 50.

56. Koepnick, "Reframing the Past", 72.

57. Wolfgang Preiss played Stauffenberg, Werner Hinz was Generaloberst Beck, Paul Esser appeared as von Witzleben, and Wolfgang Büttner as Oberst Olbricht.

58. For a more detailed analysis of the reception of the two films in the 1950s, see Peter Reichel, *Erfundene Erinnerung*, pp. 71–78.

59. For details on this failed attempt, see Joachim Fest, *Staatsstreich. Der lange Weg zum 20. Juli* (Berlin: Siedler, 1994), pp. 195–99.

60. Mommsen, *Alternatives to Hitler*, p. 35.

61. Facsimiles of the leaflets are contained in the *Begleitmaterialien zur Ausstellung "Widerstand gegen den Nationalsozialismus"* by the *Gedenkstätte Deutscher Widerstand*, Berlin, no date.

62. For a detailed analysis of these Russian experiences, see Detlef Bald, *Die Weiße Rose. Von der Front in den Widerstand* (Berlin: Aufbau, 2003).

63. Hans Konrad Leipelt was also sentenced to death and executed on 29 January 1945. He had copied the last leaflet and attempted to distribute it; he also collected money for Kurt Huber's widow after his murder. Heinz Kucharski belonged to a resistance circle in Hamburg which discussed the *Weiße Rose* leaflets; sentenced to death, he managed to escape while on transport to his execution.

64. Others in the cast include Fabian Hinrichs as Hans Scholl, André Hennicke as Roland Freisler, Florian Stetter as Christoph Probst and Johanna Gastdorf as Else Gebel, the prison inmate who shared Sophie's cell.

65. See, for example, Elmar Krekeler's review "Die Stunde der Patriotin", *Berliner Morgenpost*, 24 February 2005. See also Stefan Reinecke, "Chronist des Opfers", *die tageszeitung*, 14 February 2005. Similarly Fritz Göttler, "*Sophie Scholl. Die Letzten Tage*: ein Traum von Licht", *Süddeutsche Zeitung*, 23 February 2005; Thomas Assheuer, "In unser aller Auftrag", *Die Zeit*, 24 February 2005.

66. See Stefan Reinecke's review "Chronist des Opfers".

67. The wording here is close to the Gestapo files. See Bundesarchiv Berlin, ZC 13267, vol. 3.

68. Giorgio Agamben, *Homo Sacer. Sovereign Power and Bare Life*, translated from the Italian by Daniel Heller-Roazen (Stanford: Stanford UP, 1998).

69. Hannah Arendt, *On Violence* (San Diego, New York, London: Harcourt Brace & Copnay, 1970), p. 55.

70. Ibid., p. 56.

71. The cast included Jutta Lampe as Ruth, Maria Schrader as Hannah, Katja Rieman in the role of the young Lena Fischer, Doris Schade as the 90-year-old Lena and Jürgen Vogel as Lena's brother; the well-known Brechtian performer Jutta Wachowiak and Belgian actor Jan Decleir appeared as an elderly German – Jewish couple during the Third Reich.

72. Nathan Stoltzfus, *Resistance of the Heart: Intermarriage and the Rosenstraße Protest in Nazi Germany* (New York and London: W. W. Norton, 1996).

73. Wolf Gruner, *Widerstand in der Rosenstraße. Die Fabrik-Aktion und die Verfolgung der Mischehen 1943* (Frankfurt a. M.: Fischer, 2005); on Nazi policies for the so-called "mixed marriages", see Beate Meyer, *Jüdische Mischlinge. Rassenpolitik und Verfolgungserfahrung 1933–1945* (Hamburg: Dölling & Gallitz, 1999). Meyer also contributed to the debate around von Trotta's film, criticizing a variety of historical "errors" in "Geschichte im

Film – Judenverfolgung, Mischehen und der Protest in der Rosenstraße", *Zeitschrift für Geschichtswissenschaft* 52 (2004), 23–46. See also a shorter reprint on H-German@h-net.msu.edu (July 2004).

74. Wolfgang Benz, "Kitsch as Kitsch can", *Die Süddeutsche Zeitung*, 18 September 2003.

75. Nathan Stoltzfus, "Die Wahrheit jenseits der Akten", *Die Zeit*, 10 October 2003.

76. Koepnick, "Reframing the Past", 73 and 56; Daniela Berghahn, "Post-1990 Screen Memories: How East and West German Cinema Remembers the Third Reich and the Holocaust", *German Life & Letters* 59 (2006), 294–308.

77. Berghahn, "Post-1990 Screen Memories", 306.

78. Ibid.

79. See Evelyn Wilcock, "Rosenstraße – a response", http://www.h-net.org/~german/discuss/Rosenstrasse/Rosenstrasse_index.htm (accessed 2 February 2007).

80. Arguing historically, Meyer misses the staged choreography, see Beate Meyer, "Geschichte im Film – Judenverfolgung, Mischehen und der Protest in der Rosenstraße", http://www.h-net.org/~german/discuss/Rosenstrasse/Rosenstrasse_index.htm (accessed 2 February 2007).

81. Koepnick, "Reframing the Past", 76. For a critical appraisal of heritage films, see Matthias Fiedler, "German Crossroads: Visions of the Past in German Cinema after Reunification", in Anne Fuchs, Mary Cosgrove, Georg Grote (eds), *German Memory Contests*, pp. 127–45.

82. Fiedler, "German Crossroads", p. 143.

6   Hitler Youth autobiographies: Günter Grass's *Beim Häuten der Zwiebel* and Joachim Fest's *Ich nicht*

1. Philippe Lejeune, *Le pacte autobiographique* (Paris: Seuil, 1975); see also Lejeune, *On Autobiography*, transl. by Katherine Leary, ed. by John Paul Eakin (Minneapolis: University of Minneapolis Press, 1989).

2. Roland Barthes, "The Reality Effect", in *The Rustle of Language* (California: California UP, 1989), pp. 141–48. See also Martina Wagner-Egelhaaf who speaks of a "desire for reality". Martina Wagner-Egelhaaf, *Autobiographie* (Stuttgart: Metzler, 2nd ed. 2005), p. 8.

3. Paul de Man, "Autobiography as De-facement", *Modern Langues Notes* 94 (1979), 919–30; here, 920.

4. On "life writing" in current debates, see Marlene Kadar, Linda Warley, Jeanne Perreault, Susanna Egan (eds), *Tracing the Autobiographical* (Waterloo, Ontario: Wilfrid Laurier UP, 2005); G. Thomas Couser, *Vulnerable Subjects. Ethics and Life Writing* (Ithaca, New York, London: Cornell UP, 2004); Paul John Eakin (ed.), *The Ethics of Life Writing* (Ithaca, New York, London: Cornell UP, 2004); Paul John Eakin, *How Our Lives Become Stories: Making Selves* (Ithaca, New York, London: Cornell UP, 1999).

5. On the development of autobiography from the Middle Ages to early modernism, see Horst Wenzel (ed.), *Die Autobiographien des späten Mittelalters und der frühen Neuzeit* (Munich: Fink, 1980).

6. See Jean Starobinski, *Jean-Jacques Rousseau. La transparence et l'obstacle* (Paris: Gallimard, 1976).

7. See Jean-Jacques Rousseau, *Les Confessions I* (Paris: Gallimard, 1973), p. 31. See Ralf Konersmann, "Zeichensprache. Wahrheit und Wahrhaftigkeit bei Rousseau", *DVjs* 66 (1982), 41–62.

8. Rousseau radicalized Montaigne's declaration that his *Essays* would paint an authentic picture of himself precisely because they would expose both his "defects" and his "native form", see *The Essays of Michel De Montaigne*, transl. and ed. with an introduction by M. A. Screech (London: Allen Lane, Penguin Press, 1991), p. lix.

9. While Goethe wrote part I, II and III between 1811 and 1813, part IV was only completed in 1831 and published posthumously in 1833. On Goethe's autobiography, see Bernd Witte, "Autobiographie als Poetik. Zur Kunstgestalt von Goethes *Dichtung und Wahrheit*", *Neue Rundschau* 89 (1978), 384–92.

10. See Johann Wolfgang von Goethe, *Briefe. Hamburger Ausgabe* (Munich: dtv, 1988), vol. 4, p. 363.

11. Anthony Giddens, *Modernity and Self-Identity: Self and Society in the late Modern Age* (Cambridge: Polity Press, 1991).

12. Zygmunt Bauman, *Identity. Conversations with Benedetto Vecchi* (Cambridge: Polity, 2004), p. 23.

13. Ciarán Benson, *The Cultural Psychology of the Self. Place, Morality and Art in Human Worlds* (London, New York: Routledge, 2001), p. 10.

14. See Helmut Schelsky, *Die skeptische Generation* (Düsseldorf, Cologne: Diederichs, 1957).

15. See Frei, *1945 und Wir*, p. 12.

16. Weigel, " 'Generation' as a Symbolic Form", 272.

17. Weigel writes, "As founder generation of the new state this is the concealed first generation whose roots in the Nazi period are negated due to their age at the time. This generation came to see itself as an innocent child." Weigel, " 'Generation' as Symbolic Form", 273.

18. Martin Walser, *Ein springender Brunnen. Roman* (Frankfurt a. M.: Suhrkamp, 1998), p. 283.

19. Helmut Schmitz, *On Their Own Terms. The Legacy of National Socialism in Post-1990 German Fiction* (Birmingham: University of Birmingham Press, 2004), pp. 197–98.

20. Ibid., p. 201.

21. Part I, *Also Ordnung ist das ganze Leben* (Order is One's Whole Life, 1986) offers a portrait of the 1920s and, above all, of the mentality of the paternal generation which was disaffected by the Weimar Republic. Part III, *Wer mit den Wölfen heult, wird Wolf* (Whoever runs with the Pack becomes a Wolf, 1996), begins with the end of the war as a defining moment of liberation and moves on to explore the emerging post-war order and, above all, the intellectual climate of the 1950s.

22. Harig's narrative treatment of outsiders in the community, such as the school boy René, who was mistreated by his classmates for his apparent otherness, provides a good example of this. Harig shows that euthanasia and the disappearance of local Jews was widely known. See Ludwig Harig, *Weh dem der aus der Reihe tanzt* (Munich: Hanser, 1990). On this part of the autobiography, see Schmitz, *On their Own Terms*, pp. 159–79.

23. See also Thomas Bernhard's *Die Ursache* (The Cause, 1975), the first part of a five-part autobiography. In this text, Bernhard analyzes the repressiveness of family life and of the Austrian educational system during National Socialism. He also explores the continuity of Nazi thinking and the authoritarianism of the post-war period. See Urs Bugmann, *Bewältigungsversuch. Thomas Bernhards autobiographische Schriften* (Berne, Frankfurt a. M.: Peter Lang, 1981). On Austrian autobiography, see Klaus Amann and Karl Wagner (eds), *Autobiographien in der österreichischen Literatur. Von Franz Grillparzer bis Thomas Bernhard* (Innsbruck, Vienna: Studien-Verlag, 1998).

24. On Wolf, see Sabine Wilke, " 'Worüber man nicht sprechen kann, darüber muß man allmählich zu schweigen aufhören': Vergangenheitsbeziehungen in Christa Wolfs *Kindheitsmuster"*, *Germanic Review* 56 (1991), 169–76, Almut Finck, "Subjektivität und Geschichte in der Postmoderne. Christa Wolfs *Kindheitsmuster"*, in *Geschriebenes Leben. Autobiographik von Frauen*, ed. Michaela Holdenried (Berlin: Erich Schmidt, 1995), pp. 311–23. On Wolf's later autobiographical narratives and East German autobiography, see Dennis Tate, *Shifting Perspectives. East German Autobiographical Narratives Before and After the end of the GDR* (Rochester: Camden House, 2007).

25. Christa Wolf, *Kindheitsmuster* (Berlin, Weimar: Aufbau, 1976), p. 215.

26. On this issue, see Hans J. Markowitsch and Harald Welzer, *Das autobiographische Gedächtnis. Hirnorganische Grundlagen und biosoziale Entwicklung* (Stuttgart: Klett-Cotta, 2005).

27. Dominick LaCapra, *Writing History, Writing Trauma*, pp. 41–42. See also Dominick LaCapra, *History and Memory after Auschwitz* (Ithaca, London: Cornell UP, 1998).

28. Peter Sloterdijk, *Literatur und Organisation von Lebenserfahrung* (Munich: Hanser, 1987), p. 113.

29. Günter Grass, *Beim Häuten der Zwiebel* (Göttingen: Steidl, 2006). Subsequent references appear in the main text as *BH* followed by page references.

30. "Warum ich nach sechzig Jahren mein Schweigen breche. Eine deutsche Jugend: Günter Grass spricht zum ersten Mal über sein Erinnerungsbuch und seine Mitgliedschaft in der Waffen-SS", *FAZ*, 12 August 2006, 33–35; here, 33. [All translations of quotations from newspapers are mine, unless otherwise indicated.]

31. "It is common knowledge that our memories, our self perceptions may be and oftentimes are deceptive. We embellish, dramatize, tie up outcomes in anecdotes. I wanted to hint at all of this, to include the shady bits which all memories feature, I wanted to have this shining through the form." Ibid., 33.

32. Frank Schirrmacher, "Das Geständnis", *FAZ*, 12 August 2006, 1.

33. Gustav Seibt, "Geständnis einer Schnecke", *Süddeutsche Zeitung*, 15/16 August 2006, 11.

34. Jens Jessen, "Und Grass wundert sich", *Die Zeit*, 17 August 2006, 1.

35. Stephan Speicher, "Die zwei Rätsel des Günter Grass", *taz*, 14 August 2006, 4.

36. Christian Thomas, "örtlich betäubt", *Frankfurter Rundschau*, 14 August 2006, 3. However, in the same paper, Harry Nutt questions the very premise of the moralizing debate: Nutt raised the question as to what kind of life we ascribe to such a paradigmatic figure from the outside. Harry Nutt, "Das lange Schweigen", *FR*, 14 August 2006, 3.

37. The precise wording of the question was, "Ist Günter Grass für Sie nach seinem Eingeständnis eine Persönlichkeit, deren Wort in politischen und moralischen Fragen auch weiterhin Gewicht hat?" (Following his confession, do Günter Grass's statements on political and moral questions continue to bear weight for you?), *Der Spiegel*, 21 August 2006, 63.

38. See also Henryk M. Broder, "Der Herr der Binse", *Spiegel Online*, 14 August 2006, http://www.spiegel.de./kultur/gesellschaft/0,1518,431695,00.html (accessed on 14 August 2006). Broder polemicizes as follows: "Es ist, als würde eine Familie vor Weihnachten erfahren, dass Oma als junge Frau auf den Strich gegangen ist, ausgerechnet Oma, die sich immer als besonders sittenstreng gebärdet und den Enkeln das Tragen von Miniröcken verboten hat. Und nun fragen sich alle: Wohin mit Oma?" [It is as if a family were to find out shortly before Christmas that Grandma used to work the streets in her younger years. Grandma, of all people, who is always such a stick in the mud about decorum and who forbade her granddaughters to wear mini-skirts. Now, everyone is asking; where are we going to put her?].

39. Matthias Matussek, Volker Hage, et al., "Fehlbar und verstrickt", *Der Spiegel*, 31 August 2006, 46–66 ; here, 47.

40. Ibid., 58.

41. Ibid., 58. Accordingly the self-reflections in Grass's autobiography are dismissed as a strategy of concealment that disguise historical facts; Ibid., 60.

42. Georg Klein, "Unser armer grandioser Greis", *Die Welt*, 19 August 2006, "Die literarische Welt", 1. Also see Georg Diez, "Opa Grass. Die Enkel, die Erinnerung und die Geschichtspolitik", *Die Zeit*, 17 August 2006, 41.

43. In April 2007, the publisher Klaus Wagenbach wrote an article in *Die Zeit* in which he revealed that he recently found some notes for a Grass biography that he had jotted down in 1963. These notes contained a reference to Grass's service in the SS. For Wagenbach, this is proof that Grass had not concealed his SS membership prior to the mid-1960s. He suggests that until then Grass could rely on widespread knowledge that many youngsters were drafted into the SS as canon fodder at the very end of the war. According to Wagenbach, it is likely that Grass only stopped talking about his brief service once the atrocities committed by the SS entered the public domain. Klaus Wagenbach, "Grass hat nichts verschwiegen", *Die Zeit*, 26 April 2007.

44. Ruth Benedict, *The Chrysanthemum and the Sword: Patterns of Japanese Culture* (Cleveland: Meridian Books, 1967)

45. Another counter-narrative concerns his childhood friend Wolfgang Heinrichs, who challenged the war propaganda of the NS propaganda machine. His family derived their information from the BBC, the enemy broadcaster. The reader learns that Wolfgang Heinrichs came from a Social Democratic household: the father was imprisoned in a concentration camp and then dispatched to the eastern front as part of a so-called "Himmelfahrtskommando" (ascension commando). He survived the war and returned to the eastern sector attracted by the vision of a socialist state. However, when he challenged the enforced amalgamation of the SPD and KPD in the SED, he was once more threatened with imprisonment in Buchenwald (*BH*, 24). Again this episode shows that resistance is an exceptional concept.

46. Wolfgang Preisendanz, "Zum Vorrang des Komischen bei der Darstellung von Geschichtserfahrung in deutschen Romanen unserer Zeit", in *Das*

Komische, ed. W. Preisendanz, Rainer Warning [Poetik und Hermeneutik vol. 7] (Munich: Fink, 1976), pp. 154–64.

47. Andrew Plowman, "Between 'Restauration' and 'Nierentisch': The 1950s in Ludwig Harig, F. C. Delius, and Thomas Hettche", in Anne Fuchs, Mary Cosgrove and Georg Grote (eds), *German Memory Contests*, pp. 253–69; here, p. 259.

48. Joachim Fest, *Hitler* (Berlin: Propyläen, 1973).

49. Albert Speer, *Spandauer Tagebücher* (Berlin, Vienna: Propyläen, 1975); Joachim Fest, *Speer. Eine Biographie* (Berlin: Fest, 1999).

50. For an historical perspective on Speer's knowledge of and involvement with the Final Solution, see Matthias Schmidt, *Albert Speer. Das Ende eines Mythos* (Berne, Munich: Scherz, 1982); Susanne Willems, *Der entsiedelte Jude. Albert Speers Wohnungsmarktpolitik für den Berliner Hauptstadtbau* (Berlin: Edition Hentrich, 2002). For an evaluation of Speer in Germany's collective memory, see Stefan Krebs and Werner Tschacher, "Speer und Er. Und wir? Deutsche Geschichte in gebrochener Erinnerung", *Geschichte in Wissenschaft und Unterricht* 58 (2007), 163–73. The title of this essay refers to Heinrich Breloer's docudrama *Speer und Er* (2005), which challenged the received view of Speer as an "innocent" technocrat. Recently, the debate on Speer was ignited once more when a letter that Speer wrote on 23 September 1971 to Hélène Jeanty, the widow of a Belgian resistance fighter, resurfaced in which he admitted that he had been present at Himmler's Posen speech where the Final Solution was unveiled.

51. Joachim Fest, *Staatsstreich. Der lange Weg zum 20. Juli* (Berlin Siedler, 1994); Joachim Fest, *Der Untergang. Hitler und das Ende des Dritten Reiches, eine historische Skizze* (Berlin: Fest, 4th ed. 2002). Traudl Junge, *Bis zur letzten Stunde. Hitlers Sekretärin erzählt ihr Leben*, unter Mitarbeit von Melisssa Müller (Munich: Claasen, 2002).

52. Robert Leicht, "Ein Mikromilieu des Anstands", *Die Zeit*, 14 September 2006.

53. Markus Sander, "Joachim Fest: *Ich nicht*. Erinnerungen an eine Kindheit und Jugend", *Stuttgarter Zeitung*, 29 September 2006; Eckhard Fuhr, "Joachim Fests Jugend-Autobiografie *Ich nicht*", *Die Welt*, 13 September 2006.

54. Alexander Cammann, "Ein imaginäres Museum", *die tageszeitung*, 4 October 2006.

55. See Ingo Cornils, "Successful Failure? The Impact of the German Student Movement on the Federal Republic of Germany", in *Recasting German Identity*, ed. Stuart Taberner and Frank Finlay (Rochester: Camden, 2002), pp. 109–26.

56. On the notion of normalization, see Stuart Taberner and Paul Cooke, *German Culture, Politics and Literature into the Twenty-First Century* (Rochester: Camden House, 2006).

57. Botho Strauß, "Anschwellender Bocksgesang", in *Der Aufstand gegen die sekundäre Welt* (Munich, 1999), pp. 55–79. On Strauß as an exponent of the New Right, see Roger Woods, "On Forgetting and Remembering: The New Right Since German Unification", in Anne Fuchs, Mary Cosgrove, Georg Grote (eds), *German Memory Contests*, pp. 271–86.

58. See Martin Walser, "Erfahrungen beim Verfassen einer Sonntagsrede", in *Die Walser-Bubis-Debatte. Eine Dokumentation*, ed. Frank Schirrmacher (Frankfurt a. M.: Suhrkamp, 1999), pp. 7–29. The late Ignatz Bubis responded in his capacity as President of the Jewish Council and as a Holocaust

survivor. See Ignatz Bubis, "Rede des Präsidenten des Zentralrats der Juden in Deutschland am 9. November 1998 in der Synagoge Rykerstrase in Berlin", in *Die Walser-Bubis-Debatte*, pp. 106–13. For subsequent academic debates, see Amir Eshel, "Vom eigenen Gewissen: Die Walser-Bubis-Debatte und der Ort des Nationalsozialismus im Selbstbild der Bundesrepublik", *DVjs* 2 (2000), 333–60; Anne Fuchs, "Towards an Ethics of Remembering: The Walser-Bubis Debate and the Other of Discourse", *German Quarterly* 75 (2002), 235–47.

59. The effects of unification were also debated in terms of normalization. On this issue, see Stuart Taberner and Paul Cooke, "Introduction", in *German Culture, Politics and Literature into the Twenty-First Century: Beyond Normalization*, ed. Stuart Taberner and Paul Cooke (Rochester: Camden House, 2006), pp. 1–15. See also Stephen Brockmann's contribution in the same volume, " 'Normalization': Has Helmut Kohl's Vision Been Realized?", pp. 17–29.

60. The law stipulates that children can have dual citizenship until the age of 18 years; thereafter they have to choose one over the other unless they make a special case for maintaining two citizenships. For more legal details, see www.einbuergerung.de

61. Fischer was accused of throwing Molotov cocktails during a demonstration in 1976. He denied this and only admitted beating up a policeman. On the memory of German terrorism, see Chris Homewood, "The Return of 'Undead' History: The West German Terrorist as Vampire and the Problem of 'Normalizing' the Past in Margarethe von Trotta's *Die bleierne Zeit* (1981) and Christian Petzold's *Die innere Sicherheit* (2001)", in Taberner and Cooke (eds), *German Culture*, pp. 121–50.

62. Matthias Matussek, "Der stolze Einzelgänger", *Der Spiegel*, 12 September 2006.

63. On the significance of Augustine, see Paul Ricoeur, *Memory, History and Forgetting*, translated from the French by Kathleen Blamey and David Pellauer (Chicago: University of Chicago Press, 2004), pp. 96–102.

64. Joachim Fest, *Ich nicht. Erinnerungen an eine Kindheit und Jugend* (Reinbek: Rowohlt, 2006), p. 13. All subsequent page references appear in the text followed by *IN*.

65. The historiography of the First World War is still largely embedded in national history. On the German perspective, see Rainer Rother (ed.), *Der Weltkrieg 1914–1918. Ereignis und Erinnerung* (Berlin: Minerva, 2004).

66. Boris Barth, *Dolchstoßlegenden und politische Desintegration: das Trauma der deutschen Niederlage im Ersten Weltkrieg 1914–1933* (Düsseldorf: Droste, 2003).

67. The *Reichsbanner Schwarz-Rot-Gold* was formed in 1924 by the First World War veterans who wanted to protect the Weimar Republic against right-wing and left-wing militancy. Its members included party supporters of the Social Democratic Party, the Zentrumspartei, the Deutsche Demokratische Partei and the Trade Unions.

68. On German *Bildungsbürgertum*, see Dagmar Günther, *Das nationale Ich? Autobiographische Sinnkonstruktionen deutscher Bildungsbürger des Kaiserreichs* (Tübingen: Niemeyer, 2004).

69. Michael Grüttner, "Die nationalsozialistische Wissenschaftspolitik und die Geisteswissenschaften", in *Literaturwissenschaft und Nationalsozialismus*, ed. Holger Dainat and Lutz Danneberg (Tübingen: Niemeyer, 2003), pp. 13–39.

70. See Nobert Frei, *Karriere im Zwielicht. Hitlers Eliten nach 1945* (Frankfurt a. M.: Campus, 2001); Jörg Friedrich, *Die kalte Amnestie. NS-Täter in der Bundesrepublik* (Frankfurt a. M.: Fischer, 1984).
71. Cited after the *King James Version*, Book of Matthew, Chapter 26, pp. 33–34. See also "The Book of Mark", Chapter 14, verses 27–31.
72. Cited after the *Biblia Sacra Vulgata*, The Latin version can be accessed through www.lib.uchicago.edu/efts/ARTFL/public/bibles.
73. The exception is Robert Leicht, "Ein Mikromilieu des Aufstands", *Die Zeit*, 14 September 2006.

7 Epilogue: Germany as a threshold culture

1. Jürgen Busche, "Hat Jürgen Habermas die Wahrheit verschluckt?", *Cicero. Magazin für politische Kultur* 11 (2006), 72–77.
2. Gereon Wolters, *Vertuschung, Anklage, Rechtfertigung. Impromptus zum Rückblick der deutschen Philosophie auf das Dritte Reich* (Bonn: Bonn UP, 2005).
3. Jürgen Habermas, *Eine Art Schadensabwicklung. Kleine politische Schriften VI* (Frankfurt a. M.: Suhrkamp, 1987).
4. Andreas Zielcke, "Verleumdung wider besseres Wissen", *Süddeutsche Zeitung*, 27 October 2006.
5. Jürgen Habermas to Wolfram Weimer, 25 October 2006. The letter can be accessed online www.cicero.de/97.php?ress_id=9&item=1444 (accessed 3 March 2007).
6. Christian Geyer, "Ein Fall Habermas? Der verschluckte Zettel", *FAZ*, 27 October 2007; see also Uwe Justus Wenzel, "Verschluckte Geschichte. Eine Anekdote über Jürgen Habermas wird aufgewärmt", *Neue Zürcher Zeitung*, 28 October 2007.
7. Filbinger died on 1 April 2007, aged 93. In his funeral oration, Oettinger followed the conventions of the *de mortuis nihil ni si bene*. He said "Hans Filbinger war kein Nationalsozialist. Im Gegenteil: Er war ein Gegner des NS-Regimes. Allerdings konnte er sich den Zwängen des Regimes ebenso wenig entziehen wie Millionen andere" (Hans Filbinger was no National Socialist. On the contrary, he was opposed to the NS regime. However, like millions of Germans he could not resist the pressures of the system). Cited in "Auszüge aus der Trauerrede Oettingers auf Filbinger", *FAZ*, 12 April 2007. For a critical evaluation of Filbinger's role during National Socialism, see Robert Leicht, "Unrecht. Schlechtes Gedächtnis, gutes Gewissen – zum Tode Hans Filbingers. Ein Nachruf", *Die Zeit*, 4 April 2007; Oliver Das Gupta, " 'Filbinger hatte Handlungsspielraum' – Historiker widersprechen Oettinger", *Süddeutsche Zeitung*, 16 April 2007; Heribert Prantl, "Wenn die Geschichte ruhen will – Deutschland und die Aufarbeitung der NS Historie", *Süddeutsche Zeitung*, 16 April 2007.
8. See Bernd Dörris, "Oettingers späte Einsicht", *Süddeutsche Zeitung*, 16 April 2007; Günter Nonnenmacher, "Der Widerruf", *Frankfurter Allgemeine Zeitung*, 17 April 2007; Georg Löwisch und Lukas Wallraf, "Widerruf im dritten Anlauf", *die tageszeitung*, 17 April 2007.
9. Fritzsche, *Stranded in the Present*, p. 104.

Works Cited

Primary Works

Bernhard, Thomas, *Die Ursache* (Salzburg: Residenz Verlag, 1975).

Beyer, Marcel, *Flughunde* (Frankfurt a. M.: Suhrkamp, 1995).

Beyer, Marcel, *The Karnau Tapes*, transl. John Brownjohn (London: Secker & Warburg, 1997).

Beyer, Marcel, *Spione* (Frankfurt a. M.: Fischer, 2002).

Beyer, Marcel, *Spies*, transl. Breon Mitchell (Florida: Harcourt, 2005).

Brown, Dan, *The da Vinci Code* (London: Corgi Books, 2003).

Bruhns, Wibke, *Meines Vaters Land. Geschichte einer deutschen Familie* (Munich: Econ, 2004).

Cartwright, Justin, *The Song before it is Sung* (London: Bloomsbury, 2007).

Delius, Friedrich Christian, *Mein Jahr als Mörder* (Berlin: Rowohlt, 2004).

Dückers, Tanja, *Spielzone* (Berlin: Aufbau, 1999).

Dückers, Tanja, *Himmelskörper* (Berlin: Aufbau, 2003).

Dückers, Tanja and Verena Carl (eds), *stadt land krieg. Autoren der Gegenwart erzählen von der deutschen Vergangenheit* (Berlin: Aufbau, 2004).

Fest, Joachim, *Ich nicht. Erinnerungen an eine Kindheit und Jugend* (Reinbek: Rowohlt, 2nd edn, 2006).

Frenssen, Gustav, *Peter Moors Fahrt nach Südwest. Ein Feldzugbericht* (Berlin: Grote'sche Verlagsbuchhandlung, 1906).

Geiger, Arno, *Es geht uns gut. Roman* (Munich: Carl Hanser, 2005).

Goethe, Johann Wolfgang von, *Aus meinem Leben. Dichtung und Wahrheit. Hamburger Ausgabe*, vols 9 and 10 (Munich: dtv, 1982).

Grass, Günter, *Hundejahre. Roman* (Göttingen: Steidl, 1993 [1st edn, 1963]).

Grass, Günter, *Katz und Maus. Eine Novelle* (Reinbek: Rowohlt, 5th edn, 1964 [1st edn, 1961]).

Grass, Günter, *Die Blechtrommel. Roman* (Göttingen: Steidl, 1993 [1st edn, 1959]).

Grass, Günter, *Im Krebsgang. Eine Novelle* (Göttingen: Steidl, 2002).

Grass, Günter, *Crabwalk*, transl. Krishna Winston (London: Faber & Faber, 2003).

Grass, Günter, *Beim Häuten der Zwiebel* (Göttingen: Steidl, 2006).

Grass, Günter, *Peeling the Onion*, transl. Michael Henry Heim (London: Harvill & Secker, 2007).

Hahn, Ulla, *Unscharfe Bilder. Roman* (Munich: dtv, 2005).

Harig, Ludwig, *Ordnung ist das ganze Leben* (Munich: Hanser, 1986).

Harig, Ludwig, *Weh dem, der aus der Reihe tanzt* (Munich: Hanser, 1990).

Harig, Ludwig, *Wer mit den Wölfen heult, wird Wolf* (Munich: Hanser, 1996).

Hein, Christoph, *Landnahme* (Frankfurt a. M.: Suhrkamp, 2004).

Jirgl, Reinhard, *Die Unvollendeten* (Munich: Hanser, 2003).

Jünger, Ernst, *In Stahlgewittern* (Stuttgart: Klett-Cotta, 1978).

Jünger, Ernst, *Strahlungen I* (Stuttgart: Klett-Cotta, 1988).

Kafka, Franz, *Brief an den Vater*, with an afterword by Wilhelm Emrich (Frankfurt a. M.: Fischer, 1975).

Kafka, Franz, *Die Erzählungen und andere ausgewählte Prosa. Originalfassung*, ed. Jürgen Born, Gerhard Neumann, Malcolm Paisley and Jost Schillemeit (Frankfurt a. M.: Fischer, 1996).

Kinder, Hermann, *Im Schleiftrog* (Zurich: Diogenes, 1977).

Leupold, Dagmar, *Nach den Kriegen* (Munich: Beck, 2004).

Meckel, Christoph, *Suchbild. Über meinen Vater* (Frankfurt a. M.: Fischer, 1983).

Meckel, Christoph, *Suchbild. Meine Mutter* (Munich, Vienna: Hanser, 2002).

Medicus, Thomas, *In den Augen meines Großvaters* (Munich: Deutsche Verlagsanstalt, 2004).

Menasse, Eva, *Vienna* (Cologne: Kiepenheuer & Witsch, 2005).

Montaigne, Michel de, *The Essays of Michel de Montaigne*, transl. and ed. with an introduction by M. A. Screech (London: Allen Lane/Penguin Press, 1991).

Mulot, Sibylle, *Nachbarn* (Zurich: Diogenes, 1995).

Mulot, Sibylle, *Die unschuldigen Jahre* (Zurich: Diogenes, 2001).

Mulot, Sibylle, *Die Fabrikanten* (Zurich: Diogenes, 2005).

Overath, Angelika, *Nahe Tage. Roman in einer Nacht* (Göttingen: Wallstein, 2005).

Plessen, Elisabeth, *Mitteilung an den Adel* (Zurich, Cologne: Benzinger, 1976).

Raabe, Wilhem, *Abu Telfan oder die Heimkehr vom Mondgebirge* (Leipzig, Reclam, 1976).

Rehmann, Ruth, *Der Mann auf der Kanzel. Fragen an einen Vater* (Munich, Vienna: Hanser, 1979).

Rousseau, Jean-Jacques, *Les Confessions I* (Paris: Gallimard, 1973).

Schneider, Peter, *Vati* (Darmstadt: Luchterhand, 1989).

Sebald, W. G., *Austerlitz* (Munich: Hanser, 2001).

Sebald, W. G., *Luftkrieg und Literatur. Mit einem Essay über Alfred Andersch* (Frankfurt a. M.: Fischer, 2003).

Sebald, W. G., *On the Natural History of Destruction*, transl. Anthea Bell (London: Hamish Hamilton, 2003).

Spiegelmann, Art, *Maus I. A Survivor's Tale – My Father Bleeds History* (London: Penguin, 1987).

Spiegelmann, Art, *Maus II. A Survivor's Tale – And Here My Troubles Began* (London: Penguin, 1992).

Timm, Uwe, *Rot* (Cologne: Kiepenheuer & Witsch, 2001).

Timm, Uwe, *Am Beispiel meines Bruders* (Cologne: Kiepenheuer & Witsch, 2003).

Timm, Uwe, *In My Brother's Shadow*, transl. Anthea Bell (London: Bloomsbury, 2005).

Treichel, Hans-Ulrich, *Der Verlorene* (Frankfurt a. M.: Suhrkamp, 1998).

Treichel, Hans-Ulrich, *Lost*, transl. Carol Brown Janeway (New York: Vintage, 1999).

Vesper, Bernward, *Die Reise* (Jassa: März-Verlag, 1977).

Wackwitz, Stephan, *Ein unsichtbares Land. Familienroman* (Frankfurt a. M.: Fischer, 2003).

Wackwitz, Stephan, *An Invisible Country*, translated from the German by Stephan Lehmann, with a foreword by Wendy Lesser (Philadelphia: Paul Dry Books, 2005).

Wackwitz, Stephan, *Neue Menschen. Bildungsroman* (Frankfurt a. M.: Fischer, 2005).

Wallner, Michael, *Cliehms Begabung* (Frankfurt a. M.: Frankfurter Verlagsanstalt, 2000).

Wallner, Michael, *Finale* (Berlin: Rowohlt, 2003).
Wallner, Michael, *April in Paris* (Munich: Luchterhand, 2006).
Walser, Martin, *Ein springender Brunnen* (Frankfurt a. M.: Suhrkamp, 1998).
Weiss, Peter, *Die Ästhetik des Widerstands* (Frankfurt a. M.: Suhrkamp, 1983) vol. III.2.
Wolf, Christa, *Kindheitsmuster* (Berlin, Weimar: Aufbau, 1976).
Wolf, Christa, *A Model Childhood*, transl. Ursule Molinaro and Hedwig Rappolt (London: Virago, 1982).

Filmography

Aimee & Jaguar (Günther Rohrbach/Senator Film, 1999), directed by Max Färberböck.
Comedian Harmonists (Perathon Film, 1997), directed by Joseph Vilsmaier.
Der 20. Juli. Das Attentat auf Hitler (CCC Film, 1955), directed by Falk Harnack.
Der Untergang (Constantin Film in co-production with NDR, WDR, Degeto, ORF, EOS, RAI Cinema, 2004), directed by Oliver Hirschbiegel.
Die Flucht (ARD, 2007), directed by Kai Wessel.
Die Weiße Rose (Sentana Film, 1982), directed by Michael Verhoeven.
Dresden (ZDF, 2006), directed by Ronald Suso Richter.
Es geschah am 20. Juli (Arca, 1955), directed by Georg Wilhelm Pabst.
Flags of our Fathers (Dreamwork Pictures, Warner Bros., 2006), directed by Clint Eastwood.
Fünf letzte Tage (Pelemele, 1982), directed by Percy Adlon.
Hitlerjunge Salomon (Euro Video, 1990), directed by Agnieszka Holland.
Joyeux Noël (Nord-Ouest Productions, Artémis, Senator Film, Media Pro Pictures, 2005), directed by Christian Carion.
Letters from Iwo Jima (Warner Bros., 2006), directed by Clint Eastwood.
Mutters Courage (Sentana, 1995), directed by Michael Verhoeven.
Rosenstraße (Concorde, 2003), directed by Margarethe von Trotta.
Sophie Scholl. Die letzten Tage (Warner Brothers, 2005), directed by Marc Rothemund.
Stauffenberg. Der 20. Juli 1944 (ARD, 2004), directed by Jo Baier.

Secondary Literature

Abraham, Nicolas, "Aufzeichnungen über das Phantom. Ergänzungen zu Freuds Metapsychologie", *Psyche* 8 (1991), 691–98.
Ackermann, Anton, "Legende und Wahrheit über den 20. Juli", *Einheit* 7 (1947), 1172–82.
Agamben, Giorgio, *Homo Sacer. Sovereign Power and Bare Life*, trans. Daniel Heller-Rozen (Stanford: Stanford UP, 1998).
Alewyn, Richard, "Das Problem der Generation in der Geschichte", *Zeitschrift für deutsche Bildung* 5 (1929), 519–27.
Amann, Klaus and Karl Wagner (eds), *Autobiographien in der österreichischen Literatur. Von Franz Grillparzer bis Thomas Bernhard* (Innsbruck, Vienna: Studien-Verlag, 1998).

Applegate, Celia, *A Nation of Provincials. The German Idea of Heimat* (Berkeley: California UP, 1990).

Arendt, Hannah, *On Violence* (San Diego, New York, London: Harcourt Brace & Copnay, 1970).

Assheuer, Thomas, "In unser aller Auftrag", *Die Zeit*, 24 February 2005.

Assmann, Aleida, "Grenzen des Verstehens. Generationsidentitäten in der neuen deutschen Erinnerungsliteratur", *Familiendynamik. Interdisziplinäre Zeitschrift für systemtorientierte Praxis und Forschung* 30 (2005), 370–89.

Assmann, Aleida, "On the (In)compatibility of Guilt and Suffering in German Memory", *German Life & Letters* 59 (2006), Special Issue: Anne Fuchs and Mary Cosgrove (eds), *Memory Contests*, 187–200.

Assmann, Aleida, *Der lange Schatten der Vergangenheit. Erinnerungskultur und Geschichtspolitik* (Munich: Beck, 2006).

Assmann, Jan, "Collective Memory and Cultural Identity", *New German Critique* 65 (1995), 125–33.

Assmann, Jan, *Das kulturelle Gedächtnis. Schrift, Erinnerung und politische Identität in den frühen Hochkulturen* (Munich: Beck, 2000).

Bachmann, Doris, "Die Dritte Welt in der Literatur. Eine ethnologische Methodenkritik literaturwissenschaftlichen Interpretierens am Beispiel von Wilhelm Raabes Roman *Abu Telfan oder die Heimkehr vom Mondgebirge*", *Jahrbuch der Raabe-Gesellschaft* (1979), 27–71.

Bachmann, Ingeborg, "Literatur als Utopie", in *Ingeborg Bachmann. Kritische Schriften*, ed. Monika Albrecht and Dirk Göttsche (Munich, Zurich: Piper, 2005), pp. 329–49.

Baer, Ulrich, " 'Learning to Speak Like a Victim': Media and Authenticity in Marcel Beyer's *Flughunde*", *Gegenwartsliteratur. Ein germanistisches Jahrbuch* 2 (2003), 245–61.

Bald, Detlef, *Die Weiße Rose. Von der Front in den Widerstand* (Berlin: Aufbau, 2003).

Barnouw, Dagmar, *Germany 1945. Views of War and Violence* (Bloomington: Indiana UP, 1996).

Barth, Boris, *Dolchstoßlegenden und politische Desintegration: das Trauma der deutschen Niederlage im Ersten Weltkrieg 1914–1933* (Düsseldorf: Droste, 2003).

Barthes, Roland, *La chambre claire. Note sur la photographie* (Paris: Gallimard, 1980).

Barthes, Roland, "The Reality Effect", in *The Rustle of Language* (California: California UP, 1989), pp. 141–48.

Bartov, Omer, "Germany as Victim", *New German Critique* 80 (2000), 29–40.

Bauman, Zygmunt, *Community. Seeking Safety in an Insecure World* (Cambridge: Polity Press, 2001).

Bauman, Zygmunt, *Identity. Conversations with Benedetto Vecchi* (Cambridge: Polity Press, 2004).

Becker, Peter von, "Schmalzbomben auf Dresden", *Der Tagesspiegel*, 7 March 2006.

Becker, Peter von, "Vertreibung als Drama. Die Flucht von uns selbst", *Der Tagesspiegel*, 6 March 2007.

Benedict, Ruth, *The Chrysanthemum and the Sword: Patterns of Japanese Culture* (Cleveland: Meridian Books, 1967).

Benjamin, Walter, "Theses on the Philosophy of History", in *Illuminations*, ed. Hannah Arendt, transl. Harry Zorn (London: Pimlico, 1999), pp. 245–55.

Benson, Ciarán, *The Cultural Psychology of the Self. Place, Morality and Art in Human Worlds* (London, New York: Routledge, 2001).

Benz, Wolfgang, "Kitsch as Kitsch can", *Die Süddeutsche Zeitung*, 18 September 2003.

Benz, Wolfgang and Walter H. Pehle, *Lexikon des deutschen Widerstandes* (Frankfurt a. M.: Fischer, 2nd edn, 2004).

Berghahn, Daniela, "Post-1990 Screen Memories: How East and West German Cinema Remembers the Third Reich and the Holocaust", *German Life & Letters* 59 (2006), Special Issue: Anne Fuchs and Mary Cosgrove (eds), *Memory Contests*, 294–308.

Boa, Elizabeth, *Kafka. Gender, Class, and Race in the Letters and Fictions* (Oxford: Clarendon Press, 1996).

Boa, Elizabeth, "Introduction: notes from a symposium – notes towards 'Hingegend'", in *Anne Duden: A Revolution of Words. Approaches to her Fiction, Poetry and Essays* [*German Monitor* 56], ed. Heike Bartel and Elizabeth Boa (Amsterdam: Rodopi, 2003), pp. 1–18.

Boa, Elizabeth, "'Telling It How It Wasn't': Familial Allegories of Wish-Fulfillment in Postunification Germany", in Anne Fuchs, Mary Cosgrove and Georg Grote (eds), *German Memory Contests*, pp. 67–83.

Boa, Elizabeth and Rachel Palfreyman, *Heimat – A German Dream. Regional Loyalties and National Identity in German Culture 1890–1990* (Oxford: Oxford UP, 2000).

Bodnar, John, *Remaking America. Public Memory, Commemoration and Patriotism in the Twentieth Century* (Princeton: Princeton UP, 1992).

Boehncke, Heiner, "Clair obscur. W. G. Sebalds Bilder", in *W. G. Sebald, Text + Kritik* 158 (2003), 43–62.

Böhme, Hartmut, *Fetischismus und Kultur. Eine andere Theorie der Moderne* (Hamburg: Rowohlt, 2006).

Booth, Michael R., *English Melodrama* (London: Herbert Jenkins, 1965).

Brenner, Peter J., "Zur Entzauberung der Fremde und Verfremdung der Heimat in Raabes *Abu Telfan*", *Jahrbuch der Raabe-Gesellschaft* (1989), 45–62.

Brockmann, Stephen, "'Normalization': Has Helmut Kohl's Vision Been Realized?", in Stuart Taberner and Paul Cooke (eds), *German Culture, Politics and Literature into the Twenty-First Century*, pp. 17–29.

Broder, Henryk M., "Der Herr der Binse", *Spiegel Online*, 14 August 2006.

Brooke, Rupert, *The Poetical Works of Rupert Brooke*, ed. Geoffrey Keynes (London: Faber & Faber, 1951).

Brooks, Peter, *The Melodramatic Imagination: Balzac, Henry James, Melodrama, and the Mode of Excess* (New York: Columbia UP, 1984).

Broszat, Martin, "Resistenz und Widerstand", in *Bayern in der NS-Zeit. Herrschaft und Gesellschaft im Konflikt*, ed. Martin Broszat et al. (Munich, Vienna, 1981) vol. 4, pp. 691–709.

Bubis, Ignatz, "Rede des Präsidenten des Zentralrats der Juden in Deutschland am 9. November 1998 in der Synagoge Rykerstrase in Berlin", in *Die Walser-Bubis-Debatte: Eine Dokumentation*, ed. Frank Schirrmacher (Frankfurt a. M.: Suhrkamp, 1999), pp. 106–13.

Bugmann, Urs, *Bewältigungsversuch. Thomas Bernhards autobiographische Schriften* (Berne, Frankfurt a. M.: Peter Lang, 1981).

Busche, Jürgen, "Hat Jürgen Habermas die Wahrheit verschluckt?", *Cicero. Magazin für politsche Kultur* 11 (2006), 72–77.

Buß, Christian, "Go West, Gräfin", *Spiegel Online*, 2 März 2007.

Cammann, Alexander, "Ein imaginäres Museum", *die tageszeitung*, 4 October 2006.

Caruth, Cathy, *Unclaimed Experience. Trauma, Narrative and History* (Baltimore, London: John Hopkins UP, 1996).

Chiene Sheperd, John, *Italian Gardens of the Renaissance* (London: Academy Editions, 1994).

Collins Donahue, William, "Illusions of Subtlety: Bernhard Schlink's *Der Vorleser* and the Moral Limits of Holocaust Fiction", *German Life & Letters*, 54 (2001), 60–81.

Confino, Alon, *Germany as a Culture of Remembrance. Promises and Limits of Writing History* (Chapel Hill: The University of North Carolina Press, 2006).

Cooke, Maeve, "The Ethics of Post-Holocaust Art: Reflections on Redemption and Representation", *German Life & Letters*, 59 (2006), Special Issue: Anne Fuchs and Mary Cosgrove (eds), *Memory Contests*, 266–79.

Cornils, Ingo, "Successful Failure? The Impact of the German Student Movement on the Federal Republic of Germany", in *Recasting German Identity*, ed. Stuart Taberner and Frank Finlay (Rochester: Camden House, 2002), pp. 109–26.

Cosgrove, Mary, "Melancholy Competitions; W. G. Sebald reads Günter Grass and Wolfgang Hildesheimer", *German Life & Letters* 59 (2006), Special Issue: *Memory Contests*, 217–32.

Cosgrove, Mary and Anne Fuchs, "Introduction", *German Life & Letters* 59 (2006), Special Issue: *Memory Contests*, 3–10.

Couser, G. Thomas, *Vulnerable Subjects. Ethics and Life Writing* (Ithaca, New York, London: Cornell UP, 2004).

Das Gupta, Oliver, "'Filbinger hatte Handlungsspielraum' – Historiker widersprechen Oettinger", *Süddeutsche Zeitung*, 16 April 2007.

de Man, Paul, "Autobiography as De-facement", *Modern Langues Notes* 94 (1979), 919–30.

de Montaigne, Michel, *The Essays of Michel de Montaigne*, transl. and ed. M. A. Screech (London: Allen Lane/Penguin Press, 1991).

Derrida, Jacques, *De la grammatologie* (Paris: Minuit, 1967).

Diez, Georg, "Opa Grass. Die Enkel, die Erinnerung und die Geschichtspolitik", *Die Zeit*, 17 August 2006.

Dilthey, Wilhelm, "Über das Studium der Geschichte der Wissenschaften vom Menschen, der Geschichte und dem Staat", in *Die geistige Welt, Einleitung in die Philosophie des Lebens. Erste Hälfte: Abhandlungen zur Grundlegung der Geisteswissenschaften*, in *Gesammelte Schriften*, ed. Georg Misch (Leipzig, Berlin: B. G. Teubner, 1924), vol. 5, pp. 31–73.

Dörris, Bernd, "Oettingers späte Einsicht", *Süddeutsche Zeitung*, 16 April 2007.

Duttlinger, Carolin, "Traumatic Photographs: Remembrance and the Technical Media in W. G. Sebald's *Austerlitz*", in *W. G. Sebald: A Critical Companion*, ed. J. J. Long and Anne Whitehead (Edinburgh: Edinburgh UP, 2003), pp. 155–71.

Duttlinger, Carolin, "A Lineage of Destruction? Rethinking Photography in *Luftkrieg und Literatur*", in *W. G. Sebald and the Writing of History*, ed. Anne Fuchs and J. J. Long (Würzburg: Königshausen & Neumann, 2007), pp. 163–77.

Eakin, Paul John, *How our lives become stories: making selves* (Ithaca, New York, London: Cornell UP, 1999).

Eakin, Paul John (ed.), *The Ethics of Life Writing* (Ithaca, New York, London: Cornell UP, 2004).

Eigler, Friederike, *Gedächtnis und Geschichte in Generationenromanen seit der Wende* (Berlin: Erich Schmidt, 2005).

Enge, Torsten Olaf, *Garden Architecture in Europe; 1450–1800. From the Villa Garden of the Italian Renaissance to the English Landscape Garden* (Cologne: Taschen, 1992).

Erll, Astrid and Ansgar Nüning (eds), *Medien des kulturellen Gedächtnisses: Konstruktivität – Historizität – Kulturspezifizität* (Berlin, New York: Walter de Gruyter, 2004).

Eshel, Amir, "Vom eigenen Gewissen: Die Walser-Bubis-Debatte und der Ort des Nationalsozialismus im Selbstbild der Bundesrepublik", *DVjs* 2 (2000), 333–60.

Felman, Shoshana and Cathy Caruth (eds), *Testimony. Crisis of Witnessing in Literature, Psychoanalysis and Art* (New York, London: Routledge, 1992).

Fest, Joachim, *Hitler* (Berlin: Propyläen, 1973).

Fest, Joachim, *Staatsstreich. Der lange Weg zum 20. Juli* (Berlin: Siedler, 1994).

Fest, Joachim, *Speer. Eine Biographie* (Berlin: Alexander Fest Verlag, 1999).

Fest, Joachim, *Der Untergang. Hitler und das Ende des Dritten Reiches, eine historische Skizze* (Berlin: Alexander Fest Verlag, 4th edn, 2002).

Fichte, Johann Gottlieb Friedrich, *Reden an die deutsche Nation*, ed. Reinhard Lauth (Hamburg: Meiner, 1978).

Fiedler, Matthias, *Zwischen Abenteuer, Wissenschaft und Kolonialismus. Der deutsche Afrikadiskurs im 18. und 19. Jahrhundert* (Cologne, Weimar, Vienna: Böhlau, 2005).

Fiedler, Matthias, "German Crossroads: Visions of the Past in German Cinema after Reunification", in Anne Fuchs, Mary Cosgrove and Georg Grote (eds), *German Memory Contests*, pp. 127–45.

Finck, Almut, "Subjektivität und Geschichte in der Postmoderne. Christa Wolfs *Kindheitsmuster*", in *Geschriebenes Leben. Autobiographik von Frauen*, ed. Michaela Holdenried (Berlin: Erich Schmidt, 1995), pp. 311–23.

Finger, Evelyn, "Die Ohnmacht der Bilder", *Die Zeit*, 1 March 2007.

Finger, Evelyn, "Quotenopfer", *Die Zeit*, 8 March 2007.

Finker, Kurt, *Stauffenberg und der 20. Juli 1944* (Berlin: Union-Verlag, 1967).

Franzen, K. E., and Hans Lemberg, *Die Vertriebenen. Hitlers letzte Opfer* (Munich: Propyläen, 2001).

Frei, Norbert, *Karriere im Zwielicht. Hitlers Eliten nach 1945* (Frankfurt a. M.: Campus, 2001).

Frei, Norbert (ed.), *Hitlers Eliten nach 1945* (Munich: dtv, 2003).

Frei, Norbert, *1945 und Wir. Das Dritte Reich im Bewußtsein der Deutschen* (Munich: Beck, 2005).

Freud, Sigmund, "Über die Deckerinnerung", in *Gesammelte Werke*, ed. Anna Freud et al. (Frankfurt a. M.: Fischer, 1999), vol. 1, pp. 529–54.

Freud, Sigmund, "Der Familienroman der Neurotiker", in *Gesammelte Werke*, ed. Anna Freud et al. (Frankfurt a. M.: Fischer, 1999), vol. 7, pp. 227–31.

Freud, Sigmund, "Das Unheimliche", in *Gesammelte Werke*, ed. Anna Freud et al. (Frankfurt a. M.: Fischer, 1999), vol. 12, pp. 292–68.

Friedrich, Jörg, *Die kalte Amnestie. NS-Täter in der Bundesrepublik* (Frankfurt a. M.: Fischer, 1984).

Friedrich, Jörg, *Der Brand. Deutschland im Bombenkrieg 1940–1945* (Munich: Propyläen, 2002).

Friedrich, Jörg, *Brandstätten. Der Anblick des Bombenkrieges* (Munich: Propyläen, 2003).

Fritzsche, Peter, *Stranded in the Present. Modern Time and the Melancholy of History* (Cambridge, MA: Harvard UP, 2004).

Fuchs, Anne, "Towards an Ethics of Remembering: The Walser-Bubis Debate and the Other of Discourse", *German Quarterly* 75 (2002), 235–47.

Fuchs, Anne, *Die Schmerzensspuren der Geschichte. Zur Poetik der Erinnerung in W. G. Sebalds Prosa* (Cologne, Weimar, Vienna: Böhlau, 2004).

Fuchs, Anne, "From Vergangenheitsbewältigung to Generational Memory Contests in Günter Grass, Monika Maron and Uwe Timm", *German Life & Letters* 59 (2006), Special Issue: Anne Fuchs and Mary Cosgrove (eds), *Memory Contests*, 169–86.

Fuchs, Anne, "A Heimat in Ruins and the Ruins as Heimat: W. G. Sebald's *Luftkrieg und Literatur*", in Anne Fuchs, Mary Cosgrove and Georg Grote (eds), *German Memory Contests*, pp. 287–302.

Fuchs, Anne, Mary Cosgrove and Georg Grote (eds), *German Memory Contests: The Quest for Identity in Literature, Film and Discourse* (Rochester, NY: Camden House, 2006).

Fuchs, Anne, "Landscape and The After-Images of History in Thomas Medicus's *In den Augen meines Großvaters*", *Gegenwartsliteratur. Ein germanistisches Jahrbuch* 5 (2006), 252–71.

Fuchs, Anne, " 'Ehrlich, du lügst wie gedruckt'. Günter Grass's Autobiographical Confession and the Changing Territory of Germany's Memory Culture", *German Life & Letters* 60 (2007), 261–75.

Fuchs, Anne, " 'Ein Hauptkapitel der Geschichte der Unterwerfung': Representations of Nature in W. G. Sebald's *Die Ringe des Saturn*", in *W. G. Sebald and The Writing of History*, ed. Anne Fuchs and J. J. Long (Würzburg: Königshausen & Neumann, 2007), 121–38.

Fuhr, Eckhard, "Joachim Fests Jugend-Autobiografie *Ich nicht*", *Die Welt*, 13 September 2006.

Geyer, Christian, "Ein Fall Habermas? Der verschluckte Zettel", *Frankfurter Allgemeine Zeitung*, 27 October 2006.

Giddens, Anthony, *Modernity and Self-Identity: Self and Society in the Late Modern Age* (Cambridge: Polity Press, 1991).

Gisevius, Hans Bernd, *Bis zum bitteren Ende*. 2 vols. (Zurich: Fretz & Wasmuth, 1946).

Goethe, Johann Wolfgang von, *Briefe. Hamburger Ausgabe* (Munich: dtv, 1988), vol. 4.

Göttler, Fritz, "Sophie Scholl. Die Letzten Tage; ein Traum von Licht", *Süddeutsche Zeitung*, 23 February 2005.

Göttsche, Dirk, "Der neue historische Afrika-Roman. Kolonialismus aus postkolonialer Sicht", *German Life & Letters* 56 (2003), 261–80.

Göttsche, Dirk, "Beobachtungen zu Anne Dudens Kurzprosa und Essayistik", in *Anne Duden: A Revolution of Words. Approaches to her Fiction, Poetry and Essays* [German Monitor 56], ed. Heike Bartel and Elizabeth Boa (Amsterdam: Rodopi, 2003), pp. 19–42.

Göttsche, Dirk, "Der koloniale Zusammenhang der Dinge in der deutschen Provinz. Wilhelm Raabe in postkolonialer Sicht", *Jahrbuch der Raabe-Gesellschaft* (2005), 53–73.

Göttsche, Dirk, "Politische Sprachkritik in Ingeborg Bachmanns Kritischen Schriften", in *Schreiben gegen Krieg und Gewalt*. *Ingeborg Bachmann und die deutschsprachige Literatur 1945–1980* [Krieg und Literatur/War and Literature vol. X], ed. Dirk Göttsche, Franziska Meyer et al. (Göttingen: V& R Unipress, 2006), pp. 49–64.

Grass, Günter, "Schreiben nach Auschwitz. Frankfurter Poetik-Vorlesung", in *Der Autor als fragwürdiger Zeuge*, ed. Daniela Hermes (Munich: dtv, 1997), pp. 195–222.

Greiner, Bernd, " 'Overbombed': Warum die Diskussion über die alliierten Luftangriffe nicht mit dem Hinweis auf die deutsche Schuld beendet werden darf", *Literaturen* 3 (2003), 42–4.

Gruner, Wolf, *Widerstand in der Rosenstraße. Die Fabrik-Aktion und die Verfolgung der Mischehen 1943* (Frankfurt a. M.: Fischer, 2005).

Grüttner, Michael, "Die nationalsozialistische Wissenschaftspolitik und die Geisteswissenschaften", in *Literaturwissenschaft und Nationalsozialismus*, ed. Holger Dainat and Lutz Danneberg (Tübingen: Niemeyer, 2003), pp. 13–39.

Günter, Joachim, "Bomben-Kitsch. Dresdens Untergang im Fernsehen", *Neue Zürcher Zeitung*, 8 March 2006.

Günther, Dagmar, *Das nationale Ich? Autobiographische Sinnkonstruktionen deutscher Bildungsbürger des Kaiserreichs* (Tübingen: Niemeyer, 2004).

Habermas, Jürgen, *Eine Art Schadensabwicklung. Kleine politische Schriften VI* (Frankfurt a. M.: Suhrkamp, 1987).

Hake, Sabine, *German National Cinema* (London, NY: Routledge, 2002).

Halbwachs, Maurice, *On Collective Memory*, ed. and transl. Lewis A. Coser (Chicago: Chicago UP, 1992).

Hanfeld, Michael, "In der Wut des Feuersturms. Dresden im Fernsehen", *Frankfurter Allgemeine Zeitung*, 20 February 2006.

Harris, Stefanie, "The Return of the Dead: Memory and Photography in W. G. Sebald's *Die Ausgewanderten*", *German Quarterly* 74 (2001), 370–92.

Hassell, Ulrich von, *Vom anderen Deutschland. Aus den nachgelassenen Tagebüchern 1938–1944* (Zurich: Atlantis, 1945).

Heer, Hannes, *Vom Verschwinden der Täter. Der Vernichtungskrieg fand statt, aber keiner war dabei* (Berlin: Aufbau, 2005).

Heilman, Robert, *Tragedy and Melodrama, Versions of Experience* (Seattle, London: University of Washington Press, 1968).

Hirsch, Marianne, *Family Frames. Photography, Narrative and Postmemory* (Cambridge, MA: Harvard UP, 1997).

Höfer, Adolf, "Himmelskörper und andere Unscharfe Bilder. Romane zur Thematik der deutschen Kriegsopfer im Gefolge der Novelle *Im Krebsgang* von Günter Grass", *Literatur für Leser* 28 (2005), 147–61.

Homewood, Chris, "The Return of 'Undead' History: The West German Terrorist as Vampire and the Problem of 'Normalizing' the Past in Margaretha von Trotta's *Die bleierne Zeit* (1981) and Christian Petzold's *Die innere Sicherheit* (2001)", in *German Culture, Politics and Literature into the Twenty-First Century*, ed. Stuart Taberner and Paul Cooke, pp. 121–50.

Honold, Alexander, " 'Verlorene Generation': Die Suggestivität eines Deutungsmusters zwischen Fin de Siècle und Erstem Weltkrieg", in *Generation: Zur Genealogie des Konzepts – Konzepte von Genealogie*, ed. Sigrid Weigel, Ohad Parnes, Ulrike Vedder, Stefan Willer (Munich: Fink, 2005), pp. 31–56.

Huyssen, Andreas, *Twilight Memories. Marking Time in a Culture of Amnesia* (London, NY: Routledge, 1995).

Huyssen, Andreas, "On Writings and New Beginnings: W. G. Sebald and the Literature about the Luftkrieg", *Zeitschrift für Literaturwissenschaft und Linguistik* 31 (2001), 72–90.

Huyssen, Andreas, "Air War Legacies: from Dresden to Baghdad", in Bill Niven (ed.), *Germans as Victims*, pp. 181–93.

Jahn, Bernhard, "Familienkonstruktionen 2005. Zum Problem des Zusammenhangs der Generationen im aktuellen Familienroman", *Zeitschrift für Germanistik* 3 (2006), 581–96.

Jaspers, Karl, *Die Schuldfrage* (Heidelberg: Lambert Schneider, 1946).

Jessen, Jens, "Unternehmen *Walküre*", *Die Zeit*, 19 February 2004.

Jessen, Jens, "Und Grass wundert sich", *Die Zeit*, 17 August 2006.

John, Juliet, *Dickens's Villains. Melodrama, Character, Popular Culture* (Oxford: Oxford UP, 2001).

Junge, Traudl, *Bis zur letzten Stunde. Hitlers Sekretärin erzählt ihr Leben*, in association with Melisssa Müller (Munich: Claasen, 2002).

Kadar, Marlene, Linda Warley, Jeanne Perreault, Susanna Egan (eds), *Tracing the Autobiographical* (Waterloo, Ontario: Wilfrid Laurier UP, 2005).

Kahlweit, Cathrin, "Suchbild mit Vater", *Süddeutsche Zeitung*, 22 March 2004.

Karasek-Langer, Alfred and Elfriede Strzygowksi, *Sagen der Beskidendeutschen* (Plauen: Wolff, 1930).

Kershaw, Ian, *The Nazi Dictatorship. Problems and Perspectives of Interpretation* (London, New York: Edward Arnold, 1985).

Kettenacker, Lothar (ed.), *Ein Volk von Opfern? Die neue Debatte um den Bombenkrieg 1940–1945* (Berlin: Rowohlt, 2003).

Klein, Georg, "Unser armer grandioser Greis", *Die Welt*, 19 August 2006.

Koepnick, Lutz, "Reframing the Past: Heritage Cinema and Holocaust in the 1990s", *New German Critique* 87 (2002), 47–82.

Kofmann, Sarah, *The Childhood of Art. An Interpretation of Freud's Aesthetics*, transl. Winifred Woodhull (New York: Columbia UP, 1988).

Konersmann, Ralf, "Zeichensprache. Wahrheit und Wahrhaftigkeit bei Rousseau", *DVjs* 66 (1982), 41–62.

Krebs, Stefan and Werner Tschacher, "Speer und Er. Und wir? Deutsche Geschichte in gebrochener Erinnerung", *Geschichte in Wissenschaft und Unterricht* 58 (2007), 163–73.

Krekeler, Elmar, "Die Stunde der Patriotin", *Berliner Morgenpost*, 24 February 2005.

Krovoza, Alfred, "Psychoanalyse und Geschichtswissenschaft. Anmerkungen zu Stationen eines Projekts", *Psyche* 57 (2003), 904–37.

Kucklick, Christoph, *Feuersturm. Der Bombenkrieg gegen Deutschland* (Hamburg: Ellert & Richter, 2003).

Kuhn, Annette, *Family Secrets. Acts of Memory and Imagination* (London, NY: Verso, 1995).

Künzig, Bern, "Schreie und Flüstern – Marcel Beyers *Flughunde*", in *Baustelle Gegenwartsliteratur. Die neunziger Jahre*, ed. Andreas Erb (Opladen, Wiesbaden: Westdeutscher Verlag, 1998), pp. 122–53.

LaCapra, Dominick, *History and Memory after Auschwitz* (Ithaca, London: Cornell UP, 1998).

LaCapra, Dominick, *Writing History, Writing Trauma* (Baltimore, London: The John Hopkins UP, 2001).

Le Goff, Jacques, *History and Memory*, transl. Steven Rendall and Elizabeth Claman (New York, Oxford: Columbia UP, 1992).

Leicht, Robert, "Ein Mikromilieu des Anstands", *Die Zeit*, 14 September 2006.

Leicht, Robert, "Unrecht. Schlechtes Gedächtnis, gutes Gewissen – zum Tode Hans Filbingers. Ein Nachruf", *Die Zeit*, 4 April 2007.

Lejeune, Philippe, *Le pacte autobiographique* (Paris: Seuil, 1975).

Lejeune, Philippe, *On Autobiography*, transl. Katherine Leary and ed. John Paul Eakin (Minneapolis: University of Minneapolis Press, 1989).

Lekan, Thomas M, *Imagining the Nation in Nature. Landscape Preservation and German Identity, 1885–1945* (Cambridge, MA, London: Harvard UP, 2004).

Lennon, John and Malcolm Foley, *Dark Tourism: The Attraction of Death and Disaster* (London and New York: Continuum, 2000).

Lethen, Helmut, *Verhaltenslehre der Kälte: Lebensversuche zwischen den Kriegen* (Frankfurt a. M.: Suhrkamp, 1994).

Levy, Daniel and Natan Sznaider, *Erinnerung im globalen Zeitalter: Der Holocaust* (Frankfurt a. M.: Suhrkamp, 2001).

Leys, Ruth, *Trauma. A Genealogy* (Chicago: Chicago UP, 2000).

Littler, Margaret, "Trauma and Terrorism: the Problem of Violence in the Work of Anne Duden", in *Anne Duden: A Revolution of Words. Approaches to her Fiction, Poetry and Essays* [German Monitor 56], ed. Heike Bartel and Elizabeth Boa (Amsterdam: Rodopi, 2003), pp. 43–62.

Lloyd, Christopher, *Collaboration and Resistance in Occupied France. Representing Treason and Sacrifice* (Basingstoke: Palgrave, 2003).

Long, J. J., "History, Narrative and Photography in W. G. Sebald's *Die Ausgewanderten*", *MLR* 98 (2003), 117–37.

Long, J. J., "Monika Maron's *Pawels Briefe*: Photography, Narrative and the Claims of Postmemory", in Anne Fuchs, Mary Cosgrove and Georg Grote (eds), *German Memory Contests*, pp. 147–65.

Löwisch, Georg and Lukas Wallraf, "Widerruf im dritten Anlauf", *die tageszeitung*, 17 April 2007.

Lübbe, Hermann, "Der Nationalsozialismus im politischen Bewußtsein der Gegenwart", in *Deutschlands Weg in die Diktatur*, ed. Martin Broszat (Berlin: Siedler, 1983), pp. 329–49.

Ludden, Teresa, "History, Memory, Montage in Anne Duden's *Das Judasschaf*", *German Life & Letters* 59 (2006), 249–65.

Mannheim, Karl, "Das Problem der Generationen", in *Wissenssoziologie*, ed. Kurt H. Wolff (Soziologische Texte 28) (Berlin, Neuwied: Luchterhand, 1964), pp. 509–65.

Mannheim, Karl, "The Problem of Generations", in *Essays on the Sociology of Knowledge*, ed. Paul Kecskemeti (London: Routledge, 1964), pp. 276–322.

Markowitsch, Hans J. and Harald Welzer, *Das autobiographische Gedächtnis. Hirnorganische Grundlagen und biosoziale Entwicklung* (Stuttgart: Klett-Cotta, 2005).

Matussek, Matthias, Volker Hage et al., "Fehlbar und verstrickt", *Der Spiegel*, 31 August 2006.

Matussek, Matthias, "Der stolze Einzelgänger", *Der Spiegel*, 12 September 2006.

Mauelshagen, Claudia, *Der Schatten des Vaters: deutschsprachige Väterliteratur der siebziger und achtziger Jahre* (Frankfurt a. M., Berlin: Lang, 1995).

McLean, Stuart, *The Event and Its Terrors. Ireland, Famine, Modernity* (Standford: Standford UP, 2004).

Meinecke, Friedrich, *Die deutsche Katastrophe: Betrachtungen und Erinnerungen* (Wiesbaden: Brockhaus, 1946).

Meyer, Beate, *Jüdische Mischlinge. Rassenpolitik und Verfolgungserfahrung 1933–1945* (Hamburg: Dölling & Gallitz, 1999).

Meyer, Beate, "Geschichte im Film – Judenverfolgung, Mischehen und der Protest in der Rosenstraße", *Zeitschrift für Geschichtswissenschaft* 52 (2004), 23–46.

Mitscherlich, Alexander and Margarete Mitscherlich, *Die Unfähigkeit zu trauern. Grundlagen kollektiven Verhaltens* (Munich: Piper, 1967).

Moeller, Robert G., *War Stories. The Search for a Usable Past in the Federal Republic of Germany* (Berkeley, Los Angeles, London: University of California Press, 2001).

Mommsen, Hans, *Alternatives to Hitler. German Resistance under the Third Reich*, transl. and annotated by Angus McGeoch, with an introduction by Jeremy Noakes (London, New York: I. B. Tauris, 2003).

Naumann, Klaus, "Bombenkrieg – Totaler Krieg – Massaker. Jörg Friedrichs Buch *Der Brand* in der Diskussion", *Mittelweg 36* (2003), 40–60.

Nietzsche, Friedrich, *On the Advantage and Disadvantage of History for Life*, transl. Peter Heuss (Indianapolis, Cambridge: Hackett Publishing, 1980).

Niven, Bill, *Facing the Nazi Past. United Germany and the Legacy of the Third Reich* (London, New York: Routledge, 2002).

Niven, Bill, "Bernhard Schlink's *Der Vorleser* and the Problem of Shame", *MLR* 98 (2003), 381–96.

Niven, Bill (ed.), *Germans as Victims. Remembering the Past in Contemporary Germany* (Houndsmills: Palgrave/Macmillan, 2006).

Niven, Bill, "The GDR and Memory of the Bombing of Dresden", *Germans as Victims*, pp. 109–29.

Nonnenmacher, Günter, "Der Widerruf", *Frankfurter Allgemeine Zeitung*, 17 April 2007.

Nora, Pierre, "Generation", in *Realms of Memory: Rethinking the French Past. Conflicts and Divisions*, transl. Arthur Goldhammer (New York: Columbia UP, 1996), vol. 1, pp. 499–531.

Nutt, Harry, "Das lange Schweigen", *Frankfurter Rundschau*, 14 August 2006.

Overmans, Rüdiger, *Deutsche militärische Verluste im Zweiten Weltkrieg* (Munich: Oldenburg, 1999).

Partouche, Rebecca, "Der nüchterne Blick der Enkel. Wie begegnen junge Autoren der Kriegsgeneration? Ein Gespräch mit Tanja Dückers", *Die Zeit*, 30 April 2003.

Paver, Chloe, " 'Ein Stück langweiliger als die Wehrmachtsausstellung, aber dafür repräsentativer': The Exhibition *Fotofeldpost* as Riposte to the Wehrmacht Exhibition", in Anne Fuchs, Mary Cosgrove and Georg Grote (eds), *German Memory Contests*, pp. 107–25.

Peter, Jürgen, *Der Historikerstreit und die Suche nach einer nationalen Identität der achtziger Jahre* (Frankfurt a. M.: Peter Lang, 1995).

Piepmeier, Rainer, "Das Ende der ästhetischen Kategorie Landschaft. Zu einem Aspekt neuzeitlichen Naturverhältnisses", *Westfälische Forschungen* 30 (1980), 8–46.

Piepmeier, Rainer, "Landschaft", in *Historisches Wörterbuch der Philosophie*, ed. Joachim Ritter and Karlfried Gründer (Basel, Stuttgart: Schwabe & Coag, 1980), vol. 5, pp. 11–28.

Pilarczyk, Hannah, "Dresden, 13. Februar 1945: Ohne Anlass zu Opferdiskursen", *die tageszeitung*, 4 March 2006.

Pinder, Wilhelm, *Das Problem der Generation in der Kunstgeschichte Europas* (Cologne: E. A. Seemann, 1949).

Plowman, Andrew, "Between 'Restauration' and 'Nierentisch': The 1950s in Ludwig Harig, F. C. Delius, and Thomas Hettche", in Anne Fuchs, Mary Cosgrove and Georg Grote (eds), *German Memory Contests*, pp. 253–69.

Prager, Jeffrey, *Presenting the Past. Psychoanalysis and the Sociology of Misremembering* (Cambridge, MA: Harvard UP, 1998).

Prantl, Heribert, "Wenn die Geschichte ruhen will – Deutschland und die Aufarbeitung der NS Historie", *Süddeutsche Zeitung*, 16 April 2007.

Preisendanz, Wolfgang, "Zum Vorrang des Komischen bei der Darstellung von Geschichtserfahrung in deutschen Romanen unserer Zeit", in *Das Komische, Poetik und Hermeneutik*, ed. W. Preisendanz and Rainer Warning (Munich: Fink, 1976), vol. 7, pp. 154–64.

Prinz, Kirsten, " 'Mochte doch keiner was davon hören' – Günter Grass's *Im Krebsgang* und das Feuilleton im Kontext aktueller Erinnerungsverhandlungen", in *Medien des kulturellen Gedächtnisses: Konstruktivität –Historizität – Kulturspezifizität*, ed. Astrid Erll and Ansgar Nüning (Berlin, NY: Walter de Gruyter, 2004), pp. 179–94.

Reich, Ines and Kurt Finker, "Reaktionäre oder Patrioten? Zur Historiographie und Widerstandsforschung in der DDR bis 1990", in Gerd. R. Ueberschär (ed.), *Der 20. Juli*, pp. 158–78.

Reichel, Peter, *Erfundene Erinnerung: Weltkrieg und Judenmord in Film und Theater* (Munich, Vienna: Hanser, 2004).

Reinecke, Stefan, "Chronist des Opfers", *die tageszeitung*, 14 February 2005.

Reinhard, Wolfgang, *Lebensformen Europas. Eine historische Kulturanthropologie* (Munich: Beck, 2005).

Ricoeur, Paul, *Memory, History and Forgetting*, transl. Kathleen Blamey and David Pellauer (Chicago: Chicago UP, 2004).

Riedel, Wolfgang, *Der Spaziergang. Ästhetik der Landschaft* (Würzburg: Königshausen & Neumann, 1989).

Riehl, Wilhelm Heinrich, *Die Naturgeschichte des Volkes als Grundlage einer deutschen Social-Politik* (Stuttgart: Cotta, 1855).

Riehl, Wilhelm Heinrich, *The Natural History of the German People*, transl. David J. Diephouse (Lewiston: Mellen, 1990).

Ritter, Gerhard, *Carl Goerdeler und die deutsche Widerstandsbewegung* (Stuttgart: Deutsche Verlagsanstalt, 1955).

Ritter, Joachim, *Subjektivität* (Frankfurt a. M.: Suhrkamp, 1980).

Rother, Rainer (ed.), *Der Weltkrieg 1914–1918. Ereignis und Erinnerung* (Berlin: Minerva, 2004).

Rüsen, Jörn, *Zerbrechende Zeit. Über den Sinn der Geschichte* (Cologne, Weimar, Vienna: Böhlau, 2001).

Sander, Markus, "Joachim Fest: *Ich nicht*. Erinnerungen an eine Kindheit und Jugend", *Stuttgarter Zeitung*, 29 September 2006.

Schelsky, Helmut, *Die skeptische Generation* (Düsseldorf, Cologne: Diederichs, 1957).

Schirrmacher, Frank, "Stauffenberg: ein Geschichtsfilm ohne Geschichte", *Frankfurter Allgemeine Zeitung*, 25 February 2004.

Schirrmacher, Frank, "Das Geständnis", *Frankfurter Allgemeine Zeitung*, 12 August 2006.

Schirrmacher, Frank and Hubert Spiegel, "Warum ich nach sechzig Jahren mein Schweigen breche. Eine deutsche Jugend: Günter Grass spricht zum ersten Mal über sein Erinnerungsbuch und seine Mitgliedschaft in der Waffen-SS", *Frankfurter Allgemeine Zeitung*, 12 August 2006.

Schlabrendorff, Fabian von, *Offiziere gegen Hitler* (Zurich: Europa Verlag, 2nd edn, 1951 [1st edn, 1946]).

Schlabrendorff, Fabian von, *Offiziere gegen Hitler*, ed. Gero von Schulze Gaevernitz (Zurich: Europa Verlag, 1946).

Schlant, Ernestine, *The Language of Silence. West German Literature and the Holocaust* (New York: Routledge, 1999).

Schleiermacher, Friedrich, *Hermeneutik und Kritik*, ed. and introduced by Manfred Frank (Frankfurt a. M.: Suhrkamp, 1977).

Schmidt, Matthias, *Albert Speer. Das Ende eines Mythos* (Berne, Munich: Scherz, 1982).

Schmitt, Carl, *Ex Captivitate Salus. Erfahrungen der Zeit 1945/47* (Berlin: Duncker & Humblot, 1950).

Schmitthenner, Walter and Hans Buchheim (eds), *Der deutsche Widerstand gegen Hitler*. Vier historisch-kritische Studien von Herrmann Graml, Hans Mommsen, Hans J. Reichardt und Ernst Wolff (Cologne, Berlin: Kiepenheuer & Witsch, 1966).

Schmitz, Helmut, *On their Own Terms. The Legacy of National Socialism in Post-1990s German Fiction* (Birmingham: Birmingham UP, 2004).

Schmitz, Helmut, "Reconciliation between the Generations: The Image of the Ordinary Soldier in Dieter Wellershoff's *Der Ernstfall* and Ulla Hahn's *Unscharfe Bilder*", in Stuart Taberner and Paul Cooke (eds), *German Culture, Politics and Literature*, pp. 151–65.

Schnur, Harald, *Schleiermachers Hermeneutik und ihre Vorgeschichte im 18. Jahrhundert: Studien zur Bibelauslegung, zu Hamann, Herder und Friedrich Schlegel* (Stuttgart: Metzler, 1994).

Schönherr, Ulrich, "Topophony of Fascism: On Marcel Beyer's *The Karnau Tapes*", *The Germanic Review* 73 (1998), 328–48.

Schubert, Elke, "Die Normalität besichtigen", *Frankfurter Rundschau*, 6 April 2004.

Seibt, Gustav, "Geständnis einer Schnecke", *Süddeutsche Zeitung*, 15/16 August 2006.

Seibt, Gustav, "Fette Torte. Im Fernsehen: Maria Furtwängler in *Die Flucht*", *Die Süddeutsche Zeitung*, 1 March 2007.

Silverman, Kaja, *The Threshold of the Visible World* (London: Routledge, 1996).

Simmel, Georg, "Philosophie der Landschaft", in *Das Individuum und die Freiheit. Essais* (Berlin: Wagenbach, 1984), pp. 130–38.

Sloterdijk, Peter, *Literatur und Organisation von Lebenserfahrung* (Munich: Hanser, 1987).

Smuda, Manfred "Natur als ästhetischer Gegenstand und als Gegenstand der Ästhetik", in *Landschaft* (Frankfurt a. M.: Suhrkamp, 1986), pp. 44–69.

Speer, Albert, *Spandauer Tagebücher* (Berlin, Vienna: Propyläen, 1975).

Speicher, Stephan, "Die zwei Rätsel des Günter Grass", *die tageszeitung*, 14 August 2006.

Spence, Jo and Patricia Holland (eds), *Family Snaps. The Meaning of Domestic Photography* (London: Virago, 1991).

Starobinski, Jean, *Jean-Jacques Rousseau. La transparence et l'obstacle* (Paris: Gallimard, 1976).

Steinbach, Peter, "Vermächtnis oder Verfälschung? Erfahrungen mit Ausstellungen über den deutschen Widerstand", in Gerd. R. Ueberschär (ed.), *Der 20. Juli*, pp. 212–34.

Stoltzfus, Nathan, *Resistance of the Heart: Intermarriage and the Rosenstraße Protest in Nazi Germany* (New York, London: W. W. Norton, 1996).

Stoltzfus, Nathan, "Die Wahrheit jenseits der Akten", *Die Zeit*, 10 October 2003.

Storz, Oliver, "Ärzte, Flammen, Sensationen", *Süddeutsche Zeitung*, 7 March 2006.

Strauß, Botho, *Der Aufstand gegen die sekundäre Welt* (Munich: Hanser, 1999).

Taberner, Stuart, "Normalization and the New Consensus on the Nazi Past: Günter Grass's *Im Krebsgang* and the Problem of German Wartime Suffering", *Oxford German Studies* 31 (2002), 161–86.

Taberner, Stuart, "Representations of German Wartime Suffering", in *Germans as Victims*, ed. Bill Niven, pp. 164–80.

Taberner, Stuart and Paul Cooke (eds), *German Culture, Politics and Literature into the Twenty-First Century* (Rochester: Camden House, 2006).

Tate, Dennis, *Shifting Perspectives. East German Autobiographical Narratives Before and After the End of the GDR* (Rochester: Camden House, 2007).

Thomas, Christian, "örtlich betäubt", *Frankfurter Rundschau*, 14 August 2006.

Tuchel, Johannes, "Das Ende der Legenden. Die Rote Kapelle im Widerstand gegen den Nationalsozialismus", in Gerd. R. Ueberschär (ed.), *Der 20. Juli*, pp. 347–65.

Ueberschär, Gerd R. (ed.) *Der 20. Juli. Das andere Deutschland in der Vergangenheitspolitik nach 1945* (Berlin: Elefanten Press, 1998).

Ullrich, Volker, "Gruppenbild mit Nazis", *Die Zeit*, 19 February 2004.

Vedder, Ulrike, "Luftkrieg und Vertreibung. Zu ihrer Übertragung und Literarisierung in der Gegenwartsliteratur", in *Chiffre 2000 – Neue Paradigmen der Gegenwartsliteratur*, ed. Corinna Caduff and Ulrike Vedder (Munich: Fink, 2006), pp. 59–79.

Vogel, Sabine, "Meiner Mutter Liebe", *die tageszeitung*, 17 July 2004.

Vogt, Jochen, "Er fehlt, er fehlte, er hat gefehlt: Ein Rückblick auf die sogenannten Väterbücher", in Stephan Braese, Holger Gehle, Doron Kiesel, Hanno Lowey (eds), *Deutsche Nachkriegsliteratur und der Holocaust* (Frankfurt a. M., New York: Campus, 1998), pp. 385–99.

Wagenbach, Klaus, "Grass hat nichts verschwiegen", *Die Zeit*, 26 April 2007.

Wagner-Egelhaaf, Martina, *Autobiographie* (Stuttgart: Metzler, 2nd edn, 2005).

Walser, Martin, "Erfahrungen beim Verfassen einer Sonntagsrede", in *Die Walser-Bubis-Debatte. Eine Dokumentation*, ed. Frank Schirrmacher (Frankfurt a. M.: Suhrkamp, 1999), pp. 7–29.

Wassermann, Rudolf, "Widerstand als Rechtsproblem. Zur rechtlichen Rezeption des Widerstandes gegen das NS-Regime", in Gerd. R. Ueberschär (ed.), *Der 20. Juli*, pp. 254–67.

Weigel, Sigrid, "Téléscopage im Unbewußten: Zum Verhältnis von Trauma, Geschichtsbegriff und Literatur", in *Trauma: Zwischen Psychoanalyse und kulturellem Deutungsmuster*, ed. Elisabeth Bronfen, Birgit Erdle, and Sigrid Weigel (Cologne, Weimar, Vienna: Böhlau, 1999), pp. 51–76.

Weigel, Sigrid, " 'Generation' as a Symbolic Form: On the Genealogical Discourse of Memory Since 1945", *The Germanic Review* 77 (2002), 264–77.

Weigel, Sigrid, *Genea-Logik. Generation, Tradition und Evolution zwischen Kultur- und Naturwissenschaften* (Munich: Fink, 2006).

Weigel, Sigrid, Ohad Parmes, Ulrike Vedder, Stefan Willer (eds), *Generation. Zur Genealogie des Konzepts – Konzepte von Genealogie* (Munich: Fink, 2005).

Welzer, Harald, Sabine Moller, Karoline Tschugnall, *"Opa war kein Nazi" – Nationalsozialismus und Holocaust im Familiengedächtnis* (Frankfurt a. M.: Fischer, 2003).

Welzer, Harald, "Schön unscharf. Über die Konjunktur der Familien- und Generationenromane", *Mittelweg* 36 (2004), 53–64.

Wenzel, Horst (ed.), *Die Autobiographies des späten Mittelalters und der frühen Neuzeit* (Munich: Fink, 1980).

Wenzel, Uwe Justus, "Verschluckte Geschichte. Eine Anekdote über Jürgen Habermas wird aufgewärmt", *Neue Zürcher Zeitung*, 28 October 2006.

White, Hayden, *The Content of the Form. Narrative Discourse and Historical Representation* (Baltimore, London: John Hopkins UP, 1987).

Wilke, Sabine, " 'Worüber man nicht sprechen kann, darüber muß man allmählich zu schweigen aufhören': Vergangenheitsbeziehungen in Christa Wolfs *Kindheitsmuster*", *Germanic Review* 56 (1991), 169–76.

Willems, Susanne, *Der entsiedelte Jude. Albert Speers Wohnungsmarktpolitik für den Berliner Hauptstadtbau* (Berlin, Edition Hentrich, 2002).

Wilms, Wilfried, "Taboo and Repression in W. G. Sebald's *On the Natural History of Destruction*", in J. J. Long and Anne Whitehead (eds), *W. G. Sebald*, pp. 175–89.

Wippermann, Wolfgang, *Wessen Schuld? Vom Historikerstreit zur Goldhagenkontroverse* (Berlin: Elefanten Press, 1997).

Witte, Bernd, "Autobiographie als Poetik. Zur Kunstgestalt von Goethes *Dichtung und Wahrheit*", *Neue Rundschau* 89 (1978), 384–92.

Wittlinger, Ruth, "Taboo or Tradition: the 'German as Victims' Theme in the Federal Republic until the mid-1990s", in Bill Niven (ed.), *Germans as Victims*, pp. 62–75.

Wolters, Gereon, *Vertuschung, Anklage, Rechtfertigung. Impromptus zum Rückblick der deutschen Philosophie auf das Dritte Reich* (Bonn: Bonn UP, 2005).

Woods, Roger, "On Forgetting and Remembering: The New Right Since German Unification", in Anne Fuchs, Mary Cosgrove and Georg Grote (eds), *German Memory Contests*, pp. 271–86.

Young, James E., *At Memory's Edge. After-Images of the Holocaust in Contemporary Art and Architecture* (New Haven, London: Yale UP, 2000).

Zantop, Susanne, *Colonial Fantasies. Conquest, Family, and Nation in Precolonial Germany 1770–1870* (London, Durham NC: Duke UP, 1997).

Zielcke, Andreas, "Verleumdung wider besseres Wissen", *Süddeutsche Zeitung*, 27 October 2006.

Zitelmann, Rainer, "Position und Begriff", in *Vereinigungskrise. Zur Geschichte der Gegenwart*, ed. Jürgen Kocka (Göttingen; Vandenhoeck & Ruprecht, 1995), pp. 9–32.

Index